FUNDAMENTALS
OF
COMPUTER
SCIENCE

FUNDAMENTALS OF COMPUTER SCIENCE

Terry M. Walker
University of Southwestern Louisiana

ALLYN AND BACON, INC. BOSTON, LONDON, SYDNEY

Portions of this book were based upon INTRODUCTION TO COMPUTER
SCIENCE: AN INTERDISCIPLINARY APPROACH, by Terry M. Walker, Copyright ©
1972, by Allyn and Bacon, Inc.

Library of Congress Cataloging in Publication Data

Walker, Terry M   1938–
    Fundamentals of computer science.
    Bibliography: p.
    Includes index.
    1. Electronic data processing. 2. Electronic digital computers—Pro-
gramming. I. Title.
QA76.W19   001.6′4   75-1231

ISBN 0-205-04715-7

Second printing . . . August, 1975

TO MY WIFE
ANN

CONTENTS

4 ALGORITHM DESIGN I: FUNDAMENTAL CONCEPTS 71

5 ALGORITHM DESIGN II: LOOPING, ITERATIVE ALGORITHMS, AND EFFICIENCY 133

6

7

8

PREFACE

This book is designed as a text for a one-semester introductory course in computer science for students majoring in any subject area. It was written embracing the now generally accepted view that the first course in computer science should focus on teaching the concepts associated with problem solving. Since problem-solving concepts are so important in learning and everyday life, many persons now contend that such a course should be required of all college students, regardless of their major area.

purpose and goals of this book

One year of high school algebra is the only mathematics prerequisite for using this book. Thus it can be used as a text for a course offered to students as early as their first semester in college. In fact, because of the importance of an understanding of problem-solving concepts in the learning process and in everyday life, all college students should take the course as early as possible in their college studies.

prerequisites

Because the emphasis is on learning the concepts of problem solving, four of the first five chapters are used to introduce problem-solving concepts in detail. The approach in these four chapters is that the basic problem-solving concepts are valid for all types of problems. Therefore, the emphasis in these chapters is placed on solving problems from a variety of disciplines.

emphasis on problem solving

Another position adopted in this book is that the concepts of problem solving should not be obscured by introducing them solely through the use of a computer programming language. The basis for this position is that problem-solving concepts are important independent of the computer language that may be used to implement algorithms on a computer. In addition, it has been the author's experience that learning the rules of a particular programming language is far easier for a student than is learning how to design an algorithm for solving a class of problems. Therefore, all of the algorithms designed in this text are represented using a flowchart language in which algorithm logic stands out clearly. Nevertheless, it is desirable for students to test their algorithms on a computer. Therefore, programming language manuals for the more popular procedural-level computer languages are available for use with this book. Each of these manuals is keyed to the main text on a chapter-by-chapter basis.

flowchart and programming languages

A third view adopted is that the student should not be biased from the very beginning with the notion that numeric information is more important in computer problem solving than nonnumeric information. Thus, throughout this book, string data are treated, along with numeric data, as a natural data type. Similarly, solving problems of the nonnumeric type receives equal emphasis with the solution of numeric-type problems in all parts of this text.

numeric and nonnumeric get equal treatment

Finally, algorithm development in this book utilizes some concepts from structured programming. Thus every algorithm is preceded by a descriptive flowchart that is used to establish the fundamental logical aspects of the algorithm. In addition, only simple control structures are used in the algorithms themselves. Moreover, fancy algorithm tricks are avoided in favor of a straightforward approach in algorithm logic that is easily understood. Furthermore, trace tables are introduced to provide a student with some notions involved with verifying algorithm correctness.

structured programming concepts

This book is divided into two basic parts. The first five chapters and Chapter 9 make up the core of the text. It is the purpose of this basic core to provide the student with a minimal level of understanding about computers and a rather thorough understanding of how to design algorithms to solve problems. Chapters 6, 7, 8, and 10, which constitute the second part of the book, are applications chapters. They are included to give students an opportunity to observe the application of the principles presented in the first part of the text to problems in their areas of interest. The final chapter explores the impact of the computer on society. It is included because of the author's opinion that students should not be allowed to complete their first course in computer science without gaining some insight into the actual and potential impact of the computer on people and their institutions. Finally, there are four appendices which provide information on: (1) number systems, (2) numeric functional operators, (3) selected references, and (4) a glossary of computer terms. Let

chapter organization of book

us now take a more detailed look at some of the chapters of this book.

The first chapter is designed to give an overview of the problem-solving process. It also contains material on computer applications, which is included to motivate students in their study of subsequent chapters of the book. The second chapter provides a brief introduction to the basic notions associated with the architecture of computer systems. An analogy of the human as an information processor is used in this chapter to ease the student into these concepts. Because the intent of the book is to introduce the fundamentals of problem solving, Chapter 2 is purposely not designed to provide an exhaustive treatment on computer systems. In fact, no more than three or four lectures should be devoted to the first two chapters because of the importance of proceeding with the introduction of problem-solving techniques.

contents of Chapters 1 and 2

Chapters 3 through 5 constitute three chapters on the fundamentals of problem solving and algorithm design. Throughout these chapters it is reemphasized that we are designing algorithms to be implemented on a computer. However, the presentation is based entirely upon a flowchart language that is completely independent of the computer system used. During the coverage of Chapters 4 and 5 the instructor may want to introduce in parallel a procedural-level computer programming language using one of the companion language manuals. However, the use of a computer programming language is not mandatory since an entire course can be based around the flowchart language.

contents of Chapters 3, 4, and 5

Chapters 6 through 8 contain applications of the concepts introduced in Chapters 3 through 5 to problems from several disciplines. The various applications were organized by discipline so that it would be convenient to introduce students to applications from their particular areas of interest. All of the material in these chapters is self-contained and assumes no prior knowledge. Furthermore, all of these applications chapters are independent of each other and can be covered in any order (after having completed Chapters 3 through 5). Again, the companion language manuals can be used in parallel with any of these chapters since they are keyed to the main text on a chapter-by-chapter basis.

contents of Chapters 6, 7, and 8

Chapter 9 is the final core chapter of the text. It is designed to introduce the important concept of subalgorithms. This chapter appears where it does in the chapter sequence for several reasons. First, for motivational and learning reenforcement purposes, the author felt that several applications chapters were needed immediately following the introduction to the fundamentals of problem-solving concepts. This allows a student to gain confidence and mastery of the algorithm design process before tackling the new and often difficult topic of subalgorithms. Second, although subalgorithms are important to professionals in computer science, they are not essential to an understanding of problem-solving concepts for persons from other disciplines. Therefore, a good understanding of

contents of Chapter 9

the fundamentals of problem-solving concepts (which is achieved through practice in solving problems) was considered to be more important than learning about subalgorithms.

contents of Chapter 10

After introducing the subalgorithm concept, applications are made in Chapter 10 to the solution of problems in the physical sciences, mathematics, and engineering. In this chapter, subalgorithms are applied to the solution of several problems. This is done to reenforce the concept of a subalgorithm.

acknowledgments

The author is indebted to the many persons who have contributed, either directly or indirectly, prior to and during the development of this book. I would like to thank Dr. D. D. Hearn, Dr. E. Towster, Mr. J. D. Robertson, and the many anonymous reviewers secured by Allyn and Bacon for their thorough reading of the manuscript and for their many suggestions. In addition, I would like to express my appreciation to Mr. John McMahon, Mr. Orie Gay, and Mrs. Rebecca Terrell for their various contributions. Finally, I would like to thank my wife, Ann, who not only offered me encouragement and understanding during the preparation of this text, but typed most of the manuscript. It is to her that I dedicate this book.

Terry M. Walker

FUNDAMENTALS
OF
COMPUTER
SCIENCE

Computer Applications and Problem Solving

The first electronic computer was completed in 1946. Since that time, computers by the tens of thousands have gone into use in businesses, government agencies, scientific laboratories, and universities. This wide use of computers has created jobs by the hundreds of thousands. The availability of these jobs has meant that many thousands of persons have required training and education in the design and use of computers. A result of this need has been the creation of an area of study called *computer science*. This book is designed to introduce some of the fundamental ideas in this field.

In this chapter we will examine first some of the ways in which computers are used. Then the general notions involved in problem solving will be explored. These notions are related to the concepts of problem analysis and algorithm design, which are the primary subjects of this book.

1.1 USES OF COMPUTERS

business applications Computers are used today in all areas of society to perform a great variety of tasks. In the business world they are used to solve numerous kinds of problems. One example would be that of computing a payroll and printing payroll checks. A far different business application is the use of computers to control machinery in a production plant. For example, computers are used to control the machinery that rolls steel slabs into steel sheets. A third example is their use in airline reservations systems (Fig. 1.1). In this case, computers store all of the information about flights and the passengers that will be on those flights.

social science applications In the social sciences computers are now widely used. One example from the field of sociology is the statistical analysis of masses of data about people in an effort to identify trends and relationships that involve social groups. A psychologist might use a computer to monitor the behavior of laboratory animals during an experiment. An educator might use a computer to teach students the rules of arithmetic. Computers are being used to analyze musical scores. There have even been efforts made in the direction of using a computer to compose music.

Figure 1.1.   Airline Reservations Terminal (*Courtesy of* Braniff International)

Computers are also used extensively in the physical sciences, mathematics, and engineering. They have been quite widely used to solve equations and perform such mathematical operations as integration. Much of the research in physics that is involved with the structure and behavior of atomic particles requires computer analysis. The list of areas in which computers are being used includes virtually every endeavor of modern man.

physical science applications

An important reason for the growth in computer use is that computers help us to solve problems that we could not solve otherwise. Manned space flight and interplanetary space missions have been made possible by computers, for example, because only through high-speed calculation of space-vehicle movement can the necessary almost-immediate

power of computers

3

Figure 1.2. Computers at NASA's Mission Control Facility in Houston, Texas (*Courtesy of* International Business Machines Corporation)

course corrections be effected (Fig. 1.2). And consider the use of computers for the processing of bank checks. The task of sorting the growing volume of checks (in 1974 more than 28 billion checks were processed by the Federal Reserve System) and updating accounts would not be economically possible without computers. Thus, were it not for computers, banks would have to limit the number of checking accounts. A third example to consider is the wide use of computers in the solution of matrix problems in engineering and the physical sciences. Since many computations are required to solve a matrix problem, matrices would be of little more than theoretical interest without computers. Similarly, many currently unsolved problems in various fields will eventually be solved with the help of computers.

computer speed and accuracy   Another major reason for their widespread use is that computers can solve many problems much faster and with greater accuracy than people can. Large computers are able to perform calculations on the order of one million per second. In addition, they do this calculation with great accuracy. Because of built-in self-checking features, computers do not make errors in calculation that go undetected. The same statement cannot be made about people. A computer can add up several hundred thousand numbers of various sizes in a fraction of a minute without making any errors of calculation. Given a month and a desk calculator, it seems unlikely that a person could add up even as many as 100,000 numbers without making at least one error.

Note that although computers do not make errors, they may produce incorrect results. The reason is that people provide a computer with the steps it follows in solving a problem and the data it processes. Therefore, when either the method for problem solution or the data (or both) are in error, incorrect results will be produced.

Even with their enormous capabilities, however, computers are not yet well suited to performing creative work. A computer can help an architect in the design of a building, but it cannot develop a design for the building without the architect. Thus computers should be given tasks that they perform well, releasing people to do the things they do well. If we assign to computers jobs that require a great deal of computation and data manipulation, we will free people to identify new problems and develop solutions to both new and existing problems.

computer not creative

1.2   FUNDAMENTALS OF PROBLEM SOLVING

Each day of our lives we are faced with the need to solve many problems. The way in which we go about solving most of these problems is a very informal one. In fact, when we are solving a problem, we are rarely aware that we are involved in problem-solving activity. That is, we develop the method that we use to solve most of our problems at a subconscious level.

Another aspect of our daily need for problem solving is that there are two basic classes of problems that must be solved. These are:

basic problem classes

1. Problems that occur only once.
2. Problems that occur more than once.

For example, for many people the problem of choosing whom they are going to marry occurs only once in their lifetime. On the other hand, most of us have to select the method by which we are going to get to and from work or school thousands of times. A problem that is not likely to occur very often is usually solved anew each time it does occur. That is, in solving the problem there is little awareness of the fact that this problem has been solved before. In the case of problems that occur often, however, most people tend to develop one method (or sometimes several methods) of solution. They then use this method to solve the problem each time it occurs. For example, we probably go through the same steps in brushing our teeth every time we decide to do it.

The informal process by which we obtain rather poorly defined methods for the solution of our everyday problems is perfectly satisfactory. However, when we use a computer to solve a problem, we must develop a well-defined set of steps that leads to a problem solution. This is because a computer can only solve a problem for which it has been given a detailed set of rules that provides a solution. Developing this set of steps must, of necessity, be done by following a more formal problem-solving process.

In the remainder of this chapter we will pursue general problem-solving concepts. This will cause us to begin to think in a more formal way about the process of developing methods for problem solution. In Chapter 2 we will concern ourselves with gaining some insight into the way in which computers are organized and the methods by which they solve problems. Then we will be ready to study in greater depth the process by which we can develop computer methods to solve problems.

1.3 PROBLEM ANALYSIS

problem definition

A very important aspect of the process of developing a solution to any problem is the analysis of the problem. *Problem analysis* is the process by which the problem is defined and all of the information needed for problem solution is identified. The importance of properly defining a problem cannot be overemphasized because a method developed for solving the wrong problem will be unacceptable. This is true no matter how good the solution method for solving the wrong problem may be. For example, the best available recipe for making an apple pie will not solve our problem if the problem is really that of making a chocolate cake. Our problem, however, may actually be that of preparing a dessert. In this case the recipe for excellent apple pie will provide a dandy solution to the problem. The point is simply that even the best solution to the wrong problem is of no value to a person who needs to have a certain problem solved. There are usually an unlimited number of methods available for the solution of a given problem. To choose the best method, however, we must first adequately define the problem that needs to be solved.

Let us pursue the topic of problem definition a little further by means of another example. Suppose that we have the problem of choosing the best route to follow in driving to the local pizza parlor. We could spend a considerable amount of time in the development of a method for solving this problem. But this may not be the problem that we really want to solve. The problem may actually be that of finding the best way (note, not *route* but *way*) of going to the local pizza parlor. In this case, several alternative methods of solution are available. These would include taking a bus or taxicab or getting one of our friends to take us.

The process of defining the problem to be solved is further compli- **precision of** cated by the need to be precise in stating the problem definition. For **definition** example, in the problem of choosing a best route to follow in driving to the local pizza parlor, the word *best* is ambiguous. The reason that *best* is ambiguous is because we do not know in what sense a route is *the best route*. The best route might be the one with the shortest driving distance. Or it could be the route with the shortest driving time. A third alternative could be the route in which the fewest traffic signals are encountered. It is apparent that a number of other alternative meanings of *best route* could be given. In addition, *best* could include several of the above criteria. Thus an important part of problem definition is to define the problem using precise terms. This is necessary to prevent us from developing a method for the solution of the wrong problem because we misunderstand the problem that needs to be solved.

Precisely defining the problem for which a method of solution is sought is only the first step in problem analysis. Problem analysis also involves examining all the subproblems that may be involved in developing **subproblems** a method of solution. As an example, in the best-route-to-the-pizza-parlor problem, we may need to make decisions about alternative routes to follow at certain points. For example, a traffic jam might cause us to go a different way in reaching the pizza parlor. Thus the alternative routes and the conditions that cause us to take each of these routes must also be set out. To use another example, knowing that F.I.C.A. taxes (social security taxes) must be held out of a paycheck is not enough in a problem of computing a payroll. We also must observe that F.I.C.A. taxes are only to be withheld on annual earnings-to-date that are less than a certain amount.

Another aspect of problem analysis is to identify:

1. All of the *inputs* available for solving a problem. **inputs and outputs**
2. All of the *outputs* required as a solution to the problem.

For example, let us examine the problem of baking a chocolate cake. The inputs would be the ingredients that go into the cake, including flour, shortening, and chocolate flavoring. The output would be the chocolate cake. As another example, inputs to the best-route-to-the-pizza-parlor problem would be things such as time of day, traffic congestion encountered, and weather conditions. The output for this problem would be to arrive at the pizza parlor.

By now we are probably beginning to see that the whole area of problem analysis is very subjective in nature. A nice little method for analyzing a problem, which will always give all of the information required

7

for the solution of that problem, does not exist. We summarize the process of *problem analysis* by simply saying that it *includes*:

1. The development of a precise definition of the problem.
2. Identification of all subproblems.
3. Listing all required and available inputs.
4. Listing all desired outputs.

We will discuss the concepts associated with problem analysis in more depth in Chapter 3.

1.4   ALGORITHM DESIGN

algorithms

After a problem has been properly analyzed, we are ready to develop a method for its solution. This method of solution is embodied in what we will call an algorithm. An *algorithm* is simply a procedure consisting of a set of *unambiguous* rules that specifies a *sequence* of operations that provides the *solution* to a problem in a *finite number* of steps. As we will see, algorithms may be represented in many ways. Stated simply, however, an *algorithm* represents the logic involved in arriving at the solution to a problem.

Although the above definition of an algorithm may sound complicated, we have all used algorithms many times. One example of an algorithm would be a recipe for making a chocolate cake. Such a recipe simply contains a set of rules for:

1. Combining specific amounts of ingredients in a certain sequence.
2. Placing the combined ingredients in an oven for baking for a specified period of time.

The rules that make up the recipe must be unambiguous. Also, they must result in the output of a chocolate cake after executing a finite number of steps. These requirements are satisfied by most chocolate cake recipes.

A second example of an algorithm is a set of instructions for the assembly of a model airplane. The set of instructions tells us which parts to put together in a certain sequence so as to end up with a model of an airplane. Again, the steps must be clearly stated and specific (unambiguous). The result of executing such a set of instructions should be a model airplane.

first route-to-Tony's algorithm

Another example of an algorithm would be the method by which we follow a route to drive to our favorite pizza parlor. If we assume that we prefer the pizza at Tony's Pizza House on Johnston Street, such an algorithm might read as follows:

1. Leave our dorm and walk to our car in the parking lot.
2. Enter the car and buckle our seat belts.
3. Start the engine of the car.
4. Drive out of the parking lot to the street in front of our dorm.
5. Proceed to the freeway.
6. Follow the freeway five miles.
7. Exit from the freeway and turn right at the mailbox.
8. Proceed to the Pizza House parking lot.

Are we willing to accept this as the representation of an algorithm? The answer to this question must be *no* because the above procedure does not consist of unambiguous rules. For example, in step 5 nothing is said about which direction the freeway is once we have driven into the street. Furthermore, it does not specify to which freeway we are to proceed. There may be two or three freeways near our dormitory. Steps 6 through 8 also contain ambiguities that need to be removed.

We might ask why these ambiguities are important if we know what each step means. The answer to this question is that we generally want an algorithm to provide the solution to a problem for anyone who might wish to use the algorithm. For example, a friend of ours who lives down the hall may also enjoy the pizza at Tony's Pizza House on Johnston Street. In addition, he may want to use our algorithm for driving there to get a pizza. For him to use it successfully, however, our algorithm must be precise enough to permit him to accomplish his goal. That is, by using our algorithm our friend must arrive at Tony's Pizza House parking lot.

In later chapters, this lack of ambiguity in algorithm steps becomes particularly important. This is due to the fact that all of our algorithms will be designed to be implemented on a computer. As we will learn in Chapter 2, computers need completely unambiguous steps to follow to be able to solve a problem.

As a second attempt at an algorithm for solving the route-to-Tony's-Pizza-House problem, we might have:

second route-to-Tony's algorithm

1. Leave our dorm and walk to our car in the parking lot.
2. Enter the car and buckle our seat belts.
3. Start the engine of the car.
4. Drive out of the dorm parking lot to Elm Street.
5. Proceed north on Elm Street four blocks to the I-10 freeway interchange.
6. Turn to the right onto the freeway entrance ramp before reaching

the freeway overpass.

7. Proceed east on the I-10 freeway and exit at Johnston Street, which will be the eighth exit.

8. Turn to the right onto Johnston Street.

9. Proceed south six blocks on Johnston Street.

10. Turn to the right from Johnston Street into Tony's Pizza House parking lot and park in any available space.

The first thing that we notice about this algorithm is that the set of rules is rather precise. They would be just as meaningful to our friend down the hall as they are to us. In these algorithm steps we have given specific street names, highway numbers, and directions. This is in contrast with the very general and ambiguous rules of the earlier version of our route-to-Tony's-Pizza-House algorithm.

The above algorithm for following a route for getting to the Pizza House is represented in the English language. This method of representing an algorithm may be satisfactory in solving a relatively simple problem, such as choosing a route to Tony's Pizza House. However, in the case of more complex algorithms, the English language will prove to be an unsatisfactory means of representation. Several reasons may be given for not using English to represent an algorithm. *First,* the English language is ambiguous. For example, consider the many meanings that are associated with a word such as *love*. *Second,* the logical flow of the algorithm is not easily displayed in an English language representation of an algorithm. This point will become more important later in this chapter when we design algorithms that include branches.

flowchart language
A language widely used in computer science to represent algorithms is the *flowchart language*. The flowchart language we will use in this book consists of:

1. A set of eight standard flowchart symbols, six of which we will call *flowchart boxes*.

2. The symbols for the 26 capital (uppercase) and 26 lowercase letters of the English alphabet, associated punctuation marks, and certain special symbols.

3. The symbols for the ten decimal digits and associated mathematical symbols.

4. Rules for assembling these symbols into algorithm statements.

The *shape* of each of the flowchart boxes indicates the type of operation that is to be performed within the box. Details on the other symbols and rules for assembling them into algorithm statements will be given later in this chapter and in Chapters 4, 5, and 9.

A flowchart language representation of the second version of our route-to-Tony's-Pizza-House algorithm appears in Fig. 1.3. Only four types of flowchart symbols have been used in this flowchart:

route-to-Tony's algorithm flowchart

1. An oval box.
2. A rectangular box.
3. A circular symbol.
4. A straight line with an attached arrowhead.

Notice that each flowchart box has a small number just above it on the righthand side. These numbers are simply reference numbers which will permit us to refer, for example, to the third box in the flowchart as box 3.

Let us pause to discuss this flowchart in some detail. First, notice that boxes 1 and 12 are oval. In general, the oval boxes indicate a terminal point in an algorithm. That is, they identify a starting or a stopping point in an algorithm. Thus box 1 indicates the first step in the algorithm to be executed. Similarly, box 12 indicates that the problem solution has now been obtained and that the algorithm is at a stopping point. We will call the oval-shaped boxes *terminal boxes*. Boxes 2 through 11 are all rectangular. They describe various processing operations that are to be performed during the execution of the algorithm. These rectangular boxes are called *processing boxes*.

terminal boxes

processing boxes

The two circular symbols with the number 1 in them are called *connectors*. The purpose of a connector is to indicate the continuation of flow. There are two types of connectors:

connectors

1. Out-connectors.
2. In-connectors.

An *out-connector* is one that has a line with an arrowhead pointing to the connector circle. An *in-connector* is one that has a line leading from it that points to a flowchart box or to a flowline. Out-connectors indicate that flow is to resume in some other portion of the flowchart; an in-connector is a point in the flowchart where flow is to resume. For example, in Fig. 1.3 the connector containing the number 1 at the bottom of the left column of symbols is an out-connector. It indicates that flow is to resume with some in-connector containing the number 1. That in-connector indicates the continuation of a flow sequence that starts somewhere else in the flowchart. In this example, the continuation point is the in-connector at the top of the right column of symbols in the flowchart.

Finally, symbols in this flowchart are connected to each other by straight lines with attached arrowheads. These directed straight lines are called *flowlines*. They are used to indicate the sequence in which algorithm steps are to be executed.

flowlines

In Fig. 1.4 we have a second version of the route-to-Tony's-Pizza-

11

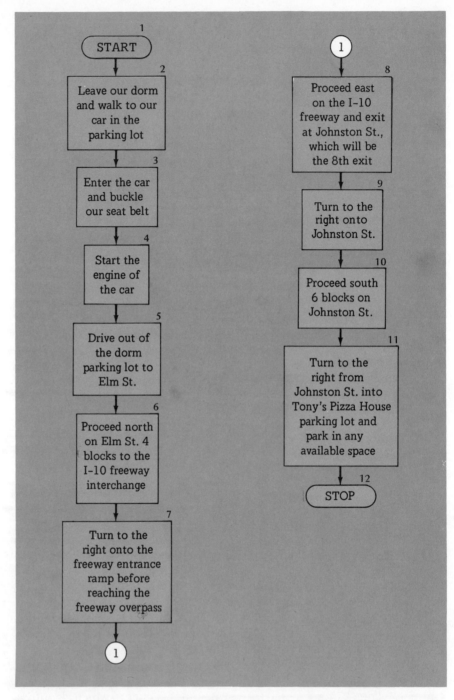

Figure 1.3. Route-to-Tony's-Pizza-House Flowchart

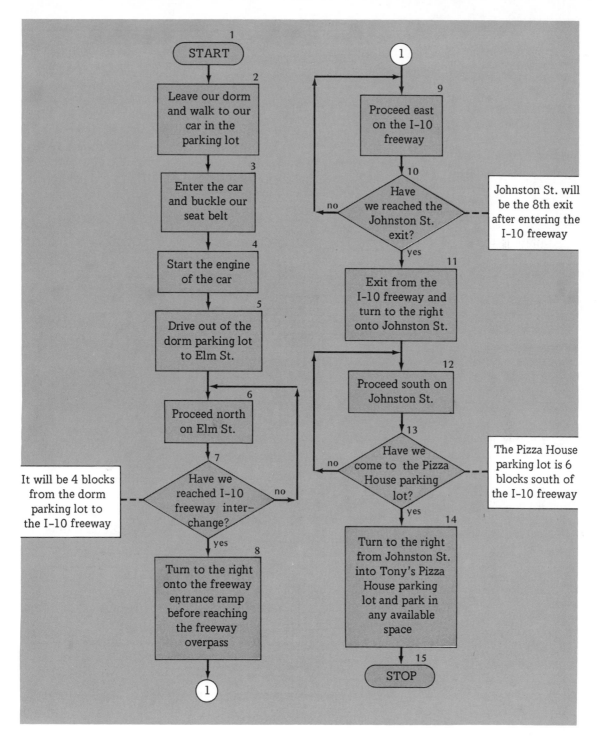

Figure 1.4. Revised Route-to-Tony's-Pizza-House Flowchart

second version of route-to-Tony's algorithm flowchart

House algorithm flowchart. This is another version of the algorithm given in Fig. 1.3. The new feature introduced is the decision process, which was implicitly included in the flowchart in Fig. 1.3. In box 6 of Fig. 1.3 we instructed the person executing the algorithm to proceed north on Elm Street to the I–10 freeway interchange. Implicit in this instruction is that the person must remain alert as to whether or not the interchange has been reached. If we have not reached the interchange, we continue traveling north on Elm Street. When we reach the interchange we are directed to turn to the right onto the freeway entrance ramp before reaching the freeway overpass. Therefore, box 6 of the original flowchart is expanded in Fig. 1.4 into boxes 6 and 7. This expansion of the step is to expressly show the decision-making process, which was implicit in Fig. 1.3. Box 6 of the new flowchart contains an action and box 7 contains a decision question. Similar expansions have been made for symbols 8 and 10 of Fig. 1.3. Notice that the *decision box* is a diamond-shaped symbol.

decision boxes

The process of repeating the execution of algorithm steps (such as repeating the execution of box 6 in the flowchart of Fig. 1.4) is called looping. In *looping* one or more algorithm steps are repeated until some decision criteria are satisfied. The topic of looping will be covered in greater depth in Chapter 5.

looping

Finally, observe that another new type of flowchart box appears in Fig. 1.4. This box is a rectangular-shaped symbol that has one end left open. These boxes are called *annotation boxes* and are used to provide descriptive or explanatory information. Notice that they are not given box numbers. In addition, annotation boxes are connected to other flowchart boxes by *broken lines* instead of flowlines. The reason for this is that annotation boxes do not contain executable algorithm steps. Thus they are *not* in the regular flow of the algorithm. The annotation box simply provides a means of relating explanatory information to a particular algorithm step. The annotation boxes in Fig. 1.4 are connected to boxes 7, 10, and 13. Information is given in each of these boxes about the geographical distance to the point at which exits will be made from each of the algorithm loops.

annotation boxes

test grade example

As a final example, we will examine an algorithm for obtaining five test grades, summing the five grades, and copying down the sum. The flowchart for this algorithm appears in Fig. 1.5. Notice in boxes 2, 3, 4, 5, 6, and 14 the appearance of boxes with a new shape, the shape of a parallelogram. The parallelogram-shaped box is called the *input/output box* and denotes such operations as copying on paper numbers to be operated upon. We will use two verbs, GET and PUT, in conjunction with the input/output box.

input/output boxes

When the verb GET appears in an input/output box, this means that an input to the algorithm is to be obtained. For example, in Fig. 1.5 someone could read us the five values to be input to the algorithm. In boxes

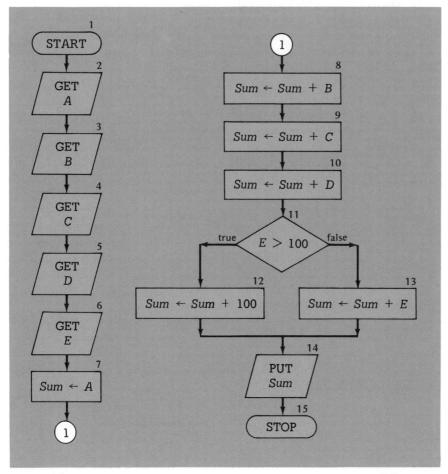

Figure 1.5.   Algorithm Flowchart for Summing Four or Five Test Grades

2 through 6 of the flowchart we show the operations for copying these numbers down and associating them with the variables* A, B, C, D, and E. Once copied, we can refer to these values symbolically by the use of the variable names A, B, C, D, and E.

The verb PUT appearing in an input/output box means that a value used in the algorithm is to be recorded on some medium. An example in our algorithm would be writing the value of the variable Sum on a sheet of paper to be handed to the instructor. This operation is performed in box 14 of Fig. 1.5.

---

* Variables and constants will be discussed more fully in Chapter 4.

The steps needed to form the sum are given in boxes 7 through 10 and boxes 12 and 13.   Notice that each of these boxes contains the variable name *Sum* followed by a left-pointing arrow.   This left-pointing arrow is

assignment operator called the *assignment operator* because it is used to assign values to variables.   In this example, values are being assigned to the variable named *Sum*.   To the right of the assignment operator in each of these boxes is either a variable or a simple arithmetic expression.   The arithmetic expressions are used to indicate that the value of one of the variables is to be added to the value of the variable named *Sum*.

In box 11 a decision must be made as to whether or not the fifth test grade (the value of the variable *E*) is greater than 100.   This decision is included because the fifth exam included a bonus question that made the total number of points possible greater than 100.   However, the teacher did not want to count more than 100 points for the fifth exam.   Therefore, if the value of the variable *E* is greater than 100, box 12 is executed, causing only 100 points to be added to the sum.   On the other hand, when the fifth exam grade is determined to be not greater than 100 (i.e., less than or equal to 100), box 13 is executed.   This causes the value of *E* to be added into the sum.   Notice that either box 12 or box 13 will be executed; in no case will both or neither of the boxes be executed.

The discussion of this and the previous section should give us some very elementary notions about problem analysis and algorithm design.   However, we are not yet prepared to develop algorithms that a computer can use to solve a problem.   This must await the more detailed discussions that begin in Chapter 3.

PROBLEMS

1. Does the algorithm of Fig. 1.4 contain any additional ambiguities?   If yes, make the necessary changes to remove them from the algorithm.

2. Develop the English language representation of an algorithm for mailing a letter.   Begin your algorithm just after the point where you sign the letter.   Assume that the letter is to be mailed at a mailbox that is two blocks away.

3. Use the flowchart symbols of this chapter to develop the flowchart representation for the algorithm of Problem 2.

4. Develop the English language representation of an algorithm for changing a flat tire on a car.   Begin your algorithm at the point where you have just

pulled off of the highway and discovered that you have one flat tire.   Allow for all contingencies in your algorithm, including the possibility that the spare tire is flat.

5. Develop the flowchart representation for the algorithm of Problem 4.

6. Develop the English language representation of an algorithm for replacing a broken pane of glass in a door.   Assume that the pane of glass is held in place on all four sides by small wooden strips, each of which is attached by five small nails.

7. Develop the flowchart representation for the algorithm of Problem 6.

8. Develop the English language representation of

an algorithm for making a long-distance telephone call. Allow for all alternatives normally involved in placing a long-distance call. Assume that you are using a touch-tone telephone and already know the number that you wish to call.

9. Develop the flowchart representation for the algorithm of Problem 8.

10. Develop an algorithm flowchart for getting dressed. Include questions about where you are

going as part of the problem.

11. Develop an algorithm flowchart for getting a date for Saturday night.

12. Modify the algorithm flowchart of Fig. 1.5 for the case in which bonus questions were also included on the first and third exams. Assume that no more than 100 points are to be counted on any one test.

SUMMARY

1. The methods people generally use to solve problems are developed at a subconscious level.

2. There are two basic classes of problems:
a. Problems that occur only once.
b. Problems that occur more than once.

3. To solve a problem, computers require a well-defined set of steps.

4. Formal problem-solving concepts exist for solving problems using a computer.

5. Problem analysis is the process by which the problem is defined and all of the information needed for problem solution is identified. Problem analysis includes:
a. The development of a precise definition of the problem.
b. Identification of all subproblems.
c. Listing all required and available inputs.
d. Listing all desired outputs.

6. The best solution to the wrong problem is useless.

7. An algorithm is a procedure consisting of a set of unambiguous rules which specifies a sequence of operations that provides a solution to a problem in a finite number of steps.

8. An algorithm should generally provide the solution to a problem for anyone who might wish to use the algorithm.

9. Algorithms are often represented using a flowchart language.

10. The flowchart symbols that have been introduced in this chapter are:
a. The terminal box:

b. The processing box:

c. The connector:

d. The flowline:

e. The input/output box:

f. The decision box:

g. The annotation box:

Introduction to Computer Systems

In Chapter 1 we established that learning how to design algorithms to be executed by computers would be our primary interest. We also developed some basic notions about what an algorithm is and how algorithms are constructed.

In this chapter we will learn something about how computers are organized and how they function. One way in which we will accomplish this will be to develop an analogy between humans and computers. Following this, we will relate what we have learned from this analogy to the structure of real computer systems.

2.1   HUMAN BEINGS AS INFORMATION PROCESSORS

Among the attributes of human beings is that they are information processors. That is, one of the things that we do as human beings is process information. Since computers are also information processors, an effective way to gain some understanding of computers is by examining the human being as an information processor.

input of information by humans

Information to be processed by a person must be in the memory portion of the brain before the processing can take place. Thus, a means must exist to *input* that information. People have several ways of inputting information. One method is *visual*, through use of the eyes. For example, in reading this book you are inputting information to your brain. Other examples of visual information input might be watching a sporting event or reading what the instructor is writing on the chalkboard. Obviously, numerous examples of visual information input could be given.

A second means that a human being has of inputting information to be processed is through *hearing*. An obvious example would be hearing what others have to say, such as hearing an instructor's lecture. Other kinds of sounds that we hear which provide information would be music, auto horns, and the rustling of the leaves in a tree. Thus the sense of hearing provides a second important way that people have for the input of information.

In addition to sight and sound as input media, there are other means of input that are also important. These would include the senses of touch, taste, and smell. Although normally we do not think of *touch* as a means of inputting information, it is a very important one. When we touch objects, we not only gain knowledge about such things as hot and cold. We also are inputting information about such qualities as the texture of an object (e.g., smooth or rough, soft or hard). With regard to *taste,* this is also an important source of information input. Through taste we learn whether something is sweet or bitter, spicy or bland, and other attributes of things that are consumed orally. Similarly, *smell* provides us with a valuable source of information input. For example, smoke produces a danger signal, while perfume might invoke pleasant thoughts. In summary, the five principal types of input for human beings are sight, sound, touch, taste, and smell. It is through these senses that information is input to the brain for processing.

When information to be processed is input, it must be stored. This storage of information takes place in a portion of the brain called memory (Fig. 2.1). When processing of information takes place, the information that results from this processing is also stored in a person's memory. Thus *memory* is a place for the storage of information, including both informa-

human memory for information storage

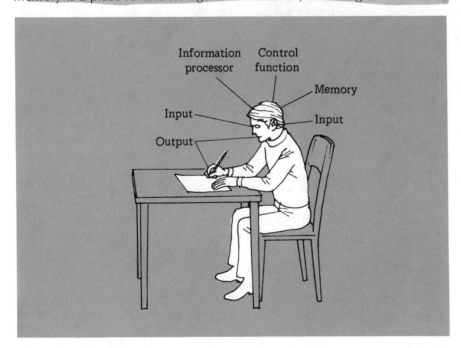

Figure 2.1.   The Human Being as an Information Processor

21

tion that has been input and information that may already have been processed. Notice that nothing has been said about the amount of time that passes between the input of certain information and the processing of that information. It is therefore not necessary that information be processed at the time that it is input. This is because one purpose for inputting information is to store it for future reference or processing.

There is still much about human memory that is not understood. For example, the capacity of human memory is not known. That is, we do not know what the maximum amount of information is that can be stored in a human memory. While it is reasonable to assume that there is some limit to the amount of information that a person can remember, this limit is apparently quite large. Another thing about human memory that is not well understood is the amount of time required to access a given item of information. That is, how long does it take for a person to remember something once the process of trying to remember it begins? Put another way, it is not known why we are able to remember some things almost immediately, whereas other things are recalled only after hours or days of thinking about them.

information processing by humans

Once the information is stored in memory, it is ready to be processed. Much of the *processing* we do as human beings involves simply the classification, storage, and retrieval of information. However, sometimes we process information in a way that changes it or in a way that produces new information. For example, we might add several numbers together, thus getting the sum, which is a new item of information. Processing that involves such things as addition is possible because in our memory we have stored addition tables, which record the sum of two digits or numbers. Another type of processing might involve rearranging things, such as taking a person's name in natural order (i.e., surname last) and placing the surname first. For example, the name Tom Brown might be rearranged as Brown, Tom. An additional and very important type of processing is that of making *decisions*. Decision making takes place in the brain and usually involves such things as comparing two numbers to determine whether one number is less than, equal to, or greater than a second number. Regardless of the kind of processing, all processing takes place in a portion of the brain. Remember from our discussion of Chapter 1 that all processing is performed using algorithms. Therefore, the steps of the algorithms executed by human beings to solve problems are also stored in a person's memory as information.

output of information by humans

A fourth aspect of information processing involves the *output* of information. When information has been processed, it is often desired that it be output. One method people have for the output of information is *vocal*. That is, information is output from memory by speaking. Another means of output is by *manually* produced messages. One type of manually produced output is a handwritten message. Another would be a message produced using a typewriter or some similar mechanical device. Less frequently used means of outputting information include facial expressions, eye contact, and body movements. In summary, the primary ways human beings have to output information are through speaking and manually produced messages. Secondary output methods include facial expressions, eye contact, and body movements.

The final thing involved in the person as an information processor is the *control* factor. That is, the input, processing, memory, and output functions must be begun, coordinated, and halted. In addition, these actions must be carried out in the proper order. For example, we cannot begin processing an item of information before it has been input. Similarly, the information that results from processing cannot be output prior to the development of that information. Therefore, the sequence in which operations are performed is important. This sequencing is determined by algorithm steps the execution of which is controlled by a portion of the brain.

human control of information processing functions

To *summarize,* human beings are information processors. As such, they must input, store, process, and output information. In addition, people must have the ability to supervise all of these information-processing functions to cause them to be performed in the proper sequence.

2.2   COMPUTERS AS INFORMATION PROCESSORS

In the previous section, we studied human beings as information processors. Now we are ready to use what we learned in that section to gain an understanding about computers. The reason that people serve as a good model for studying about computers is that computers and human beings perform similar functions in processing information.

A common error that is made when thinking about computers is that a computer consists only of the cabinets, circuitry, and other physical devices that are seen when visiting a computer center. For example, people often think that a computer consists only of the objects that you can see in the photograph in Fig. 2.2. However, this is false because the photograph shows only the hardware or physical components of the computer system. Not seen in a computer center or in the photograph of Fig. 2.2 is the second part of a computer, a part called the *computer operating system* or *software.* The computer operating system consists of a series of algorithms that are represented in the memory of the computer. These operating system algorithms are necessary because they facilitate the processing of the algorithms people write to provide a computer with the method for solving particular types of problems. They are also used to schedule the resources (computer hardware and software components) of

computer hardware

computer software

23

Figure 2.2.   IBM System/370 Computer Hardware System (*Courtesy of* International Business Machines Corporation)

the computer among these user algorithms.   The remainder of this chapter will be devoted to studying computer hardware and operating systems.

2.2.1   Computer Hardware Systems

**computer
information input**

A computer has one or more *input devices* that function in a way that corresponds with the input function of a human.   That is, these devices are designed to input information into the memory of a computer.   Among the types of input devices would be card readers, paper tape readers, magnetic tape drives, and typewriter terminals.

A *card reader* is a device that is designed to read punched cards, such as the one shown in Fig. 2.3.   Information is represented in such a card by the hole or holes punched in the various columns of the card by a device called a *card punch*.   Thus, a card reader (Fig. 2.4) functions by sensing which columns and rows in a card have had holes punched in them.   The result of this sensing is that the codes that represent the information in a card are electronically sent to the computer's memory.   Thus a card reader is connected directly to the computer's memory and processing unit.

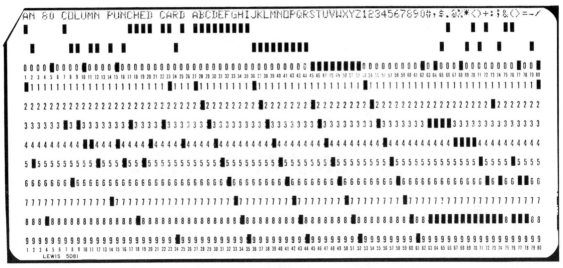

Figure 2.3   Hollerith Punched Card

Figure 2.4.   IBM 3525 Card Reader (*Courtesy of* International Business Machines Corporation)

Since a particular row and column on a punched card either does or does not contain a hole, the code that results is called a binary code. Thus, a *binary code* is one in which only two states are possible. An analogy to a binary code would be a conventional light switch, which must be either on or off; it cannot be in between these two states. However, even though the code is binary, the information represented in each card column is symbolic. That is, symbols, such as decimal digits and alphabetic characters, are being represented in each card column by use of a binary code.

A *punched paper tape reader* is very similar to a card reader. However, it reads information that is punched into a continuous paper tape. As in the case of punched cards, the information is represented in paper tape by the series of holes that have been punched into the tape by a paper tape punch. A *magnetic tape drive* is designed to read information that has been recorded magnetically on a coated plastic tape. The principle involved in using magnetic tape is similar to that used in recording audio messages on a tape recorder. The fundamental difference is that the information stored on a magnetic computer tape is represented using a binary code similar to the code used on punched cards. This coded information may have been written on a tape by a device that permits information to be entered manually on magnetic tape. Another possibility is that the information has been written on the magnetic tape as output from previous computer processing.

The *typewriter terminal* (Fig. 2.5) differs from the input devices dis-

Figure 2.5.   IBM 2740 Typewriter Terminal (*Courtesy of* International Business Machines Corporation)

cussed previously. This is because it is the only device that allows information to be entered manually directly into computer memory. That is, with punched cards, punched paper tape, and magnetic tape, the information is first entered into one of these media. Then it is read from them into computer memory. Two steps are therefore required to input information into memory. However, in the case of a typewriter terminal, the information is input directly into computer memory as it is entered into the keyboard of the terminal. In many cases this results in quite a savings of both labor and time in entering information into a computer. In addition, the chances for error may be reduced. However, no computer-readable copy of the information will be produced for future input to a computer. Thus a typewriter terminal may not always be the best device to use for the input of information. An exception to this exists in that some typewriter terminals can produce a punched paper tape while input is being made directly to computer memory. The paper tape can then be used to input that information in the future.

The *memory* of a computer stores all information electronically in the form of a binary code. The reason that a binary code is used is that two-state electronic storage devices (remember the on–off analogy of a light switch as a two-state or binary device) are much easier to construct than are storage devices that allow three or more states. Thus, for purposes of engineering efficiency and to reduce costs, computer memory devices store information using a binary code.

computer memory for information storage

The memory of a computer is usually not singular, but rather is *plural;* that is, each computer usually has more than one memory. These memories are usually segmented into two classes—*main memory* and *auxiliary memory.* The primary distinction between these two classes of memory is the source and destination of information placed in or taken from the respective memories. Thus all information placed in auxiliary memory must come from main memory, while information in main memory may come from input devices, auxiliary memory, or the central processing unit. Similarly, information output from auxiliary memory must go into main memory, while information in main memory may go to output devices, auxiliary memory, or the central processing unit. These relationships between memory classes and input/output are displayed in the information-flow diagram in Fig. 2.6. The primary reason for the distinction between main memory and auxiliary memory is cost. That is, the storage devices used for main memory are much more expensive per unit of information stored than are the devices used for auxiliary memory. Therefore, a relatively small but costly main memory is used together with a relatively large but inexpensive auxiliary memory to form the memory system of the computer.

Several different types of storage devices are used in main memory.

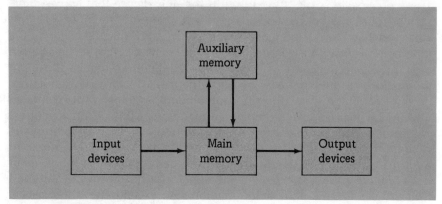

Figure 2.6. Information Flow Between Main and Auxiliary Memories and Input/Output Devices

main memory devices

By far the most common of these has been the magnetic core, which consists of a small doughnut-shaped piece of magnetic material that can have one of two states. That is, the core can be given one of two states of polarity and thus is used to represent one of two binary digits (usually a 0 and a 1). These magnetic cores are then strung together on wires to form planes of cores (Fig. 2.7) that are used to store units of information. In many recently introduced computers, core memories have been replaced by memories made of integrated circuits. These memories function similarly to core memories since they represent information in a binary form.

main memory capacity and speed

The capacity of the typical computer main memory is between 100,000 and 1,000,000 bytes (the unit of memory capable of storing one character is called a *byte*) of information. However, computers with both smaller and larger main memory capacities do exist. The amount of time required to access information stored in the typical main memory is measured in billionths of a second (one billionth of a second is called a nanosecond). Thus, many millions of characters of information can be stored and/or retrieved from main memory every second.

main memory locations

Main memory on a computer is broken up into units called *locations*. Depending on the particular model of computer, one main memory location will usually consist of from one to ten bytes of storage. Consequently, a particular piece of information may require more than one location for storage. For example, three locations would be needed to store a name consisting of eighteen letters on a computer in which each location allowed six bytes to be stored. The contents of a location will always be a binary or a binary-coded number. Certain binary codes are used to represent symbols other than numbers, such as alphabetic characters and punctuation marks. For example, the binary code 11000001 is used in IBM

Figure 2.7.   Core Memory Plane (*Courtesy of* International Business Machines Corporation)

System/360 and 370 computers to represent the letter *A* of the English alphabet.   Similarly, the code 01011011 is taken to represent a dollar sign ($).   Thus, any information that can be represented using a binary code can be stored in a computer's main memory.

Because information that has been stored in a main memory location must be retrieved later, each location in main memory is given a unique location number.   This location number is usually a binary integer and is called an *address*.   It is very important not to confuse the contents of a location with the address of that location.   That is, the address of a location tells us in which location of main memory the information is stored.   The *contents* of a location, on the other hand, tell us what that information is.   Furthermore, in general there is no relationship between the address

main memory addresses

memory location contents

29

of a location and the contents of that location. We might draw an analogy here with a post office box: the number on the box in general tells us nothing about the number of letters in that box, the size of the letters, or the contents of those letters. In the same way, the address of a main memory location tells us nothing about the contents of that location.

auxiliary memory devices

Several different types of storage devices are used for auxiliary memory. Among these are magnetic disc (Fig. 2.8), magnetic drum, magnetic core, data cells, and magnetic tape. Frequently, two or more of these

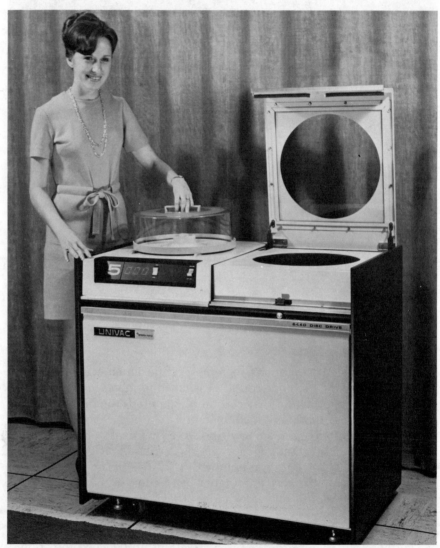

Figure 2.8. Univac 8440 Disc Drive (*Courtesy of* Sperry Univac, A Division of Sperry Rand Corporation)

types of storage devices are used on one computer system to provide the auxiliary memory.

The capacity of auxiliary memory on a typical computer system ranges from several million to hundreds of millions of characters. In fact, it is not uncommon for the auxiliary memory capacity of one computer to exceed one billion characters. The amount of time required to access information in auxiliary memory ranges from in the millionths of a second to several minutes, depending on the type of storage device. Moreover, the rate at which information can be transferred between auxiliary memory and main memory is generally in excess of 100,000 characters per second.

auxiliary memory capacity and speed

The method used to access information stored in auxiliary memory varies according to the type of device. For example, magnetic disc storage is addressable, thus allowing direct access to any item of information on a disc storage device. On the other hand, magnetic tape is generally searched serially in an associative manner. By associative, we mean that a label that describes the information we want is compared with a label contained in each group of information on the magnetic tape. This process of reading a group of information items and comparing the labels continues until a match of the labels occurs. The size of a group of information generally ranges from less than a hundred to several thousand characters.

auxiliary memory information access

The computer equivalent of the processing and control portions of the human brain is called the *central processing unit*. Thus, the central processing unit consists of components that perform such things as arithmetic and comparison operations. In addition, the central processing unit controls the operation of all of the other components of the computer hardware system. The component of the CPU (CPU is a common abbreviation for *central processing unit*) that performs operations, such as those of arithmetic and comparison, is called the *arithmetic and logical unit*. The portion of the arithmetic and logical unit that performs arithmetic operations might be thought of as an extremely fast desk calculator. This is because most computers can add several hundred thousand numbers in one second.

central processing unit

arithmetic and logical unit

The portion of the CPU that controls the operation of the remainder of the computer hardware is called the *control unit*. The control unit assures that the steps in an algorithm are executed in the proper sequence. It does this by the sequence in which the algorithm steps or instructions* are brought to the CPU for execution. This sequence is determined by the algorithm being executed. Note that the steps of an algorithm being executed by the CPU are stored in computer memory, not in the CPU. Thus, only the instruction currently being executed is generally in the CPU at any point in time. Therefore, the sequence in which instructions are executed is controlled by the order in which the CPU fetches instructions

control unit

---

* *Instructions* are the steps of an algorithm written in a computer language. The concept of instructions and computer languages will be explained in Section 2.2.2.

from main memory to the control portion of the CPU for execution.   This sequence is determined by the instructions themselves.

computer
information output

Finally, the output of information from main memory is performed using a variety of *output devices*.   Among the types of output devices used are line printers, card punches, paper tape punches, magnetic tape drives, audio devices, CRT (cathode-ray-tube) terminals, and typewriter terminals.   *Line printers* (Fig. 2.9) are devices that print numeric and alphabetic information on sheets of paper.   They generally print an entire line, consisting of from 120 to 136 or more characters, in one operation.   Such printers are capable of printing from 100 to 2000 lines per minute, with about 1200 being a fairly typical speed.   *Card punches* and *paper tape*

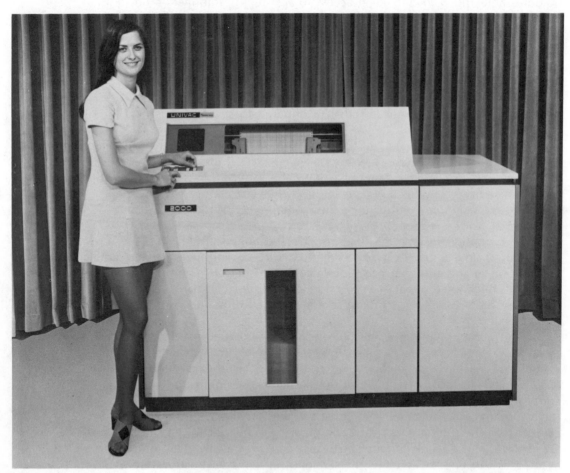

Figure 2.9.   Univac Series 0770 High-Speed Line Printer (*Courtesy of* Sperry Univac, A Division of Sperry Rand Corporation)

punches are used to punch the output information into punched cards and punched paper tape, respectively. The output produced by these devices can be used for input to the computer at a later time. *Magnetic tape drives* write information on magnetic tape. These magnetic tapes can be removed from the computer and saved as future sources of input information.

Audio devices are not often used; however, they are useful in that they produce a spoken message. A common application of audio output devices is to produce things like changes in telephone numbers and stock market price quotations. They are generally best used when the response consists of numbers. *CRT terminals* provide output that may be graphical or alphabetic in nature on devices that are built around cathode-ray tubes similar to the ones used in television sets. Finally, *typewriter terminals* are used for output when a person is working at a terminal device alternating input to the computer with output from the computer. Typewriter terminals are generally fairly slow output devices when compared with such devices as line printers. However, they are much more versatile than

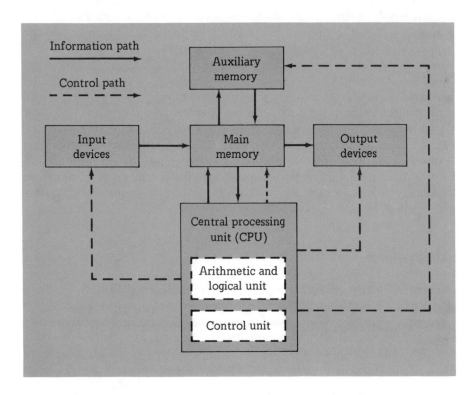

Figure 2.10. Major Component Subsystems of a Computer Hardware System

most other types of devices because they permit both input to the computer and output from the computer.

Let us *summarize* what we have learned about computer hardware systems (Fig. 2.10). Every computer must get information into its main memory in order for that information to be available for processing. An input operation is one in which information is sensed by an input device that is directly connected to the computer. Frequently used input devices include punched card readers and typewriter terminals. The information that is input goes into main memory. Main memory is organized into locations, with each location having an address. Because of the limited size of main memory, almost all computers have an auxiliary memory. Information can only be transferred between the auxiliary memory and the main memory. All processing is performed by the central processing unit. In addition, the CPU controls all parts of the computer hardware system. Finally, the information in the computer's main memory can be output through the use of output devices. The most commonly used types of output devices are line printers and typewriter terminals.

hardware reliability

A final topic that relates to computer hardware is *reliability*. Most contemporary computer hardware systems have very few failures and thus are quite reliable. Moreover, the majority of failures that do occur relate to mechanical devices, such as card readers, rather than to the electronic components. Since incorrect answers resulting from failures in the electronic components could go for a while without discovery, computer hardware incorporates many kinds of self-checking components. Thus, should a part of main memory fail, the computer would probably stop and signal the type of failure. Some computers now available even have the capacity to correct certain kinds of errors caused by hardware failure. This is done so that processing can continue when minor hardware problems occur. Therefore, we can have a great deal of confidence that the results produced by a computer are what we expect for the algorithms that we provide it with.

2.2.2   Computer Operating Systems

computer programs

An algorithm that is in a form that a computer can execute is called a *program*. The rules for writing programs and the operations that result from executing the various program steps define a computer programming language. Just as there are many natural languages (e.g., English, French, Spanish), there also exist numerous computer programming languages. The central processing unit of a computer is generally designed so that it can directly execute programs written in only one language. This language is called *machine language* (Fig. 2.11). The machine language that a particular model of computer is designed to execute will probably not

machine language programs

LOC	OBJECT CODE	ADDR1	ADDR2	STMT	SOURCE STATEMENT		
000000				1	BEGIN	START	0
000000	05C0			2		BALR	12,0
000002				3		USING	*,12
000002	5850 C00E		00010	4		L	5,A
000006	5A50 C012		00014	5		A	5,B
00000A	5050 C016		00018	6		ST	5,C
00000E	0000			7		DC	X'0000'
000010	00000007			8	A	DC	F'7'
000014	FFFFFFFC			9	B	DC	F'-4'
000018				10	C	DS	F
000000				11		END	BEGIN

Figure 2.11. Simple Machine-Language Program

be understood by another model of computer. Therefore, there is not just one machine language; instead there exist many machine languages. Thus, an algorithm written in the machine language for one computer cannot be executed on a different model of computer. This lack of compatability creates many problems.

In addition to the problems caused by the large variety of machine languages, it is not convenient or efficient for a person to write programs in machine language. One reason for this is that the steps in a machine language program must generally be written using entirely octal or entirely hexadecimal numbers.* Since we are not used to writing numbers using other than the decimal system, machine language programs would be quite difficult to develop. Another problem with machine language is that a person using it must keep track of where in main memory various information has been stored. Yet another difficulty is caused by the primitive nature of the things a computer can do in one step of a machine language program. For example, three steps are required in most machine languages to add two numbers together that are in main memory and leave the sum in main memory. Thus the development of machine language programs is a major task that generally requires the writing of thousands of program steps. All of these difficulties can be summarized by stating that machine language programs must be written using rules that conform to the design of the computer hardware.

As a result of the problems associated with the writing of machine language programs, machine-independent procedure-oriented computer languages have been developed. These languages allow programs to be written using a notation similar to the one used to describe the algorithm

procedure-oriented languages

---

* Octal and hexadecimal numbers are written using eight and sixteen symbols, respectively. This is compared with the ten symbols used in writing decimal numbers. The decimal number 27, for example, would be written in octal as 33 and in hexadecimal as 1B. Octal and hexadecimal numbers are discussed in Appendix A.

for solving a particular class of problems. Examples of these procedure-oriented languages would be FORTRAN (Fig. 2.12), COBOL, BASIC, and PL/I. A result of using these languages is that it becomes quite easy to express an algorithm in a computer language. This is because all of the algorithm steps are written in symbolic rather than numeric form. In addition, these procedure-oriented languages do not require that the location of information in main memory be maintained in developing the algorithm.

A consequence associated with procedural languages is that computers cannot directly execute algorithms written using them. That is, algorithms represented using a procedure-oriented language must be translated into machine language programs before the computer can execute them. This translation process is performed by a computer program called a *compiler.* The use of a compiler for translating programs from a procedural language to machine language is analogous to an interpreter translating a book written in Russian into English. With this background, we are now ready to discuss computer operating systems.

operating system functions Earlier in this chapter we stated that a computer *operating system* consists of a series of algorithms (often called software) that: (1) *facilitate* the processing of the algorithms that people write to tell a computer how to solve a type of problem, and (2) *schedule* the resources of the computer among these user algorithms. We have already learned in this section that an algorithm in a form that can be executed by a computer is called a program. Therefore, an operating system can be defined as a collection of computer programs. Since users very rarely write their programs for problem solution in machine language, some of the programs that make up an operating system are the compilers. Recall that these compilers are used to translate programs that users have written in procedural languages, such as FORTRAN or COBOL, into machine language programs.

compilers

utility packages Another type of program contained in an operating system is the utility package. These *utility packages* contain programs that are written to handle frequently performed user tasks. Examples of such tasks would be sorting a list of names into alphabetical order, or the output of a group of information contained in computer auxiliary memory. These utility

```
C   ***** A SAMPLE FORTRAN PROGRAM *****
      READ(5,1) A,B,C
    1 FORMAT(F10.2)
      SUM=A+B+C
      WRITE(6,2) SUM
    2 FORMAT(10X,'SUM=',F12.2)
      STOP
      END
```

Figure 2.12.   Simple FORTRAN Program

programs are very useful because they allow a user to obtain the solution to a particular type of problem without actually developing the appropriate algorithm. Thus utility programs often result in a considerable time savings for the user. In addition, a savings in computer time is often realized because the utility programs are usually written by experts that have developed the best algorithms for the particular task.

In addition to the above functions, the operating system contains programs with the responsibility of *scheduling* computer system resources* among the user's and operating system's programs. For example, there is a scheduling program that determines in what order user jobs are to be processed. Smaller computers generally do not have a scheduling problem, in that one job at a time is processed until completion. Therefore, processing of another job will not start until the previous task has been completed. This type of job scheduling is called *sequential batch processing*.

schedulers

In medium- and large-scale computers, the resources of a computer are shared by a number of jobs at one time. Such an arrangement is known as multiprogramming. In *multiprogramming*, the operating system usually inputs programs to the computer's auxiliary memory as soon as a request for processing is received. This is sometimes called a *spooling process*. At the same time, processing of programs that had been previously input is continuing. When the computer detects that it is ready to begin processing another job, the scheduling program determines which job that is waiting in auxiliary memory is to be processed next. Sometimes this is determined strictly on a first-come, first-served basis. In many systems, however, jobs are attached priorities based on such things as how much the user is willing or able to pay, or how much time will be required to process the job. Under the priority scheduling arrangement, jobs with the highest priority will be processed before jobs with a lower priority.

multiprogramming

In addition to scheduling jobs, operating systems must include *error-recovery programs*. These are necessary in order for the computer to recover from program-caused errors, which might otherwise cause the computer to come to a halt or allow incorrect results.

error recovery

Another task handled by the operating system is that of *accounting* for the use of computer resources. This accounting is required so that users of the computer can be charged for the amount of computer resources they use. In addition, the accounting system is used as a screening device to prevent unauthorized users from processing jobs. This is accomplished by assigning an account number to each user for purposes of identification. These account numbers are kept in computer memory. When a user job is input, the account number of the user must appear as one of the

resource accounting

---

* *Computer system resources* may be defined as the various computer hardware and software components that together comprise a computer.

first input items. This number is matched against the authorized account numbers in the table in computer memory. If the account number for the input job is not found in the table, the job is rejected by the computer.

time sharing

A final topic that needs to be discussed under operating systems is that of *interactive usage* (also called conversational usage or *time-sharing*). In an interactive situation, a person usually enters the information to be processed through a terminal device (such as the one shown in Fig. 2.5). Should errors occur while entering this information, the computer would immediately respond with an error message. This allows the user to correct the error and continue processing of the job. An interactive user can save programs and data that are input through a terminal. The information is saved in the computer's auxiliary memory. The saved information is called a *file*. All time-sharing operating systems have an editing program that allows a user to modify portions of the file and to make additions and deletions on the file contents.

Interactive processing is becoming more popular as time passes. In fact, today time-sharing finds wide application in both education and industry. For example, in education it is used in computer-assisted instruction; in industry airline reservations would be a widely used application.

SUMMARY

1. A computer system consists of two primary components:
a. A computer hardware system.
b. A computer operating system.

2. Information to be processed by a computer must first be input into the main memory of the computer. This operation is performed using input devices.

3. Card readers and typewriter terminals are two of the most widely used input devices.

4. The memory of a computer stores all information electronically in the form of a binary code.

5. There are two classes of computer memory:
a. Main memory.
b. Auxiliary memory.

6. Computer main memory is divided into addressable units called locations. Each location in main memory has a unique address to permit access to information.

7. Information stored in a main memory location is called the contents of the location. A typical main memory location has the capacity to store from one to ten characters of information.

8. Three of the more widely used devices for auxiliary memory are magnetic disc, magnetic drum, and magnetic tape.

9. The capacity of main memory usually ranges from 100,000 to 1,000,000 characters. Auxiliary memory capacity on most computers varies from several million to hundreds of millions of characters.

10. The arithmetic and logical unit is the computer component in which the processing of information takes place.

11. The control of all components in a computer hardware system is performed by the control unit.

12. The control unit and the arithmetic and logical unit are organized into the central processing unit.

13. Information is output from computer main memory using a variety of output devices.

14. Line printers and typewriter terminals are two of the most widely used output devices.

15. Computer hardware systems are very reliable because they include self-checking components that either signal or correct errors that might occur.

16. An algorithm in a form that a computer can execute is called a program. Programs are written using programming languages.

17. The central processing unit of a computer is capable of executing only those programs that are written using its machine language.

18. Most users write their programs using a procedure-oriented programming language because of the difficulties associated with the use of machine language.

19. Programs written in procedural languages must be translated into machine language using computer programs called compilers.

20. A computer operating system consists of a collection of computer programs that:
a. Facilitate the processing of the algorithms that people write to tell a computer how to solve a problem.
b. Schedule the resources of a computer among these user algorithms.

21. Among the types of programs contained in an operating system are:
a. Compilers.
b. Utility programs.
c. Schedulers.
d. Error recovery.
e. Accounting.

22. Multiprogramming is the scheduling strategy in which more than one user program is being processed at one time.

23. Time-sharing or interactive computing is performed using a terminal device. This type of processing exists when the computer responds immediately to user information inputs.

Elements of Problem Solving and Algorithm Design

In Chapter 1 we briefly discussed problem-solving concepts. In that chapter we learned that the solutions to most problems that people solve are obtained through an informal process. We also observed that for a computer to solve a problem the steps in the solution to the problem must be carefully set out. This notion was reinforced in Chapter 2 when we learned about the great degree of detail required by a computer to solve a problem.

In this and the seven chapters that follow, we are going to study the concepts of problem solving and algorithm design in greater depth. A number of simple problems will be analyzed and algorithms will be developed for solving these problems. Throughout the remainder of this text, we will analyze problems and develop algorithms on the assumption that the algorithms are to be executed by a computer.

problem-solving phases   Three separate phases can be identified in the process of *problem solving*. These three phases are:

1. Analysis of the problem.
2. Design of an algorithm for solving the problem.
3. Implementation of the algorithm.

When using a computer in the solution of the problem, step 3 should be restated as:

3. Computer implementation of the algorithm.

In the following three sections, we will explore in more detail each of the above three phases involved in solving a problem. Then, the final two sections of this chapter will be devoted to the considerations involved in designing an algorithm for execution on a computer and program documentation.

3.1 PROBLEM ANALYSIS

The five steps in *problem analysis* are:

1. Precisely define the problem.
2. Identify the inputs and variables of the problem.
3. Identify the outputs desired from the algorithm.
4. Determine whether or not a computer is needed to solve the problem.
5. Obtain all other information required for algorithm development.

Let us now pursue in greater detail each of these steps in problem analysis.

Problem Definition

Definition of the problem to be solved is often assumed to be a trivial step. Nothing could be further from the truth. In fact, a careful and precise definition of the problem is an absolute necessity in the process of solving a problem. It is important to note that the definition of a problem does not usually consist of just one sentence. Instead, problem definitions often require one or more pages. In addition, problem definitions often include many subproblems, which also must be precisely defined.

Several possible consequences of not developing a complete and precise definition of a problem are that the algorithm developed may solve:

1. The wrong problem.
2. A portion only of the problem that needs to be solved.
3. A more complex problem than actually needs to be solved.

The first consequence is undesirable because it means that a lot of effort has been wasted in problem analysis and the development of an algorithm for solution of the wrong problem. No matter how good the problem analysis or the algorithm, an algorithm that gives a solution to the wrong problem is of no value to us. For example, our problem may be that of baking an apple pie. In error, however, we may think that the problem is that of baking a chocolate cake. Unfortunately, the chocolate cake algorithm we develop is of little value in solving our original problem of baking an apple pie. No matter how delicious the chocolate cake may be, it still is not an apple pie. As a second example, the best algorithm for obtaining the root of a linear equation will be of no value in obtaining the roots to a quadratic equation. Similarly, an algorithm for computing employee paychecks cannot be used to register students in their classes.

wrong-problem definition

43

A generalization of this notion is that algorithms exist independently of problems. Therefore, any algorithm can be applied to solve any problem. However, unless the algorithm is designed for the particular problem that we have defined, the output it produces will be incorrect. For example, an algorithm to compute the payroll for a company will not produce inventory records on those products the company currently has in stock.

incomplete definition

The second and third consequences of not developing a complete and precise definition of the problem are really special cases of the first consequence. In the second case, the algorithm only produces a portion of the output required by the original problem because of an incomplete problem definition. For example, the problem may be that of making a frosted German chocolate cake. If in error the problem is defined to be that of baking a German chocolate cake, the algorithm developed will not produce the desired result. This is because no provision exists in the algorithm for making the frosting. As a second example, the problem may be defined in error to be that of registering students into their classes. In this case, the actual problem may be to register students into their classes and issue the bills for their registration fees. The algorithm is incorrect in this example because the bills for registration fees are not produced, something that the actual problem required.

too complex problem definition

The third consequence is bad because unnecessary effort has been used in developing an algorithm to solve a problem that is more complex than the actual problem that required solving. For example, the problem may be to bake a chocolate cake. Now, if the algorithm is designed to solve the problem of baking a chocolate cake or an apple pie, we would have solved a more complex problem than we needed to solve. As a second example, the algorithm to obtain the roots of a quadratic equation will certainly provide the root of a linear equation. But, an algorithm for solving a quadratic equation is a much more elaborate one than is needed when the original problem only calls for finding the root of a linear equation.

difficulty of problem solving

Some problems are much easier to define precisely than are other problems. For example, defining the problem of finding the roots of a quadratic equation is much easier than completely defining the problem of processing a company payroll. In general, mathematical problems are somewhat easier to define than are nonmathematical problems. The primary reason for this is that someone seeking a solution to a mathematical problem will usually have a rather precise way of thinking about and expressing the problem. For example, the person seeking a method for solving a quadratic equation probably has a rather good knowledge of the mathematics of quadratic equations. That person also has a precise language (the language of mathematics) to use in thinking about and defining the problem. On the other hand, a person seeking to solve the payroll processing problem may know quite a lot about the way the payroll is currently being processed.   However, that person does not have as precise a language as mathematics to use in thinking about and defining the problem.   This is not to say, however, that the same care should not be taken in defining a mathematical problem as is given to defining a nonmathematical one.   All problems require careful thought in the process of developing a precise definition of the problem to be solved.

From this discussion we may conclude that the major responsibility for problem definition belongs to the experts in the problem area and not with the computer specialist.   Thus the mathematician must be sure that the problem to be solved is precisely defined.   Similarly, the accountant is responsible for giving a precise definition to the payroll processing problem.   The role of the computer specialist in problem definition is primarily that of asking the problem-area expert a sufficient number of questions about the problem.   This helps assure that the problem-area expert has thought of as many aspects of the problem as is possible.   Obviously, it is very helpful and desirable for the computer specialist to have a good knowledge of the problem area.   Finally, note that the problem-area expert and the computer specialist may sometimes be the same person.   This may be good in terms of reducing the problem of two or more people communicating with each other.   On the other hand, this reduces the amount of new inputs to the problem-definition process that additional people often provide.

responsibility for problem definition

From the discussion of this section, we may conclude that a well-organized approach to problem definition does not exist.   The main rule to apply is to attempt to consider every possible aspect of each problem.   In addition, we must remain flexible so that we feel free to redefine the problem as we proceed through the other stages of problem analysis.   In fact, questions often arise during the algorithm-design stage which lead to changes in the definition of the problem.   In conclusion, the problem-definition process is more art than science.   Therefore, it is learned primarily through experience gained from having defined many problems.

problem definition an art

3.1.2   Problem Inputs and Variables

Identifying the inputs and the variables needed to solve a problem is a very important step in problem analysis.   The inputs for a problem and problem variables can often be defined during the problem-definition step.   The *inputs* for a problem consist of the data to be processed by the algorithm in arriving at a problem solution.   For example, in the payroll problem, inputs might consist of data items such as an employee's: (1) social security number, (2) name, (3) number of dependents, and (4) number of hours worked during a pay period.

inputs

variables

The *variables* for a problem would be such things as the inputs and outputs of a problem, together with any constants and intermediate results that may be needed. The concept of problem variables will be explored more fully in Section 4.2.

3.1.3   Problem Outputs

The task of identifying problem outputs or results is closely related to the definition of the problem. A considerable amount of judgment is required

amount of output

in this step because producing more output than is necessary is a waste of resources. However, producing too little output will often result in the algorithm not producing a correct solution to the problem. For example, in solving a system of linear equations, it is not usually desirable to output the values of all intermediate results. Generally, the only output desired is the set of coefficients of the system of equations and the solution values. On the other hand, just outputting the coefficient values would leave the problem unsolved because obtaining the solution values of the system of equations is the problem we wished to solve.

The greatest problem with identifying the output needed occurs in data processing problems. Often either reports are produced that are not read, or reports that may be needed by managers are not produced. In practice, there seems to be a tendency to produce too much output detail. This, in general, causes output reports to be ignored.

3.1.4   A Computer Problem?

A very important question that is often not asked is whether or not a computer should be used for the solution of a problem. Asking this question is important because computer time is expensive. In addition, developing an algorithm that a computer can use to solve a problem may often require more time than solving the problem by hand. So it may require more time and may cost more to solve a problem by use of a computer than to solve the problem manually.

criteria for using a
computer

When should computers be used to solve a problem? In general, use a computer when one or more of the following conditions are present:

1. When the computations would require so much time to perform that the cost of doing the problem by hand would exceed the cost of solving the problem using the computer.

2. When the number of computations is so great that using a computer is the only means of solution.

3. When the problem needs to be solved many times for different sets of input values.

4. When the problem is such that its solution requires repetition of a relatively small number of steps.

5. When the reliability of the output is so important that errors cannot be permitted.

As an example, we would probably never recommend using a computer to process the payroll of a company based on the first reason given above. This is because the cost of developing a computer algorithm for processing the payroll is far greater than doing the payroll by hand. Reasons 3, 4, and 5, however, more than offset reason 1 because in applying reason 1 we were just thinking about processing the payroll once. But the payroll usually needs to be processed every week of the year. Thus, once we have developed the computer algorithm, we can process the payroll at a cost much lower than the cost of doing it manually. In addition, there will generally be fewer errors when the payroll is processed by computer.

Another example involves arranging a group of numbers into ascending order. If we have only five numbers to put in ascending order, we would be well advised to sort them manually. However, if we have 150,000 numbers to sort, doing it by computer is well worthwhile because of reasons 2, 4, and 5. That is, sorting numbers involves the repeated execution of a small number of steps. In addition, it is very doubtful that anyone can correctly place 150,000 numbers into ascending order using manual methods.

In closing, let us observe that the above criteria do not hold in an introductory course in computer science. This is because textbook-type problems that are relatively simple are the only types of problems that beginning students are capable of solving in a short period of time. Many of these problems, however, can be solved faster by hand than by using a computer. Since the real purpose is learning how to solve problems using a computer and not just the solution of the problem, we are justified in using the computer for problem solution.

textbook problems

3.1.5   Obtain All Other Information

After we have identified all of the inputs, variables, and outputs associated with a problem, our last step in problem analysis will be to gather all other information about the problem. An example of this type of information might be a special case, such as the fact that social security tax is paid only on that part of an employee's yearly salary which is less than $13,200. Another example would be that the logarithm of a number is defined only for values greater than zero.

Many of these considerations may already have been included in the problem-definition step. Therefore, the primary purpose of including this final step in problem analysis is to collect as many additional pieces of information as possible before proceeding to the algorithm-design stage. This will help to ensure that the algorithm developed will provide a correct solution to the problem.

3.2   ALGORITHM DESIGN

After a problem has been properly defined and analyzed, an algorithm must be developed which provides the steps that the computer will follow in solving the problem. In Chapter 1 we informally defined the concept of an algorithm and developed noncomputer algorithms for solving several problems. Thus we already have a very limited experience in designing algorithms.

3.2.1   Properties of Algorithms

algorithms

Let us precisely define* the term "algorithm." An *algorithm* is a procedure which consists of a set of unambiguous rules specifying a sequence of operations that provides the solution to a specific class of problems in a finite number of steps. The important points in the definition are:

1. An algorithm is a procedure which is made up of a set of rules.
2. The rules that make up the algorithm must be unambiguous.
3. The operations specified by the rules must be executed in a certain sequence.
4. The procedure must give a solution to a specific class of problems.
5. The solution must be obtained in a finite number of steps.

Let us discuss these five points in more detail.

---

* This definition is as precise as can be given using a natural language such as English. For a more rigorous mathematical definition of an algorithm, see Donald E. Knuth, *The Art of Computer Programming: Vol. I: Fundamental Algorithms,* 2nd edition (Reading, Mass.: Addison-Wesley Publishing Company, Inc., 1973).

The first point was that an algorithm is a procedure made up of a set of rules. What is a procedure? Well, a *procedure is simply the set of steps that taken together gives the solution to a class of problems.* That is, the procedure is the representation of the method given by the algorithm. Thus an algorithm is really an abstraction of a method for solving a problem that we represent as the set of rules in a procedure. Notice that any algorithm may be represented as a procedure, but every procedure is not necessarily the representation of an algorithm.

procedures

The *rules* used in constructing a procedure may take many forms. They may be statements given in a natural language such as English. Another type of rule might be given by the symbols of a flowchart and their contents. Examples of these two types of procedures were given in Chapter 1. Another type of rule is a machine language instruction, such as we discussed in Chapter 2.

rules

Whatever type of rules we use for representing our algorithm, these rules must be *unambiguous*. That is, each time any person or machine that can understand the language in which the rule is written executes that rule, the rule must be interpreted to have the same meaning. Thus great care must be used when expressing an algorithm in a natural language such as English. This is because of the many meanings that a single word can have. For example, the word *love* has several meanings. There is erotic love, which is the sexual attraction of one individual for another. Another type of love is brotherly love, the warm feeling we hold for a relative or a close friend. A third type of love is the giving type of love, as represented by God's benevolent feeling toward mankind.* In a similar way, phrases constructed from words of the English language can be very ambiguous.

unambiguous

Just specifying the set of rules is not sufficient to give us the solution to a problem. The *sequence* in which the rules are to be performed is also quite important. In Chapter 1 we had examples in which the steps in a flowchart were performed in a top-to-bottom order. Only finding a connector or a decision symbol changed this sequence.

sequence

The fourth point was that an algorithm must always give a solution to a specific class of problems. This might be called the *generality attribute* of algorithms. As an example, a procedure to sum the five numbers 2, 4, 0, 7, and 8 has no generality whatsoever. It can solve only one very specific problem. A procedure to sum any five real numbers would be slightly more general but can be even further generalized. However, a procedure designed to form the sum of n real numbers would satisfy the generality condition for the existence of an algorithm. This is because the problem of summing n numbers can be considered to be a class of prob-

generality attribute

---

* The Greeks recognized these types of love by using three different words for love. Their words for the three types of love identified here were, in order: (1) eros, (2) philia, and (3) agapé.

lems.   The reason for this is that *n* can have any positive integer as a value. Thus, when *n* equals 5, five numbers would be summed.   When *n* is 8, the sum of eight values would be found.   Therefore, the algorithm would produce valid results for the general problem of adding together all of the numbers in a set.

finite number of steps

The final requirement is that the solution to a problem must be obtained in a *finite number of steps*.   This requirement simply states that execution of the algorithm must produce a solution.   This is because a procedure that does not produce a result in a finite number of steps either must: (1) not produce a result, regardless of the number of steps executed, or (2) requires an infinite number of steps in which to produce a solution. Of course, since a computer cannot execute an infinite number of steps, a procedure that requires an infinite number of steps to obtain a problem solution cannot produce a result.   Notice that this requirement does not demand that we know in advance how many steps will be executed to produce a problem solution.

3.2.2   Representation of Algorithms

In the previous section we explored the properties of algorithms and observed that an algorithm is really an abstract notion.   It is the representation of an algorithm that we use for solving problems.   A problem with which we are faced is deciding upon the language for representing our algorithms.   There are four alternatives available for representing algorithms:

1. Natural languages (such as English).
2. Computer programming languages.
3. Decision tables.
4. Flowchart languages.

Let us examine these alternatives in order to select one to use for representing the algorithms that we will develop in this text.

natural languages

A *natural language*, such as English, suffers from four basic deficiencies:

1. It is ambiguous.
2. Statements (and thus the algorithms) tend to be too long.
3. The basic logical flow of the algorithm is difficult to follow.
4. In general, computers cannot currently process algorithms that are represented in a natural language.

Under the first point, we have already noted how ambiguous a natural language such as English can be. Since ambiguous steps cannot exist in algorithms, this is a serious drawback to using a natural language. Second, the burden of writing algorithms using a natural language is too great. Thus a statement such as: "Set the value of *Sum* to be the sum of the value of *Sum* and the value of *A*" is less desirable than the flowchart language statement:

$$Sum \leftarrow Sum + A$$

The notation used here will be explained more fully in Chapter 4.

Third, the logical flow of an algorithm is difficult to follow when the algorithm is represented using a natural language. This is because a natural-language representation is serial (or linear, i.e., goes in only one direction) in nature. That is, one step is followed by another step. For example, when a branch point is reached where flow goes in one of several directions, each flow path must be followed one at a time. A major result is that loops and branches do not stand out clearly using this method of representation. This shortcoming makes a natural language a poor selection when the purpose of representing an algorithm is to communicate the logic of the algorithm to other people. Finally, we note the fact that computers cannot currently process algorithms represented using a natural language. This means that the natural-language representation would have to be translated into a computer programming-language representation for the algorithm to be processed by a computer.

A *computer programming language* can also be used to represent an algorithm. In fact, all of the algorithms that we develop in this book will be designed to be performed by a computer. Therefore, these algorithms will eventually have to be translated into a computer programming-language representation so that they can be executed on a computer. The advantages of using a computer programming language for representing an algorithm are:

computer programming languages

1. In general, computer programming languages are not ambiguous.
2. The computer programming-language representation of an algorithm generally is not cumbersome.
3. Computers can process algorithms written using a computer programming language.

There are three reasons for not using a computer programming language to represent an algorithm:

1. The basic logical flow of the algorithm is generally difficult to follow.
2. The communication of algorithm logic is restricted to those persons who understand the particular computer programming language that is used.
3. The rules associated with a computer programming language often require a long time to learn because they involve an unfamiliar notation.

The first disadvantage is because programming languages, like natural languages, are essentially serial (or linear) in nature. Thus execution of one step is normally followed by execution of the next step in the program. We might observe that this drawback becomes more serious as the logic of the algorithm becomes more complex. Therefore, if communication of the algorithm logic to others is not an important factor, direct development of an algorithm using a computer programming language may be acceptable. The second point listed is also a disadvantage, mostly because it blocks communication to others. Rather, we prefer that our algorithms be expressed in a language that is independent of any particular computer or computer programming language. The third disadvantage requires that we spend a lot of time learning a language that uses an unfamiliar notation before we can begin to learn how to construct algorithms.

decision tables   Another form of representing the rules of an algorithm is called a decision table. A *decision table* is simply a table that lists the actions to be taken for all possible conditions which may hold in a complex decision process. In Fig. 3.1 an example of a decision table is given for a portion of an algorithm. The decision table is for the case in which an employer is interested in counting the number of employees falling into certain categories based on classification by age, years of education, and current salary. Under the *Employee Characteristics* heading in the top of the decision table, the use of a colon means to compare. Thus *AGE:30* means compare the employee's age to 30. The variable *T* in the lower part of the decision table is used to tally the results of employees that fit into each of the eight categories.

Decision tables are used most often for complex decision processes. Four advantages associated with the use of decision tables are:

1. Decision tables can be easily constructed and modified because of the simplicity and flexibility of their format.
2. Decision tables are compact in their representation of a complex decision process.
3. The logic of a decision process is easily followed in a decision-table representation.

Figure 3.1.   Decision Table for Employee Characteristics

	Employee Characteristics	Rule Number							
		1	2	3	4	5	6	7	8
Condition	AGE:30	$\leq$	$\leq$	$\leq$	$\leq$	$>$	$>$	$>$	$>$
	YRS:16	$<$	$<$	$\geq$	$\geq$	$<$	$<$	$\geq$	$\geq$
	SAL:10000	$<$	$\geq$	$<$	$\geq$	$<$	$\geq$	$<$	$\geq$
Action	$T(1) \leftarrow T(1) + 1$	X							
	$T(2) \leftarrow T(2) + 1$		X						
	$T(3) \leftarrow T(3) + 1$			X					
	$T(4) \leftarrow T(4) + 1$				X				
	$T(5) \leftarrow T(5) + 1$					X			
	$T(6) \leftarrow T(6) + 1$						X		
	$T(7) \leftarrow T(7) + 1$							X	
	$T(8) \leftarrow T(8) + 1$								X

4. Computer languages are available for translating decision tables into a computer programming-language representation.

Two disadvantages associated with decision tables are:

1. Decision tables are essentially serial in nature. Thus the overall flow of the decision process is not clear in a decision table.
2. Decision tables are very cumbersome in representing simple decision situations.

Since communication of algorithm logic is so important to us in this text, the first disadvantage suggests that we drop decision tables from consideration. Furthermore, since simple decision situations are common in most algorithms, decision tables are too cumbersome for representing an algorithm.

In this text, we will use a *flowchart language* for representing our   **flowchart languages** algorithms. Advantages of using a flowchart language are:

1. The logical structure of an algorithm stands out.

2. Modular construction of algorithms is easily accomplished.
3. Flowchart representations of an algorithm are independent of any particular computer or computer programming language.
4. Flowcharts provide documentation to support the computer programming-language representation of the algorithm.

Flowcharts display the logical flow of an algorithm better than the other languages we have examined. This is because rather than being serial, as other languages are, flowcharts are *two-dimensional*. That is, flow moves not just in one dimension (up and down) but moves in two dimensions. One of these dimensions is the flow from the top to the bottom of the flowchart, and the other dimension is from one side to the other side of the flowchart. In addition, flow is shown explicitly in flowcharts through the use of flowlines and connectors. In the other languages we examined, the direction of flow is implied rather than shown explicitly. Not only does this make development of the algorithm easier. It also makes it easier to explain the structure of the algorithm to noncomputer personnel.

Flowcharts also make *modular construction* of algorithms possible. That is, the problem can be divided into different parts or subproblems. Then subalgorithms can be designed to solve each subproblem. Next, the subalgorithms are combined to solve the overall problem. For example, the subproblems in a payroll problem might be: (1) computing the gross pay, deductions, and net pay; (2) printing the paychecks; and (3) revising the payroll records to include the pay and deductions from the current pay period. An advantage of breaking a problem into subproblems is that more than one person at a time can be working on the design of the algorithm for solving the problem. This cuts down on the overall development time for designing the algorithm. Another advantage is that the logic of fairly small algorithms can be understood more readily than can the logic of large algorithms. Thus, a large problem is best solved by separating it into a series of smaller, more easily understood problems for which small simple algorithms can be developed. The concept of subalgorithms for solving subproblems will be discussed in detail in Chapter 9.

The computer and computer programming-language independence of the flowchart language is very important from the standpoint of *communication*. Flowcharts permit a person to study the logical flow of an algorithm without being familiar with a particular (or even any) computer or computer programming language. On the other hand, a person who wanted to understand the logic of an algorithm expressed in, for example, FORTRAN would have to know the FORTRAN language. Such is not the case with the flowchart representation of an algorithm. With a very minimum time requirement, anyone can pick up a properly designed flowchart and gain an understanding of the algorithm represented by that flowchart.

Furthermore, a flowchart representation of an algorithm can be easily translated into a computer programming-language representation of that algorithm.

Finally, a flowchart provides excellent *documentation* for an algorithm that has been implemented on a computer. This documentation can be important when converting a program to another computer system or into a different programming language. A flowchart can also help when removing from the algorithm logical errors that may turn up later. Finally, because of changes that may eventually occur in the problem to be solved, the algorithm itself may require alteration. When a flowchart is present, these changes in the algorithm can often be made easily without introducing errors into the algorithm. In the case where the computer program is altered directly, errors are much more likely to occur. This is particularly important, since the person who has to revise an algorithm may not be the person who originally developed it.

3.2.3   Do Algorithms Already Exist?

Once the five steps of problem analysis have been completed, we should attempt to learn if one or more algorithms already exist for solving the problem. This is an important step because if we can find a suitable algorithm for solving our problem, the process of developing a new algorithm can be omitted. Unfortunately, this step is often ignored and people duplicate the work of others in solving a problem for which an algorithm already exists.

The process of determining whether an algorithm already exists is not easily accomplished for several reasons. First, there are many places to look for algorithms that will solve particular problems. Among the sources would be:

algorithm sources

1. A professional organization publication. (For example, each month algorithms for solving various problems are published in the *Communications of the ACM.* Once each year an index of algorithms that appeared during the preceding year is published in the same source.)
2. A computer manufacturer's library of internally developed programs. (Computer manufacturers often develop libraries of programs for solving various problems. For example, IBM has a set of programs for solving mathematical and statistical problems which it calls the *Scientific Subroutine Package.* The cost of these programs varies widely.)

3. A computer manufacturer's library of user-contributed programs. (As a service to its customers, many computer manufacturers maintain a library of programs submitted by users. These are usually available to their customers at little or no cost.)

4. A colleague or competitor. (A competitor may not be willing to provide the program to us at any price.)

5. A standard package from a software house. (A software house is a business that exists to develop programs for the solution of a particular class of problems. The programs they develop are their products to sell.)

algorithm compatibility and reliability

Second, if we are able to locate an algorithm for solving a problem, we must be certain that the algorithm was designed to solve a problem exactly like the problem we have. In addition, the computer program representing the algorithm must be one that can be processed by our computer. Since programs are often written considering the characteristics of a particular model or series of computer, this is not a trivial matter. A third question concerns the reliability of the algorithm. We must be careful not to assume that an algorithm has been carefully tested by the developer. Thus, any algorithm obtained from another source should be carefully tested. Of course, the amount of testing we do depends upon how reliable we feel the source of our algorithm to be.

Despite the effort involved in searching for an already existing algorithm for solving our problem, the payoff is often great. This is particularly true in the case of large problems that involve many man-months or even man-years in their solution. Frequently, an algorithm that is designed to solve a problem which is not exactly like our problem can, with minor changes, be adapted to solve our problem.

3.2.4   An Algorithm as a Function*

Considering an algorithm to be a function may be helpful in gaining insight into what an algorithm is. Recall from algebra that the domain of a function, f(x), is the set of all possible values of the variable x for which the function is defined. Similarly, the range of a function, f(x), is the set of all possible values that f(x) may assume for all given values of x. For example, if a function is defined as

$$f(x) = x^2$$

for all real values of x, we say that $-\infty < x < +\infty$ is the domain of f(x)

---

* This section can be omitted without loss of continuity.

while $0 \leq f(x) < +\infty$ is the range.   The process of transforming a value of x into a value of $f(x)$ is said to be a *mapping* of x into $f(x)$.   The following table gives some values of x and the corresponding function values:

x	$f(x) = x^2$
-2	4
0	0
2	4
3	9

In our study of algebra, we also learned that we can have functions of two or more variables.   For example, a function for multiplying two numbers together might be indicated as

$$f(x, y) = x \cdot y$$

where $f(x, y)$ is a mapping of the product of x and y.

Now, an algorithm can be thought of as a function, since it trans- **domain** forms a set of input values into a set of output values.   The *domain* of an algorithm is the set of all input values for which the algorithm is de- fined.   Similarly, the *range* of an algorithm is the set of all possible values **range** output by the algorithm for all given input values in the domain of the algorithm.   We would then say that an algorithm defines a mapping or a function that transforms input values into output values.   As an example of an algorithm, we might have a procedure that inputs a number, forms the square of the number, and outputs that square.   In this example, the domain of the algorithm is any representable numeric value, and its range is any representable nonnegative numeric value.

Note that the input and output values of an algorithm can be any representable symbols.   They can be numbers, alphabetic characters, spe- cial characters, or any other meaningful symbols that a computer can rep- resent.   For example, we might develop an algorithm which:

1. Inputs a ten-symbol string consisting of blank spaces and/or al- phabetic characters.
2. Scans the string inserting periods wherever any blank spaces appear.*
3. Outputs the ten-character transformed string.

---

*Notice that we are using an *underline* to represent each *blank space* that may appear in a character string.   Without a rule like this it would be difficult for the reader to determine the number of blank spaces in a character string.

As an example, the input string

HI_THERE_ _

would be transformed by our algorithm to read

HI.THERE . .

The domain of this algorithm would be the set of all ten-symbol strings that contain blanks and/or alphabetic characters. The range of the algorithm would be ten-symbol strings that contain periods and/or alphabetic characters.

Finally, the relationship among the values in an input data set can be important in an algorithm. For example, we might consider an algorithm that:

1. Inputs a string consisting of ten alphabetic characters arranged in any sequence.
2. Rearranges the ten characters into nondecreasing alphabetical order using the natural order of the English alphabet (i.e., A B C · · · X Y Z).
3. Outputs the reordered ten-character string.

As an example, the input string

HITHEREDAD

would be mapped into the output string

ADDEEHHIRT

by our algorithm. Therefore, an algorithm can simply have the task of rearranging the input symbols using some criteria. The domain of this algorithm would be any ten-character sequence of alphabetic characters. The range would be any sequence of ten alphabetic characters that appear in nondecreasing alphabetical order.

We say that two algorithms are equivalent if they:

equivalent algorithms

1. Have a common domain and a common range.
2. Both algorithms produce the same output for any given input in their common domain.

Note that *equivalent algorithms* are not necessarily equal in efficiency.

Interestingly enough, it has been proved that no algorithm exists that will determine whether or not two algorithms are equivalent. That is, an algorithm does not exist which:

1. Has as its domain the set of all possible pairs of all possible algorithms.
2. Has as its range, for example, the words *yes* or *no*.
3. Performs a transformation such that *yes* is output if the pair of input algorithms is equivalent and *no* is output otherwise.

Thus, problems do exist that cannot be solved by algorithms. The study of the existence or nonexistence of algorithms for solving certain problems is called *algorithmic theory*. The study of algorithmic theory belongs to a branch of computer science known as *computability theory*.

3.3 COMPUTER IMPLEMENTATION OF ALGORITHMS

After a problem has been analyzed and an algorithm developed for its solution, the algorithm must be implemented on a computer. Implementation involves a task known as programming or coding. *Programming* is a process in which the steps of the flowchart representation of the algorithm are converted into steps in a computer programming language. There are basically three classes of programming languages which can be used for implementing an algorithm on a computer:

programming

1. Machine-oriented programming languages.
2. Procedure-oriented programming languages.
3. Problem-oriented programming languages.

We have already discussed the concept of a *machine-oriented* programming language in Chapter 2.

A *procedure-oriented* programming language relates to the procedure being coded. Thus, programs written in a procedure-oriented language are relatively independent of computer systems. That is, an algorithm coded in a procedure-oriented programming language can be executed on any computer system. The only requirement is that a translator be available to convert the procedure-oriented program into the machine language for that computer.*

---

* Recall from Chapter 2 that a program written in any language other than machine language must be translated into machine language before it can be executed by a computer.

procedure-oriented languages

Procedure-oriented programming languages can be applied to coding the algorithm for almost any type of problem. Most of the current procedure-oriented languages are, however, better adapted to certain general types of problems than they are to other types of problems. The four most popular procedure-oriented languages for processing numeric-type problems are:

1. FORTRAN (FORmula TRANslator).
2. BASIC (Beginner's All-purpose Symbolic Instruction Code).
3. ALGOL (ALGOrithmic Language).
4. APL (A Programming Language).

A popular procedure-oriented programming language for processing business-type problems is COBOL (COmmon Business-Oriented Language). A procedure-oriented language that is well adapted to processing both numeric- and nonnumeric-type problems is PL/I (Programming Language/I).

In Fig. 3.2 we show examples of statements in FORTRAN, COBOL, BASIC, PL/I, and ALGOL. Each of these statements:

1. Causes two quantities (called B and C) to be summed.
2. Multiplies this sum by a third quantity (called D).
3. Assigns the result to a variable (called A).

```
LANGUAGE                ARITHMETIC STATEMENT
--------                -----------------------------------------
FORTRAN      A=(B+C)*D
COBOL        COMPUTE A EQUALS (B PLUS C) TIMES D.
BASIC        LET A=(B+C)*D
PL/I         A=(B+C)*D;
ALGOL        A:=(B+C)*D;
```

Figure 3.2. Examples of Arithmetic Statements in Five Procedure-Oriented Languages

Notice that all of these statements relate to the procedure being performed and are not dependent on any particular computer. In addition, these statements do not require the great amount of detail required by machine language.

problem-oriented languages

Problem-oriented programming languages provide a means of programming a narrower class of problems than would be possible using a procedure-oriented language. A significant gain is usually realized, however, in using a problem-oriented language. This is because the language rules closely approximate the terms and structure of the problems themselves. Thus fewer but more powerful statements can be used in coding the algorithm. Problem-oriented programming systems are currently available for such widely diverse areas as: (1) simulation, (2) computer-assisted instruction, (3) statistics, and (4) list processing.

A critical phase in the computer implementation of an algorithm **program testing** is the program testing and debugging process. *Program testing* involves running the computer program using sets of input test data to determine whether or not the output either:

1. Coincides with answers that have previously been obtained by hand computation or some other method.
2. Is in agreement with the answers that experts in the problem field consider to be reasonable as dictated by theoretical or other considerations.

Debugging is the process of removing errors (called *bugs*) from the **debugging** computer program. There are essentially three sources of bugs in a program. First, the problem may have been poorly defined or analyzed. In this case the three stages of problem solution will need to be partially or completely repeated. Second, the algorithm may contain logical errors that require correction. The obvious result here will be that the computer program will need alteration. Third, coding errors may exist that are caused by either:

1. A failure to properly translate the algorithm steps into programming-language steps.
2. A violation of the syntactical rules* associated with the programming language.

Whatever the cause of program bugs, the process of problem analysis, algorithm design, and programming is obviously iterative. That is, one or more of these steps must be repeated until a satisfactory program is obtained for the solution of the class of problems. In practice, errors are found in so-called debugged programs for some time after their release. This, of course, is not to say that every effort should not be made to develop flawless programs. Rather, it points out that perfect products are not always the result of the efforts of the best problem-solving staffs. Therefore, some caution should be exercised in using any program, whether written by you or by another person, regardless of that person's compe-

---

* Syntactical rules are rules that tell how the statements of a language must be constructed. That is, they tell what is legal in forming statements in a language.

tence. The concepts associated with the topic of programming and program debugging will be explored further in the programming-language supplements that accompany this text. A flowchart of the problem-solving sequence appears in Fig. 3.3.

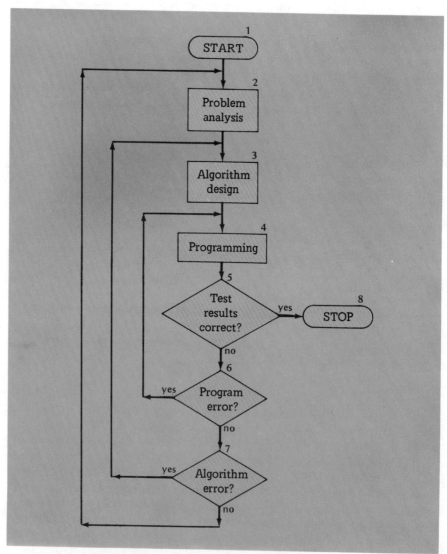

Figure 3.3. Problem-Solving Sequence Flowchart

3.4 COMPUTER CONSIDERATIONS IN ALGORITHM DESIGN

There are several considerations that relate to the fact that all of the algorithms that we will develop are designed to be executed on a computer. First, the main memory of a computer has a limited capacity.* Therefore, in designing algorithms we may not be able to use some methods for solving a problem that might otherwise give correct results. This is because the method may require more main memory capacity than is available for holding the instructions and data. For example, one method used to sort the payroll file for a company might involve loading all employee records into main memory prior to sorting the file. If our computer has a main memory capacity of 100,000 locations and our payroll file requires 400,000 locations, however, we must seek another method of solution. That is, one property of the algorithm we use for sorting must be that it does not require that the entire set of payroll information be in main memory at any one time. In general, a desirable goal is to design an algorithm that uses as little main memory as possible.

main memory capacity

A second consideration is the amount of time required for an algorithm to reach a solution to a problem. Many computers can execute hundreds of thousands of instructions per second, a very fast speed indeed. But, even a computer can be given an algorithm that requires an unreasonable amount of time to execute. Thus, when designing an algorithm, consideration should be given to using the method that minimizes computer execution time. One problem is that this rule often conflicts with the goal of minimizing the amount of main memory needed. For example, the faster sorting procedures available require that the entire set of information to be sorted be located in main memory. However, if main memory cannot hold the entire set of information, these algorithms cannot be used. Therefore, in algorithm design we must constantly balance the goal of minimizing main memory required with the desire to minimize computer execution time.

speed of execution

In Chapter 2 we learned that digital computers are finite machines. That is, numbers are usually represented using a fixed number of digit positions. In addition, the number of digit positions on most computers is usually quite limited. A consequence is that, in general, a real number cannot be represented exactly. Instead, any input value that is a real number will be stored as a finite approximation to that number. Since

finite approximations

---

* Many current computers have something called a *virtual memory*. In such computers, the size of the virtual memory rather than the size of the main memory is the limiting factor in algorithm design.

such input values are only approximations, the output will also generally be an approximation.

computational error

An additional source of error when dealing with finite approximations to real numbers is known as computational error. *Computational error* occurs because the number of digits in the result of some computation exceeds the number of digits that can be stored in a location. Thus, the result must be rounded off before it can be stored. This causes some of the significant digits to be lost. Furthermore, in many cases the input and/or computational error can, through a sequence of computations, increase until the error in the output values is so great that the results are unacceptable to the user. Even worse, the error in the results may be transparent to the user. That is, the user will not be aware that the results are in error. In this case, the incorrect results may be interpreted as true results. The topic of rounding errors will be discussed in Chapter 10.

Another factor to be considered in designing an algorithm is that the best method of manually solving a problem is not necessarily the best method for a computer to use. For example, in computing the statistical measure called standard deviation, two formulas are available. One is the definitional formula and the other is the computational formula. The computational formula is the preferred manual method because it requires fewer computations than the definitional formula. For this reason, and because it minimizes memory requirements, we might be inclined to use the same method in designing a computer-based algorithm. However, the definitional formula is to be preferred for computer solution because it minimizes computational error and, in general, produces more accurate results. Thus, in developing an algorithm, the criteria that main memory requirements and computer execution time should be minimized should not always be followed.

3.5   PROGRAM DOCUMENTATION

reasons for program documentation

An important aspect in the computer implementation of an algorithm is program documentation. Unfortunately, programs often are not properly documented in real-world situations. The reasons for thoroughly documenting a program are:

1. To make it easy for potential users to understand the purpose and logic of the program.
2. To assist persons using the program to prepare the input data correctly.
3. To allow for easy maintenance of the program.

The first point is important because a person may need to know whether a program is able to solve a problem that needs to be solved. Obviously, the best source of this information would be the person or persons who developed the algorithm and wrote the program. Therefore, the purpose of the program must be set out in the documentation. This documentation should be in both expository and flowchart form. Specific details should be included in the expository part of the documentation so that the precise purpose of the program can be easily learned. The flowchart is included to provide information about the logic used in the program. It will often be in the form of an algorithm flowchart. However, sometimes a descriptive form of flowchart is used to provide the purpose and logic of the program.

The second reason for program documentation is that input data must be provided for a program in a certain order and a specific format. In the case where punched cards are used for input, input documentation usually takes the form of card layouts. These card layouts may be diagrams of punched cards or may be expository. In either case, they describe the contents of every column of every input data card required by the program. Figures 3.4 and 3.5 provide examples of card layout in diagram and expository form, respectively. When a terminal device is used to input data to a program, similar methods can be used for input documentation.

The final purpose for documentation is necessary because algorithms and programs are dynamic instead of static. That is, the problem an algorithm is designed to solve changes as the needs of the person or the organization needing a solution to the problem change. Therefore, the algorithm and program must be altered to reflect the changes in the problem they are designed to solve. Without proper documentation this revision process will turn out to be very difficult. One reason is that making a change requires a complete understanding of algorithm logic so that the point at which the change is to be made can be identified. In addition, extreme care has to be used when changes are made so that an error is not introduced into the logic of the algorithm. Another reason for the importance of documentation is that the original designers of the algorithm may no longer be employed by the organization when the changes are to be made. Therefore, the persons who are to make the revisions will need to understand the logic of the algorithm thoroughly. Program documentation for the purpose of algorithm revision is usually provided by detailed algorithm flowcharts.

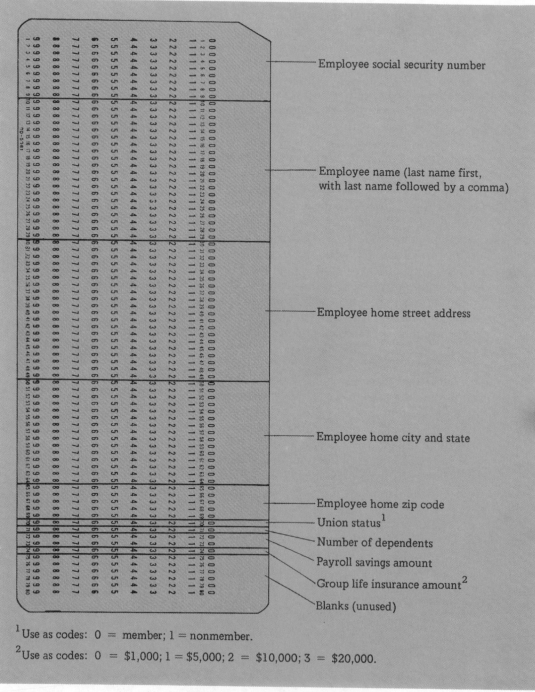

Employee social security number

Employee name (last name first, with last name followed by a comma)

Employee home street address

Employee home city and state

Employee home zip code

Union status[1]

Number of dependents

Payroll savings amount

Group life insurance amount[2]

Blanks (unused)

[1] Use as codes: 0 = member; 1 = nonmember.

[2] Use as codes: 0 = $1,000; 1 = $5,000; 2 = $10,000; 3 = $20,000.

Figure 3.4. Input Card Layout in Diagram Form

Figure 3.5. Input Card Layout of Fig. 3.4 in Expository Form

Card Columns	Field Definition
1–9	Employee social security number
10–29	Employee name (last name first, with last name followed by a comma)
30–49	Employee home street address
50–64	Employee home city and state
65–69	Employee home zip code
70	Union status (0 = member; 1 = nonmember)
71	Number of dependents
72–73	Payroll savings amount (in dollars, right-justified in field)
74	Group life insurance amount (0 = $1,000; 1 = $5,000; 2 = $10,000; 3 = $20,000)
75–80	Blanks (unused)

PROBLEMS

1. Perform all five steps of problem analysis for the problem that involves maintaining student grade records at your college or university. Make any reasonable assumptions necessary in your analysis of the problem.

2. Perform all five steps of problem analysis for the problem that involves maintaining automobile registration records in your state. Make any reasonable assumptions necessary in your analysis of the problem.

3. Perform all five steps of problem analysis for the problem that involves maintaining records on the inventory of the book store at your college or university. Make any reasonable assumptions necessary in your analysis of the problem.

4. Perform all five steps of problem analysis for the problem that involves maintaining patient records for a dentist. Make any reasonable assumptions necessary in your analysis of the problem.

5. Perform all five steps of problem analysis for the problem that involves maintaining records on the inventory of a toy store. Make any reasonable assumptions necessary in your analysis of the problem.

6. Give the domain and range for an algorithm that: (a) inputs a value for x, (b) evaluates the function $f(x) = x^4 - x^2$, and (c) outputs the values of x and $f(x)$.

7. Give the domain and range for an algorithm that: (a) inputs a pair of values, x and y; (b) evaluates the function $f(x, y) = x^2 \cdot y^4$; and (c) outputs the values of x, y, and $f(x, y)$.

8. Give the domain and range for an algorithm that: (a) inputs a fifty-symbol string consisting of alphabetic characters and blank spaces, (b) scans the string counting the number of times a vowel appears, and (c) outputs the string together with the count of the number of vowels found.

9. Give the domain and range for an algorithm that: (a) inputs a sequence of symbol strings which contains customer names, (b) rearranges the sequence of the symbol strings so that they are in nondecreasing alphabetical order by last name, and (c) outputs the resequenced symbol strings.

10. Assume that we have one algorithm which inputs a value for x, evaluates the function $f(x) = x^2$, and outputs $f(x)$, and that we have a second algorithm which performs the same task using the function $f(x) = x \cdot x$. Are these two algorithms equivalent? Why or why not?

11. Assume that we have one algorithm which inputs a value for x, evaluates the function $f(x) = x^2$, and outputs $f(x)$, and that we have a second algorithm which performs the same task using $f(x) = x^4/x^2$. Are these two algorithms equivalent? Why or why not?

SUMMARY

1. The three phases of the problem-solving process are:
a. Analysis of the problem.
b. Design of an algorithm for solving the problem.
c. Computer implementation of the algorithm.

2. The five steps of problem analysis are:
a. Precisely define the problem.
b. Identify the inputs and variables of the problem.
c. Identify the outputs desired from the algorithm.
d. Determine whether or not a computer is needed to solve the problem.
e. Obtain all other information required for algorithm development.

3. Possible consequences of not developing a complete and precise problem definition are that the algorithm developed may solve:
a. The wrong problem.
b. Only a portion of the problem that needs to be solved.
c. A more complex problem than actually needs to be solved.

4. The major responsibility for problem definition belongs to the experts in the problem area and not with the computer specialist.

5. A well-organized approach to problem definition does not exist.

6. Care must be exercised in determining what values need to be input and output in solving the problem.

7. An algorithm is a procedure which consists of a set of unambiguous rules specifying a sequence of operations that provides the solution to a specific class of problems in a finite number of steps.

8. An algorithm is an abstraction of a method for solving a problem that is represented by the set of rules in a procedure.

9. An algorithm must be designed to solve a general class of problems rather than one specific problem from a problem class.

10. Four alternatives available for representing algorithms are:
a. Natural languages.
b. Computer programming languages.
c. Decision tables.
d. Flowchart languages.

11. In this text we will use a flowchart language to represent our algorithms.

12. The advantages of using a flowchart language are:
a. The logical structure of an algorithm stands out.
b. Modular construction of algorithms is easily accomplished.
c. Flowchart representations of an algorithm are independent of any particular computer or computer programming language.
d. Flowcharts provide documentation that supports the computer programming-language representation of an algorithm.

13. If we locate an algorithm for solving our problem, we must be certain that the algorithm:
a. Is designed to solve a problem exactly like our problem.
b. Has a computer representation that can be processed by our computer.
c. Is reliable.

14. An algorithm may be thought of as a function

that maps input values into output values. Thus an algorithm has a domain of acceptable inputs and a range of possible outputs.

15. Two algorithms are said to be equivalent if they:
a. Have a common domain and a common range.
b. Both algorithms produce the same output for any given input in their common domain.

16. Computer implementation of an algorithm involves a task known as programming or coding.

17. The three basic types of computer programming languages are:
a. Machine-oriented programming languages.
b. Procedure-oriented programming languages.
c. Problem-oriented programming languages.

18. Ideally, our algorithms should require a minimum amount of main memory and a minimum amount of computer time for execution.

19. The fact that a computer can represent only finite approximations to real numbers may cause incorrect answers to be generated by an algorithm with the correct logic.

20. The best method for manually solving a problem is not necessarily the best computer method for solving the problem.

21. Program documentation is necessary because:
a. Potential users often need to understand the purpose and logic of a program.
b. Users of a program must know how to prepare input data.
c. A program must be maintained.

Algorithm Design I: Fundamental Concepts

CHAPTER

4

Now that we understand some of the basic notions about problem analysis and algorithms, we can proceed with our study of the process of designing algorithms for solving problems. In this and the following chapter, we are going to learn the basic concepts associated with designing algorithms that are represented using the flowchart language. We will assume that all of these algorithms are designed for execution by a computer. However, all of the algorithm flowcharts developed will be independent of computer and computer language. By this we mean that these algorithm flowcharts will not be designed with any particular computer or computer programming language in mind for their execution.

4.1 THE FLOWCHART LANGUAGE

The flowchart language we develop has to have symbols that can be used for writing algorithms. This need for symbols is much like the need for an alphabet of characters in a natural language. In English, for example, the alphabet is made up of the uppercase and lowercase characters (A, B, C, ..., X, Y, Z, a, b, c, ..., x, y, z). These characters are used together with certain punctuation marks (such as periods and commas) to form sentences. Similarly, a set of symbols is required in a language for a scientific area. For example, in mathematics the symbols of the alphabet include such characters as:

$$0 \quad 1 \quad 2 \quad \cdots \quad 9 \quad + \quad - \quad \times \quad < \quad \sqrt{} \quad \infty \quad \int \quad > \quad =$$

flowchart–language alphabet

In our *flowchart language* we will use the following symbols in our alphabet:

1. The symbols for the 26 uppercase and 26 lowercase letters of the English alphabet.
2. The following punctuation and grouping symbols:

$$. \quad) \quad , \quad (\quad ' \quad blank \quad ; \quad \% \quad : \quad] \quad ? \quad [\quad - \quad \$ \quad \&$$

72

3. The symbols for the ten decimal digits and the following mathematical symbols:

$$+ \quad - \quad \cdot \quad / \quad \leftarrow \quad = \quad \neq \quad < \quad \leq \quad > \quad \geq$$

4. The set of eight standard flowchart symbols (six of which we will call *flowchart boxes*) shown in Fig. 4.1.

Symbol	Symbol Name	Text Section in Which Usage Defined
	Terminal box	4.3
	Processing box	4.3
	Predefined Process box	9.1
	Annotation box	4.2, 5.2, and 9.1
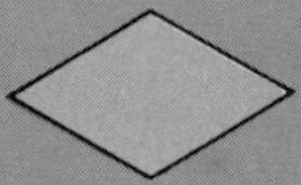	Decision box	4.5
	Input/Output box	4.4
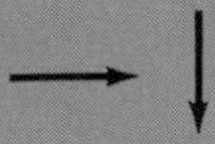	Flowline	4.3
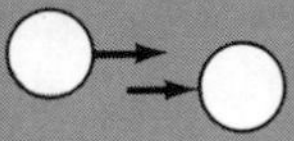	In-connector and out-connector	4.5

Figure 4.1.   Flowchart Symbols

The usage of these symbols and the various meanings they might have will be explained in this chapter and the next one and in Chapter 9.

In any language, the symbols of the alphabet for that language are

flowchart–language words

combined in various combinations to create *words*. Words have meaning, whereas characters, in general, do not have meaning. Note, however, that words are made up of one or more characters. Therefore, one symbol can represent a word and thus have meaning. But, the meaning is associated with the word, not with the single character. For example, in the English language, the letter *a* is taken to be a word as used in the phrase a *dog*. The letter *a* is also a symbol, however, which is combined with other symbols to form a word such as *tag*. In the flowchart language, the words will be made up of letters from the English alphabet, punctuation, mathematical, and grouping symbols, and/or decimal digits. When a word consists entirely of decimal digits, the decimal point and + or − signs may also be included as symbols of the word.

flowchart-language statements

Words in a language are combined, using punctuation symbols, to form *statements* or sentences in that language. We are quite familiar with the rules for forming statements or sentences in the English language. In the flowchart language, we also have statements and rules for combining words by using operators and punctuation and grouping symbols to form statements. The four basic types of statements in our flowchart language are:

1. Processing statements.
2. Control statements.
3. Declarative statements.
4. Input/output statements.

processing statements

A *processing statement* is any statement that causes information to be altered in some way. One type of processing statement is the assignment statement, which we will discuss in Section 4.3. Another kind of processing statement is one used for invoking subalgorithms, a topic taken up in Chapter 9.

control statements

A *control statement* is one that is used to sequence the steps to be executed. Control statements are the conditional branching operations, which will be discussed in Section 4.5. Terminal statements are also control statements and will be discussed in Section 4.3.

declarative statements

Declarative statements provide information about variables in the algorithm flowchart. For example, we might designate that a variable X can only assume numeric values. This use of the declarative statement will be discussed in Section 4.2.2. Another example of the use of declarative statements would be to indicate that there is a group of variables that will be referred to using one name. This use of a declarative statement will be discussed in Chapter 5 under the topic of subscripted variables.

input/output statements

An *input/output statement* is used for the input of values to computer main memory or the output of values from computer main memory. Input/output statements will be explored in Section 4.4.

4.2   CONSTANTS, VARIABLES, AND DECLARATIVE INFORMATION

Constants and variables are the two types of words used in statements in the flowchart language. Thus they are very important in the design of algorithms. In the remainder of this section we will discuss the rules for representing the various types of constants and variables in our flowchart language. Then, in Chapter 5 we will discuss another type of variable, the subscripted variable.

4.2.1   Constants

A very important kind of word in the flowchart language is called a *constant*. There are two types of constants that we will permit in our flowchart language: (1) numeric constants and (2) string constants.

A *numeric constant* will always consist of a string of decimal digits. It may or may not contain a decimal point, and also may be preceded by an algebraic sign (a + or a −). Examples of numeric constants would be:

numeric constants

$$+123 \qquad 467.523$$
$$-78 \qquad -0.000012$$
$$46532 \qquad 56700000$$

In our flowchart language, there is *no limit* on the magnitude of a numeric constant or the number of digits it may contain. Caution must be taken, however, when implementing an algorithm on a computer. This is because all computers limit the magnitude of a numeric constant and the number of digits that a constant may contain. Numeric constants are used in forming arithmetic expressions, which will be discussed in Section 4.3.

A *string constant* consists of any sequence of symbols in the flowchart language (except for the eight standard flowcharting symbols) enclosed in apostrophes ('). Since the apostrophe is used to indicate the starting and ending point of a string constant, an apostrophe may not appear as a character in a string constant. In addition, the number of blank spaces in a string constant is often difficult to determine. Therefore, we will adopt the convention in this text of using an *underline* to indicate each *blank space* in a string constant. Examples of string constants would be:

string constants

'THIS_IS_A_STRING_CONSTANT. '
'This_is_a_string_constant. '
'Dont_you_do_it! '
'123+45.6 '
'−124.675 '

Notice that the fourth example is a string constant and not an arithmetic expression. Similarly, the fifth example is a string constant, not a numeric constant. These last two examples are both string constants because they are enclosed within apostrophes. Thus the symbols used do not determine the type of the constant. The only thing that matters in identifying a string constant is whether or not the sequence of characters that make up the constant is enclosed within apostrophes. In our flowchart language, there is *no limit* on the number of characters that may appear in a string constant. In all computers, however, there will be some limit imposed upon the number of symbols that a string constant may contain.

String constants can be used in various ways. The first three examples of string constants shown above were used to represent English language statements. The fourth and fifth examples can be thought of as string constants which are being used to represent an arithmetic expression and a decimal number, respectively.

operations using constants
The operations that can be performed using numeric constants are the normal operations of arithmetic and algebra. That is, a numeric constant may be combined with another numeric constant or a numeric variable using the operations of addition, subtraction, multiplication, or division. Numeric constants can also be raised to a power or may be used as an exponent. String constants are generally operated on by processes that: (1) rearrange the symbols in the string, (2) remove symbols from the string or insert symbols into the string, or (3) alter the symbols in the string. String constants cannot be operated on arithmetically. The operations that can be performed using numeric and string constants will be discussed further in Section 4.3.

4.2.2 Variables and Declarative Information

variable names
Another important kind of word in our flowchart language is called a variable name. A *variable name* is a sequence of symbols that consists of uppercase and/or lowercase letters and/or decimal digits. The first character in a word that is a variable name *must* be alphabetic. Examples of valid variable names are:

$$A \qquad Alpha \qquad FICATax \qquad Spiritof76$$

A *variable name* is used to refer to a place* in computer main mem-

---

* A *place* is one or more consecutive main memory locations.

ory where a constant* is stored. Since constants may be numeric or string constants, variables may be numeric or string variables. Generally speaking, we should not use a variable name in an algorithm flowchart to refer to more than one type of value. The reason for this is the way in which numeric and string constants are stored and processed. We assume in the flowchart language that the number of memory locations required to represent the numeric or string constant associated with a variable name will be available. In some computer programming languages and for some computers, this assumption may not always hold true because the maximum number of characters in a string constant and the magnitude and number of digits in a numeric constant are limited on all computers.

At any point during the execution of an algorithm, a variable will have only one value stored in its main memory location (or locations). During the execution of the algorithm, however, many values (remember, only one at a time) will usually be associated with any variable name. For example, when beginning execution of an algorithm, a numeric variable named *Sum* may have the value 0, while at the end of execution *Sum* may have the value 247. In a similar manner, the value of the string variable *StudentName* may be 'Mary' at the beginning of algorithm execution, while it is 'John' at the end of algorithm execution.

values of variables

Care must be taken not to confuse the name of a variable with the value of the constant associated with that variable name. Thus we can have a variable name called *John* which we use to represent the number of apple pies that we sell during some month. The variable name in no way relates to the value that is associated with that variable. This is similar to the situation in Chapter 2, where we stated that the address of a memory location is in no way related to the contents of that location.

Another important point is that each time a variable name is given a new value, the old value of that variable name is no longer available. This is because of the destructive nature of writing a value into computer main memory locations. Recall that a variable name is simply a way of referring to a place in computer main memory. Thus, whenever a variable is given a new value, the previous value will be lost or destroyed because only one value can be in a memory location at any point in time.

Declarative information is included in an algorithm flowchart to provide information about variables used in the algorithm. One kind of information that is provided about variables is the type of constants that they may have as values. Thus a variable called *StudentName* might be declared to have only string constants as values. Similarly, we might want

declarative information

---

* In Chapter 5 we will learn that a variable name can be used to refer to a sequence of constants in main memory. In this chapter, however, we will assume that each variable name refers to only one constant at a time.

to specify that X is a numeric variable. *All* variables that appear in an algorithm flowchart in this text will be declared as to the type of values they can have. Although this is not absolutely necessary, it helps to avoid the ambiguities that would be introduced by letting the type of a variable be determined implicitly by the way in which the variables are used in an algorithm.

The *annotation box* is used to introduce declarative information into an algorithm flowchart. An annotation box is connected to the flowchart by a broken line to indicate that only declarative information is being provided. The general shape of the annotation box is that of a rectangle with one end open. Generally, the information about a particular variable will be given in an annotation box that is attached to the first step in the

declaring numeric variables

flowchart in which that variable appears. For example, if we wish to indicate that the variables A and Z can only assume numeric values, we can simply write:

$$\text{NUM } A, Z \, \vdash\!-\!-\!-$$

declaring string variables

Similarly, if *StudentName* is a variable that can have only string constants as values, we would write:

$$\text{STR } StudentName \, \vdash\!-\!-\!-$$

integer arithmetic

Another type of declarative information would be to specify that some particular numeric variable can assume only integer values. At first glance this might not seem like important information to include in an algorithm flowchart. However, consider for a moment a variable A that has been declared to be an integer variable. That is, A can assume only integers as values. In this case, the assignment statement*

$$A \leftarrow 7 \,/\, 4$$

would result in the value 1 being assigned to the variable A. This is because we have specified that A can assume only integer values, thus requiring the fractional portion of the quotient to be dropped. Had the restriction not been imposed that A could assume only integer values, the

---

* While assignment statements will not be formally discussed until the next section of this chapter, we have already seen examples of their use in Chapter 1. Simply stated, an assignment statement assigns the value of the expression on the right of the arrow to be the new value of the variable to the left of the arrow.

result of the above assignment statement would be to give A the value 1.75. Obviously, there is quite a difference between these two results.

In order to declare that a numeric variable can assume only integer values, we simply use the word NUMINT instead of NUM in the declaration of the variable. For example, the annotation box

declaring integer-valued numeric variables

NUMINT a, b
NUM c, z, f ---

would declare that a, b, c, z, and f are numeric variables, with a and b being able to assume only integer constants as values. In the absence of a declaration using NUMINT, all variables declared NUM are assumed to permit the representation of any real number.*

4.3 TERMINAL OPERATIONS, THE ASSIGNMENT STATEMENT, AND ARITHMETIC EXPRESSIONS

There are two types of operations used in all algorithm flowcharts that we will develop. They are terminal operations and assignment operations. We actually examined both of these operations in Chapter 1. Let us review them here.

The *terminal box* is an oval symbol that indicates the terminal operation. The logical starting point in an algorithm flowchart is indicated by the terminal operator

algorithm starting point

of which there will be only one per algorithm. The logical end of an algorithm, on the other hand, is indicated by the terminal operator:

algorithm stopping point

---

* In the case where we wish to represent complex numbers, we can give a declaration to that effect. Of course, a complex number can always be represented as an ordered pair of real numbers where the first number in the pair represents the real portion of the number and the second value in the pair represents the imaginary portion.

There may be only one STOP terminal operator in any algorithm developed using our flowchart language. The box containing the START terminal operator will always have exactly one flowline leading from it to indicate the direction of flow. It will never have a flowline leading into it. The STOP terminal operator, on the other hand, will never have a flowline leading from it, although it will always have one flowline leading into it.

assignment statements   In almost all algorithms, the operation that is performed most often is the assignment operation. The assignment operation is the process by which a new value is given to a variable. This operation is performed in assignment statements. An *assignment statement* is any statement that is of the form

$$variable \leftarrow expression$$

assignment operator   where *variable* is any numeric or string variable name, the left-pointing arrow ($\leftarrow$) is called the *assignment operator,* and *expression* is any arithmetic or string expression. Assignment statements always appear in the flowchart language inside of rectangular boxes. These rectangular boxes are called *processing boxes*. A processing box may have only one flowline which points to it. In addition, only one flowline may ever leave a processing box. That is, there can be only one way to enter and one way to exit a processing box.

assigning a constant   An example of an assignment statement would be

In this statement the numeric constant 13 would be the value assigned to the variable *A*. This statement would be read as: *Assign the numeric* **assignment** *constant 13 to be the new value of the numeric variable A*. Since a variable **destructive** may have only one value at a time, execution of this statement causes the previous value of *A* to be lost. Thus we say that assignment is a destructive operation. As another example, we have:

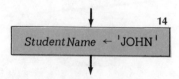

The result of executing this statement is that the value of the string variable *Student Name* is now 'JOHN'. Of course, we have assumed that the variables in these two examples have been declared somewhere in the

flowchart to be the proper types. These two examples illustrate that an expression may consist of just a single constant.

An important point to understand is that the thing to the left of the   **illegal assignments**
assignment operator must be a variable. Thus the assignment statement

is clearly incorrect. A moment of thought will tell us that this example would be nonsense anyway. The reason is that it orders the value of *A* (which is a constant) to be assigned as the value of 13. However, 13 is a constant and therefore can only have itself (13) as a value. Since *A* is a variable and can thus have any one of many values, this statement would result in a contradiction whenever *A* had a value other than 13.

Finally, there may not be more than one variable to the left of the assignment operator. This means that

is illegal because there are two variables to the left of the assignment operator. Had the desired operation been to assign the numeric constant 20 to be the value of these variables, the correct statement should have been:

Another type of expression is one that consists of a single variable.   **assigning a variable**
An example would be:

Execution of this statement would result in assigning the current value of the variable *B* to be the new value of the variable *A*. Note that after this operation is carried out, the variables *A* and *B* will both have the same value. This is because the assignment operation does not affect the values of variables to the right of the assignment operator. Another interesting observation is that we have no way of knowing whether *A* and *B* are numeric or string variables given just this one statement. It would only be in the context of the algorithm in which the statement appears that the type of the variables used in this statement can be determined. Finally, notice that the variable *B* must have been assigned a value earlier during the execution of the algorithm. Otherwise, this example would be meaningless since assignment involves the assignment of a specific constant value to a variable. However, had *B* not been given a value before executing *A* ← *B*, then the algorithm has no constant value that it can assign to *A*.

complex expressions The expression on the right of the assignment operator may be more complex than those that we have seen thus far. In fact, the expression can be any sequence of variable names and constants that is formed using the appropriate types of operators. If the variables and constants in the expression are numeric, the operators would be the arithmetic operators of mathematics and the expression would be called an *arithmetic expression*. An expression that consists of a string constant or variable, on the other hand, would be called a *string expression*. Numeric and string constants or variables may never appear together within the same expression. There are certain restrictions on the type of variable that may appear to the left of an assignment operator when a given type of expression is to the right of the assignment operator. If the expression to the right is an arithmetic expression, the variable to the left of the assignment operator must be a numeric variable. When the expression is a string expression, the variable to the left of the assignment operator must be a string variable.

flowchart box shape Before we explore the rules for constructing arithmetic expressions, let us review several points from Chapter 1. First the *shape* of a flowchart box indicates the *type of operation* that is to be performed in that box. Second, each box (except for the annotation box) in an algorithm flowchart will have a small number just above the box on the right-hand side. These **reference numbers** numbers are simply *reference numbers* that permit us to refer, for example, to the third box in the flowchart as box 3. Box numbers are usually assigned sequentially, with the first box in the flowchart being numbered box 1. Third, flowchart symbols are connected to each other by straight lines with attached arrowheads. These directed straight lines are called *flowlines*. They are used to indicate the sequence in which algorithm steps are to be executed.

flowlines

Finally, each processing box may contain one or more assignment statements. When the order in which assignment statements are to be executed is important, however, care must be taken to be sure that the assignment statements appear in the correct order. For example, the three statements required for exchanging the values of two variables, *A* and *B*, might read:

ordering of assignment statements

Notice that a third variable, *temp*, is needed in the exchange process. The reason is that three variables are needed to exchange the values of two variables. This is because assigning the value of one variable to be the value of a second variable destroys the value of the second variable. Therefore, the second variable's initial value is not available to be assigned as the value of the first variable. Thus a third variable is needed to temporarily hold the value of the first variable during the swapping process. In diagram form, the process is

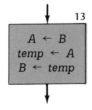

where the numbers on the arrows indicate the order of assignment.

Now, if the order of the first and second statements in the above processing box were reversed, giving

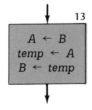

83

the exchange of the values of A and B would not take place correctly. The reason is that execution of the first assignment statement $A \leftarrow B$ will result in the value of A being destroyed before it can be assigned to be the new value of B. Similarly, exchanging the second and third assignment statements in box 12 above would also not produce the correct results in the exchange of the values of A and B. The reason is that execution of the statement $B \leftarrow temp$ will destroy the value of B before it can be assigned to A in the statement $A \leftarrow B$. In conclusion, when more than one assignment statement appears in one processing box, we must be sure to sequence the statements such that a correct result is produced. From the above example, it should be obvious that multiple assignment statements appearing in one processing box are always executed in a top-to-bottom order.

arithmetic expressions   An *arithmetic expression* in our flowchart language is a sequence of numeric variables and constants that is formed using arithmetic operators, numeric functional operators, and an operation implied by position. Parentheses may be used in an arithmetic expression to indicate the order in which operations are to be carried out. That is, parentheses will be used to group certain sequences of operators and operands into subexpressions. Essentially, the flowchart version of an arithmetic expression looks much like an arithmetic expression of algebra.

Let us now examine the rules for forming arithmetic expressions in the flowchart language.

addition and subtraction

1. *Addition* and *subtraction* are indicated by the operators + and −, respectively. For example, addition of the value of A to the value of B would be indicated by the expression

$$A + B$$

multiplication

2. *Multiplication* is indicated by the operator ·, which must always separate the two operands. The symbol × will not be permitted as a multiplication operator. This is to avoid the possibility of confusing the multiplication operator with the variable x. In addition, *implied multiplication* will *not be permitted* as it is in algebra. This rule is necessary because we permit variable names to be longer than one character in length.* Thus *ab* is taken to mean the variable *ab* rather than the operation of multiplying the value of the variable *a* by the value of the variable *b*. For example, multiplication of the value of *ASQ* by the value of *ZCUBE* would

---

* Another reason is the way in which we express subscripted variables. This topic will be taken up in Chapter 5.

be indicated by the expression

$$ASQ \cdot ZCUBE$$

3. *Division* is indicated by the division operator /. The division op-   **division**
erator ÷ will not be used, and neither will the stacked division
of algebra. As an example, the division of the value of abc by
the value of xyz would be indicated by the expression

$$abc\ /\ xyz$$

4. The operation of raising a value to a power, commonly called ex-   **exponentiation**
ponentiation, is indicated by writing the exponent of the operation
as a superscript. For example, the operation of raising the value
of xyz to the abc power would be indicated by the expression

$$xyz^{abc}$$

5. The *numeric functional operators* of mathematics can often be   **numeric functional**
expressed by use of a symbol. For example, the operation of find-   **operators**
ing the square root of the value of a would be indicated as $\sqrt{a}$.
In the flowchart language we will use special names that will be
mnemonics for the operations indicated. That is, the name chosen
for a particular functional operation will indicate the nature of that
operation. For example, the operation of finding the square root
of the value of a will be indicated in the flowchart language as
sqrt[a]. Thus the operand (or operands) of a functional operator
follows the mnemonic name and is enclosed in square brackets.
The mnemonic names for several of the numeric functional operators are given in Fig. 4.2. A complete table of functional operators

Figure 4.2.   Mnemonic Numeric Functional Operators

Operation	Mathematical Functional Operator*	Mnemonic Functional Operator*
Absolute value	$\|x\|$	abs[x]
Exponential	e^{x}	exp[x]
Natural logarithm	$\log_{e}x$	log[x]
Base-ten logarithm	$\log_{10}x$	log10[x]
Square root	$\sqrt{x}$	sqrt[x]
Truncate	x_{tr}	trun[x]

* Using x as a typical operand.

is given in Appendix B. Note that the names used as mnemonic functional references *may not be used* in an algorithm flowchart as *variable names.* This rule is necessary to avoid confusion. In addition, the argument of a numeric functional operator may be any arithmetic expression, including one that contains a reference to another numeric functional operator. For example, *sqrt*[*a* + *b*] would result in the square root of the sum of *a* and *b*.

consecutive operators

6. Two operators may not appear in consecutive positions in an expression. Thus, expressions such as *abc* + −*def* must be avoided. Instead, the correct way of stating this expression would be *abc* + (−*def*). Note that this problem will only occur in the case of the unary operator − (the *negation* operator).

To summarize, the flowchart language rules for forming arithmetic expressions are in agreement with the rules of algebra for forming arithmetic expressions with the following exceptions:

1. By rule 2, implied multiplication is not permitted in arithmetic expressions in the flowchart language.
2. By rules 2 and 3, the multiplication and division operators × and ÷ are not permitted in the flowchart language.
3. By rule 5, numeric functional operations are indicated by using mnemonic names followed by arguments enclosed in square brackets rather than by using special symbols.

operator precedence rules

The order in which operations are performed in evaluating an arithmetic expression is determined by a set of rules called *precedence rules*. By *evaluating* an arithmetic expression, we mean the process of successively reducing subexpressions to constant values until the entire expression is simply a numeric constant. For example, when encountering an arithmetic expression such as

$$A + B / C$$

we must know whether: (1) the value of A is added to the value of B, after which the sum is divided by the value of C; or (2) the value of B is divided by the value of C, and this quotient is then added to the value of A.

In our flowchart language, we will use the precedence rules of algebra, which are summarized in Fig. 4.3. An arithmetic expression is scanned four times with all operations on one level being carried out on each scan in the order indicated. Examining the table, first all numeric functional operations are evaluated in any order. If the argument to a numeric func-

Figure 4.3. Precedence Rules for Evaluating Arithmetic Expressions

Precedence Level	Operation	Order of Evaluation
1	Numeric functional reference	Any order
2	Prefix + and prefix − Exponentiation	Right to left
3	Multiplication Division	Left to right
4	Addition Subtraction	Left to right

tional reference is a subexpression, that subexpression must be evaluated, using all of the precedence rules, before the function is applied. Thus in the expression

$$sqrt[a + b - c]$$

the subexpression $a + b - c$ must be evaluated to a numeric constant before the square root can be obtained.

After all functional references have been evaluated, all prefix pluses and minuses and exponentiations are performed in a right-to-left order. Thus in the expression

$$-a^{b^{c}}$$

(1) the value of b would be raised to the value of c power, (2) then value of a would be raised to the power of the constant evaluated in step 1, and (3) the resulting constant would be negated. If the variables a, b, and c had the values 4, 3, and 2, respectively, the above expression would evaluate to the value $-262,144$ $(-4^{3^{2}}$ $=$ -4^{9} $=$ $-262,144)$.

The next step in the evaluation of an arithmetic expression will be to scan the expression in order from left to right performing all level-3 operations. Thus in the expression

$$xyz \cdot bd / rve \cdot jkl$$

(1) the value of xyz would be multiplied by the value of bd, (2) the product

in step 1 would be divided by the value of *rve*, and (3) the quotient in step 2 would be multiplied by the value of *jkl*.

In the final scan of the expression, all additions and subtractions are performed moving from left to right. For example, the expression

$$xyz + rvt - geta$$

would be evaluated by first summing the values of *xyz* and *rvt* followed by subtracting the value of *geta* from that sum. In Fig. 4.4 examples of a number of flowchart language arithmetic expressions are presented. These expressions are evaluated for the following variable values:

$$A = -2 \quad C = 4 \quad F = 4$$
$$B = 0.5 \quad D = 5 \quad X = 3$$
$$BAD = 15 \quad E = 3 \quad Y = 2$$

Figure 4.4. Examples of Flowchart Language Arithmetic Expressions and Their Evaluation

Arithmetic Expression*	Value
$X + A - 2 \cdot BAD$	-29
$(X - A/C)^Y \cdot F$	49
$(X - A)/C^Y \cdot F$	$5/4$
$X - A/C^Y \cdot F$	$7/2$
$(X^Y)^E$	729
X^{Y^E}	$6,561$
$(X + E)^{-sqrt[C]}$	$1/36$
$A - B^2/C \cdot D \cdot abs[A]$	$-21/8$
$sqrt[2 \cdot log10[D^2 \cdot C]]$	2
X^{-A}	9

*$A = -2, B = 0.5, BAD = 15, C = 4, D = 5, E = 3, F = 4,$
$X = 3, Y = 2.$

Each of these examples should be studied carefully to be certain that the precedence rules are completely understood.

precedence rules optional In closing our discussion on the evaluation of arithmetic expressions, we should note that it is not absolutely necessary that precedence rules be known when writing arithmetic expressions. The reason is that by using parentheses to group subexpressions we can force arithmetic expressions to be evaluated in any order we wish. This is because subexpressions enclosed in parentheses are always evaluated before the remainder of an expression is evaluated. Therefore, if we want to add the value of A to the value of B and divide the sum by the value of C, we can write

$$(A + B) / C$$

However, had we wanted to divide the value of B by the value of C and then add this quotient to the value of A, we could have written

$$A + (B / C)$$

Note that had we not used any parentheses but instead relied on the precedence rules, the result would have been the same as in the last example. Therefore, the parentheses in the last example are actually redundant, since the same result could have been achieved without using them. However, use of redundant parentheses offers the advantage of not having to learn a set of precedence rules. In addition, it makes a flowchart easier to understand by a person that is not particularly familiar with the flowchart language. Therefore, use of redundant parentheses is encouraged, particularly when it adds to flowchart clarity.

This completes our study of the concepts of the assignment and terminal operations. Therefore, let us develop our first algorithm flowchart. The problem we wish to solve is that of forming the sum of three numbers. The first step in the algorithm will be one that tells where execution of the algorithm is to begin. In our flowchart language, this would be a terminal symbol that contains the word START: **summing flowchart**

The next step will be to give values to the variables that will be used in forming the sum. Let us arbitrarily choose a, b, and c as the variables used to contain the values to be summed. Therefore, the next step would be

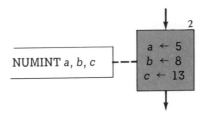

where the values 5, 8, and 13 were chosen arbitrarily. Note the necessity of declaring the type of the variables *a*, *b*, and *c* when they first appear in the flowchart. Now that the variables *a*, *b*, and *c* have been given values, the step that forms the sum can be inserted. This step would consist of a simple assignment statement that causes the three values to be added and the result to be assigned to some variable. This step would thus be

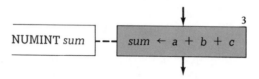

where *sum* was arbitrarily chosen as the variable name that would be assigned the result. Finally, execution of the algorithm would be terminated by a terminal box that contained the order to STOP:

All of these steps are brought together in the flowchart that appears in Fig. 4.5.

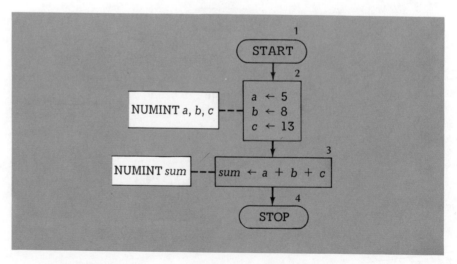

Figure 4.5. Algorithm Flowchart for Summing Three Numbers

Several comments about this algorithm need to be made. First, this algorithm is not really of any value to anyone. The reason is that it does **algorithm analysis** not contain a provision for outputting the result. The reason for not in- cluding an output step is that we have not yet studied the output state- ment. A second comment would be that this algorithm is too specific to be of value to anyone. There are two reasons for this: (1) the algorithm is designed to sum only specific values, and (2) the algorithm can be used to form the sum of exactly three values, no more and no less. The first of these problems can be solved once we learn how to indicate the input operation. On the other hand, we will only be able to solve the second problem after we have studied the decision operation. As a final comment, the above algorithm flowchart does not really represent an algorithm. The reason is that in Section 3.2.1 we stated that an algorithm is a procedure that must give a solution to a specific class of problems. Since the above flowchart provides the solution to only one specific problem, it fails as an algorithm. Therefore, we can conclude that all flowcharts are not neces- sarily the representations of algorithms. However, all flowcharts in the remainder of this book will represent algorithms.

PROBLEMS

1. Identify the type of each of the following flow- chart language constants which are legal:

a.   543.67
b.   −367.8
c.   ' BIG_TIME_SPENDER '
d.   47
e.   ' ITS_MY_TIME '
f.   −3
g. 62.3^{-845}
h.   0
i.   ' $567.6_2 '
j.   +437.65
k.   ' Tinkers_Dam '
l.   IBM_Corporation
m.   ' _ '
n.   54763259
o.   ' 42.76_ '
p.   ' Computer_Science '
q.   543.7_6
r.   −.754
s.   ' 1011011001 '
t.   −456.7

2. Identify the valid flowchart language variable names from among the following list. When a variable name is invalid, give the reason for its being invalid.

a. *Bigrate*
b. *Character String*
c. *PL/I*
d. *Z3256*
e. *OVR* ' *TM*
f. ' *Avengers* '
g. *Reference#*
h. *i*
i. *4thofJuly*
j. *K*

3. What are the values associated with each of the valid variable names in Problem 2?

4. Translate the following mathematical expres- sions into flowchart language expressions:

a. $(x - 1)(x + y + z)^2$
b. $x(y + a)(rpq(x + y) + z)$
c. $\sqrt{x + y^2} - \dfrac{x - y}{d}$

d. $a - \dfrac{b^2}{c} \cdot d + a^2 \cdot d - |a \cdot b^c|$

e. $x + f\left(\dfrac{g}{c^a} + g^{4.5}\right) + g \cdot rpq$

f. a^{b^c}

g. $(b^a)^{(c+2)}(c + h^2)^{5.7}$

h. $\dfrac{a - b}{c + d} \cdot g$

i. $a - \dfrac{b}{c + d} \cdot g$

j. $a - \dfrac{b}{c} + d \cdot g$

5. Use the following values for the variables in Problem 4 to evaluate the expressions in that problem using the precedence rules of Fig. 4.3:

$a = 2$	$f = 3.4$	$x = 2$
$b = 0.5$	$g = 1$	$y = 1$
$c = -1$	$h = 1$	$z = 1$
$d = 1.5$	$rpq = 4$	

6. Develop a flowchart for summing the five numbers 10, 7, 15, 0, and 2.

7. Develop a flowchart for evaluating the quadratic formula

$$\dfrac{-b \pm \sqrt{b^2 - 4 \cdot a \cdot c}}{2 \cdot a}$$

using 2, 5, and 3 as the values for a, b, and c, respectively.

4.4   INPUT/OUTPUT OPERATIONS

The input operation is a very important one because it is used to input the data values that an algorithm is designed to process. As we saw in the flowchart in the previous section, algorithms are severely limited without the input operation. Similarly, the output operation is very important because it provides the means of recording the results on some output medium for human use or for future computer input. Without the output operation, the results would remain in computer memory and would thus be of no value.

input/output operations   An *input* or *output operation* is indicated by a parallelogram-shaped symbol that contains either the verb GET or the verb PUT, respectively. GET boxes must contain one or more variable names of any type. On the other hand, PUT boxes must contain one or more numeric or string constants or variables. Let us examine GET and PUT boxes in that order.

GET boxes   A GET box is used to input values that are to be given to variables. Thus the GET box is the means by which values are input to locations in computer main memory. The values being input can be coming from punched cards, magnetic tape, paper tape, terminal devices, or any input medium. To an algorithm, the source of the values being input is usually not important. Instead, we simply think of the values as coming from an ordered sequence of constants. This ordered sequence of input constants

input data stream   we will call the *input data stream*. The constants that make up the input data stream are assumed to be sequenced in the order in which they are to be input. Each constant is separated from any constant that may follow it by a comma. Any spaces that occur between constants are to be ignored.

As each GET box is executed, the number of values required will be obtained from the input data stream reading from left to right. Note that all of the steps in an algorithm are in computer memory before the first step of an algorithm is executed. However, the values of the input data stream are brought into computer memory only as the values of variables using the GET operation. Thus the entire algorithm is in computer memory before the first input data stream value is input to memory. In addition, values of the input data stream are input only by executing a GET operation.

An example of a GET box would be

This input operation would cause the next value in the input data stream to be input and assigned as the new value of the variable X. If the constant obtained from the input data stream is 13.2, the new value of X would be 13.2. If the constant is 'FEVER', the new value of X would be 'FEVER'. Note that the value that X had before the GET X operation is lost after executing the box that contained GET X. Thus the GET operation is similar to the assignment operation in that both are destructive.

Another important point is that only variables can appear in a GET box. Thus the step

would be illegal because 13.2 is a numeric constant.

A final question that is always a source of confusion for the beginner is deciding whether to use an assignment operation or a GET operation to assign a value to a variable. The rule is that variables should be assigned values using an assignment statement only when the value to be assigned does not change. If the value assigned to a variable can be different from one execution of the algorithm step to another, the operation should be that of a GET box. For example, the initial value of a variable used for

assignment versus input

93

counting things should be given by an assignment statement because this initial value will usually not change from one execution of the algorithm to the next. In contrast, a variable used for the number of hours a student works should be given by a GET operation, since this value will vary among students.

input for multiple variables   More than one variable name can appear in a GET box. If there is more than one variable name, each such variable name must be separated by a comma from any variable name that follows. Execution of a GET box that contains more than one variable name causes as many constants to be read from the input data stream as there are variables in the GET box. These input values are assigned to the variables in the order in which the variable names appear in the box. For example, execution of the box

would cause the next three values from the input data stream to be assigned to the variables X, Y, and Z, respectively. Let us assume that the next three values in the input data stream are

12, 'BIG ', −7

Then execution of the above GET box would result in: (1) the variable X having the value 12, (2) the variable Y having the value 'BIG ', and (3) the variable Z having the value −7. Notice from this example that numeric and string constants can all be input using the same GET box.

PUT boxes   A PUT box is used to output constants and the values of variables. Thus the PUT box is the means by which values are output from locations in computer main memory. The values being output may be going to the paper forms on a line printer, a card or paper tape, a magnetic tape, or a terminal device. To an algorithm, the destination of the values being output is usually not important. Instead, we might think of the values as going out as some ordered sequence of numeric or string constants. This **output data stream**   ordered sequence of output constants we will call the *output data stream*. The constants that make up the output data stream are assumed to be sequenced left to right in the order in which they are output. Furthermore, the constants in the output data stream will be assumed to appear as one continuous string of characters, with no spaces appearing between consecutive constants. In addition, the apostrophes that are used to enclose string constants will not appear when string constants are moved to the output data stream.

An example of a PUT box would be

This output operation would cause the string constant **'MESSAGE'** to be placed as the next seven characters in the output data stream. Similarly, the step

would cause the numeric constant 25 to be placed as the next value in the output data stream. Since variables may also appear in a PUT box, the step

would generate the output data stream

$$TAX = \$4.25$$

assuming that the value of the variable *FICA* is 4.25 when this step is executed. Similarly, if we assume that the values of the variables *A*, *B*, and *C* are **'SPRING '**, **'_IS_SPRUNG_IN_ '**, and 1975, respectively, then execution of the PUT box would result in the output data stream:

SPRING IS SPRUNG IN 1975

An algorithm that illustrates the input/output concepts of this section appears in Fig. 4.6. Let us follow the input and output data streams as this algorithm is executed. Assume that the input data stream consists of:

0.12, −485, '_HOWDY_', '_GUMBO', 4, 10, 2, 20, '_A_STRING'

Execution of the second flowchart box would result in the variables A, X, and L being assigned the values of 0.12, −485, and '_HOWDY_', respectively. That is, execution of flowchart box 2 would result in the input of the first three constants in the input data stream. The reason that exactly three constants are input is that there are three variable names in the second flowchart box.

After flowchart box 2 has been executed, the operations indicated in box 3 will be performed. The result of these operations will be the output data stream

X = −485 HOWDY

where: (1) the characters $X=$ represent the string constant '$X=$' of box 3, (2) the characters −485 represent the value of the numeric variable X, and (3) the characters HOWDY represent the value of the string variable L. Notice that the apostrophes have been dropped from string constants in the output data stream. In addition, all of the values are put into the output data stream without spaces or commas separating them.

Execution of the step in flowchart box 4 will cause the next four values of the input data stream to be input. That is, the constants in the shaded portion of the input data stream

0.12, −485, '_HOWDY_',   '_GUMBO', 4, 10, 2 , 20, '_A_STRING'

will be input as the values of the variables V, S, U, and T. Thus execution of flowchart box 4 will result in the variables V, S, U, and T being assigned

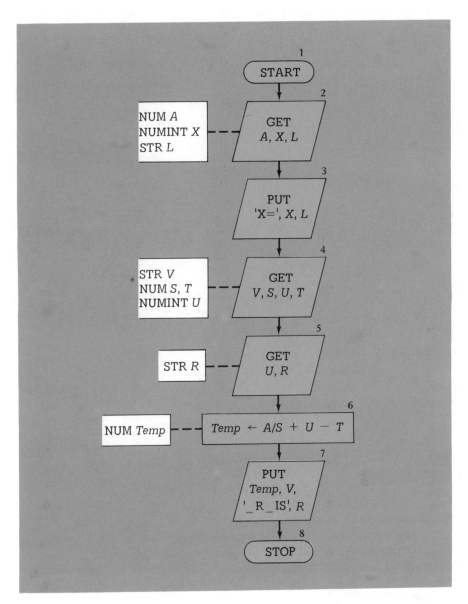

Figure 4.6. Algorithm Flowchart for Input and Output

the values ' _GUMBO ', 4, 10, and 2, respectively. Similarly, execution of the step in flowchart box 5 will cause the last two constants in the input data stream to be assigned as the values of the variables U and R. Thus U and R will have the values 20 and ' _A_STRING ', respectively, after box 5 has been executed. Notice that the value input for the variable U by the step in box 4 will be destroyed by the input operation in flowchart box 5.

The next step to be executed will be the one in flowchart box 6. The result of executing this step will be the assignment of a numeric constant to the variable *Temp*. Then the step in box 7 causes the output of four values to the output data stream. Thus the final output data stream will be

$$X = -485 \text{ HOWDY} \boxed{18.03 \text{ GUMBO R IS A STRING}}$$

where the constants in the shaded portion were output by executing flowchart box 7. Notice that the first value in the shaded portion (the numeric constant 18.03) is the result of evaluating the arithmetic expression in box 6. The second and fourth constants in the shaded portion of the output data stream are the values of the string variables V and R. Finally, the third value in the shaded portion is a string constant that appears in the PUT box itself. The last step executed in this algorithm is a STOP box, which causes algorithm execution to halt.

4.5   ALGORITHM FLOW AND BRANCHING OPERATIONS

We have already observed that the sequence in which the steps of a flowchart are executed is determined by the flowlines that are used to connect flowchart boxes. That is, a line with an arrowhead leads from one flowchart box to another in order to show the algorithm step to be executed next. In some cases, it may not be convenient to connect two flowchart **need for** boxes directly with a flowline. One case is when a second or third column **connectors** of flowchart symbols is needed on one page. Another case is when a flowchart cannot fit on one page. A third situation would be when using a flowline would cause two flowlines to cross each other. The connector (which has the shape of a small circle) is the flowchart symbol developed for use in these cases.

connectors   There are two types of connectors in the flowchart language:

1. Out-connectors.
2. In-connectors.

98

An *out-connector* is a connector that has a flowline pointing to it. An *in-connector* is a connector that has a flowline leading from it that points to a flowchart box or another flowline. An out-connector indicates that the next flowchart box to be executed is located elsewhere in the algorithm flowchart. Out-connectors may be placed next to any flowchart box in an algorithm flowchart. Often they appear at the bottom of a column of flowchart boxes. However, this is not the only place that they may be found. Every out-connector will always contain a label constant, where a label constant is simply any unsigned integer constant. An in-connector indicates a place in a flowchart where flow is to resume. In-connectors may appear anywhere in a flowchart. Often they occur at the top of a column of flowchart boxes. However, this is not the only place that they might be found. In-connectors must always contain *unique* label constants. That is, no two in-connectors in a flowchart may contain the same label constant value. In-connectors are used as reference points by out-connectors in other parts of an algorithm flowchart. That is, each time during algorithm execution that an out-connector is reached, flow will resume with the in-connector pointed to by the label constant in that out-connector.

out-connectors

in-connectors

As an example, let us consider the following flowchart skeleton:

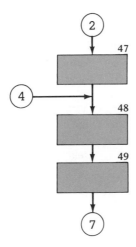

This flowchart segment contains two in-connectors and one out-connector. There must not be any other in-connectors that contain either the label constants 2 or 4 in the flowchart of which these boxes are a part. However, there may be other out-connectors that contain the label constant 7. The reason is that the values of in-connectors must be unique, whereas those of out-connectors do not need to be unique. By examining this flowchart segment, we can see that algorithm execution can resume at box 47 by having reached an out-connector that contains the label constant 2. Flowchart box 48, on the other hand, can be reached in one of two ways. First, it may be reached from box 47 by the flowline that connects these two boxes. Second, it can be reached by execution of an out-connector that references the in-connector containing the label constant 4. Finally, there must be an in-connector containing the label constant 7 somewhere in the flowchart of which this segment is a part. Thus, after execution of flowchart box 49, the next step to be executed will be the one in the flowchart box pointed to by the in-connector that contains the label constant 7.

conditional branches   A *conditional branching operation* is one in which a decision is made to determine the next flowchart box to be executed. Conditional branches are indicated in the flowchart language by the use of a diamond-shaped symbol, which is called a *decision box*. All decision boxes will have two flowlines leading from them. Which one of these two flowlines is to be followed when leaving the decision box is determined by the result of the relation or condition contained in the decision box. These relations or conditions are more or less like statements that can be answered as *true* or *false* (or *yes* or *no*). The most common type of relation is one that is used to compare two values. This comparison utilizes one of the relational operators given in Fig. 4.7. The meaning of each of the six flowchart language relational operators is given in this table and examples of their use are also included. Note that the symbols used for the relational operators are the same as those commonly used in mathematics.

Figure 4.7.   Flowchart Language Relational Operators

Operator	Meaning	Example
$=$	is equal to	$A = B$
$\neq$	is not equal to	$A \neq B$
$>$	is greater than	$A > B$
$\geq$	is greater than or equal to	$A \geq B$
$<$	is less than	$A < B$
$\leq$	is less than or equal to	$A \leq B$

A flowchart segment that illustrates a conditional branch operation would be:

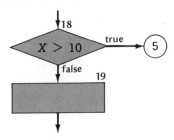

In this example, the step in box 19 would be executed following execution of box 18 when the value of the variable X is not greater than 10. On the other hand, the box following in-connector 5 would be executed next in the case in which the value of X is greater than 10. Note that a relation must be either true or false. Thus there can be only two flowlines that exit from flowchart box 18.

As a second example, the flowchart segment

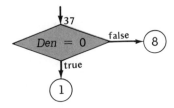

would result in a branch to in-connector 1 when the value of *Den* is equal to zero. However, when *Den* has a value that is not equal to zero, a branch to in-connector 8 results. Again, there can be only two flowlines that exit from flowchart box 37 since the value of *Den* is either equal to zero or it is not.

Another type of condition that can appear in a decision box is the end-of-file condition. This condition is used to determine whether or not the end of the input data stream has been reached while executing a GET box. Thus the decision box

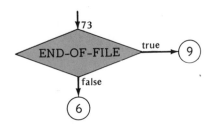

would cause a branch to in-connector 6 if the end of the input data stream has not been reached when executing the most recent GET box. On the other hand, the flowchart box following in-connector 9 would be executed next had the end of the input data stream been reached.

As a final example of a conditional branch, we have:

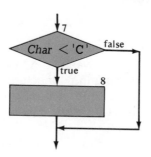

In this example, box 8 will be executed following box 7 when the value of the string variable *Char* is less than the string constant **'C'**. When the relation is false, however, box 8 will be skipped and control will pass to the step that follows flowchart box 8.

string relations   Now, in what sense can one string constant be said to be *less than* or *greater than* another constant? The answer is that in the comparison of two string constants:

1. The *shorter* of the two string constants is *extended with blanks* on the *right* until both strings are of equal length.
2. Then the constants are compared on a *character-by-character* basis beginning from the *left* of each string.
3. If every respective character pair of each string is the same, the two strings are said to be *equal*.
4. For purposes of comparing characters, the ten decimal digits are the greatest of all characters. Among themselves, the decimal digits are ordered from 0 through 9, with 0 being the least and 9 the greatest character. The next greatest characters would be the uppercase letters of the alphabet. Of these, A would be the least and Z the greatest. The lowercase letters are again ordered from a through z, and are less than any of the uppercase letters or the ten decimal digits. Special characters are usually considered to be less than other characters, with *blanks* being the least of any

character. We will not be concerned with the ordering of special characters other than blanks in this text.

5. For the leftmost pair of nonequal characters, if the character in the first string is less than the character in the corresponding position in the second string, the first string is said to be *less than* the second string.

6. For the leftmost pair of nonequal characters, if the character in the first string is greater than the character in the corresponding position in the second string, the first string is said to be *greater than* the second string.

For example, the string constant

'BIG_TIME '

is less than the string constant

'LITTLE_TIME '

since, between the leftmost nonequal characters, the letter B (in BIG) is less than the letter L (in LITTLE). Similarly,

'BIG_CLOCK '

is less than

'BIG_TIME '

since, between the leftmost nonequal characters, the letter C (in CLOCK) is considered to be less in value than the letter T (in TIME). As a final example,

'BIG_CLOCK_STRIKES '

is greater than

'BIG_CLOCK '

since, for the leftmost nonequal characters, the letter S (in STRIKES) is greater than a blank. Note that in this example the second character string had to be extended by inserting eight blank spaces (because the first constant contains eight more characters than the second constant) on the right before the comparison could be made.

PROBLEMS

8. Given the input data stream

5,6, 'Tophat_Cleaners ',467.3, 'Fortran_Code ',−78

what values would be associated with each of the variable names after execution of the following GET statements?

a. GET *a, b, c, string, numeric, code*

b. GET *x, a, b, d*
   GET *g, h*

c. GET *g, h, x, v, h*

9. Given the following values for the variables:

$$a = 46$$
$$b = 73.29$$
$$c = \text{'BIG\_VALUE '}$$
$$d = \text{'}\_\_\text{'}$$
$$f = \text{'how\_was\_that? '}$$
$$g = -56.7$$

what will be the contents of the output data stream after execution of the following PUT statements?

a. PUT ' a = ', *a, d,* ' f = ', *c*

b. PUT *f, c, c, g, a, d, d, b*
   PUT *g,* ' string = ', *g*

c. PUT *a,* ' What_did_you_say ', *f, d, g*

10. Given the flowchart sequence

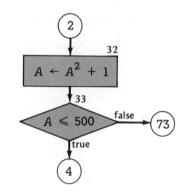

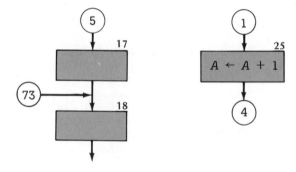

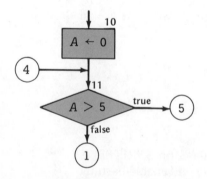

and making no additional assumptions about the remainder of the flowchart (except that box 10 will be executed first):

a. Identify the label constants.

b. Identify the in-connectors and out-connectors.

c. How many times will each of the flowchart boxes in this sequence be executed?

d. When flowchart box 18 is first executed, what will be the value of *A*?

11. Develop an algorithm flowchart for the problem of inputting four numeric values, forming the squares of the values that are positive, and outputting the values and their squares. For values that are not squared, zero should be output for the squared value.

4.6   DESIGNING ALGORITHMS

We have now studied all of the basic features of our flowchart language. In this section let us examine some problems and develop algorithms for their solution. The problems selected for analysis have all been chosen because they are familiar or because they are easily understood problems.

Each problem that we examine in this chapter and Chapter 5 will be considered in four stages. First, we will do a thorough problem analysis so that all aspects of the problem are well understood. This will be followed by a descriptive flowchart that is included to reveal the broad structure of the algorithm that we are about to develop. The third stage will be the development of a detailed algorithm flowchart that provides the detailed steps for problem solution using our flowchart language. Finally, we will verify the correctness of the algorithm flowchart logic by developing a trace table.

4.6.1   The Largest-Value Problem

For our first exercise in algorithm development, we will tackle the very simple problem of finding the largest value from among a set of numbers. For example, given the numbers

problem definition

$$5, 10, 8, -2, 6$$

our algorithm should output 10 as being the largest value. In solving this problem, we will assume that we are not interested in knowing when there is more than one value that is the largest. Thus, in the case of the number set

$$5, 10, 8, 10, 6$$

our algorithm should still output 10 as the largest value. That is, we will ignore the fact that there are two largest values equal to 10.

In solving this largest-value problem, let us proceed in stages. That is, let us begin by developing an algorithm for the case where the number set consists of only two values. Next, we will proceed to the case in which there are three numbers. Then we will develop an algorithm for the general case in which there are any number of values. For all of these cases, our problem analysis has already been performed earlier in this section. Therefore, we are ready to proceed with algorithm development.

problem analysis

Our first plan of attack is described in the descriptive flowchart given in Fig. 4.8. Notice that a descriptive flowchart is simply a way of describing

105

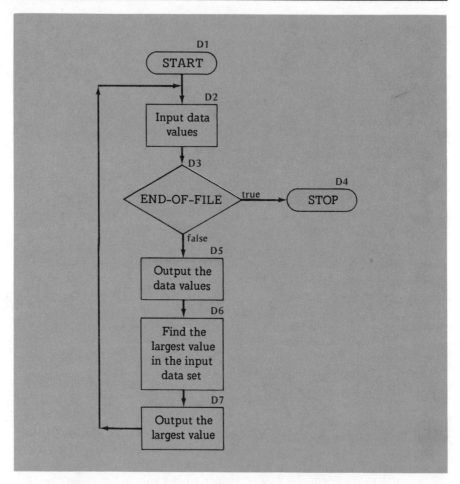

Figure 4.8. First Descriptive Flowchart for the Largest-Value Problem

in general terms the logic that our algorithm flowchart is to contain. Thus the statements of our flowchart language are not used in developing a descriptive flowchart. Instead, we simply outline the general method of problem solution using short descriptive phrases. The advantage of first developing a descriptive flowchart is that the overall sequencing of steps can be seen more easily when we are not bogged down with detail. Notice that a descriptive flowchart is not an algorithm flowchart. The reason is that the descriptive phrases tell what to do but not how it will be done. Thus they tend to be ambiguous.

descriptive flowcharts

Examining Fig. 4.8, we see that the first step in finding the largest value is to input the data values. In the case of two-number sets, this would be two values. After we make the attempt at inputting these data values, we want to determine whether or not any data values were actually input. This we do by asking if the end-of-file has been reached. If it has, we want the execution of the algorithm to stop. However, if another set of data values was actually input, then we want to output the data values that have just been input. This step is included so that the values in the data set being processed can be verified. In addition, it allows us to identify the data set for which an answer is about to be developed and output. Proceeding to descriptive flowchart box D6, we have the step for finding the largest value in the input data set. Notice in this flowchart box that all we do is say that the next logical step would be to find the largest value from among the set of values that we have just input. That is, this box contains no information on how we would go about determining which value is the largest one. Finally, we want to output the largest value after it has been determined. Once this is done, we return control to the input step so that another set of input values can be processed. Thus we are saying that we want our algorithm to be able to find the largest value in each of many data sets, not in just one data set. This is the same as saying that once we have told the computer how to solve one problem of a certain type, we will want it to be able to solve many problems of that type. Notice that the flowchart box numbers in our descriptive flowchart all have the letter D as a prefix. The reason is that this will avoid confusion with the box numbers in our algorithm flowchart when we discuss the two different flowcharts. This convention of using the letter D as a prefix will be used in all descriptive flowcharts in this book.

largest-value descriptive flowchart

Before going on to develop the algorithm flowchart for this problem, let us discuss the sequencing of steps in the descriptive flowchart. The step in box D2 appears first because data values must be input before processing can begin. This will not be true for all problems for which we develop algorithms. However, in this problem input had to occur before any other step could be executed. Otherwise, there would be no data values to process. Similarly, the test for end-of-file had to follow the input step. The reason is that we would not want to proceed with algorithm execution once all data values have been processed. It is not necessary to follow an input step with a test for the end-of-file condition. However, whenever we do perform an end-of-file test it will usually follow an input operation. The order of performing the steps in boxes D5 and D6, on the other hand, is arbitrary. That is, the data values could have been output after finding the largest value instead of before it was found. However, in problems where the input values are to be output, it is a good practice to output them immediately following the input (or end-of-file) step. Note that the step in box D7 had to follow box D6. The reason is that the largest value cannot be output until it has been found. Finally, the

sequencing of steps

flowline that leads from box D7 back up to box D2 could not appear leading from any box other than D7. This is because the processing of one data set must be completed before the processing of the next data set can begin. The reason is that inputting a set of data values destroys the previous set of data.

largest-value algorithm flowchart

In Fig. 4.9 we have the algorithm flowchart for the largest-value problem in the case in which each data set consists of only two values. To begin, flowchart box 2 is the implementation of the input step in descriptive flowchart box D2. The verb GET is used because in our flowchart language GET is the way that we indicate input operations. The variables V1 and V2 are chosen arbitrarily to store the two input data values that are being fetched from the input data stream. Since we are dealing with numeric data, an annotation box has been attached to flowchart box 2 to declare V1 and V2 to be numeric variables. In flowchart box 3, the check is made to learn whether or not any values remained in the input data stream when the GET operation was most recently executed. That is, we are asking if we have run out of values in the input data stream. If the answer is that all input data stream values had been processed before executing the GET, then box 4 is executed next. In this case, algorithm execution is ordered to stop. However, if two values were input when executing the GET, control passes to flowchart box 5. In that box, the two input values are output together with a pair of string constants that identify the input values. Notice that these string constants did not have to be the same as the variable names we used. They were chosen to be the same simply for convenience.

Descriptive flowchart box D6 has been expanded into flowchart boxes 6, 7, and 8. That is, three flowchart language steps are required to determine which of the two values is larger and assign that value to a variable to be used for output purposes. Thus, in box 6 the condition is tested that states that the first data value is greater than the second data value. If this condition is true, the step in box 8 will be executed next. In this box, the value of the first variable is assigned to be the value of the variable *Large*. However, if the condition in flowchart box 6 is false, the value of the second variable is assigned to be the value of *Large*. Notice that *Large* is declared to be a numeric variable since it is being assigned the value of a numeric variable. In addition, observe that either box 7 or box 8 will be executed after the execution of flowchart box 6. Following the execution of one of these two boxes, the output step in box 9 will be executed. Note that this PUT box includes the output of a string constant that identifies the numeric value being output. Finally, an out-connector follows box 9 to indicate that control should be transferred back up to in-connector 1. This causes flowchart box 2 to be executed following execution of box 9.

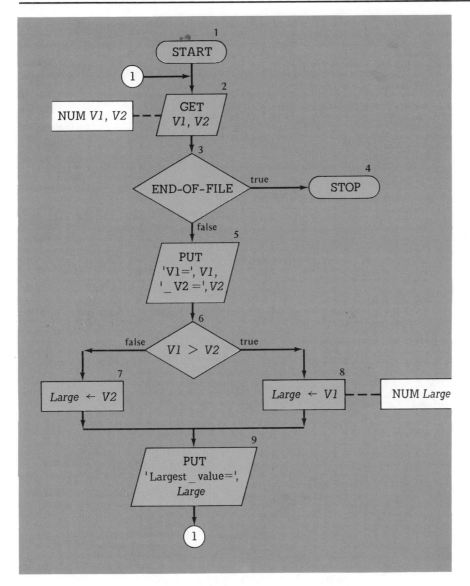

Figure 4.9. Algorithm Flowchart for the Largest-Value Problem in the Case of Two Data Values

Before proceeding to the case where there are three values in the input data set, let us develop a trace table for the algorithm of Fig. 4.9. A trace table is simply a table in which the column headings may consist of:

trace tables

109

1. The variable names used in the algorithm flowchart.
2. Conditions contained in decision boxes used in the algorithm flowchart.
3. The PUT box contents of output steps included in the algorithm flowchart.

The values contained in the trace table itself are:

1. For the columns headed by variable names, the sequence of values that have been assigned to the respective variables through either GET operations or assignment statements.
2. For the columns headed by conditions, the results of the decision for the current values of the variables. That is, these columns would contain the values of either *true* or *false*.
3. For the columns headed by PUT box contents, the sequence of values output to the output data stream by the respective PUT operation.

The trace table is created dynamically by stepping through the algorithm flowchart one box at a time. As each step is executed, the results are entered in the appropriate column of the trace table. Thus the value assigned to a variable in an assignment statement is recorded in the column headed with the name of that variable. Similarly, a value of true or false is entered in the column with a condition as a heading each time the box for that condition is executed. Thus a trace table is created one entry at a time, with each entry corresponding with the result of executing one flowchart step.

largest-value trace table   The trace table for the algorithm flowchart of Fig. 4.9 is given in Fig. 4.10. In developing this trace table, the input data stream

$$5,10, -4,-5, 6,6, 10,5$$

is assumed to have been used. Ideally, the input data stream values chosen

Figure 4.10. Trace Table for the Algorithm of Fig. 4.9

V1	V2	V1 > V2	Large
5	10	false	10
−4	−5	true	−4
6	6	false	6
10	5	true	10

in developing a trace table should be ones that cause every possible combination of branches in the algorithm to be taken.   Trace tables also assume that the correct answers are known for the input data stream used to develop the table.   The values the variables *V1* and *V2* assume in this trace table are coming from the input data stream using the GET operation in flowchart box 2.   The *true* or *false* in the condition column is determined by the relation in flowchart box 6.   Finally, the values in the column headed *Large* are being assigned by one of the assignment statements in either box 7 or box 8.

In Fig. 4.11 we have the algorithm flowchart for the case where there are three values in the input data set.   The logic of this algorithm has been based upon the descriptive flowchart of Fig. 4.8.   In fact, boxes 1 through 5 of the flowchart in Fig. 4.11 are the same as flowchart boxes 1 through 5 in Fig. 4.9, except that now three variables are used everywhere that two variables were used.   The primary difference between the flowcharts of Figs. 4.9 and 4.11 comes in the implementation of descriptive flowchart box D6.   That is, in the case of two values, only three flowchart boxes were needed, while in the case of three input values six flowchart boxes are needed to find the largest input value. Thus in Fig. 4.9 boxes 6 through 8 are used to implement descriptive flowchart box D6, while boxes 6 through 11 are used to implement the same descriptive flowchart box in Fig. 4.11.   The step in flowchart box 6 is used to determine whether the value of *V1* is greater than the value of *V2*.   If it is greater, the algorithm must determine whether or not the value of *V1* is greater than the value of *V3*.   This decision is made in box 8 of the flowchart.   When the value of *V1* is greater than that of *V3*, the condition in box 8 will be false and box 11 will be executed.   This causes the value of *V1* to be assigned to *Large* as the largest value.   However, when the condition in box 8 is true, the value of *V3* is assigned to be the value of *Large*.   An analysis of the left-hand branch out of box 6 will result in similar logic for the variables V2 and V3.   Finally, flowchart box 12 of this algorithm is identical to box 9 of the algorithm flowchart in Fig. 4.9.   The trace table in Fig. 4.12 was developed using

second largest-value algorithm flowchart

5,6,7, 5,8,3, 4,3,2, 9,5,15

as the input data stream.   This trace table is easy to understand and will therefore not be discussed.

Now the question we must ask is: What would happen if, for the case of four or five or more variables, we continue with the logic used in the algorithm flowcharts of Figs. 4.9 and 4.11?   Some thought will tell us that for each value that we add to the input data set we add one more row of decision boxes to our flowchart.   In addition, since each decision

more problem analysis

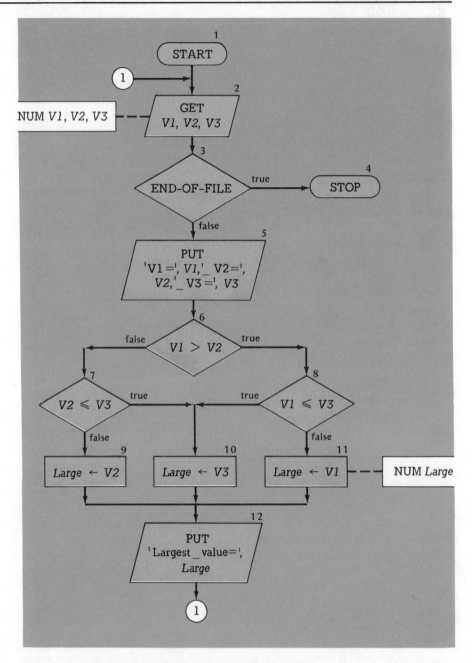

Figure 4.11. First Algorithm Flowchart for the Largest-Value Problem in the Case of Three Data Values

Figure 4.12.   Trace Table for the Algorithm of Fig. 4.11

V1	V2	V3	V1 > V2	V2 ≤ V3	V1 ≤ V3	Large
5	6	7	false	true		7
5	8	3	false	false		8
4	3	2	true		false	4
9	5	15	true		true	15

box has two outlet flowlines, each successive row of decision boxes will contain twice as many boxes as the row that is above it in the flowchart. Therefore, since for two values we had 1 decision box and for three values we had $1 + 2 = 3$ decision boxes, for four values we would have $1 + 2 + 4 = 7$ decision boxes, and for ten values we would have $1 + 2 + \cdots + 128 + 256 = 511$ decision boxes. Clearly this becomes unmanageable as the number of values becomes large. Thus we need to seek another approach to solving the largest-value problem.

Our new approach to this problem for three data values per set appears in the algorithm flowchart of Fig. 4.13. Again, flowchart boxes 1 through 5 are identical to the same boxes in Fig. 4.11. The difference comes in flowchart box 6 in which the first data value is assigned to be the value of the variable *Large*. Then, in flowchart box 7 the second data value is compared to the value of *Large* (which currently contains the first data value). If the second data value is greater than the value of *Large*, it is assigned in box 8 to be the new value of the variable *Large*. However, if the value of *V2* is not greater than the value of *Large*, flowchart box 8 is skipped. In either case, box 9 will be executed next. The condition in box 9 and the action that results from the decision is similar to the one in box 7. The only difference in this case is that the third data value rather than the second is involved in the condition and the assignment. Notice that in this algorithm we have developed a uniform way in which to treat each data value after the first one. That is, we initialize the value of the variable *Large* with the first data value. Then we successively compare each data value with the current value of *Large*. If the data value is greater than *Large*, we have a new largest value that must be assigned to be the new value of *Large*. Otherwise, we proceed to compare the next data value, and the next, and so on until all data values have been compared to the value of *Large*. Once all values have been compared, the value of *Large* can be output as the answer. Notice that with this algorithm only one decision box is added for each new data value that is included in a data set. Therefore, for ten data values per data set, we would need to have only nine decision boxes. This is quite an improvement over the

third largest-value algorithm flowchart

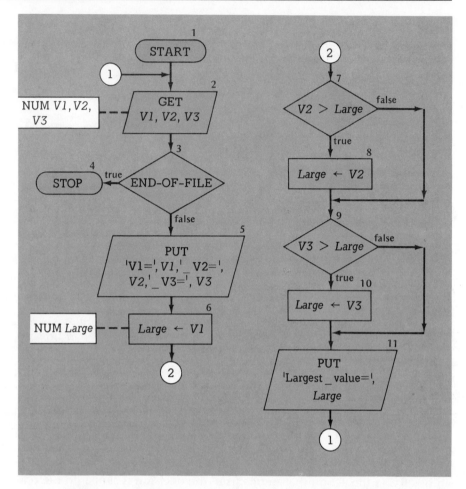

Figure 4.13. Second Algorithm Flowchart for the Largest-Value Problem in the Case of Three Data Values

number of decision boxes required in the algorithm developed in Fig. 4.11. The trace table for the algorithm of Fig. 4.13 appears in Fig. 4.14; it was developed using the same input data stream used in developing the trace table of Fig. 4.12.

more problem analysis   One major difficulty still remains with the approach taken in the algorithm of Fig. 4.13. The difficulty is that this logic produces an algorithm that is designed to handle a set number of data values, no more and no less. That is, the algorithm in Fig. 4.13 can be used to find the largest value from among three data values. However, it cannot be used to find the

Figure 4.14.   Trace Table for the Algorithm of Fig. 4.13

V1	V2	V3	Large	V2 > Large	V3 > Large
5	6	7	5	true	
			6		true
			7		
5	8	3	5	true	
			8		false
4	3	2	4	false	false
9	5	15	9	false	true
			15		

largest value from among four or five or forty data values. Thus our current algorithm has no generality to the class of problems that requires finding the largest value in a set that contains any number of values.

Figure 4.15 contains a descriptive flowchart that overcomes this difficulty. The first step to be executed in this descriptive flowchart is to input a value that provides the number of data values in the set to be processed. Notice that this step says input the number of data values—it does not say input any of the data values themselves. This step means two things: (1) we know in advance how many data values are in each data set to be processed, and (2) the data sets that we can process may have any number of data values, since the number of values is now a variable. Descriptive flowchart step D3 is included to detect whether or not more data sets remain to be processed. Obviously, should no value be in the input data stream when attempting to input the count of how many values there are in the next data set, then there must not be any more data sets to process.

The step in box D5 may be a little more difficult to explain. This step is used to initialize a variable to be used to save the largest data value found. In developing an algorithm, we initialize variables with values to get them ready for something that is to follow. In this algorithm, the thing that follows is a sequence of steps that is used to input data values and save the largest one. The way we look for the largest one is to save the largest value found so far and compare it with each successive input data value. When the comparison shows that the current input data value is larger than the largest value found thus far, then the current data value is saved as the new largest value. Should the current data value not be larger than the largest value found thus far, the current data value is ignored. These input, comparison, and save steps are represented in descriptive flowchart box D6. Returning to box D5 for a moment, we still

second
largest-value
descriptive
flowchart

115

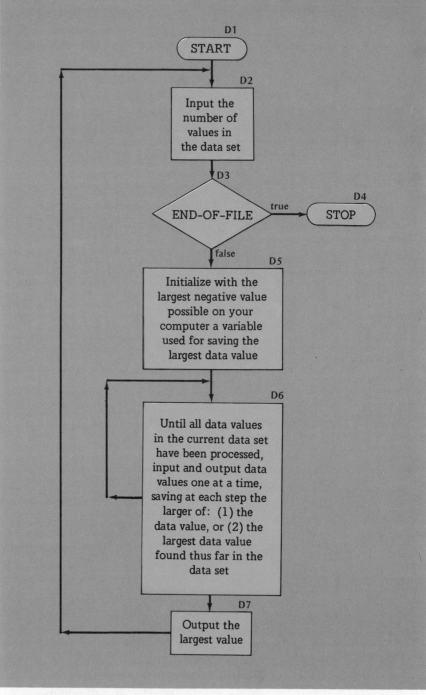

Figure 4.15. Second Descriptive Flowchart for the Largest-Value Problem

need to explain why the variable was initialized with the smallest possible value. The reason is that this forces the first input data value to be saved as the largest value found thus far the first time that step D6 is executed for a data set. Had we not performed the initialization in the way that we did, the variable we are using to save the largest value would either be undefined or not have the desired value. Thus initializing a variable is simply the step of giving a variable a starting value that causes the desired action to occur when that variable is used later in the algorithm. Implicit in box D6 is that a decision must be reached as to whether or not all data values in this data set have been processed. As long as they have not, the input-output-compare-save sequence is repeated. When all data values in the current data set have been processed, box D7 is executed, causing output of the largest value in the set. Following this step, control is returned to box D2, in which the number of values in the next data set is input.

The algorithm flowchart for the generalized largest-value problem appears in Fig. 4.16. In flowchart box 2, the number of data values in a data set is input as the value of N. Thus the variable N initially has a value that indicates how many data values there are in the data set about to be processed. Notice that N has been declared to be an integer-valued variable since a count of the number of values in a data set will always be a whole number. Flowchart box 5 contains the step to initialize the variable *Large*, which is used to save the largest value found during processing of the data set. The value -10^{15} was chosen as the initial value of *Large* since we are going to assume that no data value will be less than this fairly large negative value. If data values less than -10^{15} were possible, we would want to use whatever the smallest possible value is to initialize *Large*. The steps in boxes 6 and 7 are used to input and output one data value. This data value is stored using the variable *Value*. Notice that *Value* is declared to be a numeric variable because the algorithm is designed to process any numeric values. In box 8 of the flowchart, the condition is tested that states that the current data value is greater than the largest value found thus far. Of course, for the first data value in a data set this condition will always be true because of the initial value given to the variable *Large*. However, for the second and later data values in the data set, this condition may be either true or false. If the condition is true, the assignment statement in box 9 is executed. This causes the current data value to be assigned as the new value of *Large*. In the case where the condition is false, flowchart box 9 is not executed, thus leaving the value of *Large* unchanged. The reason for leaving the value of *Large* unchanged is that it still contains the largest data value found thus far in the data set being processed.

The step in flowchart box 10 reduces the value of N by one. This is to reflect the fact that one more data value in the data set has been

final largest-value algorithm flowchart

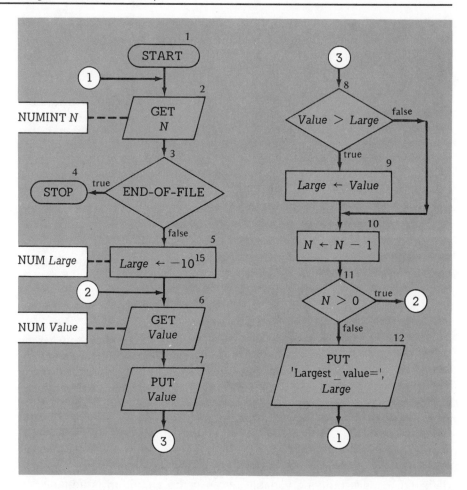

Figure 4.16. Final Algorithm Flowchart for the Largest-Value Problem

processed. Thus, after each execution of box 10, the value of N indicates how many data values in the current data set remain to be input and processed. Notice that it is perfectly acceptable for the same variable name to appear on both the right and left side of the assignment operator in the same assignment statement. This simply means that the value of the variable on the right of the assignment operator will be whatever value that variable had when execution of that assignment statement began. The value assigned to that variable will be whatever constant value the expression evaluates to using this previous value of the variable. Thus in box 10 the value of the variable N on the right will be whatever value N

had when box 10 was entered. However, the value of N when leaving box 10 will be one less than the value N had upon entering that flowchart box. In flowchart box 11 we test the condition that the value of N is greater than zero. The reason for testing this condition is that as long as it is true, then more data values in the current data set remain to be processed. Once the value of N is not greater than zero, however, all values in the current data set have been processed. In this case, the branch to flowchart box 12 is taken, which causes a string constant followed by the value of *Large* to be output. Following this output operation, a branch is taken back to in-connector 1, where a count of the number of values in the next data set is input. This processing of data sets finding the largest value of each one will continue until all data sets in the input data stream have been exhausted.

Notice that an end-of-file test is not included following the input step in box 6. The reason is that we know how many data values are in each data set. Therefore, an end-of-file cannot occur in the middle of processing a data set unless an incorrect value for N was input in box 2.

The trace table for this algorithm appears in Fig. 4.17. The input   **trace table**
data stream

$$5,\ \boxed{4,8,2,7,5,}\ 3,\ \boxed{8,7,15,}\ 6,\ \boxed{12,8,6,5,-3,2}$$

Figure 4.17.   Trace Table for the Algorithm of Fig. 4.16

N	Large	Value	Value > Large	N > 0
5	-10^{15}	4	true	
4	4	8	true	true
3	8	2	false	true
2		7	false	true
1		5	false	true
0				false
3	-10^{15}	8	true	
2	8	7	false	true
1		15	true	true
0	15			false
6	-10^{15}	12	true	
5	12	8	false	true
4		6	false	true
3		5	false	true
2		-3	false	true
1		2	false	true
0				false

was used to produce this trace table. Notice that only the values in the shaded area in this input data stream are values in the data sets for which maximum values are to be found. The values in the unshaded areas are the values of N that tell how many data values there are in the data set that follows. Of course, the values of N are distinguished from the data values by the computer because the input data stream is read by GET boxes from left to right. Notice the use of horizontal broken lines in the trace table to separate the portions of the trace table associated with the three input data sets. This trace table should be compared with the flowchart to gain a complete understanding of the logic contained in the algorithm.

4.6.2   The Depreciation Problem

problem definition   A problem often encountered in business is that of depreciating an asset. A business considers an asset to be any object of value that has a useful life longer than one accounting period. An accounting period may be for one year, six months, or some other period of time. Examples of assets would be automobiles used by salesmen, delivery trucks, buildings, machinery, and office equipment. The problem of depreciation is that of reducing the value of the asset on the company's accounting records to reflect the fact that the asset is wearing out.

problem analysis   There are a number of ways of computing depreciation that are approved by accountants. The simplest of these is the *straight-line method.* Under this method the life of the asset is divided into the cost of the asset, giving the amount that the asset depreciates each accounting period. For example, if accounting periods are for one year, an asset that cost $1,000 and has an expected life of 5 years would depreciate at the rate of $200 per year. Thus at the end of one year this asset would be worth $800, at the end of two years it would be worth $600, and so on until at the end of five years it would have no value. In tabular form, we have

Period	Value
1	$800
2	$600
3	$400
4	$200
5	$ 0

This analysis ignores the fact that assets often have what accountants call a salvage value. That is, the asset has a trade-in or junk value at the end of its useful life to the company that owns it.

descriptive flowchart

A descriptive flowchart for solving this problem appears in Fig. 4.18.

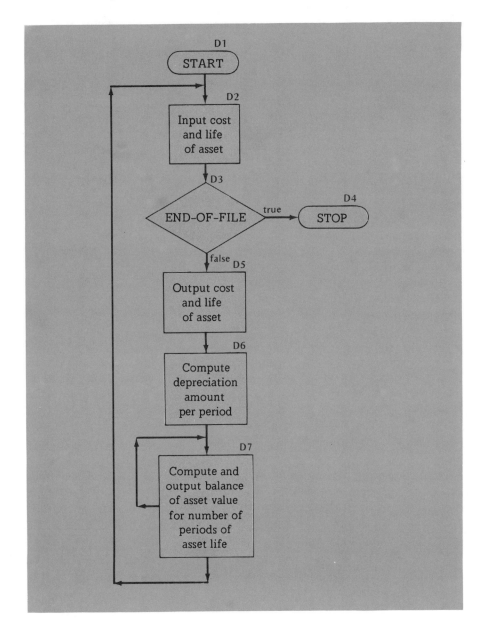

Figure 4.18. Descriptive Flowchart for the Depreciation Problem

The step in box D2 is used to input the cost of the asset and its life in terms of accounting periods. Boxes D3 and D4 are included to cause algorithm execution to stop when all of the desired depreciation tables have been processed and output. In descriptive flowchart box D5, the input values are output so that the table can be associated with the asset with those input values. The next step is to calculate the amount of depreciation for each accounting period. Once this is completed, all that remains is to compute and print the balance of the asset value at the end of each accounting period. This step is performed in box D7, where as many balances will be computed and printed as there are periods of life for that asset. When the last line of the table has been output, control is returned to box D2, where the input values for the next asset are input.

algorithm flowchart   The algorithm flowchart for this problem appears in Fig. 4.19. The first five boxes of this flowchart parallel their counterparts in the descriptive

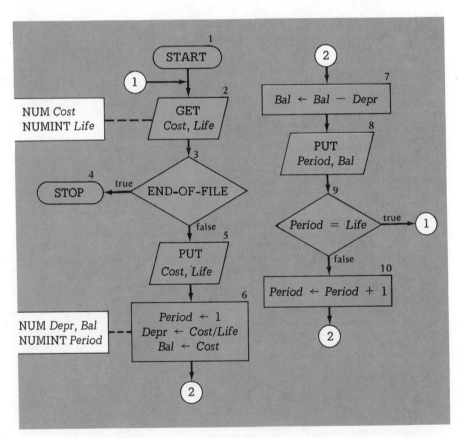

Figure 4.19. Algorithm Flowchart for the Depreciation Problem

122

flowchart. However, the statements in box 6 require an explanation. The first assignment statement in box 6 is to initialize the variable *Period* with a value of 1. This variable is used as a counter to keep track of the accounting period number for the asset balance. Since the first balance computed and output is for the end of the first accounting period, it is reasonable to initialize *Period* with 1 as its starting value. The second assignment statement in flowchart box 6 causes the amount of depreciation for each accounting period to be computed and assigned to the variable *Depr*. Thus, since the amount of depreciation is unchanged from accounting period to accounting period, we simply compute it once and assign it to be the value of a variable. The third assignment statement in box 6 is used to initialize the variable *Bal* with the cost value of the asset. This is necessary because the variable *Bal* will be used to store the current balance of the asset for each accounting period. Finally, notice that the three assignment statements in box 6 can appear in any order. This is because none of the variables on the left of the assignment operators appear to the right of the assignment operators in the statements in this box.

In box 7 the balance of the asset value is calculated by subtracting the depreciation amount from the previous balance of the asset. This value is then assigned to be the new balance of the asset. The first time that box 7 is executed for an asset, the previous value of *Bal* will be the initial cost value of the asset. However, in subsequent executions *Bal* will have the balance from the previous period as its value. Again, notice that in this assignment statement the variable *Bal* appears on both the right and the left of the assignment operator. No confusion results from this because in evaluating the expression on the right, the value *Bal* had upon entering box 7 will be used. However, on exiting from this box *Bal* will have the value resulting from evaluation of the expression. In flowchart box 8, the period number and ending balance value of the asset are output. The decision box that follows contains a condition that is included to determine if output entries have been produced for every period in the life of the asset. That is, if the condition is true that the value of *Period* is equal to the value of *Life*, a table entry for each period must have been produced. However, if this condition is not true, then the proper number of table entries have not been produced. This is because the variable *Period* is initialized at 1 in box 6 and incremented by 1 in box 10. Therefore, since the life of the asset must be a positive integer value, the value of *Period* will not be equal to that of *Life* only when the proper number of table entries have not been produced. However, once the value of *Period* is equal to that of *Life*, the depreciation table for that asset will be complete. In this case, a branch is taken to in-connector 1, where the input values for the next depreciation table are obtained. Notice that the variables *Cost*, *Depr*, and *Bal* have been declared as numeric variables since they involve dollar values that may have fractional parts. On the other hand, *Life* and *Period* are declared to be integer-valued variables since they will always represent whole numbers.

trace table   The trace table for this algorithm is given in Fig. 4.20. The input data stream

$$1000,4, \quad 5000,5$$

was used to produce this trace table. Again, the horizontal broken line has been used in the trace table to separate the results of the two input data sets. This trace table should be carefully studied using the algorithm flowchart to gain a thorough understanding of algorithm logic.

Figure 4.20.   Trace Table for the Algorithm of Fig. 4.19

Cost	Life	Period	Depr	Bal	Period = Life
1000	4	1	250	1000	
		2		750	false
		3		500	false
		4		250	false
				0	true
5000	5	1	1000	5000	
		2		4000	false
		3		3000	false
		4		2000	false
		5		1000	false
				0	true

4.6.3   The Vowel-Counting Problem

problem definition and analysis   An interesting task involved in the study of writing styles is to determine how many occurrences there are in a manuscript of each of the vowels. That is, the number of times the letter *A* appears in the manuscript, the number of times the letter *E* appears, and so on for the letters *I*, *O*, and *U* all are to be counted. In performing this task manually, we would scan the manuscript from beginning to end tallying each time we found an *A*, *E*, *I*, *O*, or *U*. An algorithm flowchart for a computer solution requires a similar approach. Let us make one simplifying assumption: all letters are uppercase. Relaxing this restriction would simply add five decision boxes to our algorithm flowchart.

The descriptive flowchart for this problem appears in Fig. 4.21. If we were doing this task manually, we would probably start by being sure that we have five clean sheets of paper on which to keep tallys of each occurrence of the five vowels. In a computer solution, we will use variables for counting the number of occurrences. Therefore, we want to be certain that each of these counter variables starts with a value of zero. Our first algorithm step would therefore be the one described in box D2. Now, our strategy for the remainder of the algorithm is a simple one. We will input one character of the manuscript at a time until there are no more

descriptive flowchart

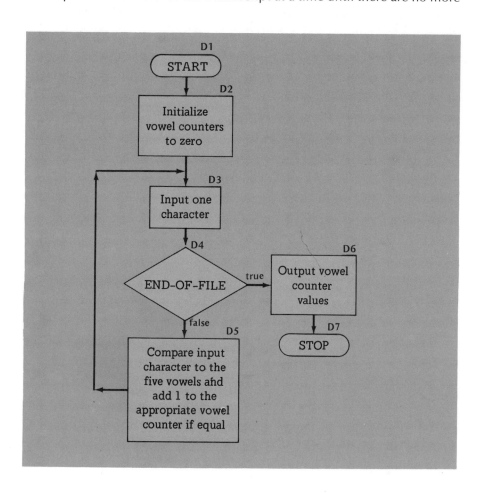

Figure 4.21. Descriptive Flowchart for the Vowel-Counting Problem

characters in the input stream. When there are no more characters in the input stream, we will print the current values of the counters and terminate execution of the algorithm. This is represented by the steps in descriptive flowchart boxes D3, D4, D6, and D7. Until the end-of-file condition occurs, each character will be checked as it is input to see if it is one of the five vowels. When it is one of the vowels, the counter for the vowel will have one added to its value to record the fact. Then control will be transferred back to box D3, where the next character is input. If the character being processed is not a vowel, we simply go back and input another character for processing. All of this logic is included in box D5.

algorithm flowchart

The algorithm flowchart for this problem is given in Fig. 4.22. Notice in box 2 that each variable name has been chosen to indicate the vowel for which it is the counter. Also observe that the five assignment statements in this box could have appeared in any order within this box. In addition, note that the five variables are declared NUMINT because counts always involve whole numbers. Flowchart boxes 7 through 16 represent the logic expressed in descriptive flowchart box D5. Notice that five decision boxes must appear in the algorithm flowchart to accomplish the comparison of the input character with the five vowels. Also, observe what occurs once any one of the equality-of-the-input-character-with-vowel conditions has produced a true result. This causes the respective counter to be increased by 1 and an immediate branch to box 3, where another character is input. In other words, comparison of the input character with the vowels ceases once it has been discovered that the input character is some particular vowel. Finally, note that string constants are output before each counter value to identify the results.

trace table

The trace table for the input data stream

'C', 'O', 'M', 'P', 'U', 'T', 'E', 'R', '_', 'S', 'C', 'I', 'E',
'N', 'C', 'E', '_', 'I', 'S', '_', 'F', 'U', 'N', '.'

appears in Fig. 4.23. Notice that the input data stream consists of the message

COMPUTER SCIENCE IS FUN.

broken up into one-character string constants. The reason for breaking this message up into these one-character constants is that the algorithm expects the input to be in the form of one-character strings. Notice in the results that the input data stream did not contain any *A* values. Therefore, the value of its counter was not changed from its initial value. Again, the trace table should be studied carefully using the algorithm flowchart and the input data stream.

126

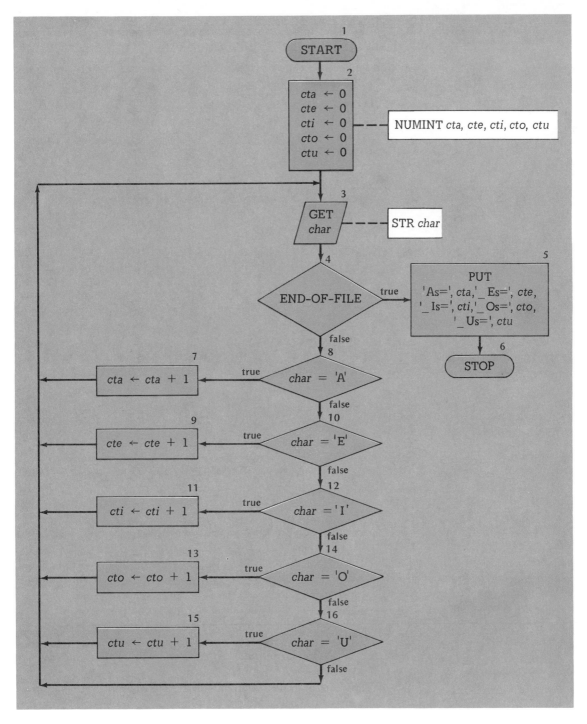

Figure 4.22. Algorithm Flowchart for the Vowel-Counting Problem

Figure 4.23.   Trace Table for the Algorithm of Fig. 4.22

cta	cte	cti	cto	ctu	char
0	0	0	0	0	' C '
			1		' O '
					' M '
					' P '
				1	' U '
					' T '
	1				' E '
					' R '
					' _ '
					' S '
					' C '
		1			' I '
	2				' E '
					' N '
					' C '
	3				' E '
					' _ '
		2			' I '
					' S '
					' _ '
					' F '
				2	' U '
					' N '
					' '

PROBLEMS

12. In flowchart box 2 of Fig. 4.16, why not use an assignment statement to assign a value to N rather than performing a GET operation?

13. In flowchart box 5 of Fig. 4.16, why not use 10^{-15} as the small value instead of -10^{15}?

14. The second assignment statement in flowchart box 6 of Fig. 4.19 can be eliminated. This can be done by replacing the variable $Depr$ in box 7 with the arithmetic expression of the second assignment statement in box 6. Would this change make the algorithm more or less efficient?

For each of the following problems, develop: (1) a descriptive flowchart, (2) an algorithm flowchart, and (3) a trace table (develop your own input data stream for each problem).

15. The problem is that of finding the largest of four numeric input values using logic that represents an extension of that used in the algorithm flowchart of Fig. 4.11.

16. The problem is that of finding the smallest value in a set of numbers. Assume that the number of values in each data set is known. The output for each data set should consist of the input values and the smallest number found in the data set. Include string constants in the output to identify the different values.

17. A teacher wants to let the computer find the area of a triangle given the length of the base and the height (or altitude) of the triangle. The area is calculated simply as the product of the base and height divided by 2. The algorithm should be designed to accept the base and height measures for a series of triangles and compute the area of each. Output should consist of the input values and their respective areas.

18. A bank has the problem of converting U.S. dollars into foreign currency and foreign currency into U.S. dollars. To convert from U.S. dollars to foreign currency, it is necessary to multiply the number of dollars by the current exchange rate between dollars and that currency. Conversion from the foreign currency is accomplished by dividing the number of units of foreign currency by the same exchange rate. In developing your conversion algorithm, assume that the input for each conversion is the number of units of currency to be converted, the current exchange rate between dollars and that currency, and either a 1 or 2, where 1 indicates the currency to be converted is dollars and a 2 indicates that it is a foreign currency that is to be converted. Output should include: (1) a string constant that states whether the currency converted is **'U.S. '** or **'FOREIGN '**, (2) the amount converted, (3) the current exchange rate, and (4) the amount of converted currency.

19. Modify the algorithm flowchart of Fig. 4.16 so that the value of N is not modified while inputting and processing the data set values. This will require the use of a counter variable that keeps track of how many values have been processed.

20. Modify the algorithm flowchart of Fig. 4.16 so that the variable *Large* is initialized with the first data value of each data set. Is this algorithm more or less efficient than the original version?

21. Modify the algorithm flowchart of Fig. 4.16 so that a count is kept of how many data sets have been processed. Before each data set is input, a heading should be output which states that:

'DATA_SET_NUMBER_'n'_FOLLOWS'

where n is the number of that data set.

22. A teacher wants to let the computer assign course grades, where the grading system used is:

0–59	F
60–69	D
70–79	C
80–89	B
90–100	A

Assume that the input is a student's name followed by his or her course average, where the average is given as an integer number. Output should consist of the student's name, course average, and course letter grade.

23. An accountant wants to use the computer to compute social security tax. The tax is calculated by taking 6 percent of the person's gross pay up to $13,200 per year. That is, social security tax is only charged on the first $13,200 of a person's income for each year. Your algorithm inputs should be a person's: (1) name, (2) accumulated earnings for the year, and (3) salary for this pay period. Output should include the input values and the social security tax.

24. Modify the algorithm flowchart of Fig. 4.16 for the case in which the number of values in each data set is not known. To accomplish this, assume that the last data value in each data set is followed by a dummy value that is equal to 10^{15}. In addition, assume that all legitimate data values must be less than that value.

25. An engineer wants to have the computer find the area of a triangle given the length of the three sides. The area is defined to be

$$area = \sqrt{T \cdot (T - X) \cdot (T - Y) \cdot (T - Z)}$$

where X, Y, and Z are the lengths of the respective sides of the triangle, and T is equal to the sum of the lengths of the three sides divided by 2. The algorithm should be designed to accept the lengths of the three sides for a series of triangles and compute the area of each. Output should consist of the input values and their respective areas.

26. A stockbroker wants the computer to add up dollar stock sales for each day. The algorithm for this problem should be developed assuming that the number of stock transactions is known.   Assume that input will be the values of these transactions, while output will consist of the values and their sum.   You should assume that the algorithm is capable of performing this task for more than one day's stock sales each time that it is used.

27. Solve Problem 26 assuming that the number of stock transactions is not known in advance.   Assume for this problem that each stock sale does not exceed $1,000,000,000.

28. A system of two simultaneous linear equations of the form

$$a \cdot x + b \cdot y = e$$
$$c \cdot x + d \cdot y = f$$

can be solved using the equations

$$x = (e \cdot d - b \cdot f)/(a \cdot d - b \cdot c)$$
$$y = (a \cdot f - e \cdot c)/(a \cdot d - b \cdot c)$$

for the case in which $a \cdot d \neq b \cdot c$.   An error message can be output should $a \cdot d = b \cdot c$.   The input in this problem will be values for the variables a, b, c, d, e, and f.   The output should consist of the input values and the two values that represent the solutions for the inputs.

29. A mathematician thinks that he has discovered an important fact and wants to use the computer to help verify that it is correct.   He has discovered that for any positive integer, N, the square of that integer (N^2) is equal to the sum of the first N odd integers.   For example, $4^2 = 16$ is equal to $1 + 3 + 5 + 7 = 16$.   The input to your algorithm should be values of N and the output should be N, N^2, and the sum of the first N odd integers.

30. Depreciation methods other than straight line are often used in depreciating an asset.   One of these methods is the sum-of-the-years-digits method.   In this method, a denominator d is formed using the formula $d = Y \cdot (Y + 1) / 2$, where Y is the life of the asset.   Then the depreciation is computed by multiplying the original cost of the asset by the number of periods of asset life remaining at the beginning of that period and then dividing this product by the denominator.   Your algorithm inputs should be original asset cost and life

in periods.   Output should be the input values and a table that shows depreciation of the asset.

31. Depreciation methods other than straight line are often used in depreciating an asset.   One of these methods is the declining balance method.   In this method a constant factor is multiplied times the remaining asset value to obtain each year's depreciation amount.   This constant factor is calculated by dividing a depreciation multiplier by the life of the asset.   Thus in the first year the constant factor is multiplied times the original cost value of the asset to obtain the first year's depreciation.   In the second year the constant factor is multiplied times the original asset cost less first year's depreciation to arrive at second-year depreciation.   And so the process continues for future years until the useful life of the asset is over.   Your algorithm inputs should be original asset cost, asset life, and the depreciation multiplier (which must be greater than 1).   Output should include input values and a table that shows the depreciation of the asset.

32. Modify the algorithm flowchart of Fig. 4.19 so that the variable *Bal* is eliminated.   This change must be made in a way that does not change the results produced by the algorithm.   Is the resulting algorithm more or less efficient than the unmodified version?

33. Modify the algorithm flowchart of Fig. 4.19 so that the condition in box 9 does not involve either the variable *Period* or *Life*.   This change must be made in a way that does not change the results produced by the algorithm.

34. A mathematician needs to solve some quadratic equations of the form

$$a \cdot x^2 + b \cdot x + c = 0$$

using the quadratic formula

$$x = \frac{-b \pm \sqrt{b^2 - 4 \cdot a \cdot c}}{2 \cdot a}$$

The inputs for this algorithm will be the coefficient values a, b, and c, while the output should consist of these input values together with the two values (the two roots) of x.   The message that imaginary roots have occurred should be output instead of the results in the case where $b^2 < 4 \cdot a \cdot c$.

35. An English professor wants to use the computer to help him count the number of words in a manuscript. This can be accomplished by counting the number of blank spaces since words are separated from each other by a blank space (we will assume that there is never more than one space between words in the manuscript). Assume that the manuscript is input one character at a time and that output is to consist of the number of words preceded by a string constant that describes this value.

36. An executive prefers that his employees use two consecutive hyphens instead of semicolons in their correspondence. Since all letters for this company are computer-edited anyway, the executive wants the computer department to write an algorithm through which all letters are processed to change all occurrences of semicolons to two hyphens. Assume that all such letters are input to the algorithm one character at a time. Output should consist of the edited letter.

SUMMARY

1. The symbols in the alphabet of our flowchart language are:

a. The symbols for the 26 uppercase and 26 lowercase letters of the English alphabet, associated punctuation marks, and certain special symbols.

b. The symbols for the ten decimal digits and the other usual symbols of mathematics.

c. A set of eight standard flowchart symbols, six of which we call flowchart boxes.

2. The words in our flowchart language consist of: (a) constants, (b) variables, and (c) certain keyword verbs.

3. The four basic types of statements in our flowchart language are:

a. Processing statements.

b. Control statements.

c. Declarative statements.

d. Input/output statements.

4. There are two types of constants and variables in our flowchart language. They are:

a. Numeric constants and variables.

b. String constants and variables.

5. A variable is a name that refers to a place in computer main memory where a constant is stored.

6. Information about an algorithm variable or an algorithm step is called declarative information and is enclosed in an annotation box. The annotation box is connected to a flowchart box by a broken line.

7. All variables in our flowchart language must be declared as to type. The three types of variables are:

a. Numeric variables (declared using NUM).

b. Integer-valued numeric variables (declared using NUMINT).

c. String variables (declared using STR).

8. The assignment statement is of the form

$$variable \leftarrow expression$$

9. The order in which assignment statements are placed within a processing box may be critical to obtaining correct results.

10. Evaluation of an expression is the process of successively reducing subexpressions to constant values until the entire expression is reduced to a single constant value.

11. Evaluation of arithmetic expressions is done using the precedence rules of Fig. 4.3.

12. A GET box contains a list of variable names that are assigned values obtained from an input data stream that consists of a list of constant values.

13. A PUT box contains a list of constants and variables the values of which are placed in an output data stream.

14. The two basic types of connectors are: (a) in-connectors and (b) out-connectors.

15. The basic branching statement is the condi-

131

tional branch, which is indicated in a flowchart by a decision box.

16. The condition contained in a decision box will be either true or false. Some of the conditions that can be tested are mathematical equality or inequality, the sequencing of string constants, and end-of-file conditions.

17. In designing an algorithm, all possible condi-

tions that are important should be considered and tests included to determine when these conditions hold.

18. Descriptive flowcharts are very useful in revealing the broad structure of an algorithm.

19. The trace table provides an effective way to test the logic of an algorithm to learn whether or not it is correct.

Algorithm Design II: Looping, Iterative Algorithms, and Efficiency

In Chapters 3 and 4 we learned about the basic aspects of problem analysis and algorithm design. In this chapter we are going to study some additional concepts of algorithm design. Among the more important concepts to be introduced in this chapter is that of looping. Actually, the three algorithms we designed in Section 4.6 contained loops. In this chapter, however, we are going to study looping as a formal process. Another important concept to be studied in this chapter is that an algorithm does not always yield an exact solution to a problem. Instead, an algorithm often yields only an approximation to the true solution. This is particularly true in the case of algorithms that solve numeric-type problems. Finally, we are going to look at some notions that relate to the efficiency of an algorithm.

5.1 LOOPING

In almost every algorithm we have developed thus far in the text, one or more steps have been executed more than once. In fact, virtually all algorithms ever designed for execution using a computer have in common that they contain one or more steps which will be executed more than once. The steps that are executed over and over in an algorithm make up what is called a loop. That is, a *loop* is a series of algorithm steps that is executed repetitively.

loops

The two reasons why the steps of an algorithm are repeated are:

1. The algorithm performs the same operations on different data items.
2. The results of the algorithm are obtained by performing operations over and over again beginning with a given set of data.

Of the algorithms examined in Chapter 4, the largest-value problem and vowel-counting problem algorithms fall primarily in the first category. This is because both algorithms essentially involved getting one or a set of data values, processing these values, and returning to the beginning of the algorithm to repeat the process on more data values. The depreciation-table algorithm, on the other hand, involved beginning with an input data set and repeating a group of steps some finite number of times. Thus the depreciation-table algorithm falls into the second category. It also qualifies for the first category, however, in that a loop is made back to repeat the table-generating process for additional data sets. Therefore, algorithms can actually contain more than one loop and also may fall into both loop categories.

Four definite components can be identified for every loop. These are: **loop components**

1. The *initialization* component, in which loop variables and other variables used in the loop are given starting values. *Loop variables* are the variables used in a loop to control the looping process. That is, loop variables are used to determine how many times the steps that make up the loop are to be repeated.
2. The *body* of the loop, which is made up of the steps to be repeated.
3. A *modification* or adjustment component in which the values of loop variables are changed in preparation for the next repetition of the loop.
4. A *test-for-loop-termination* component in which it is determined (using loop variables) whether or not the loop is to be repeated.

The initialization component must appear before any of the other three loop components. This is because it is usually necessary to a loop even though it is not one of the steps in a loop that is repeated. However, the final three loop components can appear in any order in the loop. Four possible *loop structures* are given in the flowcharts in Fig. 5.1. Structure *a* is the method used by the built-in looping facility of most dialects of the FORTRAN language. Notice that the body of the loop in structure *a* will always be executed at least once. This is because the test for loop termination is not made until after the body of the loop has been executed. In some cases, this may be a disadvantage since the steps in the body possibly may need to be skipped. Another defect in structure *a* is that the modification step will be performed even when the loop is not to be repeated. This provides for a slight inefficiency in the algorithm. **loop structures**

Loop structure *b* avoids the first of the drawbacks of structure *a* in that the body of the loop will not necessarily be performed at all under structure *b*. This is because the test-for-loop-termination component appears before the loop body. Thus under structure *b* execution of the loop may be terminated before the loop body is executed. However, loop structure *b* is less efficient than loop structure *a* in that one extra test will always be required for any given number of loop repetitions. Loop structure *c* will in general require one less execution of the modification step

135

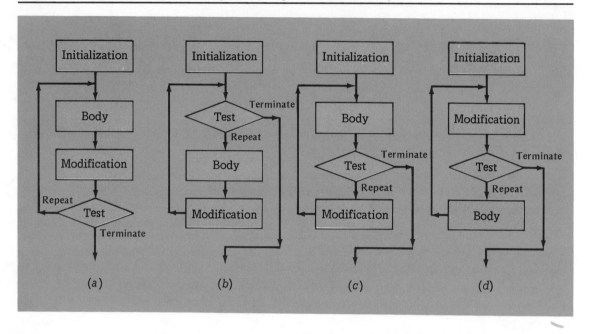

Figure 5.1 Four Possible Loop Structures

than will structures *a* and *b*. Structure *c* suffers from the first failing of structure *a*, however, in that the body of the loop will always be executed at least once. Loop structure *d* may offer individual advantages over structures *a* or *b* or *c*, but is not often used.

loop structures for a previous algorithm

Let us now identify the loop structures of the algorithm of Fig. 4.16 in Section 4.6. First, the algorithm contains two loops. One loop consists of flowchart boxes 2 and 5 through 11. This loop is used to input and output a data value and determine whether this value is greater than the largest value found thus far in the current data set. In this loop, initialization takes place in boxes 2 and 5, the loop body is in boxes 6 through 9, the modification component is in box 10, and the test-for-loop-termination component is in box 11. Therefore, this loop has loop structure type *a*. Notice that *N* is the loop variable because it is the variable that is initialized in box 2, modified in box 10, and used in box 11 to test for loop termination. Another variable, *Large*, was also initialized for this loop even though it is not a loop variable. That is, *Large* is simply a variable used in the loop, but it does not control the looping process.

The algorithm of Fig. 4.16 has a second loop, which consists of flowchart boxes 2, 3, and 5 through 12. This loop is designed to repeat for any number of data sets the process of finding the largest value in a data set. This loop does not have either an initialization step or a modification component as such because the test for loop termination is the end-of-file test in box 3. Thus termination of the outer loop occurs simply because the values in the input data stream have been exhausted. Notice that the loop body for the outer loop consists of boxes 2 and 5 through 12. Therefore, the test for loop termination is contained within the body of the loop. Thus the outer loop cannot be classified as one of the loop-structure types given in Fig. 5.1. The only case in this book in which we will not be able to classify a loop structure using Fig. 5.1 is the one involving end-of-file as the test for loop termination. Notice that this outer loop also does not have a loop variable.

One final note is that in Fig. 4.16 the inner loop (consisting of boxes 2 and 5 through 11) is completely contained within the outer loop (made up of boxes 2, 3, and 5 through 12). In cases such as this, the inner loop is said to be nested within the outer loop. That is, a *nested loop* is a loop **nested loops** that is contained within another loop. Nested loops occur very often in algorithms. In general, loops may be nested to any level. That is, loops within loops that are within other loops and so forth are permitted. The only restriction is that a loop nested within a loop must be completely contained within the loop in which it is nested. That is, all of the steps of an inner loop must be within the body of the outer loop.

5.2   SUBSCRIPTED VARIABLES

In Section 4.2.2 we learned that in designing an algorithm it is necessary to provide certain information in the flowchart about the variables used. Such information is called declarative information because it does not directly cause any action to be taken in the algorithm. In Section 4.2.2, the declarative information we included was the type of constant values that a variable name could assume. The three kinds we identified in that section were numeric variables, integer-valued numeric variables, and string variables. We declared variables to have one of these types by using an annotation box. In the annotation box we would place the words NUM, NUMINT, or STR, which are abbreviations for *numeric, numeric integer, and string,* respectively. Following each of these abbreviations the variable names in the algorithm box that were to have the respective types were listed. Also recall that the declarations were made adjacent to the box in which a particular variable is first used in the flowchart. The reason this is done as opposed to declaring all variables at the beginning of the flowchart is that it seems most natural to declare the type of a variable when it is first used.

Another very important use of the declarative statement is to specify that a variable is subscripted. Recall from algebra that we often have a variable name that has a group of values associated with it. In such a case we would place a subscript on the variable to indicate to which value of the variable we were referring. For example, we might have an ordered list of values,

$$5 \quad 6 \quad -4 \quad 2 \quad 0$$

which we might say are members of a set called *x*. To refer to the third value in the set, we would simply write x_3. In a similar way, the fifth element in the set would be referenced as x_5. Thus the subscript is an integer value that tells which element in the ordered set is being referenced. In the above example, x_3 is equal to -4 and x_5 has the value 0.

In fact, we can even be more general by using a variable as a subscript. Thus the *i*th element in the ordered set would be referenced as x_i. Therefore, if *i* is equal to 2, then x_i would be a reference to x_2, or the second element in the ordered set of values called *x*. Note that simply referring to *x* is a reference to the entire set of values. On the other hand, a reference to x_i or x_3 is a reference to only one element of the set of values.

In our flowchart language, we are going to use a slightly different way of writing our subscripts than we used in algebra. Our subscripts must be written in flowchart language as positive integer arithmetic expressions* enclosed within parentheses following a variable name. Thus the x_2 and x_i of algebra will be written in flowchart language as x(2) and x(i), respectively. In any algorithm in which subscripted variables are used, we will require that the declarative statements for the subscripted variables give the number of elements in the set of values associated with that variable. For example, the declaration

subscripted variables (margin)

flowchart-language subscripts (margin)

declaring subscripted variables (margin)

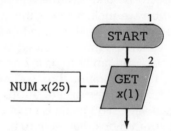

---

* A positive integer arithmetic expression can be: (1) an unsigned positive integer constant, or (2) an integer variable or any arithmetic expression that evaluates to a positive integer value.

states that x specifies a set that consists of twenty-five numeric values. Note that the subscripts are always assumed to be the set of consecutive unsigned positive integers that begin at 1 and progress through the limit given in the declaration. Furthermore, the limit given in the declaration must be a constant; it may not be a variable. As a second example of the declaration of a subscripted variable, we have

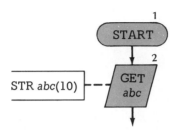

This declares abc to be an array consisting of ten elements, the values of which are string constants. Note in this example that the GET statement in box 2 will cause ten elements to be obtained from the input data stream since no subscript is placed on the variable name abc. That is, when a subscripted variable name appears without a subscript, that is a reference to the entire set of values. Generally speaking, a reference will be made to the entire set of elements in an array only in an input or output box or when communicating with a subalgorithm (a topic to be taken up in Chapter 9).

subscripted variables without subscripts

Let us now consider an example that uses subscripted variables. Suppose that we have the problem of computing class exam score averages for each student and for the class in total. Assume that each student has five test scores entering into his or her average and that each score is to be weighted equally. Furthermore, assume that the number of students in the class for which averages are to be computed is known.

exam–score problem definition and analysis

For each student in the class we will input to our algorithm the student's name and five test scores. The output from the algorithm for each student will be the student's name and test average. We will assume that all test scores are integers on the interval 0 to 100, inclusive. Following the output of the last student's name and test average, the class average is to be printed.

The descriptive flowchart for this problem appears in Fig. 5.2. The step in box D2 provides for the input of the number of students in the class. This step is needed because the number of students in the class will be used to control how many student records are input and processed. Boxes D3 and D4 are included to determine when the grades have been averaged for all classes to be processed. The first step for each student

descriptive flowchart

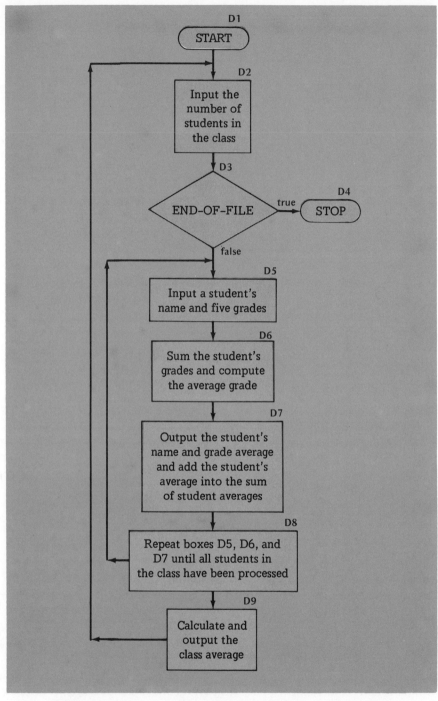

Figure 5.2. Descriptive Flowchart for Student-Test-Score Averaging Problem

will be to input a name and the student's five test scores. In box D6 the five scores are added together and the student's average test score is computed. Next, the student's name and average exam score are output, and the test score average is added into the sum of class test score averages. The step in box D8 then states that the steps in boxes D5 through D7 should be repeated for every student in this class. In our algorithm flowchart the number of times these three steps are to be repeated will be controlled by the number of students in the class, which was input in box D2. After all of the students' test scores have been averaged, the class average is computed and output in box D9. Then control is given to box D2 to begin the processing of test scores for another class of students.

The algorithm flowchart for this problem is given in Fig. 5.3. Boxes 2 through 4 of this flowchart correspond to boxes D2 through D4 of the descriptive flowchart. Notice that the variable N (which holds the number of students in a class) has been declared to have only integer values. The reason is that there will never be a fractional number of students in a class. That is, a count of the number of students in a class must always be an integer value. Flowchart box 5 contains two initialization steps. In the first statement in that box, the variable *Clsum* is initialized to a value of zero. This variable will be used to sum the test score averages of the students in the class. Since averages can contain fractional values, observe that *Clsum* has been declared to be a numeric variable. The second assignment statement in box 5 initializes the loop variable *k* with a value of 1. This variable will be used as a counter to count the number of students in the class that have been processed. Since a count of the number of students already processed must be an integer value, the variable *k* is declared to be integer-valued.

In flowchart box 6 (which corresponds with descriptive flowchart box D5) the name of a student is input to the variable *name* and the student's five test scores are input to the elements of the array variable *grade*. Notice that *name* is a string variable because it holds student names, which must be represented as string constants. Meanwhile, *grade* has been declared to be a numeric integer variable since the student test scores are all integer values. Box 7 contains two statements that are used to give initial values to the variables *sum* and *i*. The variable *sum* is used to add up the test scores for one student. Since these test scores are all numeric integer values, the variable *sum* has also been declared to be a numeric integer variable. The loop variable *i* is a counter used to count the number of grades in computing a student's average. Thus *i* is also declared to be an integer variable. The steps in flowchart boxes 8 through 10 are used to form the sum of the grades for one student. Notice the use in box 8 of the loop variable *i* as a subscript to index the individual test scores in the array *grade*. Also observe that the loop variable *i* has 1 added to it only after it has been determined in box 9 that another

algorithm flowchart

141

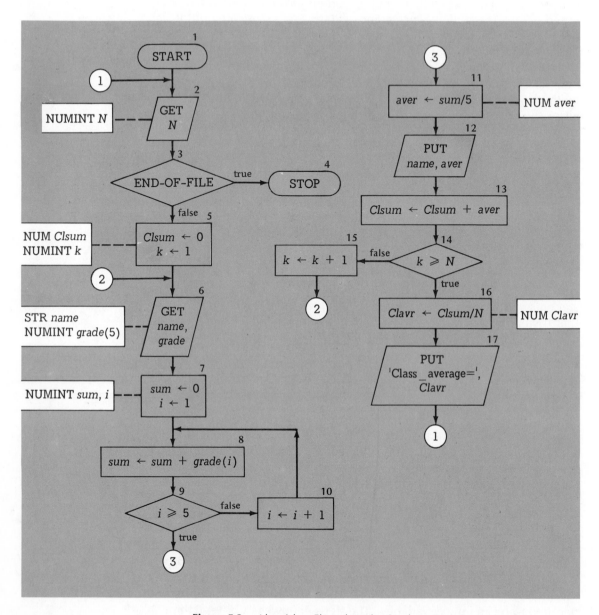

Figure 5.3. Algorithm Flowchart for Student-Test-Score Averaging Problem

execution of box 8 is needed. That is, in box 9 we are testing to learn whether or not all five test scores have been summed. When they have not been, the loop variable i is incremented by 1 in box 10 and the step in box 8 is executed again. However, when the sum of the five values has been formed, box 11 will be executed to calculate the student's test score average. Notice that even though 5 is an integer constant and *sum* an integer variable, the variable *aver* has been declared to be numeric. The reason is that the division of the numeric integer variable *sum* by the 5 can result in a value that contains a fractional part. Observe that algorithm flowchart boxes 7 through 11 correspond with descriptive flowchart box D6.

Once the student's average test score has been computed, the step in box 12 is used to output the student's name and average test score. Then in box 13 the student's average test score is added into the sum of the class test score averages. Next a test is made in box 14 to determine whether or not all of the students in this class have been processed. This is done by checking the condition that the value of the loop variable k is greater than or equal to the value of N (the number of students in the class). As long as this condition is false, more students in this class need to be processed. However, once the condition is true, processing of all of the students' test scores in this class must have been completed. In the latter case, the average of all students' test score averages is computed in box 16. Finally, the PUT statement in box 17 causes the class test score average to be output, preceded by a string constant that labels the output.

The trace table for this algorithm is given in Fig. 5.4. The input data stream used in developing this trace table is: **trace table**

4, 'B. Jones ', 80, 70, 60, 50, 60, 'L. Salt ', 90, 80, 90, 85, 82, 'R. Tall ', 90, 85, 95, 98, 99, 'B. Veck ', 75, 80, 85, 80, 79

Notice that the five values of the array *grade* are listed horizontally in the trace table, with the values separated by commas.

All of the arrays of information considered thus far have been one-dimensional. That is, the elements can be considered as a list of values that has a top element and a bottom element and zero or more elements in between. Arrays with two or more dimensions also occur and we need a way of representing them and referencing their elements. A two-dimensional array is easy to conceive of as a set of elements in which each element belongs to both a row and a column. For example, in the two-dimensional array **two-dimensional arrays**

$$
\begin{array}{rrrr}
5 & 0 & 2 & 8 \\
6 & 5 & -1 & 7 \\
-3 & 4 & 2 & 0
\end{array}
$$

Figure 5.4.   Trace Table for the Algorithm of Fig. 5.3

N	Clsum	k	Name	Grade	sum	i	$i \geq 5$	Aver	$k \geq N$	Clavr
4	0	1	'B. Jones '	80,70,60,50,60	0	1				
					80	2	false			
					150	3	false			
					210	4	false			
					260	5	false			
	64.0				320		true	64.0	false	
		2	' L. Salt '	90,80,90,85,82	0	1				
					90	2	false			
					170	3	false			
					260	4	false			
					345	5	false			
	149.4				427		true	85.4	false	
		3	' R. Tall '	90,85,95,98,99	0	1				
					90	2	false			
					175	3	false			
					270	4	false			
					368	5	false			
	242.8				467		true	93.4	false	
		4	' B. Veck '	75,80,85,80,79	0	1				
					75	2	false			
					155	3	false			
					240	4	false			
					320	5	false			
	322.6				399		true	79.8	true	
										80.65

the element with a value 4 belongs to both the third row and the second column. We would refer to that element in our flowchart language as $R(3,2)$ if the entire array was named as R. Notice that the dimensions of a two-dimensional array are the number of rows and the number of columns contained in that array. In our flowchart language we will separate the row subscript from the column subscript by a comma. In addition, by convention we will always give the row number before the column number. Thus the element in the ith row and jth column of a two-dimensional array X would be referenced as $X(i, j)$.

declaring
two-dimensional
arrays

Declaration of a two-dimensional array is similar to the declaration of a one-dimensional array. The only difference is that for a two-dimensional array both a row limit and a column limit must be given. The above two-dimensional array R could have been declared, for example, as

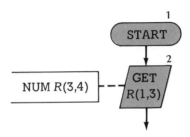

indicating that it consists of three rows and four columns of numeric values. The GET statement in this example would cause one value to be input from the input data stream to the array element in row 1 and column 3. Unlike a one-dimensional array, a two-dimensional array may not be referenced in an input or output box without explicitly giving a subscript. That is, the array element being referenced must always be specified when using a two-dimensional array in an input or output box. However, references to two-dimensional arrays need not contain subscripts when communicating with subalgorithms.

PROBLEMS

1. How many loops are there in the algorithm of Fig. 4.19? What are the loop structure types of these loops? Identify the boxes that make up each of the loops and their components. Also name the loop variable or variables for each loop.

2. How many loops are there in the algorithm of Fig. 4.22? What are the loop structure types of these loops? Identify the boxes that make up each of the loops and their components. Also name the loop variable or variables for each loop.

3. What kind of loop structure is used in each of the two loops of the algorithm of Fig. 5.3? What changes would need to be made to change both loops to each of the other three types of loop structure?

4. How many elements will each of the arrays contain given the following contents of flowchart annotation boxes?

a. NUM X(4)
b. NUM Z(50), R(23)
c. NUMINT V(25)
d. STR K(5), Z(4)
e. STR A(25,10)
f. NUMINT X(7,3), R(7)
g. NUM V(5,4,7)
h. NUM X(4,3,2,5), Y(62,4)

5. Modify the algorithm of Fig. 5.3 so that the number of exam scores for the students of each class is a variable rather than fixed at 5.

6. Modify the algorithm of Fig. 4.16 so that all of the data values of one set are stored in an array before searching for the largest value. Assume that none of the data sets to be processed will have more than 1,000 values.

7. Modify the algorithm of Fig. 4.19 so that all of the values of the depreciation table have been computed and stored in one array before any of the table values are output. Assume that the maximum life of an asset is 100 accounting periods.

8. Modify the algorithm of Fig. 4.22 so that sixty characters of a manuscript are input at a time into an array for processing. These sixty characters are then processed and the next sequence of sixty characters is input and processed. This process of inputting and processing sixty-character sequences should continue until the manuscript has been completely processed.

145

5.3   THREE EXACT ITERATIVE ALGORITHMS

iterative algorithms

In this section we will construct three iterative algorithms which provide what are essentially exact results. By *iterative algorithm,* we mean an algorithm that solves a problem by repeating certain steps one or more times. The notion of algorithms that produce exact results will be more meaningful after the study in Section 5.4 of algorithms that produce approximate results. In fact, all of the algorithms that we have developed up to now in this book have produced what are basically exact results. The only thing that may have been inexact about the results produced by these algorithms would be caused by the finite nature of numbers as represented in a digital computer. This leads to the approximation of numbers and computational errors as discussed in Section 3.4.

5.3.1   The Sequencing Problem

files, records, and fields

The concept of a file is very important in computer science. A *file* may be defined as a collection of records that relate to similar objects. Each *record* in a file is subdivided into something called fields. A *field* contains one data item. As an example, a payroll file would consist of all the data regarding payroll about the employees of a company. That is, there would be a record for each employee which gives all of the payroll data for that employee. Thus the collection of all of these employee records would provide a payroll file that contained all payroll data for the company. Now, each employee record would contain a number of data items that reside in fields within the record. For example, a payroll record might contain a field with the employee's name, another field with the employee's social security number, still another field with the employee's total earnings for the year-to-date, and so forth. Thus, all of the data items for a particular employee would be taken together as one employee record. A file therefore might be thought of as one or more drawers in a metal filing cabinet. The manila folders in these drawers would be the records, and in each manila folder are documents that are the data items for that record.

One final point on records needs to be made. The point is that generally all of the records in a file are laid out in a uniform way.* That is, if the name is in the leftmost field in one record, it will be in the leftmost field of all the records in that file. Similarly, should the social security number be the third leftmost field in one record, then social security numbers will appear in the third leftmost field in all of the other records of this file.

---

* This is not universally true. However, uniformity of record layout holds in the vast majority of data processing applications.

146

One of the most frequently performed tasks for which a computer is used involves the resequencing of the records of a file. The process of putting the records of a file into some particular order is called *sorting*.* The order into which the records of a file are sequenced is usually dependent on an item within each record called the sort item or *sort field*. Sorting almost always involves rearranging the records in the file so that the values in the sort field are in either a nonincreasing or a nondecreasing order.

For example, a payroll file generally includes a field for the employee's name and a field for the employee's social security number. Now, we could sort the payroll file into nondecreasing order using the employee's social security number as our sort field. In this case we would arrange the records of the file so that the social security number of any record is never greater than the social security number of the immediately following record. That is, the records of the payroll file would be arranged such that the first record had the smallest social security number and each succeeding record had a social security number greater than the one in the preceding record. Alternatively, the name field of each payroll record could be used as a sort field. Assuming that a nondecreasing order is desired, this would result in rearranging the records in the payroll file so that the name fields would be in nondecreasing alphabetical order. Thus the first record in the file would have the name of the employee nearest the beginning of the alphabet and the last record would have the name of the employee nearest the end of the alphabet.

In this section we will develop an algorithm for sorting a file that is stored as a one-dimensional array in main memory. That is, the file to be sorted consists of records that consist of only one item or field. Furthermore, we will assume that this field can contain a numeric value that is not greater than 10^{15} in value. The fact that the records of the file sorted in our algorithm each contain only one value does little to change the logic of our algorithm. In fact, the only change required for files whose records contain multiple fields is that the sort fields of the respective records would be compared rather than the entire record. Storage or interchange of records would continue to involve the movement of the entire record in either case.

Our approach to sequencing a list of values will use the same method as would be used were we doing the task with pencil and paper. That is, we first scan the list of values to be sorted from top to bottom to find the smallest value. After scanning the entire list, we would copy the smallest value in the list on another sheet of paper and cross out that

sorting file records

problem definition and analysis

---

* Our discussion here implies that sorting a file involves physically rearranging the records of a file. However, it is not necessary to have the records of a file physically ordered for them to be sorted. A further discussion of this notion involves the concept of linked lists, a topic that is beyond the scope of this text.

value on the original list. We would then scan the original list from top to bottom again to locate the smallest value that has not been crossed out. This value is then copied as the second entry in the sorted list and the value is crossed out on the original list. This process is repeated until all of the items on the original list have been crossed out. The new list will then contain the values of the original list sorted into nondescending order. A step-by-step example of this process for a list containing six values is given in Fig. 5.5. Note that on any pass through the original list there may be two or more entries that have the same value, and this value may be the smallest value. In this case, we will take the first of these equal values as the smallest one. The second equal value would then be selected as the smallest remaining value on the next scan of the original list.

Figure 5.5.   Step-by-Step Analysis of Two-List Sorting Method

						Pass					
1		2		3		4		5		6	
Original List	Sorted List	Original List	Sorted List	Original List	Sorted List	Original List	Sorted List	Original List	Sorted List	Original List	Sorted List
8	4	8	4	8	4	8	4	8	4	~~8~~	4
7		7	5	7	5	~~7~~	5	~~7~~	5	~~7~~	5
5		~~5~~		~~5~~	6	~~5~~	6	~~5~~	6	~~5~~	6
7		7		7		7	7	~~7~~	6	~~7~~	7
~~4~~		~~4~~		~~4~~		~~4~~		~~4~~	7	~~4~~	7
6		6		~~6~~		~~6~~		~~6~~		~~6~~	8

descriptive flowchart

A descriptive flowchart for our sequencing problem appears in Fig. 5.6. The method begins by inputting the number of values in the data set to be sorted. Then the values of the set are input into an array and output one at a time. Then the input array is searched for the smallest value. When the entire input list has been searched and the smallest value found, this value is output. The reason for outputting the value rather than storing it in a second array is that our second list is the output of our algorithm and will thus not require any further processing. If sorting the input values was an intermediate step of a larger processing task, however, we would have to store the values in the successive positions of a second one-dimensional array. The step in box D8 requires an explanation. This step states that a value larger than the largest possible value should be assigned to the array position that holds the value just output. The purpose of this step is equivalent to crossing out the smallest value in the original list. The reason is that a value larger than the largest possible value cannot be selected as one of the output values because all possible input values will be smaller than it is. Finally, the step in box D9 says that the

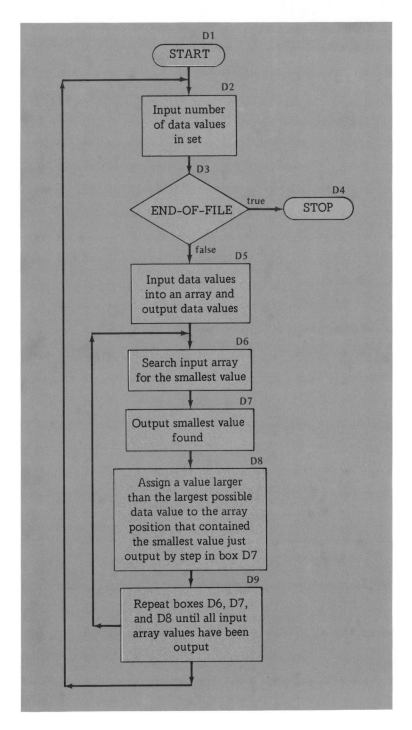

Figure 5.6. Descriptive Flowchart for the Sequencing Problem

steps in boxes D6, D7, and D8 should be repeated until all of the input array values have been output. Then control is returned to step D2, where the number of values in the next data set is input.

algorithm flowchart   The algorithm flowchart for this problem appears in Fig. 5.7. The

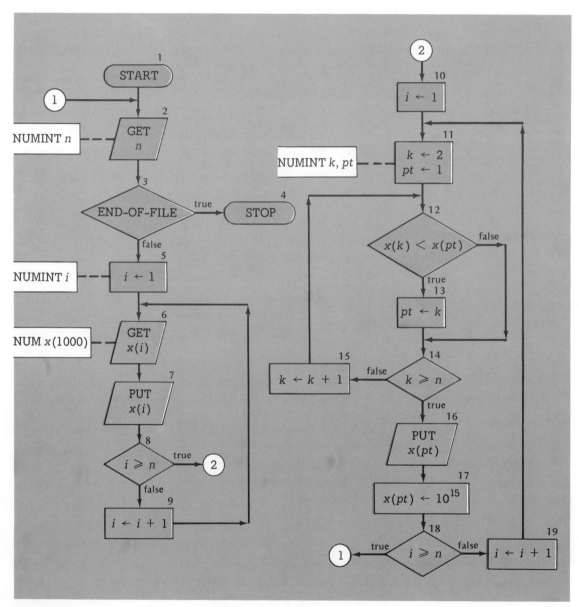

Figure 5.7. Algorithm Flowchart for the Sequencing Problem

steps in boxes 2 through 4 agree with the logic in descriptive flowchart boxes D2 through D4. Notice that the variable *n* is declared to be integer-valued since it is a count of how many numbers are in the input file. In box 5 the loop variable *i* is initialized for use in the loop of boxes 6 through 9. The steps in this loop represent the logic for descriptive flowchart box D5. That is, the steps in boxes 5 through 9 are used to input and output the list of numbers that is to be sorted. Notice that this list can contain a maximum of 1,000 values, where 1,000 was chosen arbitrarily. This fact is determined by the declarative information contained in the annotation box connected to flowchart box 6. Finally, notice that this input loop is of loop structure type c.

The steps in flowchart boxes 10 through 19 perform the functions given in boxes D6 through D9 of the descriptive flowchart. This sequence of flowchart boxes consists of two loops, where one loop is contained inside the other loop. This again illustrates the fact that nested loops in an algorithm are both permitted and useful. In the current algorithm, the outer loop consists of boxes 10 through 19, while the inner loop is made up of boxes 11 through 15. The outer loop is used to repeat the process of scanning the input array for the smallest value and outputting that value. The inner loop exists to perform the scan of the input array to find the smallest value.

The step in box 10 initializes the loop variable *i*, which is used to count the number of passes through the input array. In this algorithm, sorting the *n* input values requires *n* passes through the input array. Notice that this step is the initialization step for the outer loop. Flowchart box 11 contains two initialization steps for the inner loop. The first variable, *k*, is used to step through the input array during the scanning operation. The variable *pt* is used to point to the array element that contains the smallest value found thus far during the scan of the array. In box 12 is the step that compares the *k*th item in the input array with the element in x that was previously found to be the smallest value. When the *k*th value is less than the value that has previously been found to be the small-est on this scan of the input array, then in box 13 the value of the subscript *k* is assigned to be the new value of *pt*. Thus the variable *pt* contains a value which points to the element in the array x that contains the smallest value found thus far in the scan of the list of input values. As long as the *k*th value is not less than the *pt*th value, however, box 13 is not executed and the value of the pointer *pt* remains unchanged. That is, it still contains the value of the subscript that points to the element in the array x that has been found to contain the smallest value thus far in the scan. Box 14 contains a test for loop termination while in box 15 we have the modifi-cation step for the inner loop.

When execution of the inner loop is terminated by the condition in box 14, the value of *pt* will be the subscript of the array element that contains the smallest value in x.   In box 16 this value is output.   Then in box 17 a value larger than any possible input value is assigned to replace the *pt*th value of the array x.   This assignment is analogous to crossing out the items of the original list on a sheet of paper.   It is necessary to avoid choosing the same item again on future scans of the list.   Finally, the condition in box 18 is the test for loop termination of the outer loop, while box 19 contains the outer-loop modification step.

trace table   The trace table for this algorithm appears in Fig. 5.8.   The input data stream

$$5, 15, 7, 19, 2, 6$$

is the one used to generate this trace table.   The horizontal broken line

Figure 5.8.   Trace Table for the Algorithm of Fig. 5.7

n	i	x(i)	i ≥ n	k	pt	x(k) < x(pt)	k ≥ n	PUT x(pt)
5	1	15	false					
	2	7	false					
	3	19	false					
	4	2	false					
	5	6	true					
	1			2	1	true	false	
				3	2	false	false	
				4	4	true	false	
			false	5		false	true	2
	2			2	1	true	false	
				3	2	false	false	
				4		false	false	
			false	5	5	true	true	6
	3			2	1	true	false	
				3	2	false	false	
				4		false	false	
			false	5		false	true	7
	4			2	1	false	false	
				3		false	false	
				4		false	false	
			false	5		false	true	15
	5			2	1	false	false	
				3	3	true	false	
				4		false	false	
			true	5		false	true	19

is included to separate the input phase from the sorting phase of the algorithm. Notice in the rightmost column of the table that the array values are output by this algorithm in nondescending order.

5.3.2 The Table-Lookup Problem

A task that must be done in almost any field of study and, in fact, in everyday living involves looking something up in a table. For example, in mathematics there are tables of logarithms, tables of trigonometric functions, and so forth. In English and other natural languages, we have dictionaries which contain the definitions for the words that make up that language. In chemistry there are tables of the basic elements and their symbols. In accounting there are income tax tables. This list could go on and on.

problem definition and analysis

We can identify three basic elements when looking something up in a table. First, there is the *search argument,* which is the key to be used in searching the table. In the case of finding the logarithm of a number, the search argument would be the value of *x* for which a logarithm is being sought. When the problem is that of looking up the definition of a word in an English dictionary, the search argument would be the word for which we wish to find a definition. In the case of computing income tax, the search argument would be the taxable income of a person or company.

The table that is being searched for a value usually consists of two sets of elements:

1. A set of list arguments.
2. A set of function values.

The *list arguments* are the pieces of information that are used to access the proper *function information* in the table. In a table of logarithms, the list arguments would be the different values of *x* for which the corresponding logarithms (function values) are given in the table. The list arguments in an English dictionary would be the words in the dictionary; the function values would be the definitions associated with the various list arguments. In an income tax table, the limits on the various income classes would be the list arguments, and the corresponding tax rates and base amounts would be the function values.

Let us develop an example in which the table consists of the partial contents of an English dictionary. We might think of our table as a two-dimensional array with *n* rows and 2 columns, as shown in Fig. 5.9. Each element in our array consists of a string of symbols. The lefthand column of our table consists of the list of words in our dictionary. That is, the first column of our two-dimensional array is our set of list arguments. The

Figure 5.9. Excerpts from an English Dictionary Represented as a Table

$f(i,1)$ List Argument	$f(i,2)$ Function Value
A	first letter of the English alphabet
abound	to be in great plenty
cash	money
discourage	to dissuade
peak	the top of a mountain
strip	to deprive of covering
upset	to overturn
zoo	a zoological garden

ith element in this list will be referenced by $f(i,1)$. Thus the first subscript gives the row number and the second subscript gives the column number. The righthand column of our table consists of the list of definitions in our dictionary. Thus the second column of our two-dimensional array is our list of function values, with each definition being a function value. The ith element of the function list will be referenced by $f(i,2)$. The string constant associated with $f(i,2)$ will therefore be the definition corresponding to the word associated with $f(i,1)$. There is thus a one-to-one correspondence between the set of list arguments and set of function values.

descriptive flowchart   A descriptive flowchart for this problem is given in Fig. 5.10. Boxes D2 and D3 contain steps to input the values of the table that are to be searched. Notice that these values are input to a two-dimensional array. The step in box D4 causes a search argument value to be input. In box D7 is a step in which the search argument is compared with each successive list argument value in the table. In the case in which the search argument value is found in the column of list argument values, the corresponding function value is to be output. However, it is entirely possible that we have attempted to look for a search argument value that is not in the table. In this situation, an error message of some kind should be output. After either case, the next search argument value should be input by the step in box D4.

algorithm flowchart   The algorithm flowchart for this problem appears in Fig. 5.11. In designing this flowchart, we have assumed that the table to be searched contains no more than 500 rows of string constants. Descriptive flowchart box D2 is implemented in flowchart box 2 as a GET operation. If the dictionary in Fig. 5.9 is our input table, then the value of n would be 8. This is because there are eight rows in the table. Next the loop in boxes 3 through 6 inclusive is used to implement descriptive flowchart box D3.

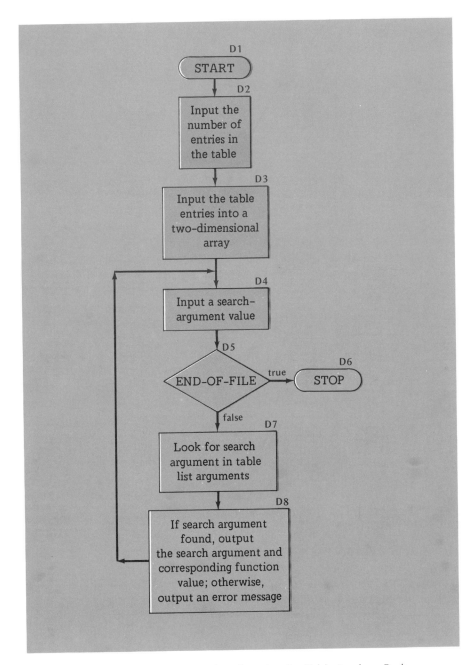

Figure 5.10. Descriptive Flowchart for the Table-Lookup Problem

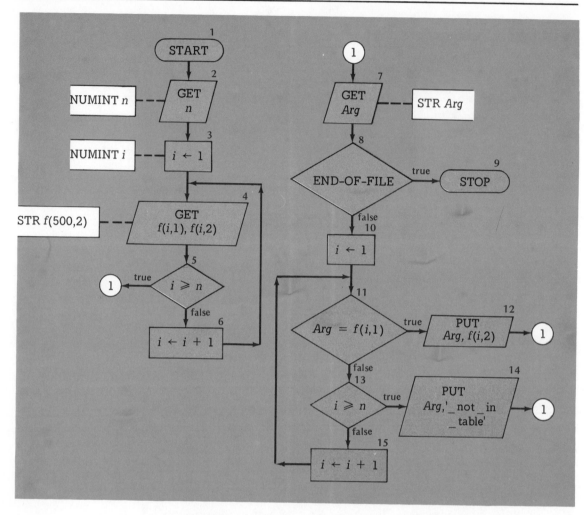

Figure 5.11.   Algorithm Flowchart for the Table-Lookup Problem

That is, the steps in this loop are used to input the table values. The initialization step is in box 3, the loop body is in box 4, the test for loop termination is in box 5, and the modification step is in box 6. Thus this table input loop is of structure type c, as classified in Fig. 5.1.

Our method of attack in searching this table for the list argument value that matches our search argument value will be to follow a *serial search* procedure. In this method the search argument value is compared to the successive list argument values beginning with $f(1,1)$. If the value of $f(1,1)$ is not equal to the search argument value, the counter i is advanced by 1. Then the value of $f(2,1)$ is compared to the search argument value.

This process continues until a value of $f(i,1)$ is found which is equal to the search argument value or until the n list argument values are exhausted. If a match between a list argument value and the value of the search argument is found, the values of the search argument and the corresponding function argument are printed in box 12. That is, when the value of an $f(i,1)$ is found which is equal to the search argument value, the values of *Arg* and $f(i,2)$ are output.

If the search argument value does not exist in the set of list arguments, however, the value of *Arg* and an error message are output in box 14. The loop for performing the serial search of the table appears in boxes 10, 11, 13, and 15. Box 10 represents the initialization step, boxes 11 and 13 are tests for exit from the loop, and box 15 contains the modification step. Thus, in this case we have a loop that does not contain a body as such. The basic loop structure, however, is essentially that of type *c*, as classified in Fig. 5.1.

A trace table appears in Fig. 5.12 for the algorithm of Fig. 5.11 using as table input the contents of Fig. 5.9, and as search argument values the words *'cash'* and *'brush'*.

trace table

5.3.3   The Prime-Number Problem

In elementary mathematics a student is often asked whether or not a given number is a prime number. Recall that for any positive integer $n > 1$, we say that n is a prime number if and only if n cannot be factored into the product of any two positive integers that are greater than 1. Conversely, if n can be factored into the product of two positive integers that are greater than 1, then by definition n is not a prime number. For example, 3 and 5 are both prime numbers since neither can be factored into the product of two positive integers. The numbers 4 and 6 are not prime, however, since 4 can be factored into the product $2 \cdot 2$ and 6 can be factored into the product $2 \cdot 3$.

problem definition and analysis

From the above definition of a prime number, it follows that a prime number is a positive integer for which the only positive integers that will divide it evenly are unity and the prime number itself. Or, reversing this, if we can find a positive integer r (where $1 < r < n$) that will divide n evenly, then n is not a prime number. Now, saying that r divides n evenly is just another way of saying that when we divide n by r the remainder will be zero. For example, 3 divides 6 evenly because the remainder is zero. On the other hand, 3 does not divide 5 evenly because the quotient is 1 and there is a remainder of 2.

Now, the condition that r be a positive integer that divides n evenly can be restated mathematically by saying that the equation

157

Figure 5.12. Trace Table for the Algorithm of Fig. 5.11

n	i	f(i,1)	f(i,2)	i ≥ n	Arg	Arg = f(i,1)	PUT Arg, f(i,2)
8	1	'A'	'first letter of the English alphabet '	false			
	2	'abound '	'to be in great plenty '	false			
	3	'cash '	'money '	false			
	4	'discourage '	'to dissuade '	false			
	5	'peak '	'the top of a mountain '	false			
	6	'strip '	'to deprive of covering '	false			
	7	'upset '	'to overturn '	false			
	8	'zoo '	'a zoological garden '	true			
	1			false	'cash '	false	
	2			false		false	
	3					true	cash money
	1			false	'brush '	false	
	2			false		false	
	3			false		false	
	4			false		false	
	5			false		false	
	6			false		false	
	7			false		false	
	8			true		false	brush not in table

$$n = r \cdot trun[n / r] \tag{5.1}$$

must hold. In Eq. (5.1) *trun* is simply the functional operator that means *drop the fractional portion of the number.* That is, only the integer portion of the division is to be used in performing the multiplication operation. For example, in the case in which $n = 7$ and $r = 5$, $trun[7/5]$ yields a truncated quotient of 1 (notice that the remainder of the division is dropped). Therefore, Eq. (5.1) would produce $7 = 5 \cdot 1$ or $7 = 5$, which is obviously not true. On the other hand, if $n = 6$ and $r = 3$, then $trun[6/3]$ produces a truncated quotient of 2 (notice in this case that the remainder we dropped is zero). Thus Eq. (5.1) yields $6 = 3 \cdot 2$ or $6 = 6$, and we conclude that Eq. (5.1) holds.

That Eq. (5.1) is a restatement of the condition that *r* be a positive integer that divides *n* evenly can be seen by dividing both sides of Eq. (5.1) by *r*.   This yields

$$n \ / \ r = trun[n \ / \ r] \qquad \qquad \textbf{(5.2)}$$

But *n/r* can equal *trun[n/r]* only when *n/r* is an integer since *trun[n/r]* is the integer formed by dropping the fractional portion of the quotient of *n/r*.   Thus *n/r* can equal *trun[n/r]* only if the fraction dropped in the truncate operation was zero.   But the fraction can only be zero if *r* is a positive integer that divides *n* evenly.   Therefore, Eq. (5.1) is equivalent to saying that *r* divides *n* evenly.   For example, when *n* = 7 and *r* = 5, Eq. (5.2) would be

$$7 \ / \ 5 \ = \ trun[7 \ / \ 5]$$
$$1.4 \ = \ trun[1.4]$$
$$1.4 \ = \ 1$$

But this equation obviously does not hold.   On the other hand, for *n* = 6 and *r* = 3, Eq. (5.2) results in

$$6 \ / \ 3 \ = \ trun[6 \ / \ 3]$$
$$2 \ = \ trun[2]$$
$$2 \ = \ 2$$

which is obviously true.

   The above analysis gives us a rather simple algorithm for deciding whether or not a given positive integer *n* is a prime number.   All that we have to do is test every positive integer *r* (for $1 < r < n$) using Eq. (5.1). If we can find any value of *r* which satisfies that equation, then *n* is not a prime number.   Otherwise, *n* is a prime number.   A descriptive flowchart for this problem is given in Fig. 5.13, and an algorithm flowchart using this method appears in Fig. 5.14.   Notice that the test in box 7 eliminates the trivial cases when *n* equals 2 or 3, since we know that 2 and 3 are both prime numbers.   Also observe the loop which consists of boxes 8, 9, 11, and 12.   This loop will be repeated a finite but unknown number of times in arriving at an answer.   In fact, this loop is simply trying all integer values of *r* (for $1 < r < n$) to see if any of them divide *n* evenly.   In this loop, box 8 represents the initialization step, box 11 represents the modification step, and boxes 9 and 12 are tests for loop termination.   Observe that there is no step which represents the body of the loop, although box 9 is a kind of a pseudo-body.   Essentially we have a loop structure of type *a* as classified in Fig. 5.1.   A trace table for this algorithm using the input data stream

descriptive and algorithm flowcharts

trace table

159

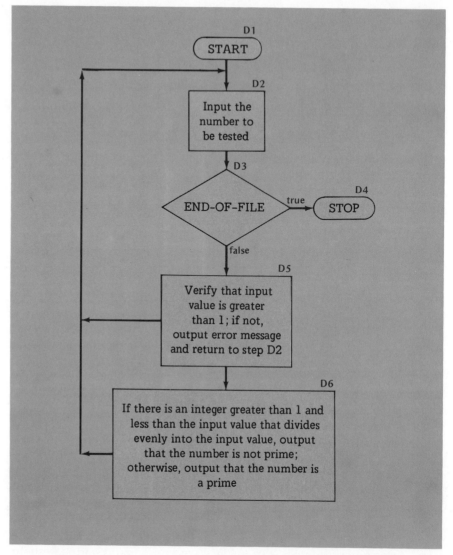

Figure 5.13. Descriptive Flowchart for the Prime-Number Problem

3, 5, 15, 13

appears in Fig. 5.15.

more problem analysis

Our analysis of this problem to date has not been as complete as it should have been to obtain an efficient algorithm. That is, an algorithm can be developed which is more efficient than the algorithm that appears

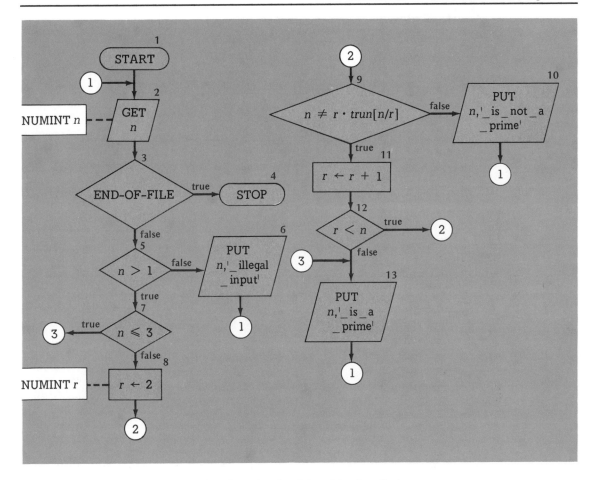

Figure 5.14. Algorithm Flowchart for the Prime-Number Problem

in Fig. 5.14. First, if *n* cannot be evenly divided by 2, then *n* cannot be evenly divided by any even integer. This is so because by definition an even integer is one that is equal to 2 or is a multiple of 2. If we use this fact in developing our algorithm, we need to test *n* by using $r = 2$ and only the higher successive odd integers $r < n$.

A second point missed in our earlier analysis is that we are always testing two divisors when we test the condition of Eq. (5.1). One divisor, *r*, we are testing explicitly. But, implicitly we are also testing the quotient of n / r as a divisor. This is so because *n* divided by *r* produces the same remainder as *n* divided by $trun[n/r]$ as long as $r \leq \sqrt{n}$. Therefore, if *r* divides *n* evenly (producing a remainder of zero), then n / r must also

Figure 5.15.   Trace Table for the Algorithm of Fig. 5.14

n	r	$trun[n/r]$	$n \neq r \cdot trun[n/r]$	$r < n$	PUT n, '_is_a _prime'	PUT n, '_is_not_ a_prime'
3					X	
5	2	2	true			
	3	1	true	true		
	4	1	true	true		
	5			false	X	
15	2	7	true			
	3	5	false	true		X
13	2	6	true			
	3	4	true	true		
	4	3	true	true		
	5	2	true	true		
	6	2	true	true		
	7	1	true	true		
	8	1	true	true		
	9	1	true	true		
	10	1	true	true		
	11	1	true	true		
	12	1	true	true		
	13			false	X	

divide n evenly. For example, 3 divides 15 evenly, producing a quotient of 5. But, the quotient 5 (which is n / r in this case) also divides 15 evenly, giving 3 as a quotient. Thus when we test r as a divisor, we are also testing n / r as a divisor. A moment's thought tells us that one of the two divisors must be less than $\sqrt{n}$ except for the case where $r = n / r$ when $r = n / r = \sqrt{n}$. Therefore, all we need to do to show that n is a prime number is to show that no integer r on the interval $1 < r \leq \sqrt{n}$ is a number that divides n evenly.

revised algorithm flowchart

trace table

Using these two additional points, we can develop the more efficient prime-number algorithm shown in Fig. 5.16. The trace table for this algorithm appears in Fig. 5.17 using the same input test data values as were used in the trace table of Fig. 5.15. At first glance, the statement that the algorithm represented in Fig. 5.16 is more efficient than the one in Fig. 5.14 seems false. The one in Fig. 5.16 has one more box and two more algorithm steps than does the algorithm of Fig. 5.14. Thus, if the criterion for efficiency is the number of steps, the algorithm of Fig. 5.14 is more efficient

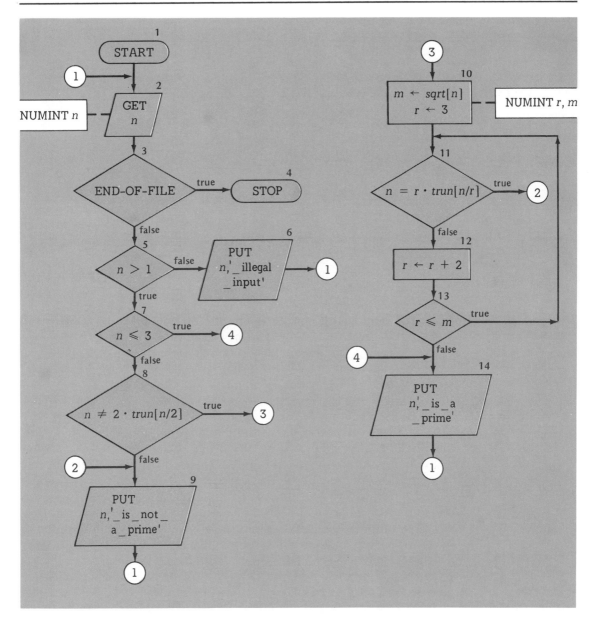

Figure 5.16. Improved Algorithm Flowchart for the Prime-Number Problem

than the algorithm of Fig. 5.16. However, comparing the trace tables for these two algorithms using the same input data stream values reveals that the algorithm of Fig. 5.16 is clearly more efficient than the algorithm of

Figure 5.17.   Trace Table for the Algorithm of Fig. 5.16

n	$n \neq 2 \cdot trun[n/2]$	r	m	$trun[n/r]$	$n = r \cdot trun[n/r]$	$r \leq m$	PUT n, '_is _a_prime'	PUT n, '_is_ not_a_prime'
3							X	
5	true	3	2	1	false			
		5				false	X	
15	true	3	3	5	true			X
13	true	3	3	4	false			
		5				false	X	

Fig. 5.14. Our measure of efficiency in this case is the number of steps that must be executed to arrive at a solution.

In fact, the difference becomes even more dramatic for larger values of n. For example, for $n = 37$, the trace table using the algorithm of Fig. 5.14 would contain a test as given in box 9 for $r = 2, 3, 4, \cdots, 36$—or thirty-five lines. The trace table for the algorithm of Fig. 5.16, however, would contain a test only for $r = 2, 3, 5$—or only three lines. For an even larger value of n, say 1,087, the difference would be 1,085 lines, as against sixteen lines in the two respective trace tables.

In the algorithm of Fig. 5.16 there is a loop consisting of boxes 10, 11, 12, and 13. Box 10 contains the initialization steps, box 12 contains the modification step, and boxes 11 and 13 represent tests for termination of the loop. Again, there is no body to the loop as such, although box 11 might be considered to be a sort of pseudo-body. Notice that in box 8 we are testing for $r = 2$, which is testing for all even integer values in one step. Also, notice that while we are using $sqrt[n]$ as a test to determine when execution of the loop can be stopped, we compute the $sqrt[n]$ only once. This computation is performed in box 10 with the result being assigned to the integer variable m prior to entering the loop proper. This value of m is then used in box 13 rather than reevaluating $sqrt[n]$ every time that box 13 is encountered. Notice that m really contains an approximation to the $sqrt[n]$ rather than the true value because it is used as a limit on the loop variable r, which is an integer variable.

principle of loop efficiency

This illustrates the general principle of *loop efficiency*, which states that only steps which are dependent on the looping process should be included in the iterative (repetitive) portion of the loop. Since the value of $sqrt[n]$ remains constant throughout the execution of the repetitive portion of the loop (boxes 11, 12, and 13), it should be computed before the first execution of those boxes occurs. On the other hand, the steps in boxes 11, 12, and 13 all depend on the value of r, which is changing each time the steps of the iterative part of the loop are executed. Thus these steps must be included within the iterative portion of the loop. In addition, observe that we are testing only odd values of r since r was initialized with a value of 3 and the increment in box 12 is now 2.

A final observation is that both Figs. 5.14 and 5.16 actually contain two loops. There is the obvious loop that we have already discussed in which we test the various values of r as divisors of n. But, there is a second loop which consists of all the algorithm steps except for the START and the STOP statements. That is, we are looping on the algorithm for finding a prime number, and within that big loop we have a smaller loop for testing different values of r as divisors of n. Also notice in both algorithms that n and r can assume only integer values, and that m can assume only an integer value in the algorithm of Fig. 5.16.

PROBLEMS

For each of the following problems, develop: (1) a descriptive flowchart, (2) an algorithm flowchart, and (3) a trace table (develop your own input data stream for each problem).

9. A mathematics teacher wants the computer to produce a multiplication table that has ten rows and ten columns. The entries in the table should be the products of the successive integers given in a row at the top of the columns and the successive integers given in a column at the left of the respective rows. Input to the algorithm should be the value of the leftmost integer in the column-heading row and the value of the topmost integer in the row-heading column. The rows and columns of integers and their products should all be stored in a single two-dimensional array that consists of eleven rows and eleven columns. Algorithm output should consist of all elements of this array except for the element in the first row of the first column.

10. A mathematician wants to use the computer to develop and output a table that contains the first n terms of the Fibonacci sequence. The first several terms in the sequence are

$$0, 1, 1, 2, 3, 5, 8, 13, 21, \ldots$$

and each subsequent term in the sequence is computed using the equation

$$F_{i+2} = F_{i+1} + F_i$$

where $i \geq 0$, $F_0 = 0$, and $F_1 = 1$.

11. To operate on strings of characters, an English professor needs an algorithm that will concatenate (join together) two strings of characters. The input to this algorithm should be: (a) two integers that provide the number of characters in each input string, and (b) two strings of characters that are each to be stored in separate one-dimensional arrays with one character per array element. The output should include both input strings as well as the concatenated string, which is to be in a third one-dimensional array.

12. A mathematics teacher wants the computer to be able to factor any positive integer into its prime factors. Recall from algebra that the prime factors of a positive integer are those prime numbers that when multiplied together give the number for which they are the prime factors. The number and its prime factors should be output by the algorithm.

13. A physicist wants the computer to perform table lookups on some numeric values that are in tabular form. However, the search arguments may not be equal to a list argument value but instead may fall between two list argument values. Should the search argument lie between the ith and $(i + 1)$th list argument values, then the function value output should be calculated using

$$f(i,2) + [f(i + 1,2) - f(i,2)] \cdot \frac{Arg - f(i,1)}{f(i + 1,1) - f(i,1)}$$

where f is a two-dimensional table of list argument and function values and Arg contains the search argument value. The assumption is made that the values in the table are sequenced so that the list argument values are in ascending order.

14. To perform some linguistics research, a professor needs an algorithm that will extract a substring from a string of characters. The input to the algorithm should be: (a) an integer value that gives the number of characters in the input string, (b) an input string of characters that is to be stored in a one-dimensional array with one character per array element, (c) an integer value that gives the length of the substring to be extracted, and (d) an integer value that specifies the symbol position in the input string (counting from the left) that marks the beginning of the substring to be extracted. Output should consist of all of the input values and the array that contains the substring.

15. A statistician wants the computer to be able to calculate the permutation of x objects taken from n objects. The definition of a permutation is

$$_nP_x = n!/(n - x)!$$

where $n! = n \cdot (n - 1) \cdot (n - 2) \cdot \cdots \cdot 3 \cdot 2 \cdot 1$. The input to the algorithm should be values for n and x, where $1000 > n \geq 0$ and $n \geq x \geq 0$.

16. The statistician of Problem 15 wants the computer to output a table of permutations for a given value of n and a set of consecutive values of x. That is, the algorithm is to input an integer value for n and a pair of integer values x_{high} and x_{low} for the upper and lower bounds for x. Then develop a table of $_nP_x$ for all values of x between x_{low} and

x_{high}. Include the value of n and the values taken on by x in the output. Also include a test to be certain that $x_{high} \leq n$ and that $x_{low} \geq 0$.

17. A mathematician wants to use the computer to develop tables of prime numbers. A method that can be used to generate such a table involves sifting a list that consists of all odd integer numbers greater than 2 and less than or equal to n arranged in ascending order. The sifting procedure involves the deletion of every kth number in the list subsequent to the value of k. That is, delete: (a) every third element after 3, (b) every fifth element after 5, (c) every seventh element after 7, and so forth. The algorithm developed should output a table containing all of the prime numbers up through n. Assume that n is always less than 100,000.

18. An English professor wants to use the computer to search for substrings in strings of characters. That is, given two input arrays that contain character strings, an algorithm is needed that determines whether or not the second string is contained in the first string. An integer pointing to the position that contains the leftmost character of the substring in the string should be output along with the two input strings. In the case in which the second string is not contained in the first string, the output pointer value should be zero.

19. A statistician wants the computer to be able to calculate the combination of x objects taken from n objects. The definition of a combination is

$$_nC_x = \frac{n!}{x!(n - x)!}$$

where $n! = n \cdot (n - 1) \cdot (n - 2) \cdot \cdots \cdot 3 \cdot 2 \cdot 1$. The input to the algorithm should be the values for n and x, where $1000 > n \geq 0$ and $n \geq x \geq 0$.

20. The statistician of Problem 19 wants the computer to output a table of combinations for a given value of n and a set of consecutive values of x. That is, the algorithm is to input an integer value for n and a pair of integer values x_{high} and x_{low} for the upper and lower bounds for x. Then develop a table of $_nC_x$ for all values of x between x_{low} and x_{high}. Include the value of n and the values taken on by x in the output. Also include a test to be certain that $x_{high} \leq n$ and that $x_{low} \geq 0$.

5.4   ALGORITHMS THAT YIELD APPROXIMATIONS

All of the algorithms that we have constructed thus far have provided what are essentially exact results. By *exact results* we mean that the technique or method used in the algorithm was designed to provide an answer that is completely correct. If there was any error in the answer, this error was not caused by the computational technique. Rather, the error was introduced because in a computer we attempt to represent real numbers by a finite number of digits. For example, in many modern computers, only the seven most significant digits of a number will fit in one memory location. Thus, inputting the real number 1234567890123 would result instead in the storage of the value 1234567000000. Another kind of error creeps in during computations as a result of having to represent real numbers using a fixed finite number of digits. This kind of error was discussed in Chapter 3 and was called computational error.

exact results

In general, algorithms designed to solve other than mathematical types of problems are designed to provide exact solutions. In many problems in mathematics, however, we choose methods of solution that are designed to provide *approximations* to the exact solutions. The reason for this choice is that in many cases the algorithms which produce exact solutions: (1) are not known, (2) are inefficient, or (3) are difficult to implement on a computer. Therefore, algorithms are designed in some cases which give only approximations to the true solutions. An example of the use of approximate methods of solution would be in finding values of the common mathematical functions, such as the square root and trigonometric functions. Because computer storage is such a scarce resource, it was decided from the very beginning of computer science not to store tables of the values for these common mathematical functions in the memory of the computer. Rather, algorithms were developed that compute approximations to these functional values.

approximate results

A basic characteristic of algorithms which generate approximations to the true solutions is that they are *iterative*. That is, they arrive at solutions by using a looping process. There is a basic distinction, however, between the looping procedures of approximate algorithms and exact algorithms. In an approximate algorithm the number of times a loop must be repeated in order to get a satisfactory solution cannot be determined analytically before a solution is computed. On the other hand, in the case of an exact algorithm, we can determine analytically the maximum number of times a loop must be repeated to yield a solution before the algorithm has been executed. In this section we will consider two such approximate algorithms, both of which are designed to produce approximations to the square root of a real number.

5.4.1   The Square-Root Problem

problem definition and analysis

Our first approach to approximating the square root of a number might be called the add-and-check method.   In this approach we begin by recognizing that the square root of all positive numbers will also be positive. Moreover, the square of an approximation to the square root of a number should be approximately equal to the number for which the square root is being sought.   Our method starts by finding the integer portion of the square root to the number.   Some thought would tell us that the integer portion would be the largest integer whose square is not larger than the number for which it is the square root.   To obtain this integer part, all that we need to do is square every integer beginning with 1 until a result exceeds the number whose square root is being approximated.   For the number 5, we would have the following sequence:

Approximation	Approximation Squared	Number
1	1	5
2	4	5
3	9	5

Thus the integer part of our approximation to the square root of 5 would be 2.

The next step would be to find the most significant fractional digit of our approximation.   This we do by successively adding 0.1 to our approximation until the square of the approximation again is greater than the number itself.   For the example involving the square root of 5, we have

Approximation	Approximation Squared	Number
2.1	4.41	5
2.2	4.84	5
2.3	5.29	5

Thus the approximation to the square root of 5 to two significant digits is 2.2.   To obtain another decimal place of accuracy, we can repeat the procedure using 0.01 as the increment.   This results in:

Approximation	Approximation Squared	Number
2.21	4.8841	5
2.22	4.9284	5
2.23	4.9729	5
2.24	5.0176	5

This produces 2.23 as our approximation to the square root of 5. Obviously this process can be repeated to produce as many digits of accuracy as are desired.

A descriptive flowchart for this approach is given in Fig. 5.18, where the flowchart produces two fractional digits of accuracy. The algorithm flowchart for this problem appears in Fig. 5.19. The steps in boxes 2 through 4 correspond with descriptive flowchart boxes D2 through D4. Similarly, descriptive flowchart box D5 is implemented in algorithm flowchart boxes 5 and 6. Flowchart box 7 is used to initialize the variable y, which is used to store the approximate value of the square root. The steps in the loop consisting of boxes 7 through 9 are used to find the integer part of the approximation. Once the square of the variable y exceeds the value of z, an adjustment is made to the value of y in flowchart box 10. The loops consisting of flowchart boxes 11 through 12 and boxes 14 through 15 accomplish the same thing for the two fractional digits of accuracy. Finally, the input value and the approximation are output in flowchart box 17. The trace table for this algorithm is given in Fig. 5.20 for the input data stream

descriptive and algorithm flowcharts

trace table

$$4, \quad 10, \quad 0.04$$

A second method which provides an approximation to the square root of a positive real number is one that involves averaging successive approximations to the square root. This method is actually a special case of Newton's method for finding the roots of an equation. In this method we are seeking an approximation to the square root of a positive real number z.

more problem analysis

An initial approximation to the square root, which we will call x_0, is needed, where x_0 should be greater than zero. Given z and x_0, we can find a better approximation, x_1, by use of the formula

$$x_1 = (x_0 + \frac{z}{x_0})/2 \qquad (5.3)$$

An even better approximation, x_2, can be obtained by evaluating

$$x_2 = (x_1 + \frac{z}{x_1})/2 \qquad (5.4)$$

We can continue this process indefinitely until an approximation is computed that is satisfactory for our needs. The general formula to compute the $(i + 1)$th approximation given z and the ith approximation is

$$x_{i+1} = (x_i + \frac{z}{x_i})/2 \qquad (5.5)$$

169

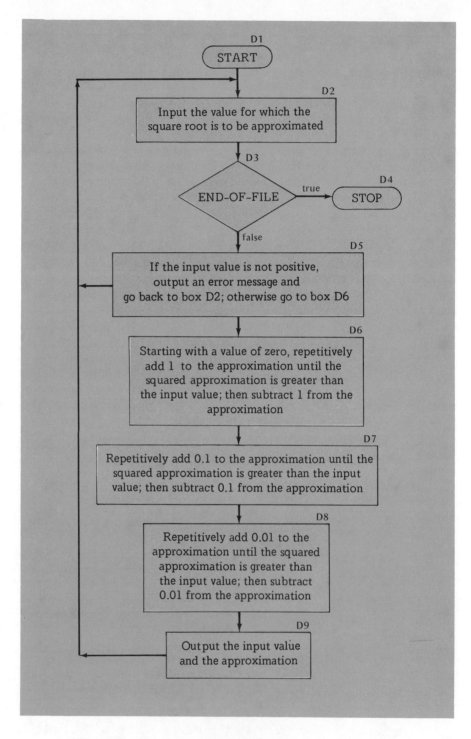

Figure 5.18. Descriptive Flowchart for the Square-Root Problem

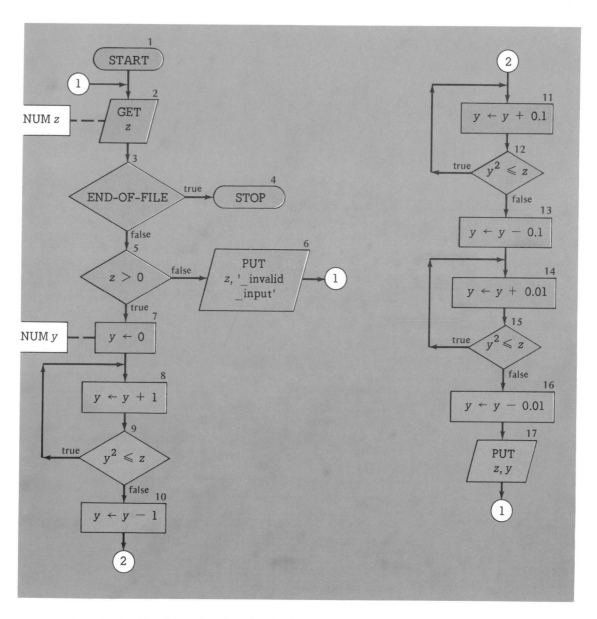

Figure 5.19. Algorithm Flowchart for the Square-Root Problem

Figure 5.20.   Trace Table for the Algorithm of Fig. 5.19

z	y	Box 9 $y^2 \leq z$	Box 12 $y^2 \leq z$	Box 15 $y^2 \leq z$
4	0			
	1	true		
	2	true		
	3	false		
	2			
	2.1		false	
	2.0			
	2.01			false
	2.00			
10	0			
	1	true		
	2	true		
	3	true		
	4	false		
	3			
	3.1		true	
	3.2		false	
	3.1			
	3.11			true
	3.12			true
	3.13			true
	3.14			true
	3.15			true
	3.16			true
	3.17			false
	3.16			
0.04	0			
	1	false		
	0			
	0.1		true	
	0.2		true	
	0.3		false	
	0.2			
	0.21			false
	0.20			

Let us use an example to test this method. Suppose that we want to find the square root of 4 using 1 as an initial approximation. Using the formula of Eq. (5.5) with $z = 4$ and $x_0 = 1$, we have the following results:

i	x_i	x_{i+1}
0	1.00	2.50000
1	2.50	2.05000
2	2.05	2.00061

We can see that just three iterations using the formula of Eq. (5.5) give us three significant digits of accuracy when comparing the approximation to the true value. Even a poor initial estimate such as using $x_0 = 100$ converges rapidly to a satisfactory estimate of the desired square root:

i	x_i	x_{i+1}
0	100.000	50.02000
1	50.020	25.05000
2	25.050	12.60500
3	12.605	6.46100
4	6.461	3.54000
5	3.540	2.33500
6	2.335	2.02400
7	2.024	2.00015

Now that we have seen that the method produces approximations to square roots, at least in the case of two examples, let us discuss what we mean by a *satisfactory approximation*. Our first inclination might be to say that when our approximation gets close enough to the true value, we will accept that value as our square root. However, this overlooks one important point—we do not know the true value. If we did know the true value, we would not need to be computing approximations to the exact result. Another alternative might be to say that an approximation is satisfactory when the value of an approximation changes very little from the value of the previous approximation. That is, if there is little difference between the values of x_6 and x_7, for example, we will take x_7 as a satisfactory approximation to the true value.

satisfactory approximations

But this forces us to decide in what sense we mean that there is little difference. One possibility might be to measure the *absolute difference* between two successive approximations:

$$|x_i - x_{i+1}| \qquad (5.6)$$

The major problem with this measure of error is that it does not take into consideration how large the error is relative to the values of the approximations. That is, for example, a difference of 2 is much larger relative to an approximation of 5 than it is to an approximation of 100. Thus, if $x_i = 3$ and $x_{i+1} = 5$, this difference of 2 represents a percentage change relative to x_{i+1} of $|(3 - 5)/5| = 40$ percent. On the other hand, if $x_i = 98$ and $x_{i+1} = 100$, this represents a percentage change relative to x_{i+1} of only $|(98 - 100)/100| = 2$ percent.

Our conclusion at this point might be that we should therefore use *percentage error* as our measure of the goodness of an approximation, where we measure percentage error as

$$|(x_i - x_{i+1})/x_{i+1}| \tag{5.7}$$

A drawback to this measure of closeness, however, is that on occasion the values of our approximations may be very close to zero. In that case, our denominator in Eq. (5.7) may become zero or close enough to zero to badly inflate our measure of relative difference. Therefore, a preferable measure of difference between successive approximations is

$$|x_i - x_{i+1}|/(|x_i| + |x_{i+1}|) \tag{5.8}$$

Since the denominator of Eq. (5.8) is the sum of the absolute values of two successive approximations, we have virtually eliminated the chance of using a zero denominator. It will be Eq. (5.8) that we will use to measure the closeness of two successive approximations in most approximate algorithms in the remainder of this text.

descriptive and algorithm flowcharts   In Fig. 5.21 we have a descriptive flowchart for this method, while the algorithm flowchart for finding an approximation to the square root of a positive real number using the formula of Eq. (5.5) is contained in Fig. 5.22. In box 2 is a step for inputting the values of: (1) z and (2) the relative difference required to terminate the iteration process. In box 3 we check to see whether any values were actually input. Box 5 contains a check to be certain that the value of z we have input is a positive number. If the value of z is not positive, our algorithm is not designed to process it. In that case, an error message is printed and we branch back to in-connector 1 to input another set of values for z and *diff*.

If the value of z is positive, however, we pass on to box 7, which contains the initialization steps for the loop of boxes 7, 8, 9, 11, and 13. Notice that the value of the initial approximation has been chosen as $x_0 = z/2$. The use of k is as an iteration counter. We will describe this in the discussion of box 11. The body of the loop is contained in box 8 and is simply an assignment statement for the formula of Eq. (5.5). Notice that since only the two most recent approximations are needed at any one time, we have used the variables x and y to stand for x_i and x_{i+1}, respectively. This choice was made to avoid the use of subscripted variables, which should be used only when absolutely necessary.

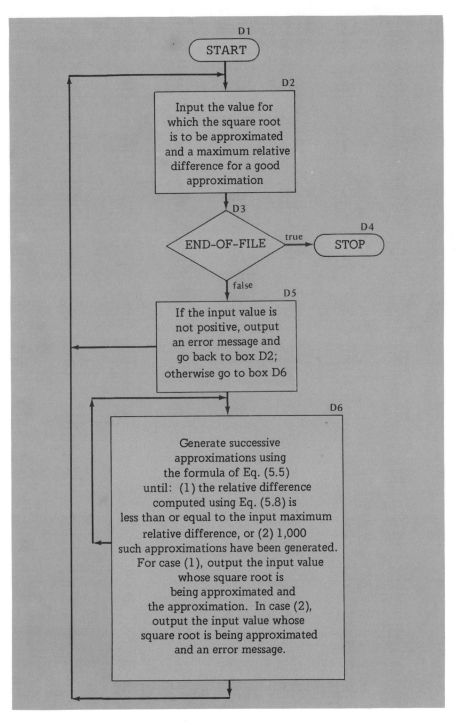

Figure 5.21. Second Descriptive Flowchart for the Square-Root Problem

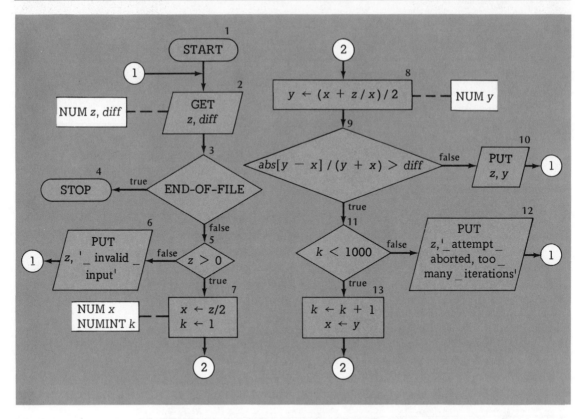

Figure 5.22. Second Algorithm Flowchart for the Square-Root Problem

The loop contains two tests for loop termination, one in box 9 and one in box 11. The test in box 9 is to determine whether the relative difference between two successive approximations is greater than the maximum relative error we are willing to tolerate. Notice that the absolute values of the two terms in the denominator are not found since we know that the values of these two variables must always be positive. The reason they must be positive is that they are both approximations to the square root of a positive number. If the relative difference is not greater than the maximum relative error we are willing to tolerate, control passes to box 10, where the values of z and the most recent approximation are output. When the relative difference is greater than the maximum difference we are willing to tolerate, control passes to box 11.

In box 11 we determine whether or not there have been 1,000 iterations of the loop. If there have been 1,000 iterations, this attempt at finding a satisfactory approximation to the square root is aborted. The reason for including this step is that it is possible to remain in our loop indefinitely because of rounding error and because an unreasonable value has been input for the maximum relative difference we will accept. That is, the step in box 11 is a safeguard against inputting a value for *diff* so small that the algorithm will never be able to satisfy the test for loop termination appearing in box 9. The step in box 12 is an error message that will be printed if we are unable to compute an acceptable approximation after 1,000 iterations of the loop.

Box 13 contains the modification steps of the loop. The first step is an assignment statement to add 1 to the iteration counter, k. The second step in box 13 is designed to assign the current approximation value to be the value of the previous approximation. Recall that x is our variable name for x_i in Eq. (5.5) and y is our variable name for x_{i+1}. This step is in preparation for looping back to the step in box 8 for the computation of the next approximation. Notice that this algorithm utilizes loop structure type c, as classified in Fig. 5.1.

Note that in this algorithm we cannot predict in advance how many times the loop of boxes 7, 8, 9, 11, and 13 will be executed in order to produce an acceptable approximation to $\sqrt{z}$. The answer to this question depends upon several things, one of which is the value input for *diff*. All that we do know is that the steps in the loop will be executed a maximum of 1,000 times. Another important point is that the value output in box 10 is only an approximation to the square root; it is not the square root. This statement will hold true in general for any situation where we are using an algorithm to generate an approximation to the true result.

A trace table for this algorithm appears in Fig. 5.23. Notice the   **trace table**
improvement in relative difference made by the final approximation in both

Figure 5.23.   Trace Table for the Algorithm of Fig. 5.22

z	*diff*	x	k	y	$\dfrac{abs[y - x]}{y + x}$
5	0.001	2.5	1	2.25	0.05263
		2.25	2	2.236	0.00310
		2.236	3	2.236	0.00001
169	0.01	84.5	1	43.25	0.32290
		43.25	2	23.579	0.29435
		23.579	3	15.373	0.21066
		15.373	4	13.183	0.07669
		13.183	5	13.001	0.00695

of these cases. In addition, note how good the approximations to the square roots are that we have generated with just three and five approximations, respectively. We say that the approximations are good since the true values (to six significant digits) are 2.23607 and 13.0000, respectively.

5.4.2   Convergence of Approximations

In both of the preceding examples of approximate algorithms we were generating a sequence of approximations to some true value. After computing any one of the approximations in these sequences we could have decided to use the most recent approximation as our solution to the problem. As an alternative, however, we could have computed additional approximations. This process of computing approximations must stop somewhere, however, for to be an algorithm a procedure must provide answers after executing a finite number of steps.

In an approximate algorithm we are never trying to compute enough approximations to obtain the true answer. But we do want our approximations to get closer to the answer as we compute more of them. That is, we want each approximation generated by our algorithm to be closer to the true answer than was the preceding approximation. When this **convergent series** holds, our series of approximations is said to be a *convergent series*. Therefore, a series of approximations is said to be convergent when the successive approximations move closer and closer to the true result. If a sequence of approximations is not convergent, it is said to be divergent. **divergent series** That is, a *divergent series* of approximations is one in which a series of successive approximations does not move us closer to the true answer.*

Besides wanting an algorithm to produce a series of approximations that converges on the true value, we want this convergence to take place rapidly. That is, we want the algorithm to produce a satisfactory approximation after generating a reasonable number of approximations. What we **rate of convergence** consider to be a reasonable number of approximations depends upon the problem that we are trying to solve. However, one absolute limit that we are faced with is the amount of computer time we can use in obtaining a satisfactory approximation. Topics such as the rate of convergence of a series of approximations are beyond the scope of this book but are covered in courses in computer science known as numerical analysis.

---

* A divergent series can occur in several ways. One way is that the successive approximations could be moving farther from the true answer. A second is that the series of approximations could be oscillating about the true answer without moving either closer to it or farther from it.

PROBLEMS

For each of the following problems, develop: (1) a descriptive flowchart, (2) an algorithm flowchart, and (3) a trace table (develop your own input data stream for each problem).

21. A certain mathematician thought that the algorithm flowchart of Fig. 5.19 was rather interesting but thought that it would be improved by making the number of fractional digits of accuracy a variable. Develop such an algorithm, where the number of significant fractional digits is an input value.

22. A mathematician decided that the algorithm of Fig. 5.19 would be more interesting if all of the inequalities used were greater than rather than less than or equal to. Make the other changes that would be necessary because of this change, assuming that the expressions in the conditions must remain on the same side of the new inequalities as they were for the old inequalities.

23. A mathematician decided that the algorithm flowchart of Fig. 5.19 could be improved by beginning with 100 instead of 1 as the initial trial value for the square root. Develop such an algorithm that begins with hundreds, then works through the tens position, and so forth.

24. A mathematician wants to generate an approximation to the mathematical constant π. This is accomplished by summing as many terms of the infinite series

$$\pi = 4 - \frac{4}{3} + \frac{4}{5} - \frac{4}{7} + \frac{4}{9} - \frac{4}{11} + \cdots$$

as might be necessary to achieve the desired degree of accuracy. Use the formula

$$error = \frac{|approx - 3.14159|}{3.14159}$$

to measure error. Design your algorithm so that as many terms are included in computing the approximation as are needed to make *error* less than some critical difference that is an input value. Also included as an input value should be a number that gives the maximum number of terms of the series to be included in computing the approximation. Output should consist of every 100th value of the approximation, as well as the final value.

25. The mathematician in Problem 24 discovered an infinite product that can be used to generate an approximation to π. This product is

$$\pi = 4 \cdot \frac{2}{3} \cdot \frac{4}{3} \cdot \frac{4}{5} \cdot \frac{6}{5} \cdot \frac{6}{7} \cdot \frac{8}{7} \cdot \frac{8}{9} \cdot \ldots$$

Use this infinite product to develop an algorithm similar to the one in Problem 24.

26. The mathematician in Problem 24 discovered another infinite series that can be used to generate an approximation to π. This series is

$$\pi = \sqrt{6 + \frac{6}{2^2} + \frac{6}{3^2} + \frac{6}{4^2} + \frac{6}{5^2} + \cdots}$$

Use this series to develop an algorithm similar to the one in Problem 24.

27. A mathematician wants to use the technique of Fig. 5.19 to develop an algorithm that finds the cube root of a number. Develop an algorithm flowchart similar to the one in that figure to compute cube roots.

28. An engineer wants to use a computer to calculate the cube root of a number. An iterative formula that can be used to calculate an approximation to the cube root is

$$x_{i+1} = (2 \cdot x_i + z/x_i^2)/3$$

Develop your algorithm using the formula of Eq. (5.8) to compute the error term. Output should consist of the input values and the final value of the approximation.

29. A statistician needs to compute the mathematical constant e, which is equal to 2.71828 accurate to six significant digits. The infinite series that can be used to compute an approximation to e is

$$e = 1 + \frac{1}{1!} + \frac{1}{2!} + \frac{1}{3!} + \frac{1}{4!} + \cdots$$

Use this series to develop an algorithm similar to the one in Problem 24.

5.5   ALGORITHM EFFICIENCY

Up to this point we have not been overly concerned about the efficiency of our algorithms. However, in the case of the prime-number problem of Section 5.3.3, we did analyze the first algorithm we developed. This analysis led to the development of a second algorithm, which was more efficient than the first one for solving the prime-number problem. Similarly, in Section 5.4 we developed two algorithms for finding an approximation to the square root of a real number. The fact that there were two algorithms which provided the same answers to a class of problems in the case of the prime number problem can be generalized to include all nontrivial problem classes. In fact, there are usually a number of algorithms which are legitimate candidates for the solution of almost any class of problems.

algorithm efficiency criteria

This fact, however, creates a serious problem for us in that we must choose the method of solution to use in the algorithms we develop. This raises the question of selecting the criteria that we should use to determine the best algorithm for solving a particular class of problems. We can identify five broad criteria:

1. Minimize the execution time of the algorithm on our computer.
2. Minimize the amount of memory that the algorithm requires.
3. Maximize the present and future flexibility of the algorithm.
4. Minimize algorithm development time.
5. Maximize the ease with which an algorithm is understood.

minimize algorithm execution time

Designing an algorithm that minimizes *execution time* may often be the most important criterion involved in judging the efficiency of an algorithm. But achieving this goal may require a great deal of algorithm development time. However, if an algorithm is executed often or if a single execution of the algorithm requires a great deal of computer time, the payoff can be substantial. Among the list of things to watch for in minimizing execution time are:

1. The frequency with which algorithm steps are executed.
2. Executing common processing steps just once.
3. Including only necessary steps within a loop.
4. Minimizing input/output operations (because input/output operations are very time-consuming).

As we noted in the prime-number problem, knowledge of the subject matter is very important in seeking efficient algorithms. The use of trace tables and other such tools can also be useful in attempting to minimize execution time by spotting changes that might be made.

The efficiency of an algorithm might also be judged by the amount of *main memory* that is required by the algorithm. For example, we often can choose between algorithms which require that: (1) all of the data be input before processing begins, and (2) only small amounts of data be in main memory at any stage in processing. The former type of algorithm is certainly less efficient in terms of main memory requirements. However, it may execute much faster than the algorithm which uses a minimal amount of main memory. Of course, the ideal is to find an algorithm that minimizes both main memory needed and execution time. Such an algorithm does not exist for most problems, however, as the two objectives often conflict with each other.

minimize main memory requirements

Maximizing the present and future *flexibility* of an algorithm is not an easy task. Accomplishing it, however, may make an algorithm efficient. The purpose in seeking present flexibility may be to design an algorithm that can provide solutions to a very broad class of problems. In most cases, the narrower the class of problems our algorithm can handle, the easier the algorithm is to develop. Future flexibility relates more to the ease with which an algorithm can cope with changes in the class of problems. This involves questions about how easily the algorithm can be changed to satisfy changing needs. Because problems are often not static, this is a more important factor in algorithm efficiency than is often realized.

maximize algorithm flexibility

An effort to minimize *algorithm development time* can sometimes cause us to develop an algorithm that is not very efficient from the standpoint of the other criteria given above. Often, however, an answer to a problem is needed by a certain time. In this case, developing an algorithm that gives correct answers may be the most efficient approach to algorithm design. In another instance, developing an algorithm that executes rapidly may not be very important if the algorithm only needs to be executed occasionally. In such a case, the cost and time spent in developing an efficient algorithm may far exceed the savings realized in executing the algorithm.

minimize algorithm development time

Another goal may be to maximize the ease with which an algorithm is understood. This criterion may provide the most efficient algorithm from a standpoint of communicating ideas to others. This ease of understanding can be very important when algorithms need revision later by a person different from the original algorithm designer. Since the problems requiring solution often change, algorithms often need revision. Therefore, in practice this criterion can be very important.

maximize ease of understanding

From the above discussion, we can see that no single definition identifies the properties that comprise an efficient algorithm. Each of the above criteria tends to conflict with one or more of the others. Therefore, each case will have to be analyzed on its own merits and its own needs. Judging algorithm efficiency is certainly very much an art. It requires a great deal of experience and the analysis of individual situations.

PROBLEMS

30. Compare the two prime-number algorithms of Figs. 5.14 and 5.16 for efficiency with respect to the five criteria listed in Section 5.5.

31. Compare the two square-root algorithms of Figs. 5.19 and 5.22 for efficiency with respect to the five criteria listed in Section 5.5.

32. A mathematician is considering one of two methods for evaluating an nth-degree polynomial. One method uses the form

$$p(x) = a_0 + a_1 \cdot x^1 + a_2 \cdot x^2 + \cdots + a_n \cdot x^n$$

where x is a real variable, n is a nonnegative integer, and the sequence $a_0, a_1, a_2, \cdots, a_n$ represents a list of real coefficients. Another method uses the form

$$p(x) = a_0 + a_1 \cdot t_1 + a_2 \cdot t_2 + \cdots + a_n \cdot t_n$$

where $t_1 = x$ and $t_k = x \cdot t_{k-1}$. Write an algorithm for each of these methods. Then develop a trace table for an input data stream of your choosing. Finally, use the five criteria of Section 5.5 to compare the efficiency of the two algorithms. In this comparison, attempt to develop some analytical formulas for the number of assignment, addition, multiplication, comparison, and total operations that would be executed in evaluating an nth-degree polynomial using each of these algorithms.

SUMMARY

1. A loop is a sequence of algorithm steps that may be executed more than once.

2. The steps of an algorithm are repeated more than once because:

a. The algorithm performs the same operations on different data items.

b. The results of the algorithm are obtained by performing operations over and over again beginning with a given set of data.

3. The four components of a loop are:

a. The initialization component.

b. The body of the loop.

c. The modification component.

d. The test-for-loop-termination component.

4. Four basic looping structures can be identified. These are shown in Fig. 5.1.

5. Information about an algorithm variable or an algorithm step is called declarative information and is enclosed in an annotation box.

6. Subscripted variables must be declared in our flowchart language so that the maximum values of the subscripts will be known within the algorithm. These declarations also provide the maximum

number of elements which may be represented in an array.

7. Subscripted variables are referenced by enclosing the subscripts in parentheses. Subscripts may be: (a) integer constants, (b) integer variables, or (c) integer arithmetic expressions.

8. When a subscripted variable appears without a subscript, this will be a reference to the entire array associated with that variable.

9. Algorithms can be classified as exact algorithms or as approximate algorithms.

10. An exact algorithm is an algorithm that is designed to provide an exact answer to a problem.

11. In an exact algorithm, it is possible before the algorithm has been executed to determine analytically the maximum number of times that a loop must be repeated to yield a solution.

12. An approximate algorithm is an algorithm that is designed to provide only an approximation to an exact answer.

13. In an approximate algorithm the number of times that a loop must be repeated to get a satis-

factory solution cannot be determined analytically before a solution is computed.

14. Approximate algorithms rather than exact algorithms are used to solve some problems because in many cases exact algorithms:

a. Are not known.

b. Are inefficient.

c. Are difficult to implement on a computer.

15. In approximate algorithms the goodness of an approximation is often computed by measuring the relative difference between successive approximations by use of the formula

$$\left| x_i - x_{i+1} \right| / (\left| x_i \right| + \left| x_{i+1} \right|)$$

16. It is important for the series of approximations computed by an approximate algorithm to converge upon an acceptable answer at a fast rate.

17. The five broad criteria for judging algorithm efficiency are:

a. Minimize the execution time of the algorithm on our computer.

b. Minimize the amount of memory space the algorithm requires.

c. Maximize the present and future flexibility of the algorithm.

d. Minimize algorithm development time.

e. Maximize the ease with which an algorithm can be understood.

Solving Problems in
Business
and Public
Administration

The largest use of computers for solving problems is in the areas of business and government. We are all familiar with some of the many ways in which computers are used. Banks use computers to process checks and to compute and print out the monthly statements for checking accounts. Department stores use computers to keep track of credit card purchases and to print monthly statements on credit accounts. Auto and life insurance companies send notices of premiums due which are computed and printed by a computer. Scheduling of such things as steel and automobile production is handled by computers. Paychecks are calculated and printed by computers, as are the reports to the Internal Revenue Service about how much an individual has earned. As another example, airline reservations are kept by a computer and are available for changes within several seconds. The federal government maintains social security tax and payment records on a computer. The Internal Revenue Service also processes income tax returns using a computer. The list of business and government uses of computers can go on and on. The main conclusion to draw is that computers are involved in virtually all aspects of business and government activity. In this chapter we are going to study something about the nature of business and government computer applications. Since government data processing is very similar to business data processing, we will use the term *business data processing* in this text to refer to both. We will also develop algorithms to solve several typical business problems.

6.1 BUSINESS DATA PROCESSING

The distinction between business and nonbusiness problems is not clearly defined. Processing large masses of data such as are involved in solving many business problems must also be done when solving such problems as space-flight calculations. On the other hand, the use of sophisticated statistical and mathematical techniques is commonly associated with engineering and the sciences. But, today such methods are also widely used in solving business problems. Applications of these mathematical tools include sales forecasting and assembly-line balancing problems. In this chapter, however, we will be interested primarily in the area commonly referred to as business data processing.

Business data processing and similar activities in the public sector involve the processing of *large amounts* of information. Information that is represented in some symbolic form (usually using numbers, letters, or special symbols) is called *data*. For example, the payroll file for a firm consists of data that represent certain relevant information about all of the employees of the firm. The reservations file of an airline consists of data that represent information on seats on all flights for a period of about one year. This includes information about all passengers holding reservations. We are thus talking about hundreds of thousands or even millions of data items.

Recall from Chapter 5 that the ordered collection of all information which is related in some way is called a *file*.* Notice that the information must be in some sequence. Thus the order of the records in a file is itself information. For example, all of the payroll information for a particular firm ordered alphabetically by last name of employee would represent a payroll file. A file is made up of records.† A *record* consists of all of the items of information related to a particular individual or element in the file. For example, a record in a payroll file would consist of all of the information related to a single employee. The individual pieces of information in a record are called *items*.† Items of information in an employee's record might include, for example, the employee's: (1) name, (2) address, (3) social security number, (4) pay rate, (5) union affiliation, and (6) earnings for the year to date. Thus the items of information in a payroll file are organized by individual employees.

The information included in a record may also be structural information. The term *structural* simply refers to information that identifies the organization or structure of a file. For example, we may include in a record a pointer to the main memory location which contains the next logical record in the file.

The term *file* is often used to mean two different things. It is sometimes given a physical meaning, such as referring to a deck of punched cards or magnetic tape reel as an input file. File is also used in a logical sense to describe a collection of records that consists of an ordered set of related information. We will use the term *file* in the logical sense in this text. Note that one or more logical files can be represented on one physical file. For example, both a payroll file and an accounts receivable file can be stored on a single magnetic disc storage unit. In this case two logical files reside on one physical file.

In Chapter 2 we learned that the main memory of a computer has a very limited capacity. Therefore, it is usually necessary to store data files

Margin notes: large data volume · file · record · items · structural information · physical versus logical files

---

* A *file* is also sometimes called a *data structure*.

† A *record* is also sometimes called a *node*.

†† An *item* is also sometimes called a *field*.

Figure 6.1. Univac Uniservo 20 Magnetic Tape Drive (*Courtesy of* Sperry Univac, A Division of Sperry Rand Corporation)

auxiliary memory

in auxiliary memory. Some commonly used *auxiliary memory media* are magnetic tape (Fig. 6.1), magnetic disc (Fig. 6.2), and magnetic drum. Magnetic tape permits the recording of information represented using a binary code on a tape very similar to that used in home tape recorders.

Figure 6.2. IBM 2314 Magnetic Disc Drives (*Courtesy of* International Business Machines Corporation)

Magnetic discs and magnetic drums are devices that also provide for the storage of information coded in a binary form. All three of these recording media allow for the storage of large amounts of information, often running into many millions of characters. A greater amount of time is required to access information stored on one of these media, however, than is required in accessing information that is in main memory. Furthermore, information stored using one of these media must be input to main memory before it can be processed.

Earlier in this section, we said that business data processing involves the processing of large amounts of information which is organized into files. An important aspect of file processing is that of maintaining the file. *File maintenance* is the process of adding new records to a file, deleting old records from a file, and modifying existing records in a file. Other file processing involves the use of the information in the file to perform a task. For example, on any given day a payroll file will contain records on all

file maintenance

189

of the persons then employed by the firm. When new employees are hired by the company, a record must be created in the master payroll file for each new employee. Similarly, if an item of information in an employee's record (such as the number of dependents) changes, this change must be recorded in the payroll file. In addition, the records of employees who are no longer employed need to be deleted from the payroll file. These are all examples of file maintenance.

file processing

The actual use of the information in the payroll file to prepare the payroll would be an example of *file processing*. Among the tasks required would be computing the employee's gross pay and all deductions. Paychecks and management reports also need to be printed. In addition, the payroll file must be updated to reflect employee earnings and deductions. This information is needed so that the proper tax forms can be prepared and payments of amounts deducted can be made to the proper agencies.

information retrieval

Another important type of file processing is called *information retrieval*. In information retrieval, the file is accessed to seek a particular type or piece of information. For example, an employee may request information about his year-to-date earnings. The process of searching the file to obtain the needed information is an example of information retrieval. Information retrieval is often performed in an online mode of operation. By *online*, we mean that the file containing the information to be retrieved is stored in the auxiliary memory of a computer and can be directly accessed at any time.

preventing file processing errors

Caution is needed when processing a file to prevent errors from creeping into the records of the file. All data that will be used to make changes in the file should be verified as to its correctness before processing is performed. As an added precaution, all records that have been changed should be listed to verify that the changes have been correctly made. Particular caution must be exercised in deleting a record from a file because of the chance that a request to delete a record will be made in error. A good practice in the case of record deletion is to maintain a file of deleted records for a fixed period of time. This will permit recovery of a record that has been deleted in error.

data verification

Another form of data verification involves testing data items during processing to check on their reasonableness. For example, if the value 92 is input for the number of hours worked during one week by an employee, this figure should be verified. Such verification might take the form of a listing of all such suspicious inputs at the end of processing. Care must be taken in choosing verification limits, however, so that not too many valid values are rejected as being unreasonable.

file security

File security is another very important aspect of file processing. By *file security*, we are referring to the need to include some provision to prevent unauthorized persons from accessing the information in a file. This is a very important problem in online systems. For example, a payroll file contains very sensitive information about employee pay rates. Thus only a small number of authorized persons should have access to the information in the payroll file.

In addition, the possibility of fraud always exists. For example, **fraud prevention** safeguards must exist to prevent someone from fraudulently increasing his own or a friend's rate of pay. Numerous cases of fraud by data processing personnel have been uncovered because such safeguards were not used. One common method to achieve file security is to associate with each file or portion of a file a certain predefined code. This code is usually called a *password* because it is similar in concept to the secret passwords sometimes used by people. The person who wishes to access a protected file must supply the proper password before the information will be made available for processing.

A final consideration in data processing problems is file backup. **file backup** *File backup* involves being able to recover the contents of a file lost due to an error in processing or when a file is accidently destroyed. As an extreme example, a fire may develop in the computer center which destroys the magnetic tape that contains the payroll file. If another copy of the information on that magnetic tape is not available somewhere, the firm is in trouble. A means of solving this problem is to keep a duplicate copy of the payroll file on magnetic tape in a fireproof vault at another location.

6.2   THE AMORTIZATION-TABLE PROBLEM

A typical problem found in business and personal finance is the problem of developing an amortization table. An amortization table is simply a list that tells what the balance on a loan is on a period-by-period basis. **problem definition** It is developed given that a certain amount is being repaid on the loan **and analysis** each period and that a portion of each payment goes for interest on the outstanding balance. To be more explicit, the balance at the beginning of the first period is the amount borrowed, which is called the *principal.* After making the first payment, the amount of the balance is reduced by the amount remaining after deducting interest on the principal for that period from the total payment. Thus, if the principal balance at the beginning of the period is $200 and the interest for the period is $10, a payment of $25 would cause the principal to be reduced by $15 (the payment amount less the interest). Therefore, the principal balance at the beginning of the next period would be $185.

Let us assume that we have the problem of developing an algorithm for generating amortization tables for loans that are repaid monthly. We will also assume that we are given: (1) a beginning principal balance, (2) a fixed annual interest rate, and (3) a fixed payment amount that can vary only for the last payment. Furthermore, assume that we want printed for each month in our schedule: (1) the date the payment is due, (2) the principal balance at the beginning of that month, (3) the portion of that month's payment going for interest, (4) the portion of that month's payment applied towards the principal, and (5) the principal balance after the payment has been made. Thus, given a loan of $3,000 at 8 percent interest repaid at the rate of $25 per month beginning on April 1, 1976, the first several lines of the amortization table would appear as in Fig. 6.3.

DUE DATE	BEGINNING BALANCE	INTEREST PAYMENT	PRINCIPAL PAYMENT	ENDING BALANCE
4/ 1/76	3000.00	20.00	5.00	2995.00
5/ 1/76	2995.00	19.97	5.03	2989.97
6/ 1/76	2989.97	19.93	5.07	2984.90
7/ 1/76	2984.90	19.90	5.10	2979.80
.	.	.	.	.
.	.	.	.	.
.	.	.	.	.

Figure 6.3. Portion of an Amortization Table

Obviously the table will continue until the amount in the rightmost column reaches zero. Since the last beginning balance plus the interest for one month may not equal the fixed payment amount, the final payment may be less than the other payments. In addition, we must guard against the case where the fixed payment amount is less than or equal to the first month's interest. In the latter case, the principal balance cannot decline and the table will never be completed.

The above analysis of the problem reveals that the inputs to the algorithm are:

1. The initial principal balance.
2. The annual interest rate.
3. The fixed monthly payment amount.
4. The due date (month, day, and year) of the first payment.

The output of the algorithm will be the amortization table, as described above.

descriptive and algorithm flowcharts   The descriptive flowchart for this problem is given in Fig. 6.4, and the algorithm flowchart appears in Fig. 6.5. Execution of the algorithm begins with a step that causes the appropriate values to be input for processing. Notice the inclusion of in-connector 1, which will permit the steps of the algorithm to be repeated for different table values. The next steps needed provide a test for end-of-file to determine when the last table has been processed and a STOP box. In the next flowchart box a

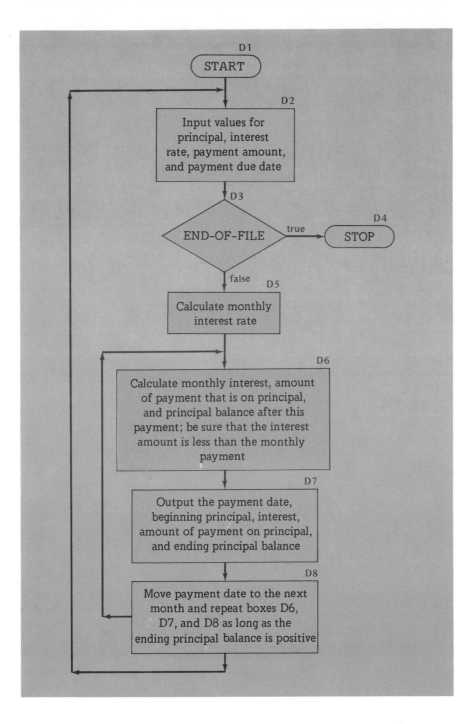

Figure 6.4. Descriptive Flowchart for the Amortization-Table Problem

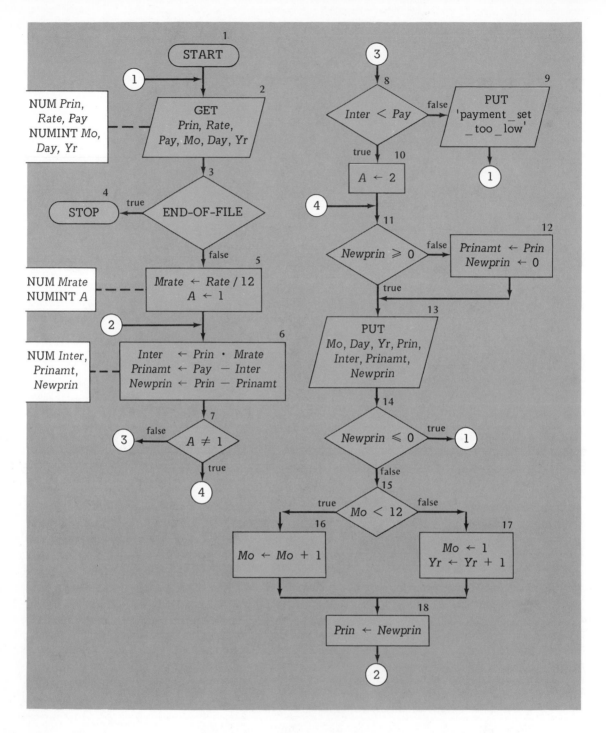

Figure 6.5. Algorithm Flowchart for the Amortization-Table Problem

monthly interest rate is computed by dividing the annual interest rate by the number of months in the year. This step is needed because the monthly interest amounts will be the ones required in the table. This step is followed by the assignment of the value 1 to the numeric variable A. The reason for this will be explained in a few moments. The next steps involve the computation of the values for the first line in the table. This is accomplished by the three assignment statements in flowchart box 6. Notice in this box how important the sequencing of consecutive assignment statements can be. Namely, the expression that assigns a value to *Prinamt* cannot be evaluated until *Inter* has been computed in the previous assignment statement. Similarly, *Prinamt* is used in the expression in the third assignment statement in the box.

The first time that the conditional branch in box 7 is reached, the variable A will have a value of 1, which was assigned in box 5. Thus the branch will be to in-connector 3. The step in box 8 is designed to be sure that the amount of interest does not equal or exceed the payment amount. This test is only required in developing the first line of the table because if the test passes the first time it will pass all subsequent times. The reason for this is that the principal balance and thus the interest will be reduced for all periods after the first if the test passes the first time. Notice that when the test passes, the variable A is given the value 2 in box 10 so that the test is bypassed on subsequent passes through the algorithm. However, when the test fails, an error message is output in flowchart box 9 and the table for the current set of input values cannot be output. Thus, in this case control is returned to in-connector 1, where the values for the next table are input.

The next step should be to output a line of the amortization table. However, before doing that we must determine whether or not the new principal balance calculated in box 6 is less than zero. If it has become negative, then before printing the line in the table the new principal balance must be set to zero and the principal payment set to the beginning principal balance for this period. When the test shows that the new principal balance is zero or positive, however, we should go ahead and print the line in the table. Notice that the new principal balance will be less than zero only when this is the last payment period. The appropriate algorithm steps appear in flowchart boxes 11, 12, and 13.

Following these steps we need to branch back to compute the next line of the table if the new principal balance is greater than zero. However, before branching back we must update the month counter and set the value of the old principal for the next period to be that of the new principal for this period. We must also test the value of our month counter to provide for the case where we move from December of one year to January of the following year. These steps are taken care of by the sequence in flowchart boxes 14 through 18. This algorithm flowchart should be studied carefully before proceeding to the next section.

PROBLEMS

1. Use the following input data stream to develop a trace table for the algorithm flowchart of Fig. 6.5:

1000.00, 0.06, 300.00, 12, 5, 74, 500.00, 0.12, 3.00, 4, 15, 75, 1000.00, 0.12, 507.51, 7, 1, 75

2. Modify the amortization-table algorithm of Fig. 6.5 so that the payment periods may be more than one month in length. This change will require the input of an additional value which gives the number of months in a payment period. For example, the input value would be 3 if payments are made only every three months. Assume that the number of months in a period is always an integer value.

For the following problems, develop: (1) a descriptive flowchart, (2) an algorithm flowchart, and (3) a trace table (develop your own input data stream for each problem).

3. An economist wants the computer to produce tables that give the present value of $1 over a certain time given a fixed rate of inflation. The present value of $1 at the end of the ith period is $P_{t-1}/(1 + r)$, where r is the constant rate of inflation and P_{t-1} (for $t = 1, 2, 3, \ldots, n$) is the present value of the dollar at the end of the previous time period. The value of P_0 is equal to 1. The algorithm inputs should consist of the inflation rate r and the number of time periods n to be included in the table.

4. An investor wants the computer to produce tables of the value of a fixed investment at each time period, where the investment accrues interest that is compounded at a fixed rate. The value of the compounded investment at the end of the ith period can be computed as $(1 + r) \cdot I_{t-1}$, where r is the interest rate per period and I_{t-1} (for $t = 1, 2, 3, \ldots, n$) is the investment value at the end of the previous period. The value of I_0 is equal to the initial investment. The algorithm inputs should consist of the initial investment, the constant interest rate, and the number of time periods for which the investment has been made.

5. A loan company manager wants the computer to be able to generate an amortization table for the case in which the amount of the periodic payment is not given. That is, algorithm input will be the annual interest rate, the initial principal amount, the due date of the first payment, the number of periods over which the loan is to be repaid, and the number of months in each payment period. The amount of each payment can be calculated using the formula

$$Payment = \frac{Prin \cdot Mrate \cdot (1 + Mrate)^n}{(1 + Mrate)^n - 1}$$

where $Prin$ is the principal amount, $Mrate$ is the interest rate for one period, and n is the number of periods over which the loan is to be repaid.

6. A marketing manager is faced with the problem of computing the breakeven point of a product. The breakeven point is that quantity of a product that must be produced for the total production and marketing costs to equal the total sales revenue. That is, the breakeven point tells the minimum quantity that has to be sold to allow the total cost to equal total income for the product. The algorithm inputs are: (1) sales price per unit, (2) quantity to be produced, (3) total fixed operating costs, and (4) variable operating costs per unit produced. The output should consist of a table whose columns consist of: (1) quantity produced, (2) total cost, (3) total revenue, (4) total profit or loss, and (5) the profit or loss per unit of product produced. A table heading should also be output which provides the input values. The *quantity produced* column should contain values that range from 0 to the number to be produced (as input). The increment for this column should be a constant, and each table should have forty entries. The *total cost* column values are computed using

$$cost = fixed + variable \cdot quantity$$

where *cost* is total cost, *fixed* is total fixed cost, *variable* is variable cost per unit produced, and *quantity* is the quantity produced. Total revenue is computed by multiplying the sales price per unit by quantity produced. The total profit is computed by subtracting column 2 from column 3, where negative results will indicate a loss. Finally, the per unit profit is obtained by dividing quantity produced into total profit.

6.3   MORE ON THE SEQUENCING PROBLEM

In Section 5.3.1 we explored the problem of sequencing a set of records in a file into a particular order. The algorithm we developed in that section was based on the two-list method. This method is called the *two-list method* because it requires two lists—an input list and an output list. These two lists are needed because the approach is basically the same as that used in manually resequencing a set of values listed on a sheet of paper. In this section we will examine another approach to the sorting problem. The method used this time, however, will take advantage of the way in which data are stored in a computer memory. A consequence of this will be that the output array will not be needed using the new approach. As in Section 5.3.1, we will assume that each record in the file consists of only one numeric value.

problem definition and analysis

The new approach to the sorting problem begins by scanning the original list to find the smallest value. The smallest value found during the scan is then interchanged with the value in the first element of the array. Next the list is scanned again, beginning this time with the second value. The smallest value found on the second scan is then interchanged with the value in the second element of the list. This process is continued, with the scan on the *i*th repetition beginning with the *i*th element in the list. After $(n - 1)$ scans of the list, the original file values will be in nondescending order. The logic of this method is illustrated in the example shown in Fig. 6.6. In this figure, a step-by-step analysis is given of the sorting of six values. Notice the use of arrows to indicate which values were interchanged on each pass through the list. In addition, observe that the horizontal broken lines indicate where the sublist begins that is to be scanned on the *i*th pass.

A descriptive flowchart for this method appears in Fig. 6.7. Notice in descriptive flowchart box D7 that the smallest value found on a pass is interchanged with the top element in the list on that pass. The fundamental advantages of this interchange sort method over the one used in the algorithm of Section 5.3.1 are that using the method of this section:

descriptive flowchart

1. The list to be searched is shortened by one element on each scan.
2. Only one array is needed instead of two, since the input array also is used to store the output array.
3. One less scan of the input list is required because on the last scan the final interchange (if one is needed) must leave the last two array positions in the proper order.

The algorithm flowchart for the interchange sort appears in Fig. 6.8. The steps in boxes 1 through 9 cause the values to be sorted to be input into an array and output. In fact, these steps are identical to the first nine

algorithm flowchart

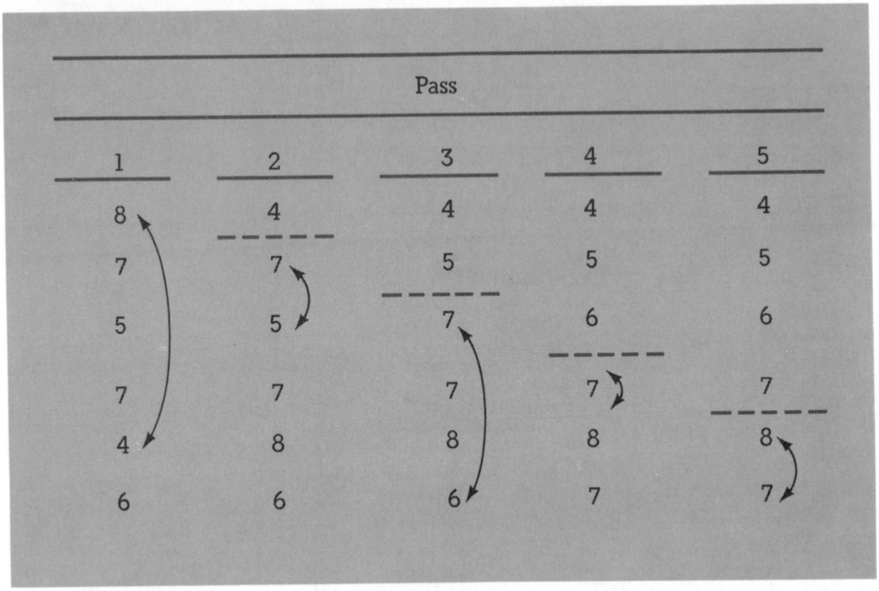

Figure 6.6. Step-by-Step Analysis of the Replacement Sorting Method

boxes in the previous sorting algorithm of Fig. 5.7. The flowchart boxes in which the sort is performed are 10 through 17. This sequence consists of two loops. The outer loop consists of boxes 10 through 17 while the inner loop is made up of boxes 11 through 15. The loop counter i for the outer loop is initialized in box 10. Box 11 contains the steps for initializing the inner loop counter k and the pointer variable pt. The step in box 12 compares the kth item in x with the element in x that was previously found to be the smallest value. When the kth value is less than the value that has previously been found to be the smallest on this pass of the input array, then in box 13 the value of the subscript k is assigned to be the new value of pt. Thus the variable pt contains a value that points to the element in the array x that contains the smallest value found thus far in this scan of the list of values. As long as the kth value is not less than the ptth value, however, box 13 is not executed and the value of the pointer pt remains unchanged. That is, it still contains the value of the subscript that points to the element in the array x that has been found to contain the smallest value thus far in this scan. Flowchart box 14 contains a test for

Figure 6.7. Descriptive Flowchart for the Sequencing Problem ▶

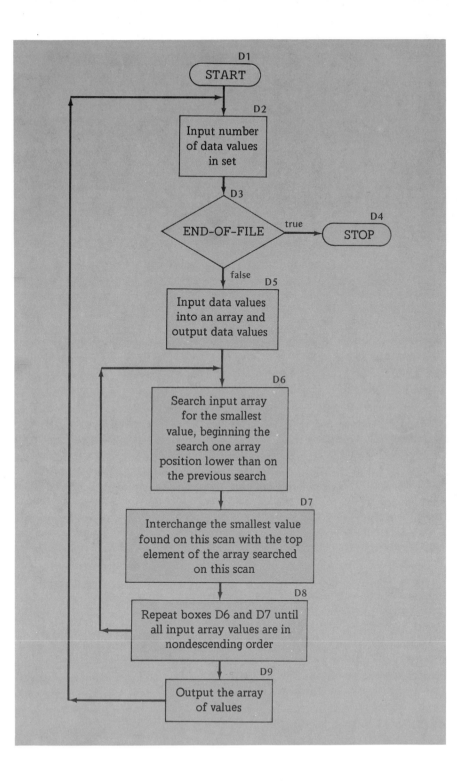

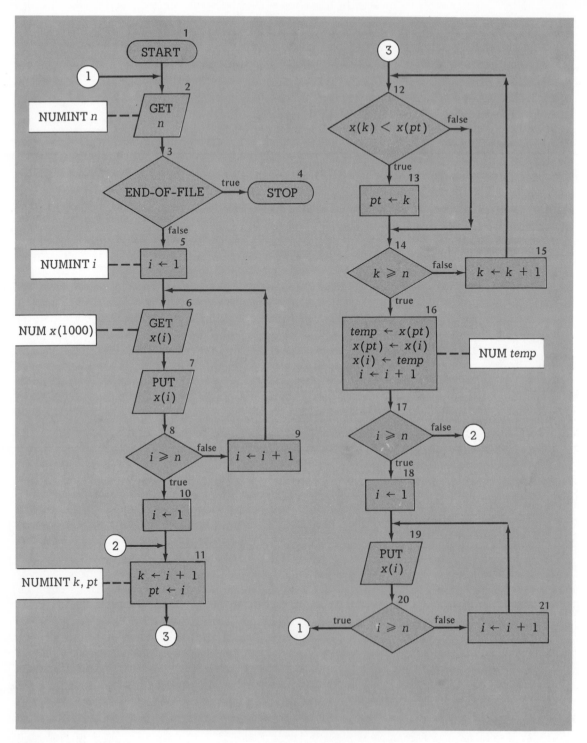

◄ **Figure 6.8.** Algorithm Flowchart for the Sequencing Problem

loop termination, and in box 15 we have the modification step for the inner loop.

When execution of the inner loop is terminated by the step in box 14, the value of *pt* will be the subscript of the array element that contains the smallest value in *x* on this pass. In box 16 this value is exchanged with the first element of the array *x* that was checked on this pass. That is, on the *i*th pass, the smallest value found beginning with the *i*th value will be interchanged with the *i*th value. Notice that three assignment statements are required to interchange two values. This is because of the destructive nature of the assignment operation. The variable used for a temporary swap location is named *temp*. The last step in box 16 is the modification step of the outer loop, and box 17 contains the test for loop termination. Finally, the steps in flowchart boxes 18 through 21 output the *n* values of the input array, with the values now being in nondescending order. When this operation has been completed, control is passed to in-connector 1, where the next set of values to be sorted is input.

PROBLEMS

7. Use the following input data stream to develop a trace table for the algorithm of Fig. 6.8:

$$10, 7, -5, 42, 67, 35, 18, 72, 4, -6, 4$$

For the following problems, develop: (1) a descriptive flowchart, (2) an algorithm flowchart, and (3) a trace table (develop your own input data stream for each problem).

8. Another sorting strategy that can be used involves scanning the file and comparing the sort fields in consecutive record pairs. During the scan, records would be exchanged in any pair when the sort-field values in those records were not in the desired order. After completing one scan of the list, the record with the largest sort-field value will be the bottom record in the list. Another scan of the list is then performed, this time excluding the last list element. This procedure is repeated, with one element being dropped off of the list on each successive scan, until the scan includes only the first two elements of the array. This sort method is called an *exchange sort.*

9. Two improvements can be made to the exchange sort algorithm developed for Problem 8. First, a variable can be included that is used to determine whether or not any records were exchanged on a particular pass through the file. The only case in which no records are exchanged on a pass is when the records are already in the desired order. When this case holds, the sorting process is completed and output of the sorted values can be performed. A second change would be to recognize the fact that all records are in order beyond the last records interchanged on the most recent scan of the file. Thus the sort fields of a file need only to be scanned up to the $(k - 1)$th record on a pass through the file when the *k*th record was the last one exchanged on the previous scan of the file. Develop an algorithm that includes these two modifications of the exchange sort algorithm developed for Problem 8.

6.4   THE CREDIT-CARD BILLING PROBLEM

At the beginning of this chapter we observed that file maintenance and processing are a very important part of business data processing. File maintenance and processing often involve adding records to or deleting records from a file, changing the values in certain fields of certain records in the file, and printing reports based on current information in the file. A file that contains permanent information is called the *master file*. Another type of file is the transactions file. A *transactions file* consists of records that contain temporary information used to update or revise the records of the master file.

problem definition and analysis

A typical problem is that of designing an algorithm for maintaining the credit-card master file for an oil company. A descriptive flowchart for such an algorithm appears in Fig. 6.9 for the Greasy Oil Company. The records of the credit-card master file contain information about all holders of Greasy credit cards. Each night the Greasy credit-card master file is updated by the transactions that have been received in the data processing center during that day. The transactions are written onto a transactions file during the day as they are received. Thus the transactions are in a more-or-less random order. Therefore, the first step taken each evening after receipt of the last transaction is to sort the transactions file records using the customer's account number as the sort field. Completion of the sort will leave the transactions records ordered from the smallest to the largest account number received during the day (we will assume that the credit-card master file is already ordered by customer account number). Furthermore, let us assume that the records of the Greasy Oil Company master and transactions files are stored sequentially on two separate reels of magnetic tape.

descriptive flowchart

Examining the descriptive flowchart in Fig. 6.9, the step in box D2 inputs the current date. The current date is needed to know when to send customers their monthly statements on account. The input step in box D3 would not normally be performed in a real-life situation. However, in this text we are going to assume that in a beginning class the students will not be allowed to use magnetic tapes. Therefore, we are simulating the magnetic tape for the master file records by inputting the values of the master file into arrays. Then the proper record in the master file is accessed by selecting the correct subscript to point to the element in the array that is to be processed next. Since records would be input from magnetic tape sequentially, this means that the subscript would take on the successive integer values from 1 to n to simulate the input of records from magnetic tape.

Box D4 causes one transactions record to be input from the input data stream. The fetching of the next master file record in box D5 simply involves incrementing the master file subscript by 1. This causes the next

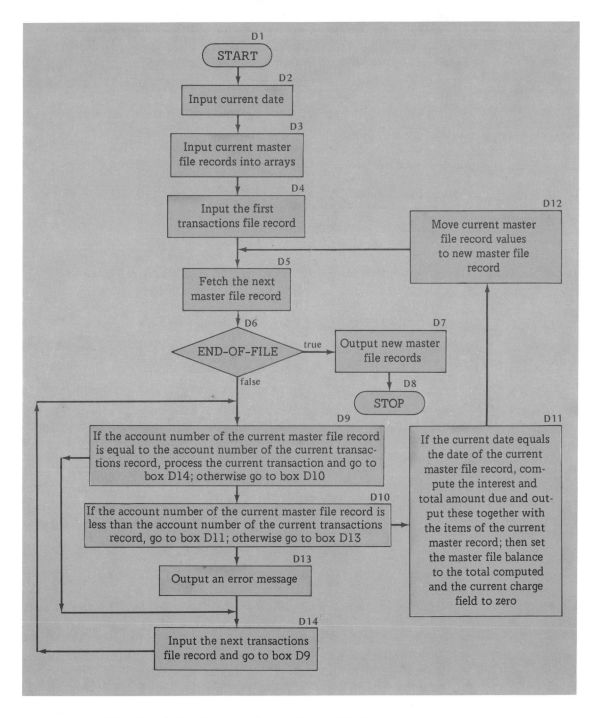

Figure 6.9. Descriptive Flowchart for the Greasy Oil Company
Credit-Card Billing Problem

master file array elements to be referred to in the various algorithm steps. When end-of-file is encountered in the master file, the output of the contents of the new master file records occurs in box D7. This step would also not be included in a real-life situation. However, in a learning situation, it is instructive to be able to see the changes that have occurred while processing the master file. The steps in boxes D9 through D14 should be studied carefully. They will not be discussed because they should be easy to understand. For the logic in Fig. 6.9 to work correctly, a dummy record with an account number larger than any active master file account number must appear after the last live record in the transactions file. This is needed to complete output to the new master file of old master file records for which there were no transactions.

master file records   Each record of the master file contains the following data fields:

1. Customer account number *(mact)*.
2. Customer name *(mname)*.
3. Customer address *(maddr)*.
4. Customer city, state, and zip code *(mcity)*.
5. Previous month's balance *(mpbal)*.
6. Current charges for this month *(mchge)*.
7. Billing date *(mdate)*.

The italicized names in parentheses will be the variable names used in our algorithm to identify these fields in the records of the master file. Notice that every variable name in the list begins with the letter *m* to indicate that this is a field of a master file record.

transactions file records   Each record in the transactions file contains the following data fields:

1. Customer account number *(tact)*.
2. Transaction code *(tcd)*:
    a. A value of 1 indicates a charge sale.
    b. A value of 2 indicates a payment on account.
    c. A value of 3 indicates that the account has been closed.
3. Transaction amount *(tamt)*.

Again, the italicized names in parentheses in this list are variable names used in our algorithm to identify these fields in a record of the transactions file. Notice that every variable name in the list begins with the letter *t* to indicate that this is a field of a transactions file record.

Another assumption that we will make is that the records of the transactions file for any given account number are also ordered by transaction code. Thus, for any account number, all type 1 transactions will be processed first, all type 2 transactions second, and type 3 transactions third. Of course, all three or even two of the types of transactions need not occur during any day.

Let us now examine the algorithm flowchart for this problem, which appears in Fig. 6.10. The step in box 2 inputs the current date, which is **algorithm flowchart** recorded simply as the day of the month. For example, on March 29, the value input for *Date* would be 29. The steps in the loop consisting of boxes 3 through 6 are used to input the master file records into their respective arrays. Thus, these steps correspond with box D3 in the descriptive flowchart. Notice that each item in the master file records is input to a separate array, where the name of the array indicates the values that it holds. Also observe that each array has been arbitrarily declared to have fifty elements. Thus up to fifty master file records can be processed by this algorithm. Of course, in real life the master file records would be input from magnetic tape, in which case no limit would be placed on the number of master file records permitted.

The two assignment statements in box 7 are used to initialize the counter variables m and n. The variable m is used to point to the current master file record being processed. That is, the variable m is given a value and used as a subscript to access all of the fields of one record in the master file. Similarly, the variable n is used to point to the most recent record in the new master file. A further explanation of the use of n and the concept of a new master file must await our discussion of box 34 of the flowchart.

Box 8 contains a step that causes one transactions file record to be obtained from the input data stream. Note that each item of the transactions file record is assigned to a different variable. The step in flowchart box 9 is equivalent to the one in box D5 of the descriptive flowchart. That is, by incrementing m by 1, the next master file record is being fetched. This is true because m is used as a subscript that points to the elements of the arrays which represent the master file record currently being processed. The condition in box 10 is used as a check for end-of-file on the master file. That is, a dummy record will be included following the last valid record in the master file. This dummy record will contain an account number value of zero to indicate the end of the master file. Such a dummy record is often called a *trailer record* because it trails the last valid record in the file.

When the condition in box 10 is true, processing of all master file records is not complete. In this case, the step in box 17 is used to learn whether or not the account numbers of the current master and transactions file records are equal. When the two account numbers are equal, a branch is taken to in-connector 5. If the value of *tcd* is determined in box 21 to be 1, the branch is taken to box 22, where the current charge field of the current master file record is updated by *tamt* (the transaction amount). A value of 2 for *tcd* causes the step in box 24 to be executed next. The step in box 24 causes the previous balance field of the current master file record to be reduced by the amount of the payment received

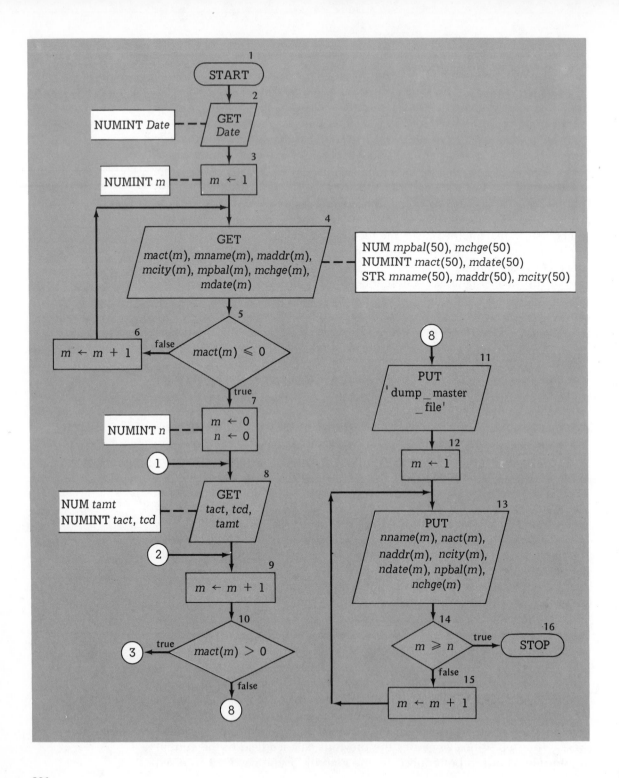

Figure 6.10. Algorithm Flowchart for the Credit-Card Billing Problem (at left, below, and continued on page 208)

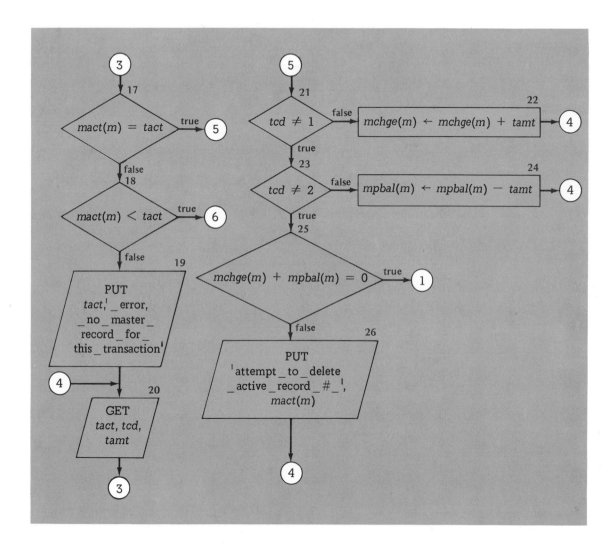

207

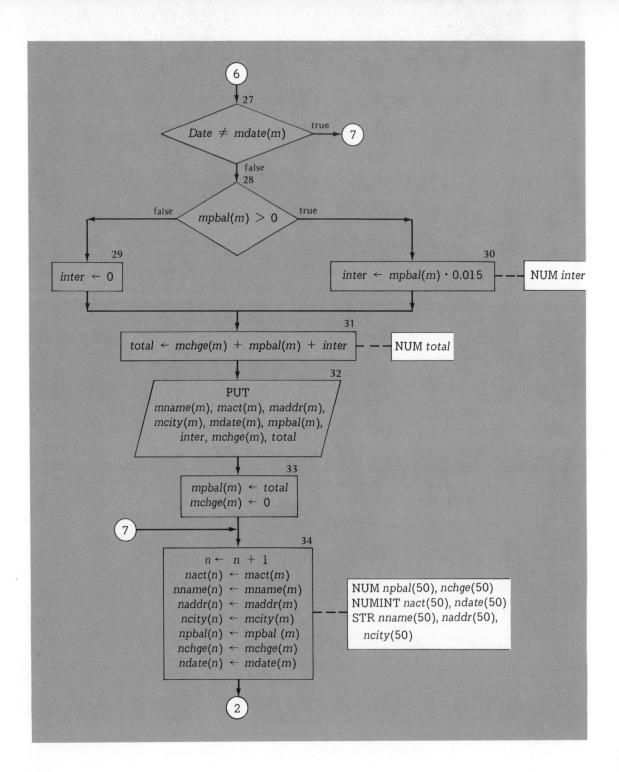

208

◄ Figure 6.10, *continued*

on account. Notice that the field *tamt* of the current transactions file record is used to input both purchases on account and payments on account. How the algorithm interprets the value of *tamt* depends entirely upon the value input for *tcd*. Following execution of the step in box 22 or 24, control is passed to box 20 through in-connector 4. In box 20, the next transactions record is input for processing.

If the value of *tcd* input is 3, we have a request to delete the current record from the master file. Note that in this case a value of zero should be in the transactions record for *tamt* since that field is not relevant. Such a request is probably a result of a customer closing his account. Our first thought might be that the operation of deleting a master file record can be performed simply by not outputting the master file record to the new master file tape. This would be a blunder, however, because we would certainly not wish to delete the record of a customer who still owes money on his account. Thus, in box 25 we have included a test to decide whether or not the sum of the previous balance and current charges is equal to zero. If the sum of these balances is not equal to zero, we output an error message in box 26 and branch to in-connector 4 to input the next transactions file record. Since there are probably not going to be any more transactions records for the same account, the test in box 18 for the next transactions record will probably cause a branch to in-connector 6. This will result in this master file record being placed in the arrays that are used to simulate the new master file tape.

When the test in box 25 indicates that the sum of the current charges and previous balance is equal to zero, control is passed to in-connector 1, where the next transactions file record is input and the next master file record is fetched. The effect of inputting these two records is to delete the most recent master file record from the master file. This is because by inputting the next master file record we have destroyed the current master file record, which thus cannot be output to the new master file.

Should the two account numbers not be equal in box 17, a test is made in box 18 to determine whether the account number of the current master file record is less than the account number of the current transactions file record. When the value of *mact* is less than the value of *tact*, the current transaction must go with a master file record that has not yet been input.* This condition will occur only if there are no more transactions records for the current master file record. In this case, we need to output this master file record to the new master file, which is contained in the arrays that have *n* as the first letter of their variable names. Then the next master file record should be input for processing. First, however,

---

* Recall that the two files are in sequence by account number.

we must compute and output the customer's statement if today is that person's billing date.

In box 27 we have a test to see if today is the billing date for this account by comparing the master file record billing date with the current date stored in *Date*. If today is this customer's billing date, his balance is computed in box 31. Then the customer's statement is output to the printer in box 32. The step in box 29 is used to compute the customer's interest if his balance for the previous month was paid in full during this period. This step is also executed if he had a negative balance that resulted from an overpayment or credit for returned merchandise. If that balance was not paid during this billing period, however, interest at 1.5 percent per month is computed in box 30 and added into the total due. In box 33 the previous balance field of the current master file record is updated and the current charge field set to zero. This is to prepare this record of the master file for processing during the next billing period. In box 34 the updated current master record is output to the arrays that contain the new master file.

Notice that if the test in box 27 indicates that today is not this customer's billing date, box 34 is the next box executed. Thus the new master file record is output whether or not this is the customer's billing date whenever the value of *mact* is less than the value of *tact*. After the new master file record has been output in box 34, we take a branch to in-connector 2 to input the next old master file record. Note that our algorithm requires that the last transactions record be a dummy record with an account number larger than any active master file account number. This is needed to finish transferring to the new master file any master file records for which there are no transactions records.

When the test in box 18 shows that the value of *mact* is greater than the value of *tact*, box 19 is executed next. Note that *mact* will be greater than *tact* only when we have a transactions record that has an account number with no corresponding master file record. The reason for this is that the master file and transactions file are in nondescending order by customer account number. Therefore, this is an error condition which requires that an error message be output in box 19. This error was probably caused by an invalid account number in a transactions record. Similar tests to detect errors in input values should be included in all algorithms. The next transactions record is input in box 20 and a branch taken to in-connector 3, where the account numbers of the current master and transactions file records are again compared.

Finally, when the condition in box 10 is false, the end of the master file has been reached. At this point the old master file has been processed and the contents of the new master file are contained in the arrays that have *n* as the first letter of their variable names. The step in box 11 of the flowchart causes a heading to be output. Then the loop in boxes 12 through 15 causes the contents of the arrays that represent the new master file to be output, one record at a time. Thus, these steps coincide with box D7 of the descriptive flowchart.

The above algorithm was designed for a simplified file maintenance problem for purposes of instruction. In a real credit-card master file maintenance situation, we would need to include such transaction steps as:

1. Adding records for new customers to the file.
2. Changing things such as name or address in existing account records.
3. The development of summary reports for management, such as total charge sales for the day.

In addition, we might wish to wait some period of time before deleting an account from the master file. This would permit processing of charge tickets not yet received in the data processing center. Or, we may wish to delete from the master file accounts upon which there have been no transactions for some period of time. Another possibility would be to copy on an inactive master file tape the records deleted from our current master file.

In addition to other types of transactions that we might process against our master file, we might also use it for other things. For example, we might use our credit-card master file as a mailing list for sending out promotional pieces. However, the above algorithm should provide some idea of the processing and maintenance of files in a business environment.

PROBLEMS

10. Assume that the transactions and master file records are stored on magnetic tape, and develop a trace table for the algorithm of Fig. 6.10. The records on the transactions file magnetic tape are:

(10, 1, 4.75), (11, 2, 5.63), (12, 1, 16.35), (12, 1, 4.25), (12, 2, 21.75), (12, 3, 0), (47, 2, 18.94), (47, 3, 0), (56, 2, 14.08), (99, 0, 0)

The records on the master file magnetic tape are:

(10, 'J._JONES ', '2 ELM ', 'CITY__77045 ', 8.03, 12.35, 30), (12, 'T_ZOE ', '4_ASH ', 'CITY__77052 ', 4.75, 4.67, 5), (47, 'A_CAR ', '4_TOP ', 'CITY__77024 ', 0, 18.94, 20), (56, 'S_LAMP ', '8_OAK ', 'CITY__77043 ', 14.08, 0, 30), end-of-file

Assume that *Date* = 30.

For the following problems, develop: (1) a descriptive flowchart, (2) an algorithm flowchart, and (3) a trace table (develop your own input data stream for each problem).

11. Design an algorithm for processing the payroll of the Sunshine Shrimp Co. Assume that each master file record contains in order an employee's: (1) social security number, (2) name, (3) home address, (4) pay rate, (5) number of dependents, (6) union dues amount, (7) year-to-date social security tax withheld, and (8) year-to-date federal income tax withheld. In addition, each transactions record contains an employee's: (1) social security number, and (2) hours worked for this pay period. Both the transactions file and master file should be assumed to be stored on separate magnetic tapes as sequentially organized files. In addition, both the transactions and master file records are in ascending order by social security number. Gross pay is calculated by multiplying the first forty hours worked times employee pay rate, and everything over forty hours worked by one-and-one-half times the pay rate. Social security tax is calculated at 6.0 percent of the gross salary on the first $13,200 earnings per year. Income tax withholding is computed by taking the gross pay less ten dollars for each dependent claimed times 20 percent. Net pay is calculated by deducting from gross pay: (1) union dues, (2) social security tax, and (3) income tax. The updated master file records should be output to magnetic tape after each transactions file record is processed. An employee's paycheck should be printed on the printer. Each paycheck should consist of the current date, the employee's name and home address, gross pay, itemized deductions, and net pay.

12. Develop an algorithm for processing student records at Dixie University. Assume that each master file record contains in order a student's: (1) student number, (2) name, (3) campus address, (4) major, (5) a list that will hold up to sixty four-digit course numbers and their respective grades, (6) total credit hours passed, and (7) cumulative grade-point average. The first two items in a transactions record are a student number and a transactions code. The three possible transactions codes mean to input and process: (1) 1—a change in name, address, or major; (2) 2—a new-student master file record; or (3) 3—a list of courses and respective grades. When a transactions code of 1 or 2 is processed, name, address, and major data fields must be input. If any one or two of these fields contains all blanks, that item in the record should not be altered on a code of 1. When the transactions code is 3, course numbers and grades must be input. A course number of 0000 indicates that no more course numbers and grades remain to be processed for this student. Note that in all three transaction types, the transactions record is variable in length. When the transactions code is 1 or 2, then the appropriate changes should be made in the respective master file record. When the transaction is of type 3, then we want to: (1) enter the course numbers and grades in the master file record; (2) update the total credit hours passed and grade-point average fields; (3) print a grade report that contains the student's name, address, student number, major, courses and grades for the current term, and cumulative grade-point average; and (4) put in a scholastic probation file the name and student number of any student whose cumulative grade-point average is below 2.0. Assume that a new master file record is to be produced for each transaction record and thus there is only one transaction per student. The system used for computing grade-point averages is A = 4, B = 3, C = 2, D = 1, and F = 0. Only these five grades are possible. Simulated magnetic tapes should be used for the current master file, the transactions file, the new master file, and the scholastic probation file.

6.5   INTEGRATED MANAGEMENT INFORMATION SYSTEMS

The integrated-systems approach to problem solving is one in which all sources and uses of data in the entire system are considered. An objective of an integrated management information system is to collect data from as few points as are necessary. The same data item should never be collected more than once in the business. The contents of management reports that are generated by the system should be determined by the relationships among the various kinds of information. In addition, a given data item should be processed as few times as possible. In an integrated management information system we generally will try to consolidate files and processing as much as is possible. We no longer think of processing a payroll and processing inventory as two separate tasks. They are integrated together in one management information system.

In summary, an *integrated management information system* is a system that is designed by considering the whole of information sources and needs within an organization. This can be contrasted with a system in which these sources and needs are broken up into mutually exclusive processing tasks. In this nonintegrated type of management information system, data items are often duplicated on several data files. In addition, the same processing steps are often repeated in several algorithms. The result of this duplication is inefficiency. As an example, a payroll file would be maintained that did not use the information in the sales file to calculate sales commissions. Rather, the information on which sales commission calculations are based would be generated separately for the payroll file. Such duplication is costly and can be avoided.

6.5.1 Example of an Integrated Information System

In this section let us construct a descriptive flowchart that illustrates how data collected at one point can serve several functions in the information system. The problem and the resulting information system will be somewhat restricted to keep it manageable. However, it illustrates some of the more important considerations in designing an integrated management information system.

Our source of information in this example will be the points of sale in the Superb Department Store. The data collected for each type of item sold are as follows:

sales record contents

1. The quantity of the item sold.
2. The stock number of the item.
3. The dollar amount of the item sold.
4. The employee number of the clerk making the sale.
5. The date of the sale.
6. The account number of the purchaser.
7. The ticket number of the ticket on which the sale is recorded.

The quantity of the item sold is always stated in per-unit terms, depending on the units used for pricing the product. For example, when items are marked with a price on each item, the quantity would be the number of this item sold. On the other hand, if an item is sold in bulk and priced by the pound, the quantity would be the number of pounds sold. If the transaction represents a return of merchandise, this value will be a negative quantity.

The stock number of an item sold contains three types of information. First, it serves to identify the type and model of the item. Second, it is used to identify the department that stocks this item. The stock number identifies the department because the two leftmost digits of the six-digit decimal stock number provide a departmental code. Finally, if the stock number is zero, this indicates sales tax. Item 3 (dollar amount) is self-explanatory except for one thing—a return of merchandise will be entered with a negative value for the amount of the sale. This permits us to process returns in the same manner as we process sales.

Item 4 (employee number of the clerk) is also self-explanatory. The date of the sale is given as the day of the year counting from January 1 as day one. Thus February 5 would have 36 as its date. The account number of the purchase is the customer's charge-account number with the Superb Department Store. For cash sales the value of this number will be zero. Item 7 in the list (ticket number of the sale) does not need an explanation.

data collection   The above data items are assumed to be captured at each sales station by a cash register. The data items are entered into the cash register by the clerk when the sale is made. For each entry the cash register produces on a magnetic tape cassette (which can be used as computer input) a record containing the data listed above. Periodically these tapes are collected and processed by the computer in the data processing center of the Superb Department Store using an algorithm that is based on the descriptive flowchart of Fig. 6.11.

descriptive   In box D2 of the flowchart, a sales record is input into main memory
flowchart   from the tape. Box D3 contains a test for end-of-file on the sales file. In box D5 a test is made to determine if the current sales record contains simply sales tax. If it is sales tax, the cumulative sales tax is increased by the amount of the tax for this sale. Then control is returned to box D2, where another sales record is input.

For all records that do not involve sales tax, we next execute the step in descriptive flowchart box D6. This step updates the total sales field of the payroll record of the clerk who made this sale by adding in the amount of the sale. The reason for recording the amount of sales for each employee is that Superb pays its clerks commissions based on their total sales. Essentially this step is carried out by retrieving this employee's record from the employee master file and adding the amount of this sale to the total sales field of this record. Then it stores this record back in the employee master file.

After executing the step in box D6, we proceed to box D7. In this box, the record for the product with this sales record stock number is

Figure 6.11.   Descriptive Flowchart for the Integrated Sales Data ▶
Information System

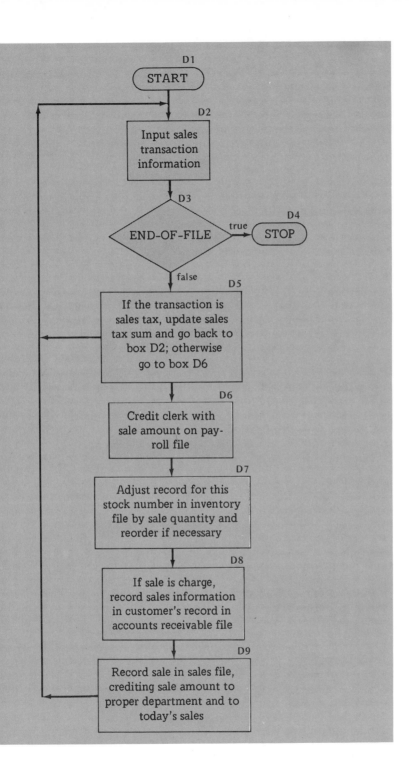

fetched from the inventory master file and the quantity-on-hand field in that record is updated. The updated quantity-on-hand value is also checked to see if it is below some preset level. If it is, an order might automatically be placed to replenish the inventory of this item. Then the updated record would be placed back into the inventory master file.

In box D8 a test is used to determine whether or not the sale was a charge sale. When it is a charge sale, the customer's record in the accounts receivable file is updated. The information recorded would probably include the date of the sale and the ticket number. These data are stored in the accounts receivable record to help in tracing errors and to aid in answering customer questions.

The final step to be executed is contained in descriptive flowchart box D9. The purpose of this step is to record the sale by department and in total for the Superb Department Store. This might be accomplished by first generating the number of the department in which the sale was made. Recall that the stock number is a six-digit decimal number that has as its two leftmost digits the number of a department. Therefore, dividing the value by 10,000 and truncating the result gives us the two-digit department number. For example, given a stock number of 267,832 and dividing this by 10,000, we have department 26 as our result. There is no need to maintain monthly, quarterly, or year-to-date sales figures since these can be easily derived by summing the daily sales figures.

The important point to pick up from this example is that the entire business organization and its information needs must be considered when designing a management information system. Files should be designed that consider the relationships among information. This means that the data items from what once were considered to be separate files should be consolidated into one file. The collection of files for an integrated management information system is often called a *data base*. This term is used to imply the integrated management information system concept.

6.5.2   The Total System Concept

Another topic closely related to an integrated management information system is the concept of a total system. A *total system* is an integrated **real-time** management information system that operates in real-time. By *real-time* we mean an information system in which outputs are available in time to affect the process that generates future inputs. For example, if sales during a Washington's Birthday special are greater than expected, management probably did not call in enough clerks to handle all of the customer load. A consequence of this could be customer ill-will and lost sales for the store. In a real-time system, management will have this information early enough in the day to call in off-duty clerks to handle the overload of customers.

The time span between the time that information is generated and the time when the information has been processed and made available does not in itself determine whether or not a system is operating in real-time. Instead, the important criterion is whether or not the necessary information is available when management requires it so that the information influences the decision-making process. If the information always is available soon enough, the system is operating in real-time. When the information is not available to management when needed, however, then the system is not operating in real-time.

In most situations, *online processing* is required to achieve real-time system performance. By online, we mean that the input goes directly into the computer system for processing at the time it originates. This is opposed to the approach in which data are collected or batched over a period of time and periodically input and processed in batches. In an online situation, the data are processed at the time it originates. As an example, our integrated system for processing sales data in Section 6.5.1 would be online if the cash registers were tied directly to a computer. In this case, the sales data would go directly into the computer for processing. This is opposed to the method that we described in Section 6.5.1 in which data were batched on a tape cassette at each cash register and then processed periodically. Be careful not to confuse online with real-time. *Online* is a physical concept stating that a device is connected directly to a computer. *Real-time*, on the other hand, is a dynamic relationship that involves the availability of information in time to affect future inputs.

online processing

One final observation is that a real-time information system is *not* necessarily a total system. That is, we can process data in real-time for one part of an organization or one function within an organization. But this does not give us a total system. To have a total system we must have an integrated management information system operating in real-time.

SUMMARY

1. The distinction between business and non-business problems is not clearly defined.

2. Business data processing involves the processing of large information files.

3. An ordered collection of records containing related information is called a file. A record is a group of separate data items that are associated with one individual or element in the file. In addition, a record may contain structural information.

4. Auxiliary memory media such as magnetic tape, magnetic disc, and magnetic drum are needed because computer main memory has such a limited capacity.

5. Two important types of file processing involve file maintenance and information retrieval.

6. When performing file maintenance, care must be taken to avoid the loss of records or information because of an error in the data or an error in the processing.

7. File security is very important because of the

confidential nature of the information kept on most files. In addition, the possibility of fraud always exists through the manipulation of data in the file.

8. File backup is very important to ensure survival of an organization when a part or all of one or more of its data files is destroyed.

9. The file that contains permanent information is called the master file. The file that contains information used to update the master file, which is processed with the aid of master file records, is called the transactions file.

10. An integrated management information systems approach is one in which all aspects of information flow and usage within a business are considered when solving a problem.

11. The objectives of an integrated management information system are to collect data from as few points as are necessary and to process those data as few times as possible.

12. A real-time information system is one in which outputs are available in time to affect the process that generates future inputs.

13. A total system is an integrated management information system that is operating in real-time.

14. Online processing is usually required to achieve real-time systems performance.

15. Online processing means that inputs go directly to the computer system as they originate. Online processing can be contrasted with batch processing, in which input data are collected over a period of time and periodically input in batches to the computer.

16. A real-time information system is not necessarily a total system.

Solving Problems in the Social Sciences and Arts

Most of the early uses of computers were in the physical sciences and engineering. Next came the application of computers in the solution of problems in government and business data processing. In recent years the computer has begun to be used to solve problems in the social sciences and arts. The areas in which they have been used range from sociology and psychology to music and the languages. In sociology, computers are used to summarize and analyze data collected about various groups. Meanwhile, computers are used to compose musical scores and to analyze such things as writing style.

Many problems in the social sciences involve the collection and analysis of large amounts of data. The analysis usually involves an area known as *statistics*. An industrial psychologist, for example, might collect data on the responses of the employees of a firm given certain changes in their work environment. The data collected might then be analyzed in an effort to determine which conditions produced the most employee output. A sociologist might collect data on how preschool training affects children from socially deprived homes. A political scientist may analyze data on voting patterns in an effort to predict political trends. An economist may be interested in the effect that money supply has on the rate of inflation. The list of applications in the social sciences can be extended almost without limit. In fact, to date the limit has been the creativity of social scientists in selecting applications for the computer.

In this chapter we are going to examine methods for solving some simple problems from several of the social sciences and arts. There are many more-complicated problem-solving methods available for application to the solution of problems in these areas. However, this chapter will give some notion as to how computers can be applied to solve problems in the social sciences and arts.

7.1   THE STATISTICAL-ANALYSIS-OF-TEXT PROBLEM

problem definition and analysis   A typical problem in the study of languages involves the statistical analysis of textual material. The statistical analysis of text can be performed in many ways. One example would be computing averages, such as the average number of words that appear in a sentence. Another example might be the average number of sentences contained per paragraph. A third example might include the average number of vowels used per word or per sentence. All of these statistics tend to vary from writer to writer and to provide a series of indexes of writing style.

In this section we will develop an algorithm that analyzes text in order to determine statistical measures of style. The three things that we will count in our analysis are the total number of sentences, the total number of words, and the total number of characters contained in the text. The output will consist of the total number of sentences contained in the text, the average number of words per sentence, and the average number of characters per word. The algorithm is designed to handle multiple texts. The end of a text is signaled by the appearance of a slash where the first character of a new sentence would begin. A new text is always begun in a new eighty-character input group. Eighty characters are input at a time into a one-dimensional array of one-character strings. After processing this eighty-character group, another group of eighty characters is input. This process continues until the appearance of a slash where a new sentence would begin. The algorithm assumes that only one blank space separates words in the text. In addition, all commas, semicolons, and hyphens are to be ignored. A period, indicating the end of a sentence, always follows a nonblank character. Furthermore, this period is assumed to be followed by two blank spaces.

The descriptive flowchart for this problem appears in Fig. 7.1; the algorithm flowchart for this problem is given in Fig. 7.2. In box 2 the variables *ns*, *nw*, and *nc* (which will be used to count the number of sentences, number of words, and number of characters, respectively) are given initial values. The character pointer *k* is also initialized in box 2. Why the value 81 is chosen as the initial value of *k* will be explained when we discuss box 7. The step in box 3 is used to input a line consisting of eighty characters. This input line is immediately output in box 6 if the end-of-file is not reached. Finding the end-of-file in box 4 will occur only when no more texts remain to be processed. In box 7, *k* is initialized in preparation for scanning the string of characters stored in *line*. When the step in box 7 is executed for the first line of a text, *k* will have the value of 81. Thus, in this case *k* will be assigned the value 1 in box 7. On subsequent executions, however, *k* may be equal to 82 or 83 as well as to 81. This point will be cleared up after discussing the steps in boxes 12 and 13, as will the purpose for the step in box 8.

descriptive and algorithm flowcharts

Figure 7.1.   Descriptive Flowchart for the Text-Analysis Problem (page 222)

Figure 7.2   Algorithm Flowchart for the Text-Analysis Problem (page 223)

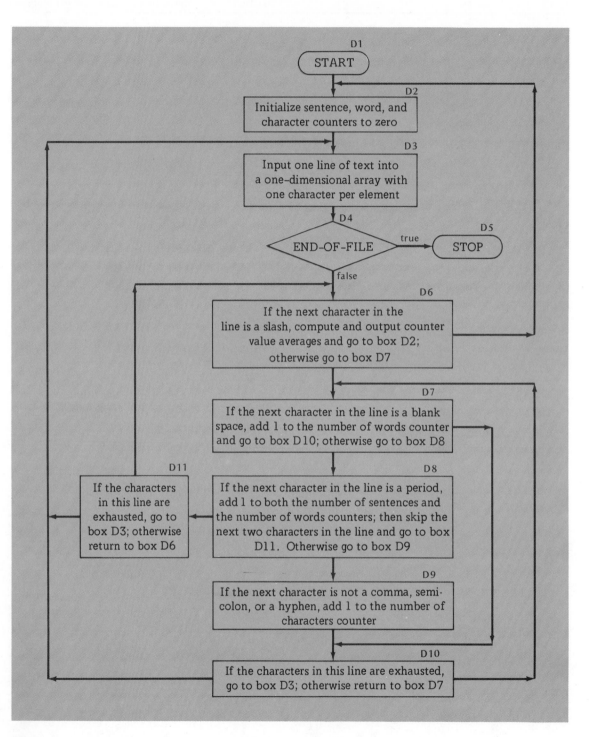

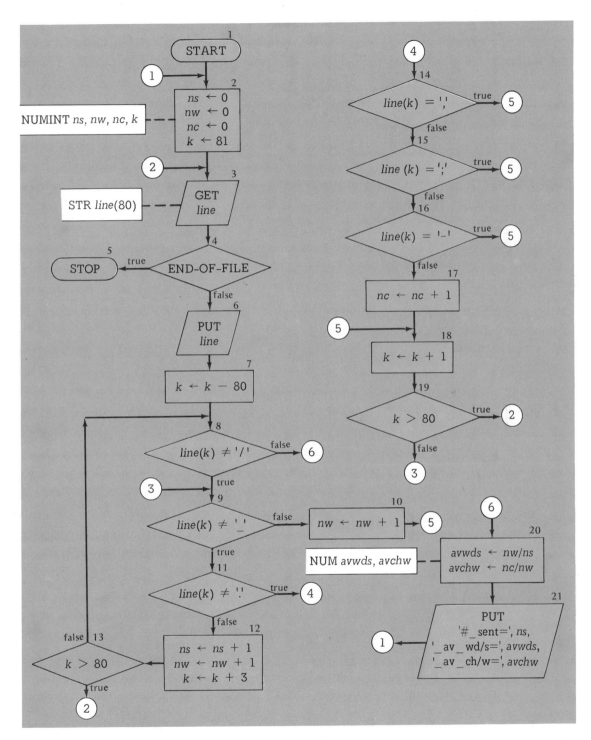

The loop consisting of boxes 9 through 19 is used for scanning the characters of the array called *line*. The comparison operation in box 9 is used to determine whether or not the kth character in the line is a blank. If it is a blank, the kth character marks the end of a word. In this case, the word counter nw is incremented by 1 in box 10 and a branch is taken to in-connector 5 where preparation is made to process the $(k + 1)$th character. When the kth character is not a blank, the comparison in box 11 is made to determine if the current character is a period. If it is a period, we have both the end of a sentence and the end of a word. Thus the variables ns and nw must both be incremented by 1, with these steps being performed in box 12.

The last step in box 12 increments the character pointer by 3. Because a period is always followed by two blanks, k should be pointing to the first character of the next sentence after executing the last assignment statement in box 12. Since incrementing k by 3 may cause k to be greater than 80, however, we test for this possibility in box 13. If k is greater than 80, this means that the first character of the next sentence is in the next eighty-character line to be input. Therefore, in this case a branch is taken to in-connector 2, where the next line of eighty characters is input. Notice that this time execution of the step in box 7 will not necessarily result in the assignment of the value 1 to k. Rather, k will be assigned the value 1 only when the period occurred in position 78 of the previous line. If the period fell in positions 79 or 80 of the previous line, however, k will be assigned the value 2 or 3, respectively, in box 7. Now, if we reached box 8 immediately after having found a period in the previous line, we must check the first nonblank character in the new line to determine if it is a slash. If the kth character in the new line is not a slash, processing continues in box 9. When it is a slash, however, a branch is made to in-connector 6, where the summary statistics are calculated and printed.

Now, if the value of k was not greater than 80 after having found a period, the first character of the next sentence must be in the current eighty-character line. Thus we branch to box 8 to see if the kth character is a slash, indicating the end of the current text being processed. If it is a slash, a branch is taken to in-connector 6 where the summary statistics are calculated and output in boxes 20 and 21. Then a branch is made to in-connector 1, where the variables are initialized for the next text to be processed. When the first character of the next sentence is not a slash, however, processing of the kth character continues in box 9.

When the comparison in box 11 indicates that the kth character is not a period, a branch is made to in-connector 4. In the three comparisons in boxes 14, 15, and 16, we test to see if the kth character is a comma, semicolon, or a hyphen. If it is not any one of these three symbols, it must be a character to be counted. Thus, in box 17 nc is incremented by 1. After executing the step in box 17 or finding that the kth character is a comma, semicolon, or hyphen, the character pointer *k* is incremented by 1 in box 18 so that the next character in *line* can be processed. In box 19 we have a comparison to determine whether the next character is on the current line or the following line. As long as *k* has a value less than or equal to 80, the next character to be processed is on the current line. Otherwise, it is on the next line.

The approach taken in this algorithm should now be clear. We first check the *k*th character to see if it is one of several key characters. That is, we check a character to see if it is a blank, a period, a comma, a semicolon, or a hyphen. If it is none of these, the symbol is assumed to be a valid character and is counted as such. When a character is a blank, this signals the end of a word. A period indicates the end of a word and a sentence. In the special case of a period, we also check the third character after the period to learn if it is a slash. This is done since a slash indicates the end of a text. We check for a character that is a comma, semicolon, or hyphen because these characters are to be ignored.

In addition, notice that no provision is made in the algorithm for counting such things as paragraphs or chapters. Many other types of analysis could have been performed on the structure of the text.

PROBLEMS

1. Use the following as an input data stream to develop a trace table for the algorithm flowchart of Fig. 7.2:

'COMPUTER_SCIENCE_IS_A_VERY_
DIFFICULT_BUT_INTERESTING_SUBJECT.__
IT_IS_VERY_SIMILA ','R_TO_MATHEMATICS_
IN_SOME_RESPECTS,_BUT_DISSIMILAR_
IN_OTHERS.__/_____','
THIS_IS_A_SHORT_TEXT.__IT_HAS_SHORT_
SENTENCES_CONSISTING_OF_RATHER_
SHORT_WORDS._',' _/_____

_____
_____ '

For the following problems, develop: (1) a descriptive flowchart, (2) an algorithm flowchart, and (3) a trace table (develop your own input data stream for each problem).

2. Develop an algorithm that: (1) inputs a name consisting of a first name, a middle name or initial, and a last name, in that order; (2) forms a string consisting of the last name followed by the first and middle initials, each followed by a period; and (3) outputs both the input and edited names. Assume that: (1) input names appear left-justified in the input stream, (2) one blank separates the first and middle names and one blank separates the middle and last names, and (3) the last name is immediately followed by a comma.

3. Develop an algorithm similar to the one described in Problem 2. Assume that the middle name or initial may or may not appear and that there may be more than one middle name or initial. Each name will be separated from its successor by one blank and the last name is again followed by a comma. Output for each name should consist of the input name followed by an edited name that consists of last name followed by an initial and a period for the first and each middle name.

4. Develop an algorithm similar to the one of Fig. 7.2 to count the number of times each of the vowels A, E, I, O, and U occur. Then output the total number of times each vowel appears in the text and

225

the average number of times each vowel appears in a sentence and in a word.

5. Develop an algorithm similar to the one in Fig. 7.2 for a single text that is divided into paragraphs and chapters. Each paragraph is to be terminated by a period-blank-blank-slash sequence and each chapter by a period-blank-blank-asterisk sequence. The text will be terminated by the end-of-file indicator. The following are to be computed and printed after each respective unit:

a. For each paragraph: (1) the number of sentences, (2) the average number of words per sentence, and (3) the average number of symbols per word.

b. For each chapter: (1) the number of paragraphs, (2) the average number of sentences per paragraph, (3) the average number of words per sentence, and (4) the average number of symbols per word.

c. For the entire book: (1) the number of chapters, (2) the average number of paragraphs per chapter, (3) the average number of sentences per paragraph, and (4) the average number of words per sentence.

6. Develop an algorithm similar to the one of Fig. 7.2 in which the occurrences of the words ' AND ', ' BUT ', and ' OR ' are counted. Output should consist of the number of occurrences of each of these words in each text and the average number of times any of these words appears in a sentence.

7. An interesting problem involves the justification of type lines. Let us assume that words are not to be divided between lines and that every line is to be both left- and right-justified. Any extra blanks required to achieve left- and right-justification should be distributed evenly between the words of a line. Assume that there are no new paragraphs, pagination is not a concern, and that the number of character positions per line is an input value that does not exceed 80. Develop an algorithm to perform type-line justification as described above. Assume the existence of an input data stream from which one character at a time is to be input and processed.

8. Modify the assumption of Problem 7 to permit new paragraphs and require the formation of new pages. The occurrence of a new paragraph is indicated by the appearance of an asterisk immediately following any period. New paragraphs should be indented five spaces. Each page should consist of twenty lines, pages should be separated by a blank line, and the first line of each page should give the page number left-justified. Develop an algorithm for this problem.

7.2   THE USE OF STATISTICS TO SUMMARIZE DATA

The first step in social science research usually involves the collection of data concerning the various attributes of the item being studied. This results in the accumulation of a large number of data values that individually do not provide the researcher with much information about the item under study. The reason is that it is difficult for a person to comprehend the meaning of a large mass of data. For example, it is very difficult for a sociologist to draw any conclusion about the educational level of the inmate population of the state prison given the number of years of formal schooling completed by each of the 1,000 inmates at the prison. This is because all that the sociologist sees is 1,000 numbers—more values than an individual can easily comprehend. Thus a need exists to have a means of summarizing collections of raw data, such as the number of years of schooling of prison inmates.

In this section we will examine two basic methods for summarizing raw data. The first of these methods involves grouping the data together into classes and then counting the number of values that falls into each class. Such statistical summaries are called *frequency distributions*. Since the number of classes chosen for a frequency distribution is usually rather small, the researcher is better able to deal with ten or fifteen summary numbers than with the large mass of raw data.

frequency distributions

The second method that we will explore involves computing *summary statistical measures* which are descriptive of the collection of values being studied. Among the statistical measures computed is the *average* of the raw data, which will hopefully be a typical value. Values such as averages are called *measures of central tendency*. Also computed are statistical measures that tell the extent to which the raw data values are spread out. These values are called *measures of dispersion*.

summary statistical measures

7.2.1   The Frequency-Distribution Problem

Several decisions need to be made when organizing raw data values into a frequency distribution. First, we must decide how many groups or classes we want the frequency distribution to have. If there are too many classes, we still have the problem of drawing any meaningful conclusions about the data because the volume of numbers is difficult to comprehend. On the other hand, the use of too few classes will hide the information we are seeking by making the classes so broad as to be almost meaningless. Thus the number of classes used must be chosen carefully. As a second consideration, we must decide the way in which we want to represent the distribution. One way is to give *raw frequencies*, which provide a count of the number of raw data values that fall into each class of the frequency distribution. Another alternative is to compute *relative frequencies*, which give the proportion of the total frequencies that fall into each class.

problem definition and analysis

Let us now design an algorithm that inputs raw data values and constructs a frequency distribution for these values. The algorithm will be designed so that any number of data sets can be input one at a time and frequency distributions developed for each. In addition, the input data values will be assumed to be less in magnitude than 10^{14}. This will permit us to place a value greater than or equal to 10^{14} after the last value in each data set except the last to indicate the end of that data set. The last data set will be terminated by following it with a value greater than or equal to 10^{15}. Each class in the frequency distribution generated by our algorithm will be assumed to be of the same length. For each class, our algorithm will compute both the frequency and the relative frequency with which a raw data value falls within that class.

RAW DATA ON NUMBER OF YEARS OF SCHOOLING
COMPLETED BY 25 PRISON INMATES

6.8	12.3	8.9	14.6	7.5
10.2	9.0	11.4	8.5	8.0
16.0	11.4	15.5	7.8	11.0
12.0	7.2	10.4	8.5	10.6
9.9	17.5	14.2	9.4	13.5

Figure 7.3. Raw Data on the Number of Years of Schooling Completed by 25 Prison Inmates

FREQUENCY DISTRIBUTION

CLASS	CLASS BOUNDARIES	FREQ.	REL. FREQ.
1	0.6800E 01 UP TO 0.8583E 01	7	0.28
2	0.8583E 01 UP TO 0.1037E 02	5	0.20
3	0.1037E 02 UP TO 0.1215E 02	6	0.24
4	0.1215E 02 UP TO 0.1393E 02	2	0.08
5	0.1393E 02 UP TO 0.1572E 02	3	0.12
6	0.1572E 02 UP TO 0.1750E 02	2	0.08

Figure 7.4. Frequency Distribution for the Raw Data of Fig. 7.3*

As an example, the raw data values in Fig. 7.3 give the number of years of schooling completed by twenty-five inmates on a prison farm. The output that appears in Fig. 7.4 provides the frequency distribution which our algorithm generated for these raw data values.

descriptive and algorithm flowcharts

The descriptive flowchart for this problem is given in Fig. 7.5, while the algorithm flowchart appears in Fig. 7.6. In box 2 the counter n, which is used to count the number of data values in a data set, is initialized at 1. The variable Mx is used to hold the maximum value found in the data set. In box 2 Mx is initialized with a value of -10^{14}, since this value is less than any legitimate data value permitted. This forces the value of x(1) to be assigned to Mx when the first step in box 5 is first executed for each data set. Similarly, initializing the minimum location Mn with 10^{14} forces the value of x(1) to be assigned to Mn when the second step in box 5 is first executed for a data set.

In boxes 3, 4, and 5 we have a loop in which a raw data value is:

---

* The class boundaries are given using computer floating-point constants. These are simply constants in which the two-digit number to the right of the letter E represents a scale factor that tells the true location of the decimal point in the constant to the left of the E. For example, 0.6800E 01 is actually 6.8. Similarly, 0.1215E 02 is really 12.15.

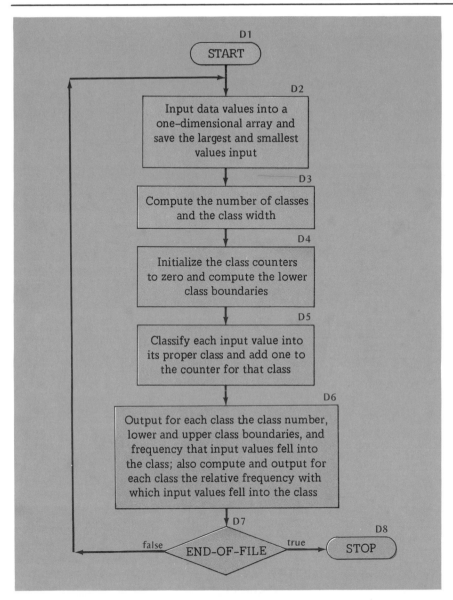

Figure 7.5. Descriptive Flowchart for the Frequency–Distribution Problem

Figure 7.6. Algorithm Flowchart for the Frequency–Distribution Problem (pages 230 and 231)

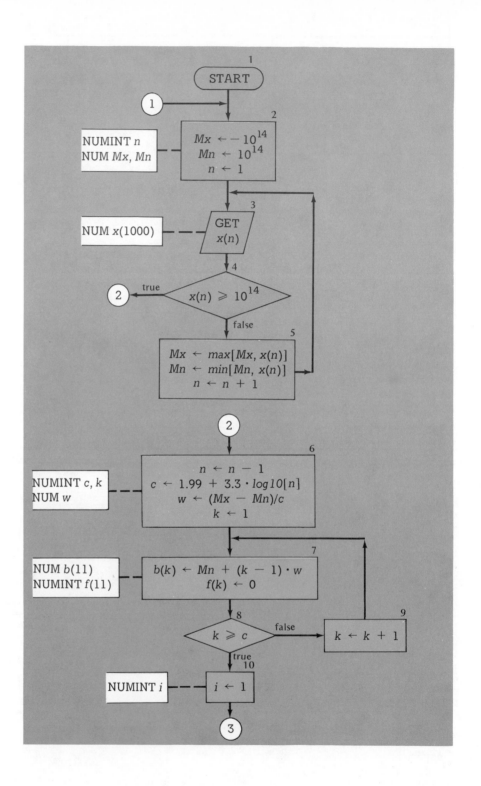

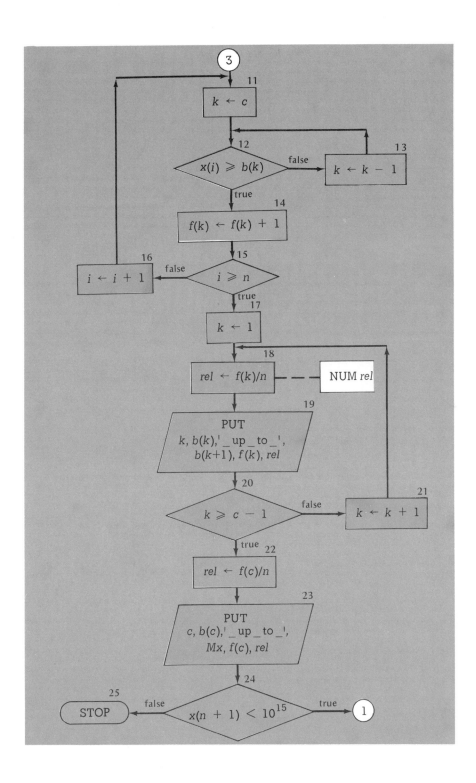

(1) input, (2) counted, and (3) checked to see if it is the maximum or minimum from among the data set values input thus far. Notice that each data value is placed into a one-dimensional array rather than immediately being placed into one of the classes of the frequency distribution. The reason for this approach is that we cannot determine the boundaries or even the lengths of the various classes until the range of the data has been learned. That is, we cannot determine the class boundaries until we know which are the largest and smallest values in the data set. In addition, we cannot decide upon the number of classes to use in the frequency distribution until the number of raw data values in the data set has been determined. Notice the use in box 5 of the functional operators *max* and *min*. The functional operator *max* returns the larger value from among its pair of arguments, while *min* returns the smaller of its two argument values.

The first step in box 6 reduces the counter n by 1 since n includes a count of the sentinel value (the sentinel value is the trailer record value that is greater than or equal to 10^{14}). The second statement in box 6 uses a statistical formula known as Sturges' rule to compute c, the number of classes to be used in developing the frequency distribution. Sturges' rule is actually expressed by the formula $1 + 3.3 \cdot \log_{10} n$, and when used the number obtained is rounded up to the next highest integer. Adding 0.99 to the formula of Sturges' rule and truncating the answer (recall that assigning a value to an integer-valued variable causes the value to be truncated) produces essentially the same result. In the third statement in box 6, the width w of each class is computed by dividing the difference between the largest and smallest raw data values by c. The last step in box 6 initializes the loop counter k for the loop of boxes 7, 8, and 9.

The loop consisting of boxes 7, 8, and 9 is designed to compute the lower class boundaries for each class of the frequency distribution. In addition, the counters for the frequencies $f(k)$ for each class are initialized at zero in this loop. The first step in box 7 is used to compute the lower class boundaries $b(k)$. This is accomplished by simply adding the appropriate multiple of the class width to the value of Mn. Notice that the maximum number of classes is 11 since n must be less than 1000 (using Sturges' rule for $n = 1000$, we have $1 + 3.3 \cdot \log_{10} 1000 = 10.9$, thus giving 11 classes).

Boxes 10 through 16 contain an outer loop that is used to classify the raw data values into their respective classes. An inner loop consisting of boxes 11 through 13 is used to determine into which class a particular data value falls. The statement in box 10 initializes the outer loop counter i. Box 11 contains the initialization step for the loop variable k of the inner loop. In box 12 we determine whether the ith data value is greater than or equal to the lower boundary of the kth class. Since k is initialized at c and is decreased by 1 for each iteration of the inner loop, we are determining successively whether it is in the cth class, the $(c - 1)$th class, and so forth down to the first class. Notice that we terminate execution of the inner loop as soon as we determine that our data value is greater than or equal to the lower class boundary of the kth class. Thus the loop variable k does not determine the number of times the inner loop is executed. Rather, this is determined by the lower class boundaries of the respective classes together with the data value. After the class into which a value of $x(i)$ falls has been determined in box 12, the frequency counter $f(k)$ for the kth class is incremented by 1 in box 14. Boxes 15 and 16 contain the outer loop test-for-loop-termination and loop-incrementation steps, respectively.

In boxes 17 through 21 we have a loop for outputting the values for the first $(c - 1)$ classes of the frequency distribution. Then in boxes 22 and 23 we have two steps that output the values for the last class of the distribution. This had to be a separate step because we are only storing the lower class boundaries of the respective classes. Notice in box 19 that we are using the lower class boundary of the $(k + 1)$th class as the upper class boundary of the kth class. In addition, notice that the relative frequencies are computed in the statements of boxes 18 and 22 by taking the ratio of the raw frequencies $f(k)$ to the total number of values n. This approach to computing relative frequencies requires fewer steps than would have been needed had they been computed in the loop of boxes 10 through 16. Finally, in box 24 we test to see if the sentinel value of the most recent data set processed is less than 10^{15}. If it is, then another data set remains to be processed, causing us to branch back to in-connector 1. Otherwise, we end execution of the algorithm with the step in box 25.

Several observations need to be made about this algorithm. First, when data values cluster together in certain portions of the range of the data values, equal class widths may not be desirable. Second, in some situations the researcher may have good reasons for choosing certain class boundaries or a number of classes different from that produced by Sturges' rule. Our algorithm is not designed to handle these situations. In addition, our algorithm is designed to handle up to 1,000 data values per set. This can be easily altered by increasing the declared lengths of the arrays. However, the main memory capacity of a computer is limited and cannot be exceeded. Thus there is an upper limit to the number of data values that can be processed by this algorithm. In addition, since all data values must have been examined before the class boundaries can be set, we must input all of the data values before classifying the data. An alternative here might be to output these values to some auxiliary memory medium as they are input. Finally, the algorithm is designed to handle only numeric information. For it to be able to process other types of information would require major revision.

more problem analysis

7.2.2   The Summary-Statistical-Measures Problem

problem definition and analysis

In this section we will examine an algorithm that computes summary statistical measures from raw data. The two most widely used types of summary measures are: (1) measures of central tendency, and (2) measures of dispersion. Measures of central tendency provide a single value from a data set which is interpreted as being a typical value from that set. The most widely used measure of central tendency is the *mean* or average of a set of data. A measure of dispersion, on the other hand, tells how spread out the raw data values are. There are a number of measures of dispersion available. The most widely used of these, however, is the *standard deviation.*

There are actually a number of different types of means. The most widely used of these is the *arithmetic mean,* which is computed by: (1) simply adding up all of the data values in a set, and (2) dividing that sum by *n,* the number of data values in the set. That is, for *n* data values, the arithmetic mean is formed as

$$M = \frac{\Sigma x}{n} \tag{7.1}$$

where $\Sigma x = x_1 + x_2 + \cdots + x_n$. Therefore, the symbol Σ simply means to sum or add together all of the values in a set. The *standard deviation* is an average which measures the dispersion of the individual data values about the arithmetic mean. It is computed as the square root of the arithmetic mean of the squared differences of each value from the arithmetic mean of the data values. If we denote the arithmetic mean given in Eq. (7.1) as *M,* the standard deviation is computed as

$$std = \sqrt{\Sigma(x - M)^2/n} \tag{7.2}$$

where $\Sigma(x - M)^2 = (x_1 - M)^2 + (x_2 - M)^2 + \cdots + (x_n - M)^2$.

descriptive and algorithm flowcharts

Let us develop an algorithm that uses Eqs. (7.1) and (7.2) to compute the arithmetic mean and standard deviation of the values of a data set. The descriptive flowchart for this problem appears in Fig. 7.7; the algorithm flowchart is given in Fig. 7.8. The first step in box 2 sets to a value of zero the summing variable sx, which is used in computing the mean. The second step in that box initializes the loop counter n to a value of 1. In the loop consisting of boxes 3, 4, 6, and 7, the data values are input, tested, output, summed, and counted. Since the individual data values are needed in computing the standard deviation, they are stored in a one-dimensional array as they are input in box 3. The end of a data set is being

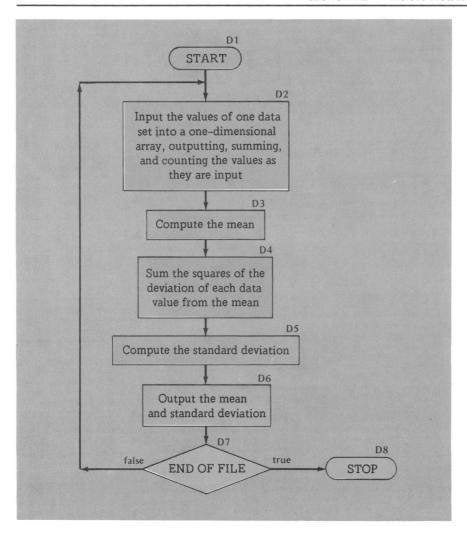

Figure 7.7.   Descriptive Flowchart for the Mean and Standard-Deviation Problem

tested for by the step in box 4. This algorithm is similar to the frequency distribution algorithm in that all data sets except the last are followed by a sentinel value greater than or equal to 10^{14}. The last data set, however, is ended by including a sentinel value greater than or equal to 10^{15}. In box 7 a data value is added to a running sum sx and the counter n is incremented by 1.

   After all of the values of a data set have been input, output, summed, and counted, we transfer control to box 5. The first step in that box reduces

235

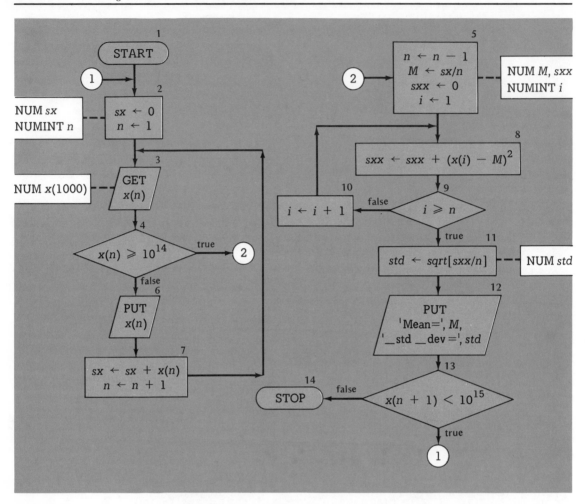

Figure 7.8. Algorithm Flowchart for the Mean and Standard-Deviation Problem

n by 1 since the nth value input was the sentinel value. The arithmetic mean M is then computed and the summing location sxx set to zero. The reason for setting sxx to zero is so that it can be used to sum the squared deviations from the mean in the second loop. The final statement in box 5 initializes the loop counter i for the second loop. The loop in boxes 8 through 10 simply sums the squared deviations from the mean. In box 11 the standard deviation is computed using the formula of Eq. (7.2). The output in box 12 includes the mean and standard deviation and identifying labels for each. Finally, in box 13 we determine whether or not any data sets remain to be processed.

Several comments should be made about this algorithm and about the problem of computing the arithmetic mean and standard deviation from a set of data. First, raw data are often grouped into frequency distributions before computing the mean and standard deviation when manual methods are being used. Since a portion of the original information is lost when summarizing data in a frequency distribution, this is to be discouraged when computing these measures. In fact, the main historical reason for grouping data when computing the mean and standard deviation was to reduce the amount of computation. With a computer, this is no longer a consideration. Second, when computing the standard deviation manually, a "short-cut formula" is usually used. This short-cut formula, however, causes appreciably greater computational error than does Eq. (7.2). Therefore, its use is to be discouraged. Finally, the algorithm developed in Fig. 7.8 requires that all of the data values be stored internally. Since computer memory capacity is limited, this may not be possible with some of the larger data sets.

more problem analysis

PROBLEMS

9. Use the following input data stream to develop a trace table for the algorithm flowchart of Fig. 7.6:

5, 1, 4, 7, 3, 2, 8, 6, 9, 5, 10^{14}, 10, 15, 20, 25, 10, 13, 14, 16, 18, 4, 10^{15}

10. Use the input data stream given in Problem 9 to develop a trace table for the algorithm flowchart of Fig. 7.8.

For the following problems, develop: (1) a descriptive flowchart, (2) an algorithm flowchart, and (3) a trace table (develop your own input data stream for each problem).

11. Modify the algorithm of Fig. 7.6 so that up to 100,000 data values per data set can be processed by the algorithm.

12. Develop an algorithm similar to the one in Fig. 7.6 for constructing a frequency and relative frequency distribution. Assume that the class boundaries are to be input rather than generated by the algorithm.

13. Develop an algorithm that is designed to develop a frequency and relative frequency distribution for alphabetic data. Assume that all data consist of uppercase alphabetic characters and that class boundaries are to be input. The algorithm should construct the classes using regular alphabetical order.

14. When data values are obtained in what is essentially random order, we can usually expect the distribution of a sample of these values to be similar to the distribution of all of the values. With this in mind, design an algorithm that inputs the first 200 values of a data set and uses these to construct the boundaries of the frequency distribution. Assume that an approximation to the number of data values is known before inputting a data set and is used to determine the number of classes. All data values should be used in constructing the frequency and relative frequency distribution except for those which fall outside of the class boundaries constructed using the first 200 values. These data values should be discarded, with a count being kept of the number of values not used.

15. Develop an algorithm for computing the arithmetic mean and standard deviation of a set of data values assuming that all of the data values cannot be stored in memory at one time. The formula for computing the standard deviation is

$$std = \sqrt{\Sigma x^2/n - M^2}$$

where M is the arithmetic mean and $\Sigma x^2 = x_1^2 + x_2^2 + \cdots + x_n^2$. All other assumptions used in developing the algorithm of Fig. 7.8 are still valid.

16. The median of a set of data values that are in nondecreasing order is defined to be the

$$[(n + 1)/2]\text{th}$$

value in the set. When the number of values, n, is odd, this value is unique. However, when n is even, the two middle values are often averaged in computing the median. The range of a set of values is defined to be the difference between the largest and smallest value in the set. Develop an algorithm that inputs sets of values one at a time and finds and outputs the median and range of those values. Assume that there are up to 1,000 values in a data set and that all of these values are less than 10^{14} in magnitude.

17. Two measures of central tendency that are sometimes used are the geometric mean (GM) and the harmonic mean (HM). They are defined as

$$GM = \sqrt[n]{x_1 \cdot x_2 \cdot x_3 \cdot \ldots \cdot x_n}$$
$$HM = n/\Sigma(1/x)$$

where $\Sigma(1/x) = 1/x_1 + 1/x_2 + \cdots + 1/x_n$. Develop an algorithm that can input an unlimited number of data values in each data set and com-

pute their arithmetic, geometric, and harmonic means. Use the sentinel values of Fig. 7.8 to indicate the end of each data set.

18. Two measures of dispersion that are sometimes used are the root mean square (RMS) and the mean deviation (MD). They are defined as

$$RMS = \sqrt{\Sigma x^2/n}$$
$$MD = \Sigma|x - M|/n$$

where $\Sigma|x - M| = |x_1 - M| + |x_2 - M| + \cdots + |x_n - M|$. Develop an algorithm that can input, one at a time, data sets consisting of up to 1,000 values and compute the root mean square, mean deviation, and standard deviation for each data set.

19. The skewness, or tendency of data values to pile up more at one end of a distribution than at the other end or the middle, can be measured by computing

$$sk = \frac{\Sigma(x - M)^3}{n \cdot (std)^3}$$

where $\Sigma(x - M)^3 = (x_1 - M)^3 + (x_2 - M)^3 + \cdots + (x_n - M)^3$ and std is the standard deviation. Develop an algorithm for computing the arithmetic mean, standard deviation, and index of the skewness sk of a set of values. Use the sentinel values of Fig. 7.8 and assume that each data set contains up to 1,000 values.

7.3   BIVARIATE RELATIONSHIPS AND THE PREDICTION PROBLEM

**problem definition
and analysis**

All of the problems in the previous section involve data that are associated with one variable. Such problems are said to be *univariate*. For example, the data used in the examples of Figs. 7.3 and 7.4 involved the number of years of schooling of prison inmates. In many problem situations in the social sciences, however, problems involve data associated with two or more variables. When there are only two variables involved, the problem is said to be *bivariate*. The nature of bivariate problems is such that they usually involve a study of the relationship between the two variables involved. In this section we will study the problem of fitting a straight line to bivariate data.

Suppose that an economist has the problem of predicting the amount of inflation that will result from allowing the money supply to grow at various rates.   Furthermore, assume that the economist has historical data that he can study to determine the relationship between these two variables.*   In a problem such as this, we would probably fit a regression equation of the form

$$y = a + b{\cdot}x \qquad (7.3)$$

to our data.   Then we could predict the amount of inflation by simply evaluating our regression equation for a given growth rate in the money supply.   The points on the graph in Fig. 7.9 indicate what such historical

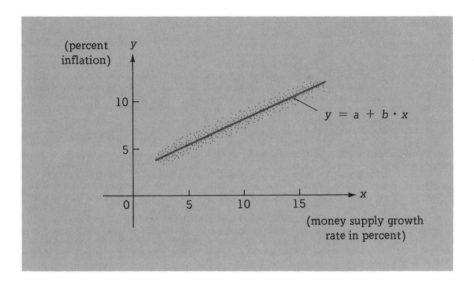

Figure 7.9.   Data Points and a Linear Regression Line

data might look like represented graphically.   The regression equation of Eq. (7.3) also appears in this graph.   For example, suppose that we denote the percentage rate of inflation as the variable y and the percentage growth in the money supply as the variable x.   Using the equations

$$b = \frac{\Sigma (x - M_x)(y - M_y)}{\Sigma (x - M_x)^2} \qquad (7.4)$$

and

$$a = M_y - b \cdot M_x \qquad (7.5)$$

---

* We are making some simplifying assumptions in this example.   For example, we are ignoring the fact that there would probably be a delay before the change in the money supply affects the amount of inflation.

where

$$\Sigma(x - M_x)(y - M_y) = (x_1 - M_x)(y_1 - M_y) + (x_2 - M_x)(y_2 - M_y)$$
$$+ \cdots + (x_n - M_x)(y_n - M_y)$$

and

$$\Sigma(x - M_x)^2 = (x_1 - M_x)^2 + (x_2 - M_x)^2 + \cdots + (x_n - M_x)^2$$

we can compute values for the regression coefficients a and b. In these two formulas, M_x and M_y are the arithmetic means of the x and y data values, respectively. These formulas give coefficients for an equation that provides what is known as a *least-squares fit*. The reason it is called a least-squares fit is that the sum of the squared deviations of the data points from the resulting equation is less than it would be for any other equation that could be constructed.

descriptive and algorithm flowcharts   A descriptive flowchart and an algorithm flowchart for computing these least-squares regression coefficients appear in Figs. 7.10 and 7.11, respectively. In designing this algorithm we assume that there are not more than 999 pairs of values in a data set. In box 2 the variables sx and sy, which are used for summing the x values and y values, respectively, and the counter n are initialized. The loop consisting of boxes 3, 4, 6, and 7 is designed to input, output, sum, and count the data values and check for the end of a data set. The step in box 3 is designed to input the nth pair of values, and box 4 checks for a sentinel value indicating the end of a data set. Notice that a pair of values must be input when inputting a sentinel x value even though the y value of the pair is never used. In box 6 the nth pair of data values is output. Box 7 contains two steps that sum the values of x and y and a third statement that increments the counter n. When a value of x is found that is greater than or equal to 10^{14}, a branch is taken to box 5. The first step in box 5 reduces the count of data pairs by 1 since the pair of values containing the sentinel is not a valid data pair. The next two steps calculate the arithmetic means Mx and My of the values of x and y, respectively. The fourth and fifth steps in box 5 then initialize the summing locations sxy and sxx. These two variables are used to compute the sums for the numerator and denominator of Eq. (7.4).

The last step in box 5 initializes a counter i which is used in the loop consisting of boxes 8, 9, and 10. In box 8 the first step is used to form the sum of the products of the deviations of the variables x and y from their respective means. This sum is the numerator used in the formula of Eq. (7.4). The second step in box 8 is used to form the sum of the squared deviations of the x values from their mean. The steps for loop termination and modification are in boxes 9 and 10, respectively. In box 11 the coefficients a and b of the regression equation are computed.

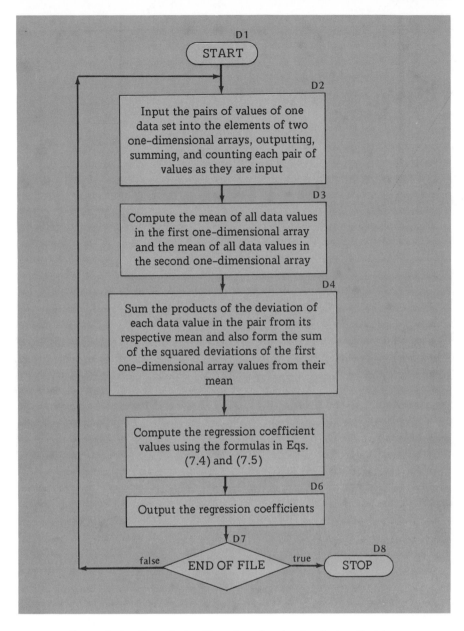

Figure 7.10. Descriptive Flowchart for the Prediction Problem

The equation is output in box 12. The step in box 13 is used to determine whether the sentinel value for the current data set is less than 10^{15}. If it is less than 10^{15}, at least one more data set remains to be processed, thus causing a branch to in-connector 1. Otherwise, all data sets have been processed and algorithm execution is terminated in box 14.

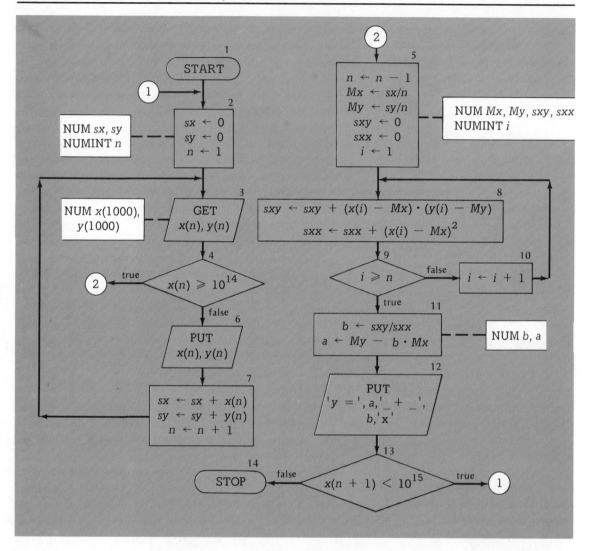

Figure 7.11. Algorithm Flowchart for the Prediction Problem

more problem analysis

Notice that only data sets with less than 1,000 pairs of values can be processed by this algorithm. Should data sets with 1,000 or more values need to be processed, either the amount of storage allocated to the arrays x and y would need to be increased or a different algorithm designed. An alternative method of computing the value of b uses the formula

$$b = \frac{\Sigma\, xy/n - M_x{\cdot}M_y}{\Sigma\, x^2/n - M_x^2} \qquad (7.6)$$

where
$$\Sigma xy = x_1 \cdot y_1 + x_2 \cdot y_2 + \cdots + x_n \cdot y_n$$

and
$$\Sigma x^2 = x_1^2 + x_2^2 + \cdots + x_n^2$$

The method using the formula of Eq. (7.4) is preferred, however, since it results in less computational error than does the formula of Eq. (7.6).

PROBLEMS

20. Use the following input data stream to develop a trace table for the algorithm of Fig. 7.11:

1, 2, 3, 3, 2, 4, 10^{14}, 0, 0, 1, 4, -3, 2, -7, 5, 0, 10^{15}, 0

For the following problems, develop: (1) a descriptive flowchart, (2) an algorithm flowchart, and (3) a trace table (develop your own input data stream for each problem).

21. Use Eqs. (7.5) and (7.6) to develop an algorithm flowchart for computing the coefficients a and b of a linear regression equation. That is, assume that all of the pairs of data values cannot be stored in main memory at one time.

22. The correlation coefficient r can be used to measure the degree of linear correlation between two sets of variables x and y. The formula for calculating r is:

$$r = \frac{n \cdot \Sigma xy - \Sigma x \cdot \Sigma y}{\sqrt{[n \cdot \Sigma x^2 - (\Sigma x)^2] \cdot [n \cdot \Sigma y^2 - (\Sigma y)^2]}}$$

where: (1) n is the number of data pairs; (2) the Σxy, Σx, Σy, Σx^2, and Σy^2 are defined above; and (3) the value of r always satisfies $-1 \le r \le 1$. Develop an algorithm for computing the correlation coefficient; assume that the number of data values in a data set is not known prior to processing. That is, you should utilize the sentinel values used in the algorithm of Fig. 7.11 to signal the end of a data set.

23. An alternative formula for computing the correlation coefficient of Problem 22 is:

$$r = \frac{\Sigma (x - M_x)(y - M_y)}{\sqrt{\Sigma (x - M_x)^2} \sqrt{\Sigma (y - M_y)^2}}$$

where $\Sigma (x - M_x)(y - M_y)$, $\Sigma (x - M_x)^2$, and $\Sigma (y - M_y)^2$ are defined above. Develop an algorithm that uses this formula; assume that there is only enough room in main memory to store up to 1,000 pairs of data values.

24. Assume that we have n pairs of values (n unknown but less than 1,000) for which we wish to develop a bivariate frequency distribution. The number of classes into which each of the variables should be divided should be determined by truncating the result of using the formula

$$c = \sqrt{1.99 + 6.6 \cdot \log_{10} n}$$

Thus each pair of data values will be classified into one of c^2 classes. Develop an algorithm flowchart to input n data pairs and develop and output a frequency distribution.

25. A measure of association between bivariate data often used in the social sciences is r_s, Spearman's rank correlation coefficient. In this method, n pairs of data values are individually ranked from 1 through n. That is, all of the values of the variable x are ranked from smallest to largest using the rank values 1 through n, and the values of the y variable are ranked similarly. Then each of the differences d between the ranks of each of the paired values are calculated, giving n values of d. Next, r_s is computed by use of the formula

$$r_s = 1 - 6 \cdot \Sigma d^2 / (n^3 - n)$$

where $\Sigma d^2 = d_1^2 + d_2^2 + \cdots + d_n^2$. As with the case of r, the values of Spearman's rank correlation coefficient always satisfy $-1 \le r_s \le 1$. Develop an algorithm for computing r_s; assume that less than 1,000 pairs of data values are in each input data set.

26. A measure of association between bivariate data often used in the social sciences is r_k, Kendall's

243

rank correlation coefficient. In this method, n pairs of data values are individually ranked from 1 through n. That is, all of the values of the variable x are ranked from smallest to largest by use of the rank values 1 through n, and the values of the y variable are ranked similarly. Then the pairs of ranks are sorted such that the ranks of the x variable are in natural order (i.e., $1, 2, \ldots, n$). Next the sum S is formed using the ranks of the y variable as follows: (1) take all possible pairs of y ranks which include the first y rank, adding 1 to S whenever the first y rank is less than the other y rank in the pair

and subtracting 1 from S whenever the first y rank is greater than the second y rank; (2) repeat step (1), starting with the second y rank; and (3) repeat the process, starting with the next y rank on each scan of the list of y ranks. Once S has been formed, r_k can be computed by use of the formula

$$r_k = S/[n \cdot (n - 1)/2]$$

The values of r_k satisfy $-1 \le r_k \le 1$, but r_k is not usually equal to r_s. Develop an algorithm for computing r_k assuming that less than 1,000 pairs of data values are in each input data set.

7.4   CANNED PROGRAMS FOR THE SOCIAL SCIENCES

In the first three sections of this chapter we have examined algorithms to solve four simple problems in the social sciences. However, as we noted in Chapter 3, it is not always necessary to develop an algorithm for solving a problem that we need to solve; someone may already have developed

canned programs   one. The computer program that is an implementation of such an algorithm is popularly called a *canned program*.

In the case in which an algorithm already exists for the solution of our problem, all that we need to do is:

1. Get a copy of the algorithm and its associated documentation.
2. Be sure that the computer implementation of the algorithm was designed to run on a similar computer to ours (same series, capacity, and components).
3. Verify that the problem the algorithm is designed to solve is the same as the problem we have to solve and that the output produced satisfies our needs.
4. Prepare the data in the format and use the control cards that are assumed by the algorithm.
5. Execute the algorithm using our data to produce the desired results.

Of course, we must make the critical assumption that the source of the algorithm is reliable. Therefore, we can assume that the algorithm has been carefully tested so that it produces correct results for the class of problem that it is designed to solve. Moreover, the methods used in the algorithm to produce results will hopefully be the best ones available for solving that type of problem.

A number of canned programs have been developed that are available for most computer systems. Three of the most popular of these packages of canned programs are:

popular statistical program packages

1. The Biomedical Package (often called BMD), which was developed in the early 1960s at U.C.L.A.
2. The statistical routines that are included in the Scientific Subroutine Package, which is distributed by IBM Corporation.
3. The Statistical Package for the Social Sciences (often called SPSS), which was originally developed at Stanford University and is now used at many computer installations.

Besides these three packages, there are several packages designed for interactive usage from remote terminals. Two of the more widely used interactive packages are IMPRESS, which was developed at Dartmouth College, and APL STATPAK.

Each of the above statistical packages consists of a large number of canned programs. These canned programs provide the capability for performing many types of statistical operations of interest to social scientists. Since most of them are written in FORTRAN (the Scientific Subroutine Package is also available in PL/I), these packages can even be adapted to machines other than the ones for which they were originally designed. In addition to this portability, each of the programs in these packages is extremely well documented. Therefore, a person can learn how to use the canned programs without becoming familiar with the logic of the algorithms or the source code itself. Consequently, canned programs are generally very easy to use and thus are important tools for social scientists.

SUMMARY

1. The use of computers in the social sciences and arts has been increasing rapidly in recent years.

2. A computer can be used to analyze text for such purposes as the determination of writing style. This is accomplished by collecting statistics on selected structural properties of the text.

3. Many problems in the social sciences involve the collection and analysis of large amounts of data.

4. Most analysis of data in solving problems from the social sciences involves the use of statistical techniques.

5. One means of summarizing data involves the construction of frequency distributions.

6. Summary statistical measures, particularly those which measure central tendency and dispersion, are often used in summarizing masses of raw data.

7. Two formulas are usually available for computing many statistical measures. The one that will usually minimize computational error is the one that involves taking deviations from the mean.

8. In developing an equation for purposes of pre-

245

dicting the value of one variable given the value of a second variable, we use regression analysis.

9. A measure of the linear relationship between two variables is given by the correlation coefficient.

10. A canned program is one that has already been written by someone else to solve a particular class of problem.

11. Several libraries exist which consist of canned programs designed to solve problems in the social sciences. The three most popular libraries are the Biomedical Package (often called the BMD package), the Statistical Package for the Social Sciences (often called SPSS), and the Scientific Subroutine Package (often called SSP).

Solving Problems in Education

Education is an area that offers a great deal of opportunity for the use of computers to solve problems. In earlier chapters we have examined some of these problems and their solutions. For example, in Section 5.2 we developed an algorithm for averaging student test grades, which is a very common problem for teachers in all aspects of education. Similarly, in Chapter 6 we examined concepts of file processing, which is important in education because of the need to keep student records. Statistical problems, similar to the ones in Chapter 7, also occur in education. This is because of the need to evaluate student groups, teaching techniques, and other things that involve statistics.

Although all of the applications mentioned in the previous paragraph are important in education, they are not a part of the main purpose of education. That is, they do not directly relate to the process of teaching people things they do not already know. In this chapter we will examine two applications from the main line of education. The first application will be in the area of computer-assisted instruction, while the second relates to guidance counseling.

8.1 THE LEARNING-HOW-TO-DO-ADDITION PROBLEM

A very important application area for computers in education involves computer-assisted instruction (computer-assisted instruction is often abbreviated CAI). The essence of computer-assisted instruction is using the computer to introduce new concepts to a student and to test the student's comprehension of those concepts. Computer-assisted instruction has thus far been applied primarily to rote learning situations, that is, to teaching things that are primarily factual. For example, common applications of computer-assisted instruction have been in teaching arithmetic, remedial grammar, and certain factual aspects of history. Since computer-assisted instruction is still in its infancy, we can expect it to be used to teach more difficult subjects in the future.

When the algorithms have been carefully prepared and tested, computer-assisted instruction has proved to be a popular means of teaching from the student viewpoint. One apparent reason for this is the fascination that people have for machines (and particularly computers). Another reason is the fact that a properly developed computer-assisted instruction algorithm will cause the computer to display what seems to be an almost unlimited amount of patience.

Let us now develop a simple algorithm for the computer-assisted instruction of addition. The input and output to this algorithm will be assumed to be through an online terminal device. This is the case in all computer-assisted instruction because of the need for the computer and the student to interact with each other. The descriptive flowchart for this problem appears in Fig. 8.1. The first step is to input the student's name. This step is performed in most computer-assisted instruction algorithms for two reasons. First, the student's name is often needed so that the computer can keep a record of the student's performance during a CAI session. Second, a personal touch is added when the computer responds to the student using his or her name.

descriptive flowchart

In box D3, we have a step for inputting a number that tells the algorithm the largest terms to be used in the addition drill. The step in box D4 will cause the computer to output the terms for the addition of all number pairs from 0 up to the value input in box D3. With each number pair, the sum of the pair of values will also be output. Once the various pairs of values and their sums have been given, a test of how well the student remembers the sums is needed. This step is performed in box D5. Notice that for each number pair presented to the student, three chances are given to provide the correct answer. That is, the student may give two incorrect answers for one problem before giving the correct answer. Each time an incorrect answer is given, it is necessary to output a message to the student. For the first two incorrect answers, this message should inform the student that the response is incorrect and that another try is allowed. When the third wrong answer is given, an incorrect answer message followed by the correct answer should be output. By printing the correct answer, the student can learn the correct sum for the number pair.

Box D6 contains a step to compute the percentage of the total number of problems that were answered correctly on one of the three trys allowed for each. Note that the student is not penalized for having as many as two wrong answers for any problem. This may not be realistic in that some penalty should be imposed for incorrect answers on a first or second try. Once the percentage of correct answers has been computed, one of four possible grade messages is output. Then, in box D7 a branch is taken to the STOP box whenever a student has performed in an *excellent* manner on the addition test. When less than excellent performance is found in box D7, a test is made in box D9 to determine if addition test results were *fair* or *good*. When they were fair or good, the student is given the option of repeating the lesson and test or stopping. When the student decides to repeat the lesson and test, a branch is taken to box D3. In the case where the student does not wish to repeat the

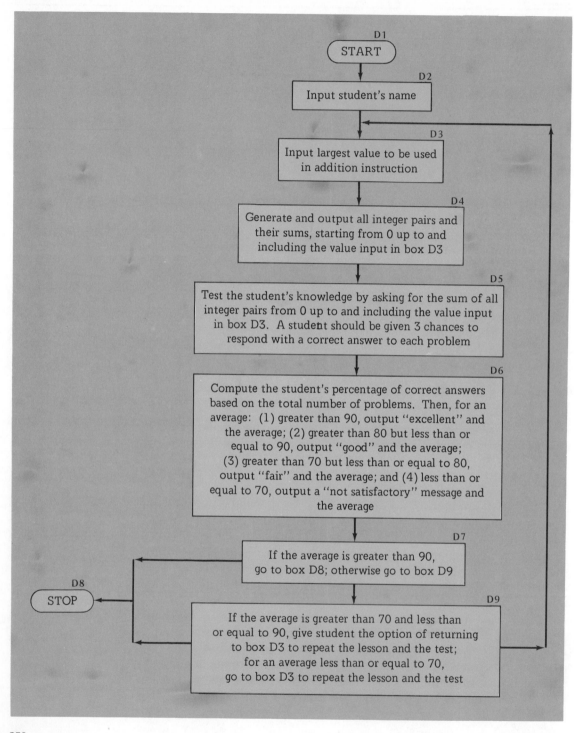

START — D1

Input student's name — D2

Input largest value to be used in addition instruction — D3

Generate and output all integer pairs and their sums, starting from 0 up to and including the value input in box D3 — D4

Test the student's knowledge by asking for the sum of all integer pairs from 0 up to and including the value input in box D3. A student should be given 3 chances to respond with a correct answer to each problem — D5

Compute the student's percentage of correct answers based on the total number of problems. Then, for an average: (1) greater than 90, output "excellent" and the average; (2) greater than 80 but less than or equal to 90, output "good" and the average; (3) greater than 70 but less than or equal to 80, output "fair" and the average; and (4) less than or equal to 70, output a "not satisfactory" message and the average — D6

If the average is greater than 90, go to box D8; otherwise go to box D9 — D7

STOP — D8

If the average is greater than 70 and less than or equal to 90, give student the option of returning to box D3 to repeat the lesson and the test; for an average less than or equal to 70, go to box D3 to repeat the lesson and the test — D9

◀ **Figure 8.1.**   Descriptive Flowchart for the Learning-How-To-Do-Addition Problem

lesson, a branch is taken to the STOP box. For the situation in which performance was unsatisfactory, repeating the lesson and test are mandatory. Thus, a branch to box D3 is taken in this case. Notice that this descriptive flowchart does not contain a test for end-of-file. The reason is that execution of the algorithm is to be repeated until the student satisfactorily passes a test on the lesson material. Of course, a student can end a terminal session at any point by simply turning the terminal off, thus causing the end of algorithm execution.

Output for a sample learning session for this problem is contained in Fig. 8.2. The algorithm flowchart appears in Fig. 8.3. Boxes 2 and 3

algorithm flowchart

```
WHAT IS YOUR NAME? TERRY WALKER
HELLO TERRY WALKER. TODAY WE ARE GOING TO STUDY ADDITION.
WHAT IS THE LARGEST TERM? 2

   0+  0=  0
   1+  0=  1
   2+  0=  2
   0+  1=  1
   1+  1=  2
   2+  1=  3
   0+  2=  2
   1+  2=  3
   2+  2=  4


NOW YOU WILL BE TESTED ON WHAT YOU HAVE JUST LEARNED.

   0+  0=?  0
   0+  1=?  0
WRONG! TRY AGAIN.  1
   0+  2=?  2
   1+  0=?  0
WRONG! TRY AGAIN.  1
   1+  1=?  2
   1+  2=?  3
   2+  0=?  1
WRONG! TRY AGAIN.  3
WRONG! TRY AGAIN.  2
   2+  1=?  2
WRONG! TRY AGAIN.  0
WRONG! TRY AGAIN.  1
THAT MAKES 3 WRONG ANSWERS! THE ANSWER IS   3
   2 +2=?  4
GOOD WORK TERRY WALKER. YOUR AVERAGE WAS 88. DO YOU WANT TO TRY AGAIN? NO
```

Figure 8.2.   Output for a Sample Learning Session

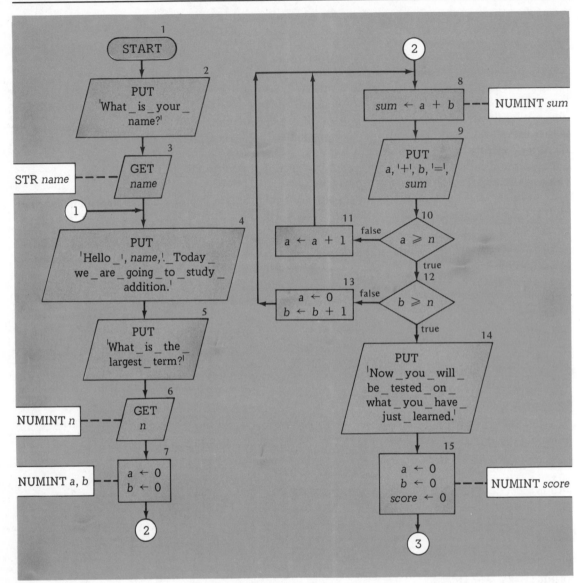

Figure 8.3. Algorithm Flowchart for the Learning-How-To-Do-Addition Problem (above, right, and page 254)

in the flowchart correspond with box D2 in the descriptive flowchart. Notice that a message was output to the student by box 2 telling what kind of input information is next required. This is a common practice in cases in which the input comes from an interactive terminal. Note that

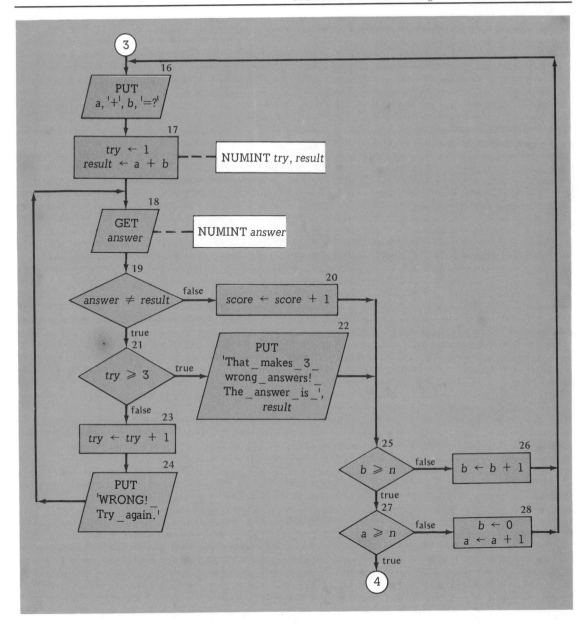

Figure 8.3, *continued*

flowchart box 5 also prompts the student with respect to the input re-
quested by execution of the step in box 6. The assignment statements
in box 7 are used to initialize the loop variables a and b. These loop
variables are used in the loop consisting of boxes 8 through 13 to output

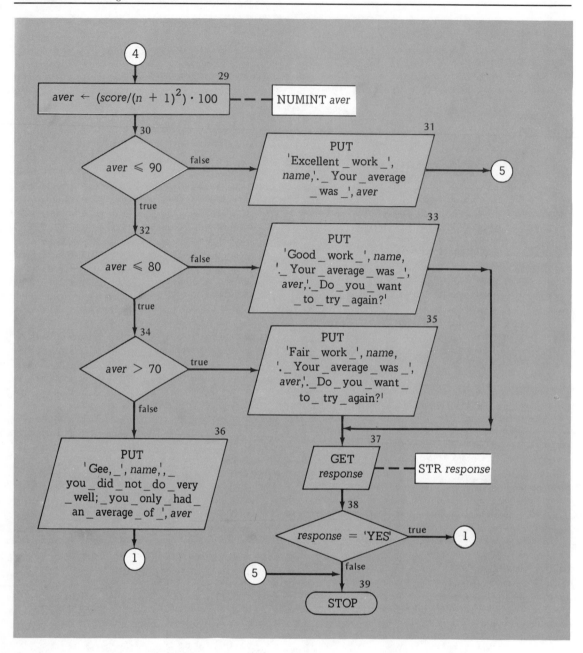

Figure 8.3,   *continued*

the number pairs and sums for the lesson. Notice that the value of *a* changes most rapidly since it is the variable of the inner loop. Thus flowchart boxes 7 through 13 correspond with descriptive flowchart box D4.

Flowchart boxes 14 through 28 are used to implement box D5 of the descriptive flowchart. Box 14 simply outputs a header message; the steps in flowchart box 15 are used to initialize the loop variables *a* and *b* and the score-keeping variable *score*. In box 16 the number pair is output for which a sum is to be input. A variable *try*, which is used to count the number of attempts at providing a correct answer, is initialized in box 17. In addition, the correct answer is computed in flowchart box 17 and assigned to the variable *result*. This avoids the necessity of recomputing the correct answer when more than one attempt is needed for the same number pair. Box 18 contains the input step for obtaining the student's attempt at a correct answer. In flowchart box 19 the student's attempt is checked to determine whether or not it is equal to the correct result. If it is equal in value, box 20 is executed to add 1 to the number of correct answers already provided by this student. However, when the attempt is in error, a test is made in box 21 to determine whether or not this represents the third attempt at a correct answer to this problem. If it does, execution of box 22 causes an appropriate message and the correct answer to be output. In the case where this was not the third incorrect attempt, the attempt counter is incremented by 1 in box 23 and the error message is output in box 24. Then a branch is taken back to flowchart box 18, where the value for another attempt is input. Whenever a correct answer is recorded in box 20 or the error message for three incorrect attempts is output in box 22, the test for termination of the inner loop is executed next. Notice that the second variable *b* varies most rapidly in the case of testing (the loop of boxes 15 through 28) while the first variable *a* varied most rapidly in the case of teaching (the loop of boxes 7 through 13). This change in the order of output of the number pairs between teaching and testing was done on purpose so that testing would be performed with a different problem order from learning.

In flowchart box 29 we have a step that computes the student's average score as a percentage value. The reason for the multiplication by 100 of the quotient of the number of correct answers and the total number of problems is that a whole percentage answer is desired. Notice that declaring *aver* to be an integer-valued variable means that any fractional part of the average will be lost. The tests in flowchart boxes 30, 32, and 34 are used to determine whether the student performed in an excellent, good, fair, or unsatisfactory way. When the performance was excellent, an appropriate message is output in box 31 and algorithm execution is halted by branching to box 39. When the test in flowchart boxes 32 or 34 determines that performance was good or fair, the appropriate message is output by either box 33 or 35. Then a response is input in box 37 to the question of whether or not the lesson and test are to be repeated. When they are to be repeated, a branch is taken to in-connector 1, where the output of the lesson begins anew. Otherwise, algorithm execution is stopped by the step in box 39. When the student's average is determined in box 34 not to be above 70, an appropriate message is output in box 36 and a branch taken to in-connector 1 to repeat the lesson and test. Notice that the only way to halt algorithm execution is by scoring above 70 on the test over the material.

canned programs for CAI

Before leaving the topic of computer-assisted instruction, we should observe that there is a rapidly growing interest in this important application area. Furthermore, this trend should be promoted with the appearance of problem-oriented languages (such as IBM's *Coursewriter*) that make the development of teaching packages a relatively easy task. In addition, some educational institutions and groups have developed (or are in the process of developing) computer-assisted instruction packages for a number of common learning areas. Among these are remedial mathematics and remedial English grammar for incoming college students with knowledge deficiencies in those areas. Thus, the future of computer-assisted instruction appears to be very promising even through CAI is still in its infancy.

8.2   THE CAREER-CHOICE PROBLEM

problem definition and analysis

An important function in any educational institution is that of guidance counseling. One important aspect of guidance counseling is that relating to assisting students in choosing a career. In doing career counseling at the high school level, one obvious question is whether or not a student is college bound. Criteria usually used for determining this are:

1. Test score on native intelligence, usually called IQ tests.
2. Overall high school grade average.
3. Score on scholastic achievement tests, such as the SAT (Scholastic Aptitude Test) or the ACT (American College Testing Program) tests.

When it has been determined that a student is likely to succeed in college, the student's interest can be measured to determine a major field of study. In addition, both college-bound and non-college-bound students need to have guidance on the choice of a career field. The two surveys most often used to project career fields and majors in which a person would most likely be successful are the Kuder Occupational Interest Survey and the Strong Vocational Interest Blank. Both of these surveys contain a number of questions that have been correlated with the responses of people in various career fields and majors who are happy with their choices. Therefore, a student's responses to these questions can be used to predict how well a person might enjoy a particular occupation or major. The major fields and occupations used on the Kuder test are shown in Figs. 8.4 and 8.5, respectively. Note that they are classified by sex.

In this section we will develop an algorithm for the problem of

Figure 8.4.   Table of College Majors

Women		Men	
Code	Major	Code	Major
1	Art and art education	1	Agriculture
2	Biological sciences	2	Animal husbandry
3	Business education and commerce	3	Architecture
4	Drama	4	Art and art education
5	Elementary education	5	Biological sciences
6	English	6	Business accounting and finance
7	Foreign languages	7	Business and marketing
8	General social sciences	8	Business management
9	Health professions	9	Economics
10	History	10	Elementary education
11	Home economics education	11	Engineering, chemical
12	Mathematics	12	Engineering, civil
13	Music and music education	13	Engineering, electrical
14	Nursing	14	Engineering, mechanical
15	Physical education	15	English
16	Political science	16	Foreign languages
17	Psychology	17	Forestry
18	Sociology	18	History
19	Teaching sister, Catholic	19	Law (graduate school)
		20	Mathematics
		21	Music and music education
		22	Physical education
		23	Physical sciences
		24	Political science and government
		25	Pre-med, pharmacology, and dentistry
		26	Psychology
		27	Sociology
		28	U.S. Air Force cadet
		29	U.S. military cadet

Figure 8.5.   Table of Occupations

Women		Men	
Code	*Occupation*	*Code*	*Occupation*
1	Accountant	1	Accountant, certified public
2	Bank clerk	2	Architect
3	Beautician	3	Automobile mechanic
4	Bookkeeper	4	Automobile salesman
5	Bookstore manager	5	Banker
6	Computer programmer	6	Bookkeeper
7	Counselor, high school	7	Bookstore manager
8	Dean of women	8	Bricklayer
9	Dental assistant	9	Building contractor
10	Department store saleswoman	10	Buyer
11	Dietitian, administrative	11	Carpenter
12	Dietitian, public school	12	Chemist
13	Florist	13	Clothier, retail
14	Home demonstration agent	14	Computer programmer
15	Home economics teacher, college	15	Counselor, high school
16	Interior decorator	16	County agricultural agent
17	Lawyer	17	Dentist
18	Librarian	18	Electrician
19	Math teacher, high school	19	Engineer, civil
20	Nurse	20	Engineer, electrical
21	Nutritionist	21	Engineer, heating/air conditioning
22	Occupational therapist	22	Engineer, industrial
23	Office clerk	23	Engineer, mechanical
24	Physical therapy	24	Engineer, mining and metal
25	Primary school teacher	25	Farmer
26	Psychologist	26	Florist
27	Psychologist, clinical	27	Forester
28	Religious education director	28	Insurance agent
29	Science teacher, high school	29	Interior decorator
30	Secretary	30	Journalist
31	Social caseworker	31	Lawyer
32	Social worker, group	32	Librarian
33	Social worker, medical	33	Machinist
34	Social worker, psychiatric	34	Mathematician
35	Social worker, school	35	Math teacher, high school
36	Stenographer	36	Meteorologist
37	X-ray technician	37	Minister
		38	Nurseryman
		39	Optometrist

Figure 8.5, *continued*

Women		Men	
Code	Occupation	Code	Occupation
		40	Osteopath
		41	Painter, house
		42	Pediatrician
		43	Personnel manager
		44	Pharmaceutical salesman
		45	Pharmacist
		46	Photographer
		47	Physical therapist
		48	Physician
		49	Plumber
		50	Plumbing contractor
		51	Podiatrist
		52	Policeman
		53	Postal clerk
		54	Printer
		55	Psychiatrist
		56	Psychologist, clinical
		57	Psychologist, counseling
		58	Psychologist, industrial
		59	Psychology professor
		60	Radio station manager
		61	Real estate agent
		62	Sales engineer, heating/air conditioning
		63	Science teacher, high school
		64	School superintendent
		65	Social caseworker
		66	Social worker, group
		67	Social worker, psychiatric
		68	Statistician
		69	Supervisor/foreman, industrial
		70	Travel agent
		71	Truck driver
		72	Television repairman
		73	University pastor
		74	Veterinarian
		75	Welder
		76	X-ray technician
		77	YMCA secretary

**descriptive
flowchart**

assisting a student in the selection of a career.   The descriptive flowchart for this problem appears in Fig. 8.6.   We will again assume that the career counseling is performed by a student sitting at an online terminal.   Thus input and output occur at the terminal in an interactive mode.   In descriptive flowchart box D2, the student's name and sex are input.   The step in box D5 is for the input of the student's IQ test score, high school grade-point average, and the five ACT test scores.   The ACT test scores input are percentiles based on all students that took the test nationwide.   The five ACT scores cover the subject areas of English, mathematics, social studies, and natural sciences, plus a composite (overall) score.   In box D6 we determine whether or not the student is properly prepared and capable of succeeding in college.   Experience has shown that high school students with an IQ of less than 110 do not usually succeed in college.   Similarly, it has been observed that to perform at a satisfactory level in college a student must have at least 2.3 as an overall academic-subject high school grade-point average.   Finally, students with an ACT test composite national percentile ranking of less than 30 generally have difficulty succeeding in college work.   Therefore, if a student fails to satisfy any of these three criteria, a branch is taken to box D9, where a career projection is made.

For college-bound students, we proceed to box D7 and output the *go to college* message.   In addition, the name of any academic area for which the student ranks below the 30th percentile should be listed.   The reason is that the student will require remedial work in those areas.   Next box D8 will be executed.   The first step in this box requires that the Kuder major test score values be input into an array.   Then the largest major score and its associated numeric major code are output.   This is followed by the output of every score (and its associated numeric major code) in which the difference between that score and the first score output is not greater than 0.06 in value.   The numeric major codes are those shown in Fig. 8.4.   The maximum difference of 0.06 between the largest score and the lowest score on majors in which a person would probably succeed has been determined by experimental results.   Thus any of the majors represented by the codes listed by box D8 would be ones in which the student shows an interest and an aptitude.

Box D9 begins with the input into an array of the Kuder occupational interest test scores for the student.   Then the largest occupational interest score and its associated numeric occupational code are output.   Following this every score (and its associated numeric occupational code) is output in which the difference between that score and the first score output is not greater than 0.06 in value.   The numeric occupational codes are those given in Fig. 8.5.   Again, every occupation represented by the codes listed by box D9 would be ones in which the student has an interest and an aptitude.   Output for a sample counseling session at a terminal appears in Fig. 8.7.

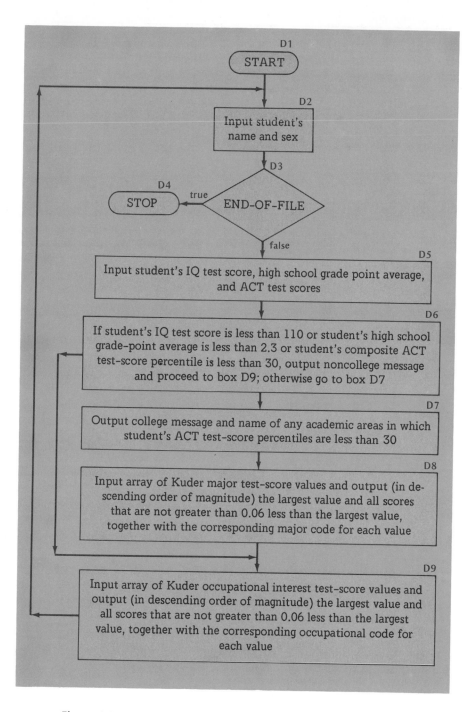

Figure 8.6. Descriptive Flowchart for the Career-Choice Problem

```
WHAT IS YOUR NAME AND SEX? TERRY WALKER,M
INPUT IQ, GPA, AND ACT SCORES: 140,3.9,93,99,29,96,95
TERRY WALKER, YOU WILL PROBABLY BE SUCCESSFUL IN COLLEGE. HOWEVER,
   YOU WILL NEED REMEDIAL WORK IN: SOCIAL STUDIES
INPUT MAJOR SCORES (IN ORDER): 0,0,0.21,0,0.18,0.22,0.27,0.49,0.47,
0,0,0,0.43,0,0,0,0,0,0,0.48,0.51,0,0,0,0.46,0,0.36,0.41,0,0
MAJOR CODE= 20 SCORE= 0.51
MAJOR CODE=  8 SCORE= 0.49
MAJOR CODE= 13 SCORE= 0.48
MAJOR CODE= 19 SCORE= 0.48
MAJOR CODE=  9 SCORE= 0.47
MAJOR CODE= 24 SCORE= 0.46
INPUT OCCUP SCORES (IN ORDER): 0.27,0.15,0,0.24,0.17,0,0,0,0.28,0,
0,0.18,0,0.48,0,0,0,0,0,0.46,0,0,0,0,0,0,0,0,0,0.44,0.45,0,0,0.48,
0.23,0,0.22,0,0,0,0,0,0.34,0,0,0.27,0,0,0,0.18,0,0,0,0,0.18,0,0.23,
0,0,0.15,0,0,0,0.21,0,0,0,0.41,0,0.19,0,0,0,0.15,0,0,0,0
OCCUPATION CODE= 14 SCORE= 0.48
OCCUPATION CODE= 34 SCORE= 0.48
OCCUPATION CODE= 20 SCORE= 0.46
OCCUPATION CODE= 31 SCORE= 0.45
OCCUPATION CODE= 30 SCORE= 0.44

WHAT IS YOUR NAME AND SEX?
```

Figure 8.7. Output for a Sample Career-Counseling Session

algorithm flowchart

The algorithm flowchart for this problem appears in Fig. 8.8. Flowchart boxes 2 through 5 correspond with descriptive flowchart boxes D2 through D4. The reason for inputting the student's sex will be given when we discuss flowchart boxes 21 through 45. Descriptive flowchart box D5 is implemented in algorithm flowchart boxes 6 and 7. Notice that the use of an interactive terminal virtually requires that we include steps similar to the one in box 6. The reason is that the user of this program must be prompted with regard to the input information that is needed. In this case we may even have somewhat of an ambiguous situation in that the prompting message does not tell the student in what order to input the ACT test scores. A more detailed message might therefore be required in a real-life program for this problem. In algorithm flowchart boxes 8 through 11 we have the steps necessary to accomplish the contents of descriptive flowchart box D6. Similarly, descriptive flowchart box D7 is implemented by algorithm flowchart boxes 12 through 20. Notice that each academic area percentile rank must be checked individually to determine areas in which remedial work may be needed.

Figure 8.8. Algorithm Flowchart for the Career-Choice Problem ▶
(continued on pages 264, 265, 266)

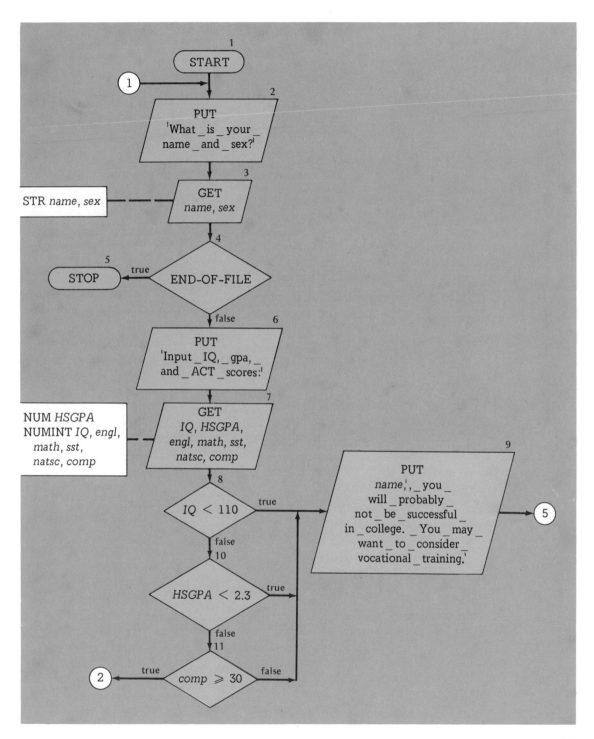

263

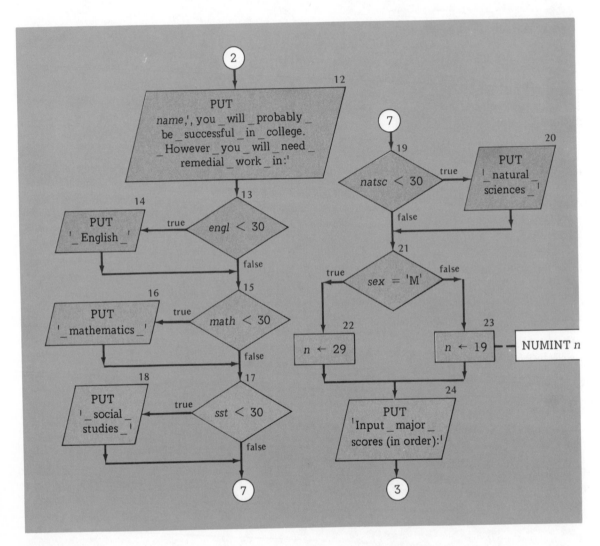

Figure 8.8, *continued*

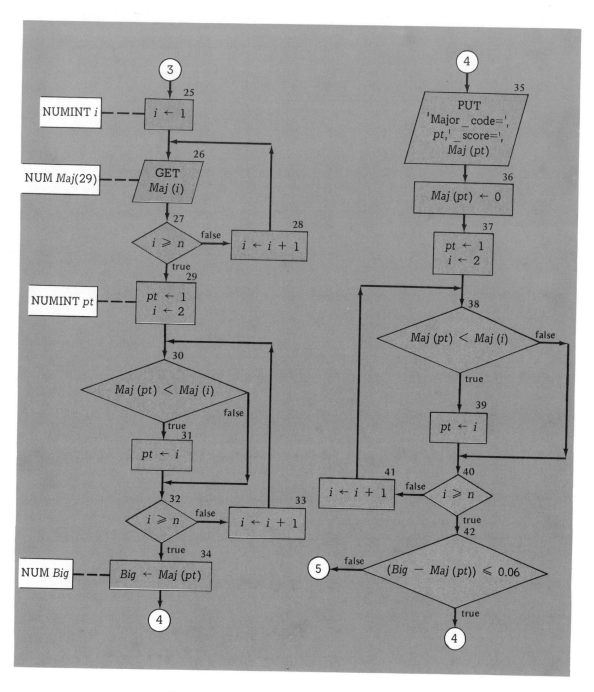

Figure 8.8, *continued*

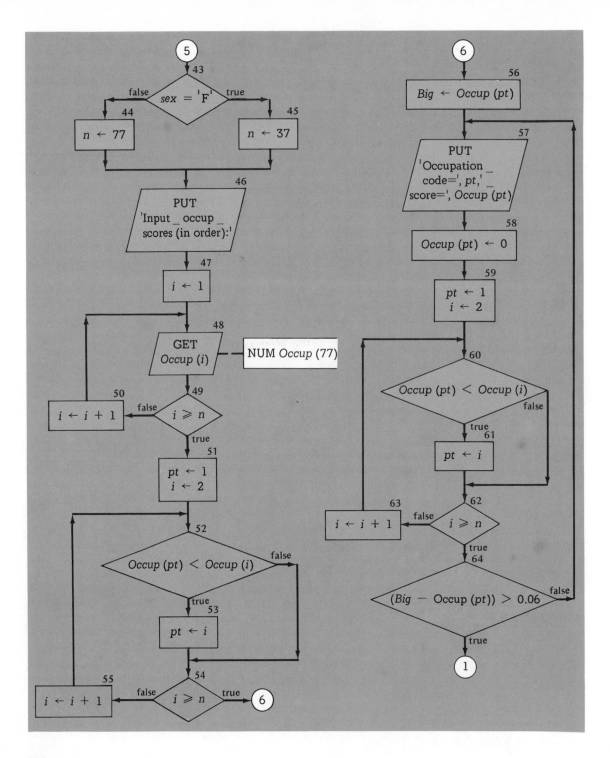

◀ **Figure 8.8,** *continued*

The purpose of the test in flowchart box 21 is to be able to assign the correct value to the variable n. The variable n is used to indicate how many times the steps are to be repeated in the loops of boxes 25 through 28, boxes 29 through 33, and boxes 37 through 41. The number of times these loops are to be repeated is different for males and females. This is because there are only 19 majors for females, whereas there are 29 majors for males. In flowchart box 25 we have a step to initialize the loop variable i that will be used in the loop of boxes 25 through 28. The purpose of this loop is to input the Kuder major scores for the student being counseled. Of course, we are assuming that the student has already completed the Kuder survey and the scores are available.

Box 29 initializes the loop counter i and a variable pt which is used as a pointer to the largest value in the array of major scores. The variable pt is initialized with a value of 1 because the search for the largest value will start assuming that the largest value is in the first element of *Maj*. Then the loop of boxes 29 through 33 compares every other value in the array with the largest value found thus far in the array (which is pointed to by the variable pt). Anytime during execution of this loop that the largest value found thus far is less than the current value being examined, the variable pt is assigned the value of the subscript of this new largest value that has been found. Thus, when the loop exit is made to box 34, the value of pt will be the subscript of the element of the array *Maj* that contains the largest value. This largest value is assigned in box 34 to the variable *Big* for use in the test in box 42. Then in box 35 the code for the largest score and the value of that score are output. Notice that the code for the largest score is simply the subscript of the element in the array that held the largest value. This is because we input the scores in order of their codes. Therefore, the subscripts are the same as the codes.

In algorithm flowchart box 36 the element in the array *Maj* that contained the largest value is assigned the value zero. The reason for assigning it this value is that the loop of boxes 37 through 41 is used to locate the largest remaining value in the array. Thus we need to give the element that contained the largest value a value of zero so that we do not find the same value again on our next search through the list. Notice that the method used in this loop to find the largest remaining value is identical to that used in the loop of boxes 29 through 33. Once exit is made from the loop to box 42, a test must be conducted to determine whether or not this largest remaining score is more than 0.06 less than the largest score in the original list. If it is, then we are done listing probable majors. However, when the difference is less than 0.06, a branch is taken back to in-connector 4, where the major code and score are output, this major-score element is assigned a value of zero, and a search is made of the array for the largest remaining value. Thus, descriptive flowchart box D8 required algorithm flowchart boxes 21 through 42 to be implemented.

The implementation of descriptive flowchart box D9 is effected in algorithm flowchart boxes 43 through 64. The logic involved in these steps is identical to that contained in flowchart boxes 21 through 42. The only difference is that in boxes 21 through 42 we are processing major scores, whereas in boxes 43 through 64 occupation scores are being processed.

PROBLEMS

1. Use the input data of Fig. 8.2 to develop a trace table for the algorithm flowchart of Fig. 8.3.

2. Modify the algorithm flowchart of Fig. 8.3 based on the following assumptions: (a) the lower bounds of the addition table (i.e., the initial values given to *a* and *b*) are input by the student rather than fixed at a value of zero, (b) the lower and upper bounds are not necessarily the same on both variables, (c) the number of trys allowed per problem is an input variable rather than fixed at 3, and (d) the average is computed as the number of correct answers divided by the number of answers input, with this quotient multiplied by 100.

3. Use the input data of Fig. 8.7 to develop a trace table for the algorithm flowchart of Fig. 8.8.

4. Modify the algorithm flowchart of Fig. 8.8 by assuming that the actual major fields and/or occupation names are to be output rather than their codes.

For the following problems, develop: (1) a descriptive flowchart, (2) an algorithm flowchart, and (3) a trace table (develop your own input data stream for each problem).

5. A geography teacher needs an algorithm that will allow students to learn about the capital cities of various countries and states. A learning session should begin (after the usual opening formalities, such as learning the student's name) by instructing the student on the capital cities of a group of states. Then the student should be tested on retention of the facts involved by being given the name of a state (or country) and having to respond with the name of the capital city. No more than four attempts should be provided to answer any question correctly. Use the criteria of the algorithm of Fig. 8.3 in determining whether or not the lesson for that group of states (or countries) needs to be repeated. Grades should be computed as 100 times the ratio of the total number of correct answers and the total number of times the student input an answer. The states and countries should be entirely input prior to the beginning of each student session.

6. A computer science professor would like to have an algorithm that drills students on the precedence rules for arithmetic expressions, as discussed in Section 4.3. The algorithm should begin by outputting the precedence rules. Then the student should be tested by the output of various expressions that he or she must evaluate and input an answer. The expressions used for testing should be input, together with the correct answers and the values to be used in evaluating those expressions. Grades should be computed as 100 times the ratio of the total number of correct answers and the total number of times the student input an answer. No more than four attempts should be provided to answer any question correctly. Use the criteria of the algorithm of Fig. 8.3 in determining whether or not the lesson should be repeated.

7. A history professor would like to have an algorithm that outputs historical text a paragraph at a time, then poses questions to the student on facts contained in that paragraph. A student may provide an incorrect answer to any question no more than three times and no more than seven incorrect answers to the questions on any one paragraph. Should either of these rules be violated, the contents of that paragraph should be output again and the student retested on the material. The student's grades should be computed using 100 times the ratio of the total number of correct answers to the questions of all paragraphs and the total number of questions asked over all paragraphs. The paragraphs and questions should be entirely input prior to the beginning of each student session.

8. A college academic counselor needs an algorithm to counsel students on such things as the selection of minors, majors, and elective courses. Algorithm input will be a student's transcript, which consists of: (a) the student's name; (b) the departmental abbreviation, course number, and grade for each course the student has completed; and (c) the student's preferred major and minor department. Assume that grades are valued as: A = 4, B = 3, C = 2, D = 1, and F = 0, and that Ws and Is are to be ignored. The algorithm should begin by inputting all student information given above. Then the student's overall grade-point average and the grade-point average for courses taken in each department should be computed. Next, the student's grade-point average for all courses taken in the major and minor stated preference departments should be compared with the student's overall grade-point average. When the overall grade-point average is greater than that in either or both of the departments for which the

student has stated a preference, a message should be printed. This message should advise the student that his or her choice may represent a poor selection. Then alternative departmental majors and/or minors should be suggested, listed in order of decreasing departmental grade-point averages. In selecting these alternative majors and/or minors, only departments having a grade-point average above the student's overall grade-point average should be listed. Finally, departments from which electives might be selected should be listed from among those for which the student has a grade-point average above 0.5 point above his or her overall grade-point average. However, the student's preferred major and minor departments should not be listed in the suggested elective departments.

9. A guidance counselor wants to develop an algorithm that integrates the Kuder major results into the algorithm of Problem 8. Develop such an algorithm by taking at most the student's six best departments based on grade-point average and six best departments based on Kuder scores. Then take the departmental ranks from both the grade-point average list and the Kuder score list and sum them for the respective departments. In forming the sum, double the rank from the Kuder score list and use a rank of seven for a department that does not appear in one list but is in the other list. Then rank the departments by increasing rank sum whenever a preferred major and/or minor shows a subpar grade-point average.

S U M M A R Y

1. The area of education offers a great deal of opportunity for the use of computers.

2. Some applications examined in earlier chapters that could be related to education are:

a. Student grade averaging.

b. Student record keeping.

c. Statistical evaluation of student groups and teaching techniques.

3. Computer-assisted instruction, which is the use of computers for teaching and testing, is a very important computer applications area in education.

4. Most applications of computer-assisted instruction thus far have been confined to rote-learning situations.

5. The fascination most people have for computers

probably offers one explanation for the success of computer-assisted instruction.

6. Computer-assisted instruction is always performed in an interactive mode, using an online terminal device for input and output.

7. In developing algorithms for computer-assisted instruction, it is very important to provide some personal touches to give the computer certain humanistic traits.

8. Computers can be used quite well in the area of academic and career counseling.

9. A general principle to follow in computer-assisted counseling is not to provide the counseled student with just one result. Instead, the person should be presented with a list of alternatives.

10. While computer-assisted counseling has not been widely used, it offers a great deal of promise for future development and application.

Algorithm Design III: Subalgorithms

As we have seen in the three previous chapters, the concepts introduced in Chapters 4 and 5 have given us all of the tools we actually need to design algorithms. However, one concept still needs to be covered so that our task of algorithm design can be made as easy as possible. The concept is the subalgorithm.

9.1   FUNDAMENTAL SUBALGORITHM CONCEPTS

subalgorithm defined

The term "subalgorithm" is actually a short way of saying subordinate algorithm. A *subalgorithm* is therefore simply an algorithm that is subordinate to another algorithm. Since we have defined an algorithm to be a procedure that provides the solution to a class of problems, a subalgorithm must be a procedure that provides a solution to a class of subproblems. The steps of a subalgorithm can always be inserted directly into the sequence of steps of the algorithm to which the subalgorithm is subordinate. However, we will concentrate in this text on subalgorithms that exist independently of the algorithms to which they are subordinate.

when to use a subalgorithm

There are three cases when we might want to use a subalgorithm. These are:

1. When the steps of a subalgorithm are to be performed in two or more places in an algorithm to which the subalgorithm is subordinate.
2. When the steps of a subalgorithm are to be performed in two or more algorithms.
3. When a large algorithm is to be designed.

In the first case, we have a subproblem that needs to be solved in several places in an algorithm. In addition, this subproblem often involves different variables each time it requires solving. For example, in many numerical algorithms, square roots of different numbers must be found at different points. That is, at one point in the algorithm we may want to find $\sqrt{x}$ and at another point we may need to find $\sqrt{y}$. One approach to this situation might be to include the steps for finding the square root at each of these points in the algorithm. This does not provide a good solution, however, because it causes the algorithm to contain many more steps than are necessary. A better approach is to develop a subalgorithm for finding the square root of any number. Then a reference to this subalgorithm can be made at each point in the algorithm where a square root must be found.

Another case where subalgorithms may be used is one in which the same steps are to be performed in several algorithms. An example would be that in many numerical algorithms there is a need to find the logarithm of a number. One alternative in this case is to develop the steps for finding the logarithm in every algorithm in which a logarithm is needed. This solution is very time consuming, however, and is rather like reinventing the wheel each time it is needed. A better approach would be to develop a subalgorithm for finding logarithms. Then, each time an algorithm we are writing requires computing a logarithm, all we need to do is reference the subalgorithm that finds logarithms.

The final case in which subalgorithms can be used to advantage is when we are developing algorithms for the solution of large problems. In almost every case, large problems can be broken down into a series of small subproblems. Then subalgorithms can be developed to solve each of the subproblems. Finally, a main algorithm can be developed which ties all of the subalgorithms together to obtain a solution to the overall problem. This approach is desirable because the subalgorithms are smaller and therefore easier to design and test than would be one giant algorithm —the mind is better able to cope with problems of a narrow scope than it is with extremely large and complex problems. Another advantage to this approach is that we can have different people working at the same time on the development of subalgorithms for the solution of the various subproblems. This will generally shorten the time required to develop the algorithm for solving the overall problem. To some extent, this is the technique that we have been using when we develop descriptive flow-charts—breaking the problem down into its simplest parts.

Now that we have shown a need for developing subalgorithms, we will consider the flowchart language rules for defining subalgorithms. In our discussion we will refer to an algorithm that calls upon a subalgorithm to solve a subproblem as the *invoking algorithm*. The subalgorithm that is called upon is called the *invoked subalgorithm*. The points in an invoking algorithm where subalgorithms are invoked or called upon are called *points of invocation*. For example, if a subalgorithm for finding square roots is available, any algorithm which uses that subalgorithm would be the invoking algorithm. The invoked subalgorithm in this case would be the square-root subalgorithm. Any place in the invoking algorithm where the square-root subalgorithm is referenced is called a point of invocation. This is all represented in the flowchart diagram in Fig. 9.1. In this diagram, the dotted lines represent flow between the invoking algorithm and the invoked subalgorithm.

invoking and invoked subalgorithms

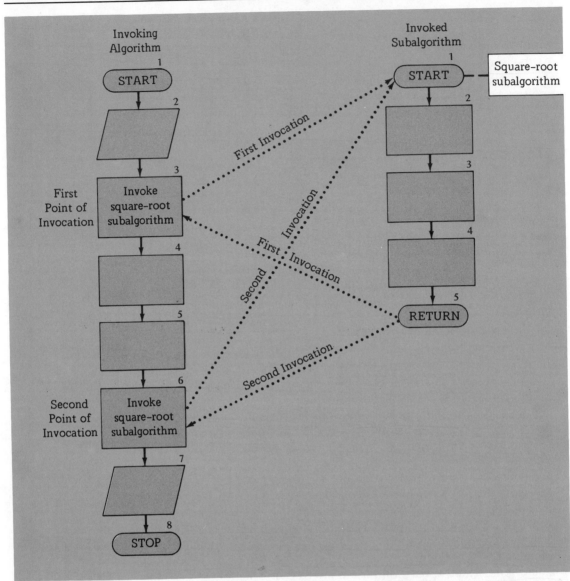

Figure 9.1.   Concept of Subalgorithm Invocation

Note that an invoking algorithm may itself be a subalgorithm since subalgorithms may invoke other subalgorithms. Therefore, a particular subalgorithm may sometimes be called the invoking subalgorithm. Care must be taken not to confuse the concept of an invoking subalgorithm with that of an invoked subalgorithm. The invoking subalgorithm will

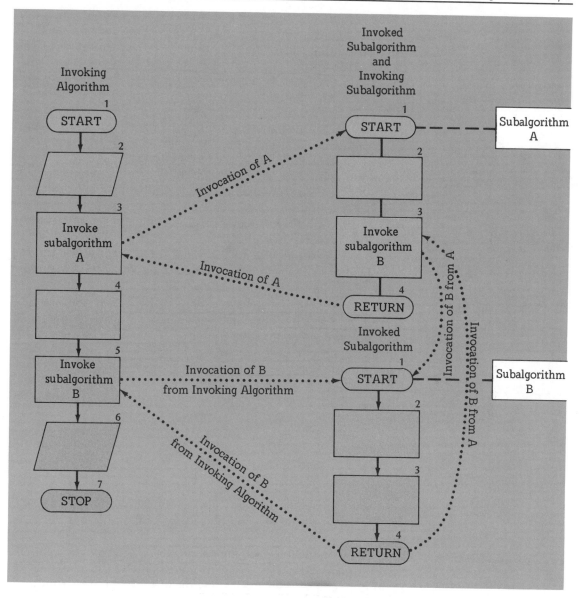

Figure 9.2. Concept of Multiple-Level Subalgorithm Invocations

always be the subalgorithm that uses the invoked subalgorithm to solve a subproblem. This concept is illustrated in the flowchart diagram of Fig. 9.2. Again, the dotted lines represent flow between the invoking and invoked algorithms. Notice in this example that Subalgorithm A is both an invoked subalgorithm of the invoking algorithm and also an invoking sub-algorithm to Subalgorithm B. In addition, observe that Subalgorithm B has been invoked by both the invoking algorithm and by Subalgorithm A. This shows that a subalgorithm may be invoked by more than one algorithm.

passing data to and from subalgorithms

We stated earlier that we are interested in studying only those sub-algorithms which are defined independently from their invoking al-gorithm. This independence means, for example, that the variables used in the subalgorithm are not known in the invoking algorithm. Similarly, the variables of the invoking algorithm are not known in the subalgorithm. Thus we need a means for passing necessary information between an in-voking algorithm and its invoked subalgorithms. Furthermore, this flow must be in two directions. That is, data from an invoking algorithm that are to be processed in an invoked subalgorithm must be made available to the subalgorithm, and results computed in a subalgorithm need to be returned to the invoking algorithm. For example, a square-root subal-gorithm needs to be supplied with the value for which the square root is to be found. It also needs to have a means of returning the square root of that value to the proper point in the invoking algorithm.

naming subalgorithms

Every subalgorithm must have a unique name that identifies the point where it may be entered. That is, execution of subalgorithm steps can begin at only one point in a subalgorithm.* The point where execution of the subalgorithm may begin is called an *entry point*. An entry point consists of an annotation box containing an entry name and formal param-eter list. This annotation box is attached by a broken line to the START box in the subalgorithm and is called an *entry point*. For example, the flowchart sequence

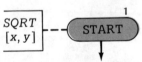

is an entry point to a subalgorithm with the entry name *SQRT*. We will permit any legal variable name to be used in naming the entry point of a subalgorithm.

parameter lists

The means by which communication between invoking algorithm and invoked subalgorithm takes place is the *parameter list*. A parameter list that appears at the point of invocation in an invoking algorithm is known as an *actual parameter list*. A *formal parameter list*, on the other hand, appears in an invoked subalgorithm following the entry name in an annotation box. Algorithms and subalgorithms may have as many actual parameter lists as there are points of invocation. However, a subalgorithm

---

* In our flowchart language, we will allow only one entry point to a subalgorithm. However, some authors (and some programming languages) allow multiple entry points to a subal-gorithm. The current trend is to discourage multiple entry points.

may have only one formal parameter list since there is only one entry point to a subalgorithm.

A subalgorithm may be invoked in one of two ways: (1) implicitly or (2) explicitly. An implicitly invoked subalgorithm is called a function subalgorithm; an explicitly invoked subalgorithm is called a general subalgorithm. A *function subalgorithm* is invoked *implicitly* by the appearance of the name of its entry point in an arithmetic expression in the invoking algorithm. This entry-point name may be followed by an actual parameter list that is enclosed in square brackets. The action taken is to transfer control to the START box in the subalgorithm having an entry point with that entry name. When execution of subalgorithm steps reaches a terminal box with the verb RETURN in it, control is transferred back to the point of invocation in the expression in the invoking algorithm. Evaluation of that expression then continues from the point of invocation.

function subalgorithm invocation

A *general subalgorithm* is invoked *explicitly* by the appearance of the name of its entry point in a predefined process box in an invoking algorithm. This name may be followed by an actual parameter list that is enclosed in square brackets. The action taken is to transfer control to the START box of the subalgorithm with an entry point of that name. Control is returned to the invoking algorithm at the step that follows the point of invocation in the invoking algorithm. This return of control takes place when a terminal box that contains a RETURN verb is executed in the invoked subalgorithm. Processing of the invoking algorithm then continues from that point.

general subalgorithm invocation

Invoking a subalgorithm and returning from a subalgorithm to the point of invocation may be thought of as special cases of a branch. That is, invoking a subalgorithm simply causes a branch to the entry point in the subalgorithm which has the same entry-point name as the one given at the point of invocation. Similarly, execution of a RETURN box in the invoked subalgorithm causes a branch back to the place following the point of invocation in the invoking algorithm.

The parameter lists used when referencing subalgorithms are very similar in function to the GET and PUT operations associated with input and output. That is, an actual parameter list is a means for outputting values from an invoking algorithm to an invoked subalgorithm. It is also used for inputting values from an invoked subalgorithm to an invoking algorithm. Similarly, the formal parameter list provides a means for inputting values to an invoked subalgorithm from an invoking algorithm. In addition, the formal parameter list permits values to be output from an invoked subalgorithm to an invoking algorithm.

Whether a formal parameter is an input or output item depends entirely upon how it is used in an invoked subalgorithm. If the value associated with the formal parameter is used in processing operations in a subalgorithm, it is an *input parameter*. On the other hand, any formal parameter that is given a value during the execution of a subalgorithm is an *output parameter.* Since the value associated with a formal parameter may be changed during execution of an invoked subalgorithm, a formal parameter may be both an input and an output parameter.

actual parameter lists

The *actual parameter list* may contain either of the following:

1. Arithmetic expressions.
2. String constants or variables.

Note that the simplest form of an arithmetic expression would be a constant or a variable name. If the expression is anything other than a variable name or a constant, the expression is evaluated and that value is used as an output to the invoked subalgorithm.* That is, a constant is developed as the value for that actual parameter expression. Note that an actual parameter value that is a constant cannot be changed by the invoked subalgorithm. The reason for this is the same as the fact that a constant is not permitted to appear to the left of an assignment operator. If the expression is simply a variable name, the variable name may be used to output a value to an invoked subalgorithm or to input a value to an invoking algorithm. Furthermore, the variable name may be an array name without a subscript. In this way an entire array of values can be output to an invoked subalgorithm or input to an invoking algorithm by the use of one actual parameter.

The method by which control is returned from an invoked subalgorithm to an invoking algorithm is as follows. The terminal box that signifies the final step to be executed in a subalgorithm contains the verb RETURN. This indicates that control is to be returned from the invoked subalgorithm to the point in the invoking algorithm just beyond where the subalgorithm was invoked.

The formal parameter list appears enclosed in square brackets following the name of the entry point to the subalgorithm. This subalgorithm entry-point name and formal parameter list are enclosed in an annotation box that is attached by a broken line to a START box in an invoked subalgorithm. This annotation box and START box together indicate the entry point to a subalgorithm. As we noted earlier, all of the subalgorithms that we develop in this book will have only one entry point. Therefore, a subalgorithm may have only one START box. In addition, the first box executed after invoking a subalgorithm must be the START box.

formal parameter lists

The *formal parameter list* may contain either of the following:

1. Arithmetic variable names.
2. String variable names.

---

* Other methods for handling parameter passage exist. However, they are beyond the scope of this book.

In the case of arithmetic or string variable names, the variables may be used for inputting values to an invoked subalgorithm or outputting values from an invoked subalgorithm. The variable names may be the names of arrays. Thus an entire array of values can be input to an invoked subalgorithm or output from an invoked subalgorithm.

We now need to examine the way in which actual parameters relate to formal parameters. In general, the following rules must hold with respect to actual and formal parameter lists: **relation of actual and formal parameters**

1. The number of parameters in the actual parameter list must be the same as the number of parameters in the formal parameter list.
2. The types of the corresponding parameters in the actual and formal parameter lists must be identical.

Thus, if there are five parameters in the formal parameter list, there must be five parameters in the actual parameter list. Furthermore, if the leftmost formal parameter is a numeric variable name, the leftmost actual parameter must be a numeric variable or an expression that evaluates to a single numeric value. Similarly, if the second parameter from the left of the formal parameter list is a string array name declared to have ten rows and five columns, the second actual parameter must be a string array name that is declared to have ten rows and five columns.

The actual and formal parameters are related to each other in a one-to-one correspondence based upon their relative positions in the parameter lists. Assume that the actual parameter list in an invoking algorithm is

$$[abc, d(4,2), r + v^2, 2, \text{'BIG'}]$$

and the formal parameter list of an invoked subalgorithm is

$$[x, y, z, kz, r(5)]$$

If we make certain assumptions about the types of the five parameters, the relationship between the parameters would be as follows:

1. Every place in the invoked subalgorithm where the variable x is used, the value or values associated with the variable abc from the invoking algorithm will be referenced. Thus, if we assign a value to x in the invoked subalgorithm, the value of abc in the invoking algorithm will be changed. Note that x and abc can be arrays, in which case more than one value would be involved.
2. A reference to y in the subalgorithm will be a reference to the element in the fourth row and second column of the array d in the invoking algorithm. Notice that y must be a simple variable

279

that represents only one value (i.e., y is not an array variable) since the actual parameter is one specific element of the array d.

3. The expression $r + v^2$ in the invoking algorithm will be evaluated and the resulting numeric constant will be used as the value for the formal parameter z in the invoked subalgorithm. Notice that since this expression will be evaluated to a constant, the variable z may not be assigned a value in the invoked subalgorithm.

4. A reference to the numeric variable kz in the invoked subalgorithm will result in the use of the numeric constant 2 in the subalgorithm. Again, the variable kz in the subalgorithm cannot be assigned a value.

5. The string constant **'BIG'** would be used everywhere in the invoked subalgorithm where the fifth element of the string array variable r is referenced. Again, the array element $r(5)$ in the subalgorithm cannot be assigned a value.

9.2 GENERAL SUBALGORITHMS

A general subalgorithm is one that is invoked explicitly by giving in a predefined process box the name of a subalgorithm entry point followed by an actual parameter list. The action taken by the invocation of a general subalgorithm is to associate the actual and formal parameters as described in Section 9.1. Then control is transferred to the START box associated with the entry point in the invoked subalgorithm. Execution of the subalgorithm then takes place in the same manner in which the steps of any algorithm would be executed. Any values of actual parameter variables that are changed through their associated formal parameters in the invoked subalgorithm will remain changed upon return to the invoking algorithm. All variable names used in the subalgorithm but not appearing in the formal parameter list are known only in the subalgorithm. Furthermore, only variable names and connectors appearing in the subalgorithm are known within the subalgorithm. Thus values can be passed between the invoking algorithm and the invoked subalgorithm only through the parameter lists. The values of as many variables in the actual parameter list as we desire can be changed in the invoked subalgorithm.

problem definition   As an example of two general subalgorithms, let us develop:

1. An invoking algorithm that is designed to process an organization's payroll.
2. A general subalgorithm for computing gross pay.
3. A general subalgorithm for computing payroll tax deductions.

descriptive flowcharts   Three descriptive flowcharts for the payroll problem appear in Fig. 9.3. In the left-hand column is the invoking algorithm descriptive flow-

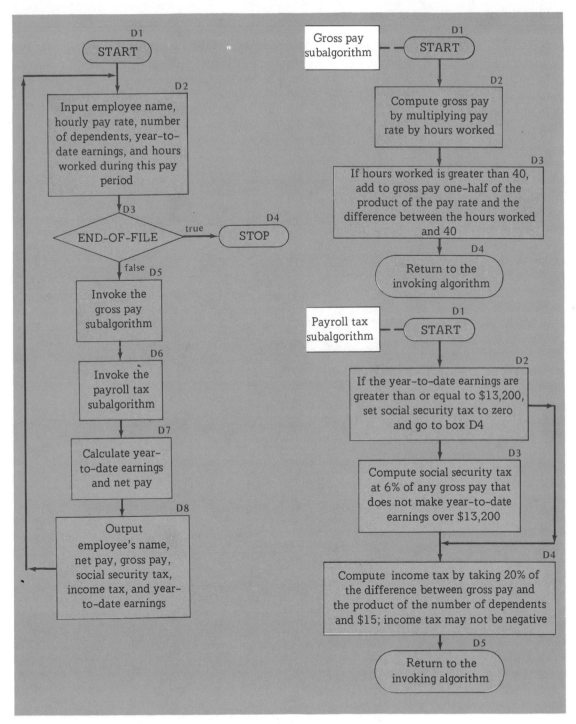

Figure 9.3. Descriptive Flowcharts for the Payroll Problem

chart. The rightmost column contains the descriptive flowcharts for the gross pay subalgorithm and the payroll-tax subalgorithm. The steps in all three of these descriptive flowcharts should be easy to understand and therefore will not be discussed.

invoking algorithm flowchart

The flowchart for the invoking algorithm is given in Fig. 9.4. In box 2 the employee's name, hourly pay rate, number of dependents, year-to-date earnings, and hours worked during this pay period are input. Except

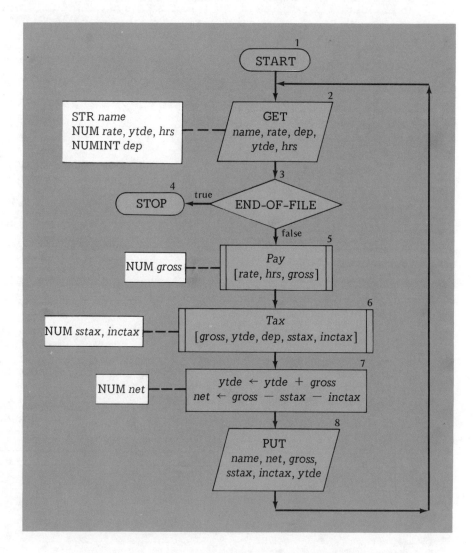

Figure 9.4. Invoking Algorithm Flowchart for the Payroll Problem

for the case of end-of-file, box 5 will be executed next.   In this box a general subalgorithm with the entry-point name *Pay* is invoked.   Notice the use of the predefined process box to indicate the invocation of a general subalgorithm.   The parameters used are the two input numeric variables, *rate* and *hrs,* and the numeric variable *gross*.   The parameters *rate* and *hrs* are used to output the rate of pay and hours worked to the subalgorithm *Pay*. The variable *gross* is used to input to the invoking algorithm the gross pay that was computed in the subalgorithm.   Before proceeding, let us examine the subalgorithm invoked in box 5.

The subalgorithm *Pay* is given in Fig. 9.5.   Notice the annotation box to the left of the START box.   The presence of this annotation box informs us that this is the flowchart for a subalgorithm.   The entry-point name for this subalgorithm is *Pay.*   The formal parameters are the variables *r, h,* and *amt.*   Thus the variable *r* in this subalgorithm is a reference to the variable *rate* in the invoking algorithm.   The reason is that *r* is the formal parameter that corresponds with the actual parameter *rate.*   Similarly, a reference to *h* and *amt* in the subalgorithm are also references to the variables *hrs* and *gross* in the invoking algorithm.   Upon entering the subalgorithm from the point of invocation (box 5 in the invoking algorithm), flowchart box 2 in the subalgorithm is executed.   This box assigns to the variable *amt* the product of the variables *r* and *h.*   Since *r* is the

first subalgorithm flowchart

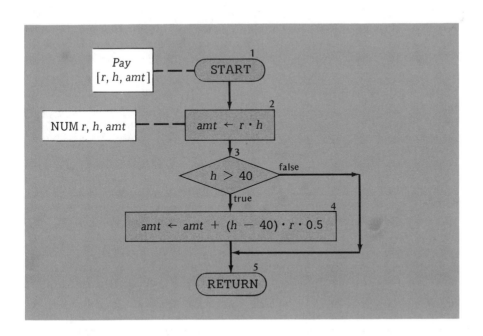

Figure 9.5.   Subalgorithm Flowchart for Computing Gross Pay

pay rate and h the number of hours worked, the value assigned to amt is the gross pay for the pay period, not including overtime. In flowchart box 3 a test is made to determine whether or not the employee worked more than forty hours. If the employee did work more than forty hours, the statement in box 4 is used to add to the gross pay an extra half of the pay for all hours worked over forty. In the case in which there was no overtime, box 4 is not executed. Execution of box 5 causes a return to be taken to the invoking algorithm. Upon return, the actual parameter $gross$ will have the value of the employee's gross pay. Execution of the invoking algorithm will then continue with flowchart box 6.

second subalgorithm flowchart
When flowchart box 6 is executed, this results in invocation of the subalgorithm with the entry-point name Tax. The actual parameters for this invocation are $gross$, $ytde$, dep, $sstax$, and $inctax$. The actual parameters $gross$, $ytde$, and dep are used to output values to the subalgorithm and the parameters $sstax$ and $inctax$ are to input values back to the invoking algorithm. The subalgorithm Tax appears in Fig. 9.6. The formal parameters are listed within square brackets in the annotation box to the left of the START box. In flowchart box 2, a test is made to determine whether or not year-to-date earnings are less than \$13,200. The reason for this test is that social security tax is only charged on the first \$13,200 earned by an employee in each year. Thus, if the employee has already earned at least \$13,200 this year, the social security tax is zero. This assignment takes place in box 3. When the year-to-date earnings are less than \$13,200, we have to determine if all of this pay period's amount is liable to social security tax. That is, a tax is charged only on that amount that is less than \$13,200. This test is made in box 4 by determining whether the sum of year-to-date earnings and the gross for this pay period is greater than or equal to \$13,200. If it is, box 5 is executed to compute the social security tax on only the amount up to \$13,200. When the sum is less than \$13,200, box 6 is executed. In this box social security tax is computed simply as 6 percent of gross pay.

Once social security tax has been determined, we are ready to calculate income tax withholding. This is computed on the net pay, which consists of gross pay less \$15 for each dependent that the employee has. The tax rate used in box 7 to calculate income tax withholding is 20 percent. In box 8 a test is made to be sure that the income tax withholding amount computed in box 7 is not negative. Of course, it only becomes negative when the gross pay is small relative to the number of dependents the employee has. When the income tax amount is determined to be negative, the variable inc is set to zero in box 9. With the execution of box 10, control is returned to the invoking algorithm following the point of invocation. Notice that the income and social security tax values were passed back to the invoking algorithm as the values of the actual parameters $inctax$ and $sstax$, respectively.

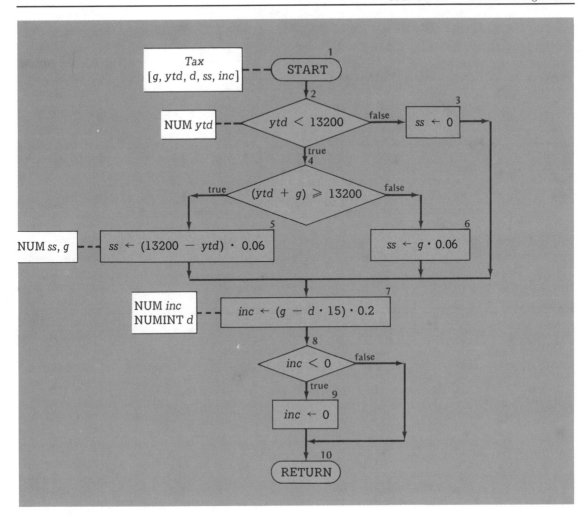

Figure 9.6. Subalgorithm Flowchart for Computing Payroll Tax Deductions

The next step to be executed in the invoking algorithm is the first statement in flowchart box 7. This statement increases the amount of year-to-date earnings by the amount of gross pay for this pay period. The second statement in box 7 calculates the net pay as the gross pay less social security tax and income tax. Finally, in box 8 the amounts calculated are output, and a branch is taken back to flowchart box 2 where the next employee will be processed. A trace table for this algorithm and two subalgorithms appears in Fig. 9.7. The input data stream used to construct this trace table is

trace table

285

Figure 9.7. Trace Table for the Algorithm Flowcharts of Figs. 9.4, 9.5, and 9.6.

	Invoking Algorithm								Pay Subalgorithm			Tax Subalgorithm				
name	rate	dep	ytde	hrs	gross	sstax	inctax	net	r	h	amt	g	ytd	d	ss	inc
'J._DOE'	2.00	3	7200.00	45					2.00	45	90.00					
											95.00	95.00	7200.00	3	5.70	10.00
					95.00	5.70	10.00	79.30								
			7295.00													
'B._LOW'	7.00	4	13100.00	40					7.00	40	280.00					
					280.00	6.00	44.00					280.00	13100.00	4	6.00	44.00
								230.00								
			13380.00													
'V._MOE'	1.50	8	4000.00	44					1.50	44	66.00					
											69.00	69.00	4000.00	8	4.14	−10.20
					69.00	4.14	0.00									0.00
								64.86								
			4069.00													
'L._TOE'	10.00	2	14100.00	35					10.00	35	350.00					
					350.00	0.00	64.00					350.00	14100.00	2	0.00	64.00
								286.00								
			14450.00													

' J._DOE ',2.00,3,7200.00,45,   ' B._LOW ',7.00,4,13100.00,40,
' V._MOE ',1.50,8,4000.00,44,   ' L._TOE ',10.00,2,14100,35

Notice that the data selected cause every branch of the subalgorithms to be tested.

9.3   FUNCTION SUBALGORITHMS

Function subalgorithms are quite similar to general subalgorithms except for the manner in which they are invoked. Whereas a general subalgorithm is invoked explicitly, a function subalgorithm is invoked implicitly. That is, a function subalgorithm is invoked by the appearance in an arithmetic expression of the name of its entry point followed by its actual parameter list.

The three main differences between a general and a function subalgorithm are:

1. A function subalgorithm is invoked implicitly by giving the name of its entry point and an actual parameter list in an arithmetic expression, whereas a general subalgorithm is invoked explicitly using a predefined process box.
2. A function subalgorithm returns a numeric constant to the point in the expression where it was invoked.
3. A function subalgorithm return causes control to be returned to the expression from which the subalgorithm was invoked. In the case of a general subalgorithm, however, a return causes control to be returned to the step after the point of invocation.

The numeric constant is returned to the point of invocation through the RETURN box of the invoked subalgorithm. This is accomplished by enclosing an expression in square brackets following the verb RETURN in the invoked subalgorithm. The values of actual parameters may be changed in a function subalgorithm just as they were in general subalgorithms. It is simply that in a function subalgorithm a return also causes a value to be returned to the point of invocation. All of the rules regarding formal and actual parameters given with regard to general subalgorithms hold for function subalgorithms.

The problem that we will use as an example for developing a function subalgorithm is that of converting a number expressed using Roman numerals to its decimal equivalent. The symbols that we will use as Roman numerals are I, V, X, L, C, D, and M. All other symbols will be considered invalid. Recall that the decimal equivalents of the above Roman numerals

problem definition and analysis

are 1, 5, 10, 50, 100, 500, and 1,000, respectively. From elementary school we recall that to convert a number represented using Roman numerals to its decimal equivalent we begin by scanning the string of Roman numerals from left to right. If the magnitude of the decimal equivalent of the ith numeral R_i is greater than or equal to the magnitude of the decimal equivalent of the $(i + 1)$th numeral R_{i+1}, then the decimal equivalent of R_i is added to a sum. Otherwise, R_i is subtracted from the sum.

descriptive flowcharts

The descriptive flowcharts for this problem are given in Fig. 9.8. In the invoking algorithm, the number to be converted is input into an array expressed as a fixed-length string of Roman numerals. This string is then printed followed by its decimal equivalent. We will assume that the Roman numeral representation of a number is followed by the number of blank spaces required to complete a fixed-length string. The conversion of the number from a string of Roman numerals to its decimal equivalent is performed in the function subalgorithm.

invoking algorithm flowchart

Let us begin with the invoking algorithm of Fig. 9.9. The step in box 2 is designed to input into the string array, R, the Roman numerals representing a number. Box 5 contains a step that initializes a counter n. The operation in box 6 is to determine whether or not the nth symbol of the string is a blank. If the nth symbol is a blank, the count of the number of digits in the current string of Roman numerals is complete and the conversion subalgorithm can be invoked in box 8. However, if the nth symbol is not a blank, we have not counted all the symbols in the string associated with the current number. In that case, we update the value of the counter n in box 7. Notice that the test for exit from our loop does not involve testing the counter n. The loop can be terminated only by encountering a blank symbol. Observe that the last string to be converted must be followed by a blank, as must the other input strings. This is because a blank serves to terminate each Roman numeral string.

Once a blank space has been found, execution of the step in box 8 of the invoking algorithm occurs. The first statement in this box causes the counter n to be reduced by 1 because it includes the blank space in the count. Next, the subalgorithm with an entry point named *Conv* is invoked in the expression in the second assignment statement in box 8. Notice that the actual parameter R is a one-dimensional string array. This is because we can use an array name without a subscript as an actual parameter and as a formal parameter. Thus an entire array of values can be passed between an invoking algorithm and an invoked subalgorithm.

subalgorithm flowchart

The flowchart for the subalgorithm for performing the conversion appears in Fig. 9.10. The formal parameters for this subalgorithm are S, m, and err. Notice that the formal parameter S is declared to have the same type and number of elements as did its corresponding actual parameter R. Similarly, m and err are the same type of variables as are their corresponding actual parameters, n and sw. The steps in box 2 of the

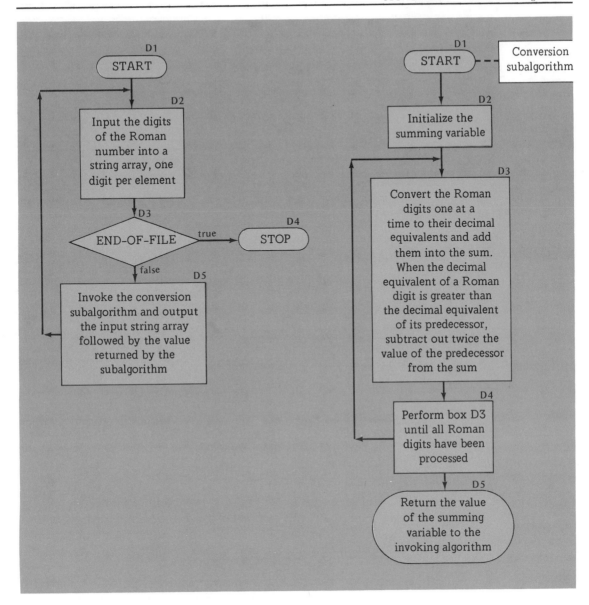

Figure 9.8. Descriptive Flowcharts for the Roman-Number Conversion Problem

subalgorithm initialize: (1) the summing variable *Sum*; (2) the variable *Prev*, which is used to hold the decimal equivalent of the previous symbol; and (3) the loop counter *i*. The loop for accomplishing the conversion consists

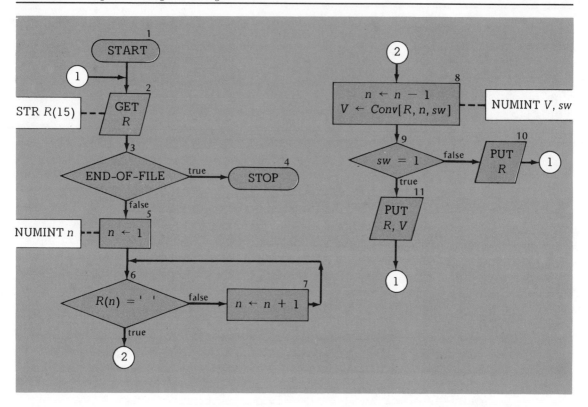

Figure 9.9. Invoking Algorithm Flowchart for the Roman-Number Conversion Subalgorithm

of boxes 3 through 15 and 17 through 22. Tests for loop termination appear in boxes 15 and 21, while box 22 contains the modification step.

Boxes 3 through 7, 13, and 15 are used to determine which one (if any) of the Roman numerals we are currently processing. For example, if the numeral is a V, the condition in box 3 will be true, whereas the comparison in box 4 will produce a result of false. Having determined that the current symbol is a V, the decimal equivalent of V is assigned to the variable d in box 9. Then control is transferred to in-connector 3. Note that if all seven conditions tested for a Roman numeral result in true, an error message is printed in box 16. Then the variable err is assigned a value of 2 prior to returning to the invoking algorithm. This assignment is to indicate the fact that a data error has occurred during execution of the subalgorithm. After the decimal equivalent has been assigned to d in the case of valid numerals, this value is added into Sum in box 18.

In box 19 a comparison is made to determine if the decimal equiva-

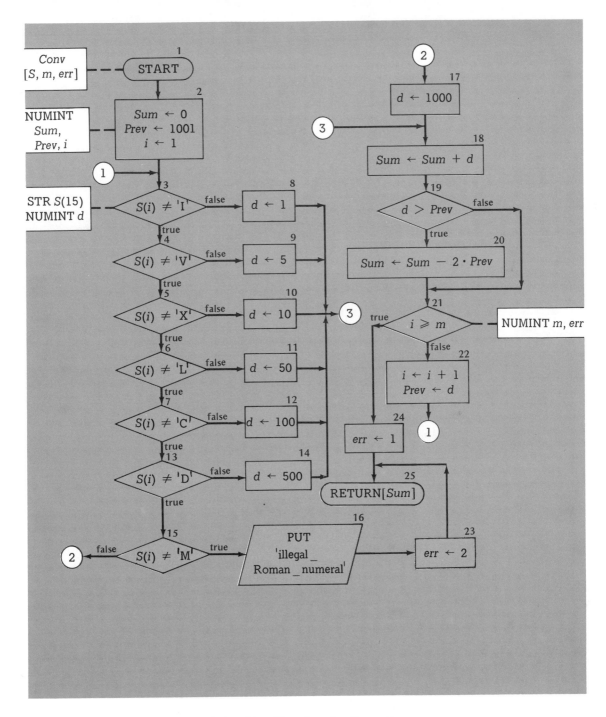

Figure 9.10. Function Subalgorithm Flowchart for Converting a Roman Number to Its Decimal Equivalent

lent of the current Roman numeral is greater than the decimal equivalent of the previous numeral. When this condition is true, the value of the decimal equivalent of the previous Roman numeral should have been subtracted rather than added. We correct this in box 20 by subtracting from *Sum* twice the value of the decimal equivalent of the previous Roman numeral. That is, we subtract out the decimal value for the previous Roman numeral once because we added it into the sum when it should have been subtracted. Then we subtract it out a second time because its value was to have been subtracted from the sum. Notice that box 20 will always be bypassed the first time through the loop since we initialized *Prev* with the value 1001 in box 2. Box 20 is also not executed when the decimal value for the current Roman numeral is less than or equal to the decimal value for the previous numeral.

In box 21 a test is made to determine whether or not all of the Roman numerals in the string have been processed. If they have, the error variable *err* is assigned a value of 1 to indicate that no data error has occurred while executing the subalgorithm. Then a return is taken through box 25, causing the value of *Sum* to be returned to the point of invocation in box 8 of the invoking algorithm. If all of the Roman numerals in this number have not been processed, then in box 22 the loop counter *i* is incremented by 1 and the decimal value for the current numeral is assigned to be the decimal value for the previous numeral.

Upon returning to the invoking algorithm, the value of the variable *Sum* in the invoked subalgorithm will be assigned as the value of the variable *V*. This is because the value of *Sum* is the one returned through the RETURN box of the subalgorithm. In addition, either a 1 or 2 will be returned as the value of the actual parameter *sw*. This variable is tested in flowchart box 9 of the invoking algorithm to determine whether or not a data error occurred during execution of the subalgorithm. If one did occur, the Roman number is output in box 10 and a branch is taken to in-connector 1. This is because a value of 2 will have been returned as the value of *sw*. Otherwise, flowchart box 11 will be executed, causing the Roman number and its decimal equivalent to be output.

trace table   A trace table for this algorithm and subalgorithm appears in Fig. 9.11. The input data stream used in developing this trace table was

'M','D','V','C','_','_','_','_','_','_','_','_','_','_','_',
'X','L','I','_','_','_','_','_','_','_','_','_','_','_','_'

As a final note to function subalgorithms, we observe that all of the functional operators defined in Chapter 4 are simply function subalgorithms. We did not show the subalgorithms for each of these functional operators, but rather have left some of them as exercises.

Figure 9.11. Trace Table for the Algorithms of Figs. 9.9 and 9.10

Invoking Algorithm			Conv Subalgorithm						
R(n)	n	PUT	Sum	Prev	i	S(i)	d	Box in Which d Assigned Value	err
'M'	1	'M'							
'D'	2	'D'							
'V'	3	'V'							
'C'	4	'C'							
' _ '	5								
	4								
			0	1001	1	'M'	1000	17	
			1000	1000	2	'D'	500	14	
			1500	500	3	'V'	5	9	
			1505	5	4	'C'	100	12	
			1605						
		1595	1595						1
'X'	1	'X'							
'L'	2	'L'							
'I'	3	'I'							
' _ '	4								
	3								
			0	1001	1	'X'	10	10	
			10	10	2	'L'	50	11	
			60						
			40	50	3	'I'	1	8	
		41	41						1

PROBLEMS

For each of the following problems, develop: (1) a descriptive flowchart, (2) subalgorithm and invoking algorithm flowcharts, and (3) a trace table (develop your own input data stream for each problem).

1. An education professor often needs the range of scores on examinations, where the range is defined to be the largest score less the smallest score. The invoking algorithm should be used to: (a) input the test scores into an array, (b) output the test scores, (c) invoke a general subalgorithm that finds both the maximum and minimum values in the set, and (d) outputs the maximum and minimum values followed by the range. Assume that the number of scores in each set is unknown but not greater than 500. Also, each data set except the last is followed by a value of 998; the last data set is followed by the value 999.

2. Develop an invoking algorithm that: (a) inputs the value *n* of data values in a list; (b) inputs the list of numeric data values into a one-dimensional array, outputting the data values as they are input; (c) invokes a general subalgorithm that sorts the values into nondescending order using the interchange sort method described in Section 6.3; and (d) outputs the list of sorted values. You will also need to develop the general subalgorithm for performing the sort.

3. An English professor needs a subalgorithm that scans a sequence of characters until it finds a substring of those characters. When the substring is found, the subalgorithm should record the position of the leftmost character of the substring in the string, counting from the left of the string (assume that the leftmost character in the string is numbered 1). If the substring is not found in the character sequence, a value of zero should be recorded. Thus, for the character sequence TOM AND BILL, the value recorded for the substring AND would be 5 because AND begins in the fifth position from the left of the string. The invoking algorithm should: (a) input a value for the number of characters in the character sequence; (b) input the characters in the sequence into a one-dimensional string array, with one character per element; (c) input a value for the number of characters in the substring; (d) input the characters in the substring into a one-dimensional string array, with one character per element; (e) invoke a general subalgorithm that performs the scan and returns the pointer as described above; and (f) outputs the character sequence, the substring, and the pointer value.

4. Expand the payroll problem of Section 9.2 to include deductions for: (a) union dues, (b) payroll savings, (c) hospitalization insurance, and (d) retirement. Each of these deductions are optional and may be subscribed to in any combination. Union dues are a flat $5 per month, whereas payroll savings can be any amount desired by the employee. Hospitalization insurance is $10 plus $1.50 for each dependent up to a maximum of three dependents. Retirement is computed as a flat 6 percent of gross pay. Develop general subalgorithms for computing: (a) hospitalization insur-

ance, (b) retirement, and (c) year-to-date earnings and net pay. Also revise the invoking algorithm accordingly.

5. A chemist often needs to look up in a table the values of certain functions for a given argument. The invoking algorithm should: (a) input the table values into a two-dimensional array, the first column of which contains the list argument values and the second column of which has the function values; (b) input search argument values and invoke a function subalgorithm that returns the appropriate function value; and (c) output the search argument and function values. Assume that any search argument value not equal to one of the list argument values is in error.

6. A mathematician wants a subalgorithm that can compute an approximation to the cube root of a number *z* using the iterative formula

$$x_{i+1} = (2 \cdot x_i + z/x_i^2)/3$$

The invoking algorithm should: (a) input the value of *z* and a critical value of the maximum relative difference that will be allowed for a good approximation, (b) invoke the cube-root-function subalgorithm, and (c) output the value of *z* and the approximation returned by the subalgorithm.

7. Modify the algorithm and subalgorithm of Figs. 9.9 and 9.10 so that the subalgorithm is used only for converting a Roman numeral into its decimal equivalent. That is, the subalgorithm will return a value *d* that represents the decimal equivalent for some Roman numeral.

8. Develop a function subalgorithm that converts a Roman number to its decimal equivalent. The formal parameter list should be assumed to be the same as the one for the subalgorithm of Fig. 9.10. However, the subalgorithm for this problem should cause the string that contains the Roman numerals to be scanned from right to left during the conversion operation. Assume that the algorithm of Fig. 9.9 is used to invoke the subalgorithm you design.

9. Develop a function subalgorithm that converts a Roman number to its decimal equivalent. The formal parameter list should be assumed to be the same as the one for the subalgorithm of Fig. 9.10. However, the seven one-character strings that contain the Roman numerals should be stored in a one-dimensional array and their seven decimal equivalents stored in a second one-dimensional array. A loop should be used for looking up the decimal equivalent associated with each Roman number digit, scanning the Roman number from left to right during the conversion operation. Assume that the algorithm of Fig. 9.9 is used to invoke the subalgorithm you design.

10. Solve Problem 5 by assuming that a search argument value may not necessarily equal some list argument value in the table. Instead, the value of the search argument may fall between the *i*th and (*i* + 1)th list argument values. If the search argument value falls between the *i*th and (*i* + 1)th list argument values, the value output should be computed as

$$f(i,2) + [f(i + 1,2) - f(i,2)] \cdot \frac{Arg - f(i,1)}{f(i + 1,1) - f(i,1)}$$

where *f* is a two-dimensional array of list arguments and function values and *Arg* is the search argument value. Notice that this subalgorithm only has meaning when the table values and search argument are numeric values. Moreover, the table is assumed to be organized such that the list argument values are in ascending order.

11. Modify the algorithm developed in Section 8.2 so that all operation sequences that are repeated in the algorithm are performed by invoking a subalgorithm. Notice that this will require the development of a general subalgorithm for inputting array values and a function subalgorithm for finding the largest remaining value in an array.

SUMMARY

1. A subalgorithm is an algorithm that is subordinate to another algorithm and that provides a solution to a class of subproblems.

2. The three cases when we might want to use a subalgorithm are:
a. When the steps of a subalgorithm are to be performed in two or more places in an algorithm to which it is subordinate.
b. When the steps of a subalgorithm are to be performed in two or more algorithms.
c. When a large algorithm is to be designed.

3. An algorithm that calls upon a subalgorithm to solve a subproblem is called an invoking algorithm.

4. A subalgorithm that is called upon to solve a subproblem is called the invoked subalgorithm.

5. The point where execution of a subalgorithm may begin is called an entry point. The entry name of a subalgorithm must be unique.

6. A parameter list that is used in the invoking algorithm is called the actual parameter list. An actual parameter list in our flowchart language is enclosed in square brackets and may contain:
a. Arithmetic expressions.
b. String variables or constants.

7. A formal parameter list is given along with the name of an entry point in a subalgorithm. A formal parameter list in our flowchart language is enclosed in square brackets and may contain:
a. Arithmetic variable names.
b. String variable names.

8. The actual and formal parameters are related to each other in a one-to-one correspondence based upon their relative positions in the parameter lists.

9. An explicitly invoked subalgorithm is called a general subalgorithm. It is invoked by the appearance in a predefined process box of an entry-point name followed by an actual parameter list.

10. An implicitly invoked subalgorithm is called a function subalgorithm. It is invoked by the appearance in an arithmetic expression of an entry-point name followed by an actual parameter list.

11. A function subalgorithm always returns a numeric constant to the point in the invoking algorithm expression where it was invoked. Results may also be returned to the invoking algorithm through the actual parameter list, as in the case of a general subalgorithm.

Solving Problems in the Physical Sciences, Mathematics, and Engineering

Problems in engineering and the physical sciences have in common that they are by nature mathematical. Furthermore, they are often problems that require a great deal of computation. In fact, the amount of computation required in solving most such problems is usually so great that a computer provides the only means of solution. Typical problems include finding the roots of an equation, solving systems of simultaneous equations, and evaluating definite integrals.

Many of the algorithms used to solve mathematical problems are designed to provide approximate rather than exact solutions. The reason that methods which yield approximate results are used is that algorithms which provide exact results are analytical rather than numerical in nature. Since analytical algorithms are usually very difficult (if not impossible) to design, numerical algorithms that yield approximate solutions are generally used.

In this chapter we are going to examine algorithms for solving problems from several areas relevant to engineers, mathematicians, and physical scientists. However, just as some of the solution methods that we examined in previous chapters are relevant to engineers and physical scientists, the solution methods developed in this chapter have applications in business and the social sciences. Thus we are being too restrictive if we state that these problems and their associated algorithms pertain only to engineers or physical scientists. In this chapter we are going to cover integer functions, problems of rounding errors, digital graphing, methods for finding the roots of an equation, the area-under-a-curve problem, and the solution of problems using simulation techniques.

10.1 INTEGER FUNCTIONS AND ROUNDING ERRORS

In an earlier chapter we observed that caution must be exercised in processing numeric data because of the approximate nature of most numbers represented in a computer. In this section we will make some more observations about this problem, which we will call rounding error. First, however, we will examine the four integer functions that are used when rounding numeric values.

10.1.1   Integer Functions

Integer functions are used to round real numbers to integer values or finite approximations to real numbers. The four integer functions are: (1) the ceiling function, (2) the floor function, (3) the truncation function, and (4) the rounding function. For any real number x, these four functions are defined as follows:

1. The ceiling of x is defined to be the least integer that is greater than or equal to x. In flowchart language, the ceiling of x can be found by using the functional operator ceil[x].

2. The floor of x is defined to be the greatest integer that is less than or equal to x. In flowchart language, the floor of x can be found by using the functional operator floor[x].

3. The value of x truncated is defined to be the integer nearest to the origin. That is: (a) for positive values of x, x truncated is equal to floor[x], while (b) for negative values of x, x truncated is equal to ceil[x]. In flowchart language, the value of x truncated is found using the functional operator trun[x].

4. The value of x rounded is defined to be the value of the integer nearest to x. Thus, for x a decimal number, x rounded is equal to floor[x + 0.5]. The flowchart language functional operator for x rounded is round[x].

ceiling

floor

truncate

round

Examples of the results for these four integer functions are given in Fig. 10.1.

Figure 10.1.   Examples of the Integer Functions

x	ceil[x]	floor[x]	trun[x]	round[x]
52.3	53.0	52.0	52.0	52.0
−52.3	−52.0	−53.0	−52.0	−52.0
52.7	53.0	52.0	52.0	53.0
−52.7	−52.0	−53.0	−52.0	−53.0
52.5	53.0	52.0	52.0	53.0
−52.5	−52.0	−53.0	−52.0	−52.0

The integer functions may seem to be rather limited in application since we may often wish to round values to something other than integers. For example, we may wish to round the value 5,257 to the nearest hundred. Or, we may wish to truncate 4.6787 to the nearest thousandth. But these objectives can be accomplished using the integer functions. All that is necessary is the proper scaling of the number to be rounded before applying the integer function. Then, after rounding the scaled value, simply

integer functions for rounding

299

scale the result using the reciprocal of the scale. For example, to round 5,257 to the nearest hundred, we would first multiply 5,257 by 10^{-2} (10^{-2} is equal to 1/100), which produces 52.57. Then we would round 52.57, which gives 53. Finally, we would multiply 53 by 10^2 (10^2 is the reciprocal of 1/100), which produces 5,300 as our result. Taking the example of truncating the value of 4.6787 to the nearest thousandth, we have

$$trun[4.6787 \cdot 10^3] \cdot 10^{-3} = trun[4678.7] \cdot 10^{-3}$$
$$= 4678 \cdot 10^{-3}$$
$$= 4.678$$

10.1.2   Rounding Errors

causes of rounding errors

In earlier chapters we observed that computers can only represent finite approximations to real numbers. That is, there is a limitation on the number of significant digits that the computer representation of a real number may contain. Thus, while floating-point numbers on many current computers can attain values as large as 10^{75} in magnitude, these numbers can have a maximum of only sixteen significant decimal digits. The rest of the digits in the number will be implied zeros that are produced by a scale factor that is stored as part of the number. Another important aspect of computer design is that numbers are not represented in a computer using the decimal number system. Instead, they are represented using the binary or some coded-binary system. Furthermore, in floating-point numbers the significant digits are almost always stored as a fraction. This can create problems since a decimal fraction does not necessarily have an exact equivalent in the binary number system. The consequence of this means of representation is that during conversion from decimal to binary the original value may be changed slightly. This problem can be demonstrated rather easily by simply inputting a decimal value to a computer and then immediately causing the computer to print that same value.

input and output errors

As a result of these two aspects of computer design, we have three basic types of rounding errors: (1) input errors, (2) output errors, and (3) computational errors. Input errors are a result of both the finite length of computer floating-point numbers and the problem of conversion from decimal to binary representation. Output errors are caused by the conversion from binary to decimal representation. Computational errors, which occur during computations, are entirely a result of the finite length of computer floating-point numbers. The effect of these errors on results varies from algorithm to algorithm and data set to data set. However, we can safely conclude that we are often using approximations to true values in solving a problem. This is true even in the case in which the algorithm is logically designed to produce exact results. Notice that what we say

computational errors

in this section about rounding error applies only to floating-point numbers. Numbers represented as binary integers do not suffer from problems of rounding error; neither do numbers stored as decimal values on computers that permit the representation of decimal numbers. This is not to say that binary integers or decimal numbers are to be preferred over floating-point numbers, since all three have their uses. For example, binary integers and decimal numbers cannot be as great in magnitude as can floating-point numbers.

A consequence of computational error is that the associative and commutative laws of mathematics are in general not valid in performing computer arithmetic. That is, the order in which arithmetic expressions are evaluated will affect the result. For example, the associative law of addition states that $(A + B) + C = A + (B + C)$. That this law may fail when using computer arithmetic can be easily illustrated. To simplify our example, let us assume that our computer uses only three significant digits to represent floating-point numbers and truncates results. Let us first form the sum of the expression $(0.00524 + 0.0883) + 2.44$. The result of adding the first and second values is 0.0935, which when added to 2.44 gives 2.53 as a sum. Now, let us form the sum of the same expression except in a different order: $0.00524 + (0.0883 + 2.44)$. The result of adding the second and third values is 2.52, which when added to 0.00524 gives 2.52 as a sum. Since 2.52 is not equal to 2.53, this demonstrates that the associative law for addition does not always hold in performing computer arithmetic. A similar statement can be made for the commutative law of addition and the associative and commutative laws for multiplication. Since the true sum of the above three numbers is 2.53354, we might induce that it is preferable to add numbers in order of increasing magnitude. In fact, as a general rule, whenever there is a sizable difference in the magnitude of numbers being summed, they should be added in order of increasing magnitude. This permits the values that are of smaller magnitude to accumulate in the final sum.

mathematical laws invalid

order for addition

Another source of computational error is caused by taking the difference of two numbers that are nearly equal in magnitude. The error is introduced because of the loss of significant digits when such a difference is computed. As an example, let us assume that we have as an arithmetic expression $1 - \sin^2 x$.* This expression looks innocent enough. However, the term $\sin^2 x$ approaches 1 as x approaches $\pi/2$. Thus, if x is assumed to be a floating-point number with six significant digits and is equal to 1.57, we have: $1 - \sin^2(1.57) = 1 - (0.999999)^2 = 1 - 0.999998 = 0.00001$. The result of evaluating this expression is thus a number with only one significant digit. However, an elementary trigonometric identity states that

nearly equal differences

---

* Knowledge of trigonometry is not required to appreciate the concept introduced in this example.

$\sin^2 x + \cos^2 x = 1$, or $1 - \sin^2 x = \cos^2 x$. Therefore, $\cos^2 x$ is mathematically equivalent to the arithmetic expression $1 - \sin^2 x$. But the two expressions are not computationally equivalent because $\cos^2 (1.57) = (0.000796326)^2 = 0.000000634135$ retains six significant digits. Therefore, care must be exercised in stating arithmetic expressions to avoid taking the difference of two values of nearly equal magnitude.

Let us now examine the results of executing on a computer the algorithm for Problem 28 of Chapter 4 (p. 000), which is designed to solve a pair of simultaneous linear equations. The table in Fig. 10.2 provides results for two input data sets. The two sets of equations represented by these data sets are:

$$\text{Data set 1:} \quad \begin{cases} x + y = 5 \\ 0.999999x + y = 7 \end{cases}$$

$$\text{Data set 2:} \quad \begin{cases} x + y = 5 \\ 1.00001x + y = 7 \end{cases}$$

Note that the only difference between the two pairs of equations is in the coefficient for x in the second equation. Three sets of results are given in Fig. 10.2 for each pair of equations. The columns headed 7 s.d. refer to the fact that the computer used floating-point numbers with seven significant digits in performing the computations. Similarly, floating-point numbers with sixteen significant digits were used in developing the answers in the columns headed 16 s.d. The results in the columns headed True were performed on a desk calculator and are exact results.

Taking the results for data set 1 first, the differences in the values for x and y in the two leftmost columns can be attributed entirely to computational error. The same statement holds for the differences in values for x and y in columns four and five. Notice that using sixteen instead of seven significant digits tends to solve much of the problem of computational error in these examples. This conclusion is reached since results

Figure 10.2   Results from Computer Execution of the Algorithm of Problem 28 of Chapter 4 to Illustrate Effects of Rounding Error

| Variables | Data Set 1 | | | Data Set 2 | | |
	7 s.d.*	16 s.d.	True	7 s.d.	16 s.d.	True
x	−1973790	−2000000	−2000000	209715	200000	200000
y	1973800	2000000	2000005	−209710	−199995	−199995

* s.d. = significant digits.

obtained using sixteen significant digits are equal to the true results except for the value of the variable y in the first data set. In general, the greater the number of significant digits used in performing computations, the less significant the amount of rounding error. Since there is a limit to the number of significant digits that can be used on computers, for larger problems computational error can still be great enough to cause significant errors in results.

Another matter to note in this example is the vast difference between the true results for the two data sets used. The difference in the coefficients between the two sets is one that could have resulted from a slight measurement error, for example. When small changes in one or more values of a data set cause large changes in the results in the context of a particular problem, the data set is said to be *ill-conditioned*. In the case of ill-conditioned data sets, increasing the number of significant digits does not reduce the sensitivity of the results to small changes in the input data values. Instead, every effort should be made to assure the accuracy of the input data. In addition, when ill-conditioned data are suspected, results should be accepted and interpreted with extreme caution. The reason for the big difference in results in our example is that we are dealing with what are essentially parallel lines. This causes a substantial shift in the point of intersection when a small change in the value of a coefficient occurs.

ill-conditioned data

As another example, suppose that we solved the quadratic equation $x^2 + 325678x - 0.02 = 0$ on a computer using the quadratic formula

$$x = \frac{-b \pm \sqrt{b^2 - 4 \cdot a \cdot c}}{2 \cdot a}$$

(10.1)

Performing our computations using floating-point numbers with both seven and sixteen significant digits, we would obtain the following results:

Significant Digits	x_1	x_2
7	$-6.25000 \cdot 10^{-2}$	$-3.25678 \cdot 10^5$
16	$6.13945 \cdot 10^{-8}$	$-3.25678 \cdot 10^5$

Notice how increasing the number of significant digits from seven to sixteen improves the result for the root x_1. In fact, the sign of the result actually changes when increasing the precision used in performing the computations. The error in this case is caused by the fact that the two terms in the difference $-b + \sqrt{b^2 - 4 \cdot a \cdot c}$ are nearly equal. This problem can be solved in this example by using an alternative formula for computing the root x_1. Using the formula $x_1 = c/(a \cdot x_2)$ and only seven significant digits, we obtain $x_1 = 6.14104 \cdot 10^{-8}$, which is quite close to the result using sixteen significant digits. This example again confirms the need to be very careful in taking the difference between two nearly equal quantities.

The data used in the above examples have been purposely chosen to illustrate the kinds of errors that can appear in the solution to problems using a computer. Even more alarming is the fact that both methods used in these examples are ones that mathematically are supposed to give exact results. If we have errors like these with algorithms which are expected to give exact results, just imagine how bad the situation can be with algorithms that are designed to give only approximate results. Fortunately, most real-world problems do not involve data that are as ill-conditioned as those used in our examples. However, in designing algorithms we must be alert to prevent rounding errors from becoming excessive. Furthermore, even though algorithm efficiency is an important consideration, accuracy of results must always come first in algorithm design.

comparison of values   A final consideration caused by the approximate nature of computer data relates to the comparison of values. Comparing two floating-point values for equality is a delicate operation. Thus, while the exact values may be equal, we are comparing two approximate values that may not be equal. Therefore, we would be well advised to accept two values as being equal to each other if their absolute difference is less than some small value. For example, we might accept the value of A as being equal to the value of B if $|A - B| < e$, where e is a small value that is determined in the context of the problem. A reasonable value for e in many problems might be 10^{-6}.

PROBLEMS

1. Develop a function subalgorithm that uses only the *trun* functional operator to find the ceiling of the value of x.

2. Develop a function subalgorithm that uses only the *trun* functional operator to obtain the value of x rounded.

3. Develop an invoking algorithm that uses the four functional operators *ceil, floor, trun,* and *round* to find the ceiling and floor of x, x truncated, and x rounded to any precision. The precision desired should be input as an integer along with the value of x that is to be operated upon.

4. Form the sums of $0.0054 + 0.00803 + 2.44$ and $2.44 + 0.00803 + 0.0054$; use only three significant digits in your computations. The difference in the two sums verifies that the commutative law of addition does not hold when performing computer arithmetic.

5. Form the products of $(4.23 \cdot 0.456) \cdot 0.987$ and $4.23 \cdot (0.456 \cdot 0.987)$; use only three significant digits in your computations. The difference in the two products verifies that the associative law of multiplication does not hold when performing computer arithmetic.

10.2   THE DIGITAL GRAPH-PLOTTING PROBLEM

The solution of some mathematical problems, such as finding the roots of an equation, is often made easier by graphing a function.   Although an accurate plot of a continuous function is often desirable, an approximation to the graph of a function is usually adequate for the analysis of most problems.   Since computers are finite machines, we must be satisfied in computer-controlled graphing with approximations to continuous functions.   Devices are available which plot continuous graphs of functions. These devices are rather expensive, however, and thus are not found in most computer installations.   Therefore, we will use a line printer for producing a digital graph of a function.

problem definition and analysis

In digital graphing, it is best to plot the y axis horizontally on the continuous forms of the printer and to plot the x axis vertically.   One reason for this is that the function $y = f(x)$ may assume the same value for more than one value of x.   Therefore, plotting the y axis horizontally requires that only one data point be printed per line of output.   A second reason is that the number of print positions on a single line is fixed, whereas there is virtually no limit on the number of lines that can be printed. Therefore, the density of the plot [i.e., the number of data points printed in a given portion of the domain of $f(x)$] and the length of the domain of $f(x)$ plotted can be varied much more easily when the x axis is plotted vertically.

The concept of digital plotting is easy to understand. In each line we output to the printer we will print one symbol that represents a value of $f(x)$ for some value of x.   Before we begin the plotting process, we must compute all of the data points that are to be used in the plot.   The reason for this is that we must know the maximum and minimum value of $f(x)$ in the portion of the domain of the function to be plotted in order to divide the print line into m equal-length intervals.   The values of x for which values of $f(x)$ are to be computed is determined by inputting the upper and lower limits of the portion of the domain of the function to be plotted and the number of data points n to be included in the plot.   Given this information, a value of $f(x)$ is computed at equal intervals over this domain of $f(x)$, where the interval is taken as the upper minus the lower limit divided by $(n - 1)$.   Once the data points have been generated, a line is printed for each data point with one symbol being placed in the print line position that corresponds with the interval of the range associated with that data point.

Let us illustrate these ideas with an example. Suppose that our print line contains nine print positions and that we wish to plot the function $f(x) = x - 1$ on the interval $0 \leq x \leq 4$ using five data points. The length of our intervals for x in this case is computed as $(4 - 0)/(5 - 1) = 1$.

305

Notice that we divide the domain by $(n - 1)$ rather than n to obtain the length of our intervals since there are only $(n - 1)$ intervals between n data points. Next we need to compute the values of $f(x)$ for each value of x. This results in the table given in Fig. 10.3. Then we must subdivide the print line into intervals of the range of $f(x)$ for printing the values from the table.

Figure 10.3.   Sample Plot Results for $f(x) = x - 1$

i	x_i	$f(x_i)$	−1.25	−0.75	−.025	0.25	0.75	1.25	1.75	2.25	2.75	3.25
1	0	−1	*									
2	1	0			*							
3	2	1					*					
4	3	2								*		
5	4	3										*

The length of an interval can be computed in our example as $[3 - (-1)]/(9 - 1)$. We divided the range of $f(x)$ by the number of print positions less 1 because we are going to center the minimum and maximum values in the lower and upper intervals, respectively. This strategy means that we will have an extra one-half interval in both the lower and upper intervals. Thus our interval length is being computed for only $(m - 1)$ of the intervals where m is the total number of intervals desired. The final step in plotting the function is to determine into which of the intervals each value of $f(x)$ falls. Then we print a line with a symbol in the print position that corresponds with that interval. The graph for our example appears beside the table in Fig. 10.3, where the horizontal scale gives nine intervals for the nine print positions. Notice that each print line is given beside its respective value of $f(x)$ in the table.

descriptive and algorithm flowcharts   In Fig. 10.4 we have a descriptive flowchart and in Fig. 10.5 an algorithm flowchart for generating a plot of a function of one variable. This algorithm uses a print line with 101 print positions and is designed to plot up to 200 data points. The input values for the variables *x1* and *x2* provide the lower and upper limits, respectively, of the domain of $f(x)$ to be plotted. The input value for n gives the number of data points to be plotted while fn is an integer that indicates the function to be plotted from among the functions given in a subalgorithm called f. The loop in boxes 5 through 8 causes blanks to be placed in all of the elements of the one-dimensional array *line*. This serves to initialize the print line that will be used for the

Figure 10.4.   Descriptive Flowchart for the Digital Graph-Plotting Problem ▶

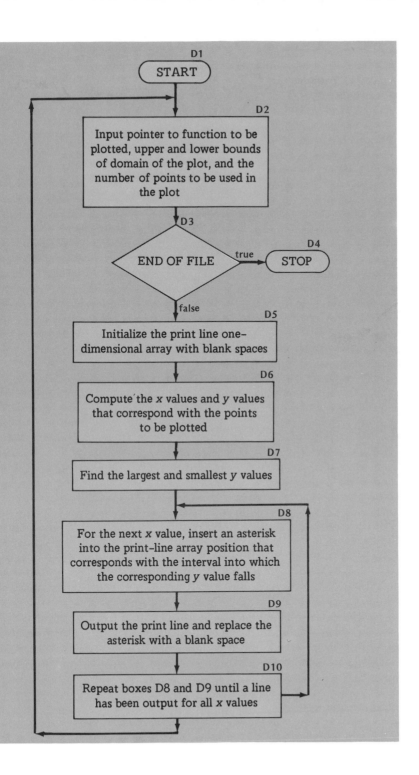

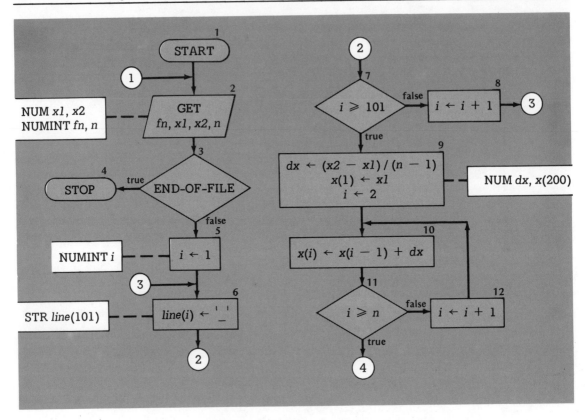

Figure 10.5. Algorithm Flowchart for the Digital Graph-Plotting Problem (continued, opposite page)

plot of the function. In the first statement in box 9 the interval dx for the xs to be used in the plot is computed. The second step in that box then assigns the lower limit of x to the first data point abscissa $x(1)$, while the third step in box 9 initializes the loop counter i. The loop of boxes 10, 11, and 12 then generates the other $(n - 1)$ values of x to be used in the plot.

In box 13 the general subalgorithm with the entry name f is explicitly invoked. This subalgorithm, which is given in Fig. 10.6 for several example functions, then returns the n values of $f(x)$ in the one-dimensional array y for the n values of x given in the array x. Notice that the parameter fn is used as a numeric variable that points to the function in f that is to be evaluated in generating the n data points. Any number of such functions of any type can be placed in the processing boxes of the subalgorithm f as long as the appropriate decision boxes are added.

Returning to the invoking algorithm, the first two steps in box 14

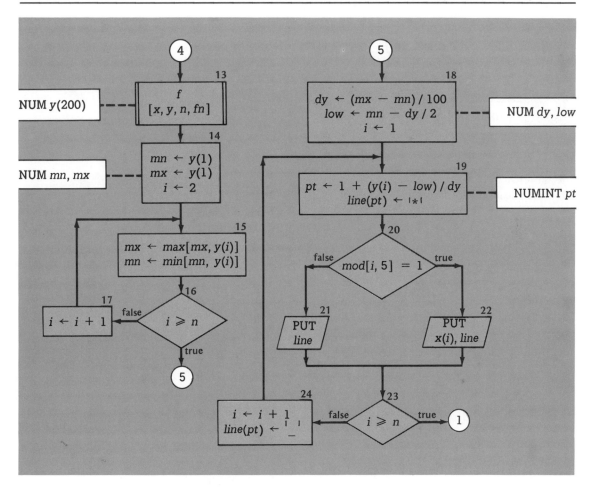

Figure 10.5, *continued*

are used to initialize the variables *mn* and *mx*. These variables will be used to find the minimum and maximum y values, respectively. The third statement in box 14 initializes the variable *i*, which is used as the loop counter in the loop of boxes 15 through 17. Notice the use of the *max* and *min* functional operators in the two statements in box 15. The first statement in box 18 assigns to *dy* the value of the length of an interval corresponding to one position in the print line. The lower limit of the lower class of the print line is then set in the second step of box 18 by subtracting one-half the length of an interval from the minimum value of y. As we will see in box 19, a value of *y(i)* will fall into the interval associated with the *pt*th print position whenever the following inequality is satisfied:

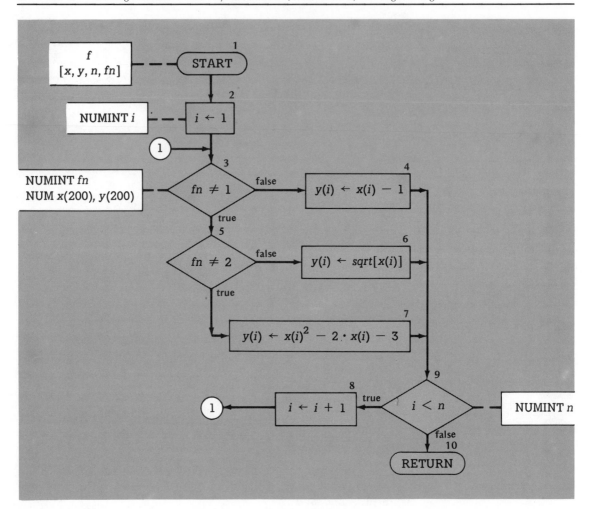

Figure 10.6. Subalgorithm Flowchart to Generate Function Values

$$low + (pt - 1) \cdot dy \le y(i) < low + pt \cdot dy \qquad \textbf{(10.2)}$$

The third step in box 18 is used to initialize the loop counter i, which is used in the loop consisting of boxes 19 through 24. The first step in box 19 assigns to pt a pointer value that points to the interval into which the ith value of y falls. This statement is equivalent to computing a value for pt that allows $y(i)$ to satisfy the inequality of Eq. (10.2). In the second step in box 19 an asterisk is assigned to the print position in *line* that corresponds with the interval into which $y(i)$ fell. Thus, after executing this step, *line* will contain 100 blanks and 1 asterisk, with the asterisk representing the data point for the data pair $(x(i), y(i))$.

The comparison in box 20 is used to determine whether to print the value of $x(i)$ with the ith line or just the line itself. Notice that the condition $mod[i,5] = 1$ will be true only when $i = 1, 6, 11, 16, \ldots$. That is, box 22 will be executed only for every fifth line output, and box 21 will be output for the four lines in between. This is because $mod[i,5] = i - 5 \cdot trun[i/5]$.

The step in box 23 tests to see if all of the n data points have been plotted. If they have, then control is returned to in-connector 1. Otherwise, in box 24 the loop counter i is incremented by 1 and the asterisk in the $p$tth print position in *line* is replaced by a blank in preparation for setting up the next print line.

A plot generated by the computer implementation of Figs. 10.5 and 10.6 for the input values $x1 = -2$, $x2 = 4$, $n = 41$, and $fn = 3$ is given in Fig. 10.7. Notice that by examining this plot we can determine not only the shape of the function but also such things as:(1) a negative root exists at approximately $x = -1$, (2) a positive root exists at approximately $x = 3$, (3) one minimum of $f(x)$ occurs (at approximately $x = 1$) in the portion of the domain of $f(x)$ of interest, and (4) there are two maximum values of $f(x)$ occurring in the portion of the domain of $f(x)$ of interest, and they are at the two endpoints, $x = -2$ and $x = 4$. Thus the digital plot for a function can be very useful in the analysis of that function.

PROBLEMS

6. Use the following as input data values to develop a trace table for the algorithms of Figs. 10.5 and 10.6:

$$x1 = 2, x2 = 5, n = 10, fn = 1$$

7. The solutions to two transcendental equations or a polynomial and a transcendental equation are often difficult to obtain analytically. The points of intersection can be approximated rather accurately, however, by plotting the equations on one graph and observing the points of intersection. Develop an algorithm that plots either one or two functions of one variable on one graph. When two functions are plotted, a list should be printed below the graph of the values of x for which the values of $f(x)$ fell into the same interval for both functions. Use an asterisk as the symbol for plotting the first function and a plus sign as the symbol for graphing the second function.

10.3 THE ROOTS-OF-AN-EQUATION PROBLEM

A problem that occurs often in applied mathematics is that of locating the roots of an equation. The roots of an equation are defined as those values of x for which an equation of the form $f(x) = 0$ is satisfied. For example, the equation

problem definition and analysis

311

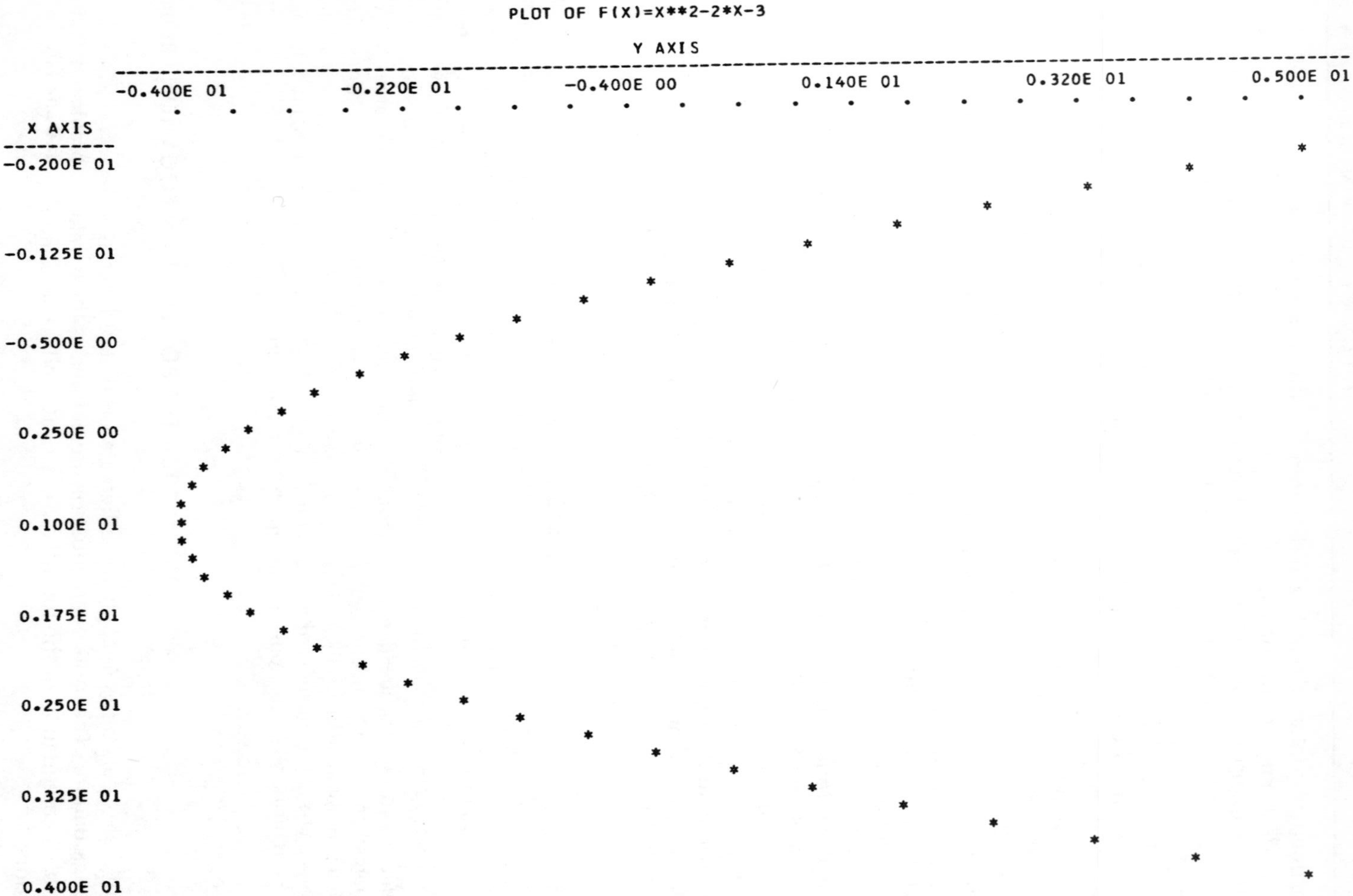

Figure 10.7. Computer Digital Plot of $f(x) = x^2 - 2 \cdot x - 3$ on the Interval $-2 \leq x \leq 4$

$$f(x) = x^2 - 2x - 3$$

contains two roots, $x_1 = -1$ and $x_2 = 3$. That is, $f(-1) = 0$ and $f(3) = 0$. Now, an equation may have either real roots or complex roots or both. We will limit ourselves in this text to solving equations with real coefficients and finding only the real roots to an equation. In general, real roots occur at the points where the function $f(x)$ crosses the x axis, since it will be at those points that $f(x) = 0$.

The types of functions that we find in applied mathematics can be classified as being either polynomial equations or transcendental equations. A polynomial is an equation that has the general form

$$f(x) = a_0 + a_1x + a_2x^2 + \cdots + a_nx^n \qquad \textbf{(10.3)}$$

A transcendental equation, on the other hand, is an equation that cannot be evaluated for any given argument by a finite number of additions, subtractions, multiplications, divisions, or exponentiations. Types of transcendental equations involve the logarithmic, exponential, trigonometric, and hyperbolic functions. Several examples would be: $f(x) = \log x$, $f(x) = e^{-x}$, and $f(x) = \sin x$.

A polynomial of degree n will always contain n roots, all of which will not necessarily be different. If the coefficients of a polynomial equation are all real, any complex roots that exist will always occur in pairs. These pairs of roots will take the form $x = a + b \cdot i$ and $x = a - b \cdot i$ and are called *complex conjugates*.* In finding the roots of a polynomial, Descartes' rule of signs can be helpful. This rule states that for k, the number of sign changes between consecutive coefficients in a polynomial, there will be k or $k - 2$ or $k - 4$ or ... positive real roots. Similarly, if we replace x by $-x$ in the polynomial and count the number of sign changes k, there will be k or $k - 2$ or $k - 4$ ... negative real roots. For example,

$$f(x) = x^3 - x^2 + 2x - 3 \qquad \textbf{(10.4)}$$

has $k = 3$ sign changes $(+ - + -)$ for x and $k = 0$ sign changes $(- - - -)$ for $-x$. Therefore, $f(x)$ in Eq. (10.4) has: (1) three positive real roots, or (2) one positive real root and two imaginary roots. Graphing a polynomial function can often be helpful in determining the number and approximate locations of the roots of an equation.

A transcendental equation may possess either real or complex roots or both. In addition, the number of roots may be either finite or infinite. Thus graphing the function may be the best method of determining the number and approximate locations of the roots of a transcendental equa-

---

* In each of these cases $i = \sqrt{-1}$.

tion. We will consider the method of bisection for finding approximations to the real roots of an equation of the form $f(x) = 0$. We will assume that the functions we deal with are continuous in the neighborhood of interest in applying the bisection method.

The logic of the bisection method for finding approximations to the real roots of an equation is very easy to understand. In using this method, we assume that exactly one real root x lies in the interval $u \leq x \leq v$. The method of bisection is based upon the fact that if a function crosses the x axis once in an interval bounded by u and v, the signs of $f(u)$ and $f(v)$ will not be the same. Thus to find an approximation to the root of an equation we can: (1) bisect the interval in which the root lies and determine in which of the two subintervals it is that the signs of the endpoints are different, (2) bisect this subinterval to find another subinterval in which the signs of the endpoints are different, and (3) continue this process of bisecting subintervals until a satisfactory approximation to the root is obtained.

The method of bisection is illustrated graphically in Fig. 10.8 for the function $f(x) = x - 1$ using as endpoints $u = 0.5$ and $v = 2$. The graph of the function appears in Fig. 10.8(a). Notice that our root x is in fact in the interval $u \leq x \leq v$ and that $f(u)$ is negative while $f(v)$ is positive. Now bisecting the interval means that we divide the interval into two halves. Denoting the midpoint of the interval as m, we compute m to be equal to $(2 + 0.5)/2 = 1.25$. Now the root x lies in either the right or left subinterval. To learn in which subinterval x lies, we simply need to evaluate $f(m)$ and compare its sign to the signs of $f(u)$ and $f(v)$. The left subinterval contains the root if the signs of $f(u)$ and $f(m)$ are different while the right subinterval will contain the root if the signs of $f(m)$ and $f(v)$ are different. In Fig. 10.8(b) we can see that the left subinterval contains the root since $f(u) < 0$ while $f(m) > 0$. Thus our new endpoints are $u = 0.5$ and $v' = 1.25$.

Next, we subdivide our new interval in (b), getting a midpoint m' that is equal to $(0.5 + 1.25)/2 = 0.875$. Now, the root x lies in either the right or left subinterval. Evaluating $f(m')$ and comparing its sign to $f(u)$ and $f(v')$, we learn that the root lies in the right subinterval. This is because $f(m') < 0$ while $f(v') > 0$. In Fig. 10.8(c) we again subdivide the interval, with the new midpoint being $m'' = (0.875 + 1.25)/2 = 1.0625$. This time the root x can be seen to lie in the left subinterval, which is bounded by $u' = 0.875$ and $v'' = 1.0625$.

Since the root of this equation can easily be seen to be $x = 1$, it is clear that our interval is converging on the root. In fact, after repeating the bisection process only three times, we have already arrived at an approximation to the root that may be satisfactory for some purpose. Just how many times the bisection process must be repeated to attain a satisfactory approximation to a root depends primarily upon: (1) the width of

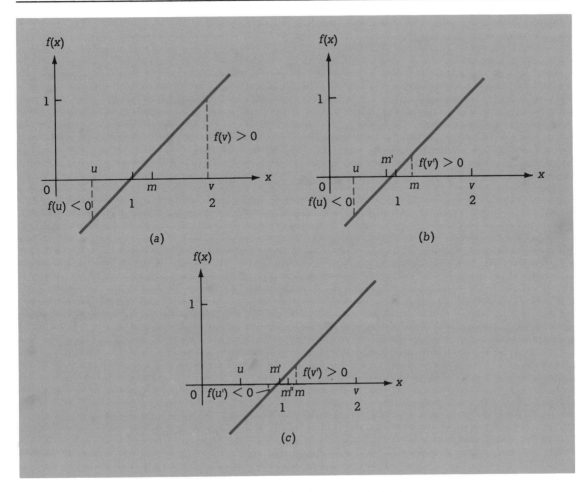

Figure 10.8. Graphical Interpretation of the Bisection Method

the first interval, and (2) what will be considered a good approximation. The digital graphing algorithm of the previous section provides a means of getting good initial values for the endpoints u and v of our interval. Our test for how good an approximation is will be the ratio set out in Eq. (5.8) of Section 5.4.1:

$$abs[u - v]/(abs[u] + abs[v]) \qquad\qquad (10.5)$$

where u and v are the endpoints of the most recent subinterval. When the above ratio is less than or equal to a predetermined value for the relative absolute difference, the most recent midpoint computed will be taken as our approximation to the root.

In Fig. 10.9 we have a descriptive flowchart and in Fig. 10.10 an algorithm flowchart that uses the method of bisection to find an approximation to the root in the interval $u \leq x \leq v$ for an equation given in the subalgorithm f. The values of the input variables u and v are the bounds of the interval that is assumed to contain the root. The value of the maximum relative absolute difference that will be accepted for a good approximation is associated with the variable d. Another input value is fn, an integer that indicates for which of the functions in the subalgorithm f we are seeking an approximate value of the root.

The two steps in box 5 assign to s and t the values of $f(u)$ and $f(v)$, respectively. The subalgorithm f, which is implicitly invoked in these two steps, returns a value of the function evaluated using the value of the first actual parameter. The subalgorithm f is given in Fig. 10.11 for several functions.

In boxes 6 and 8 are comparison operations to compare the product of s and t to zero. If the product is positive, this means that the signs of s and t are the same. This is an error condition, since $f(u)$ and $f(v)$ cannot have the same signs if only one root lies in the interval $u \leq x \leq v$. In box 7 an error message is output, with control being returned to in-connector 1. When the product of s and t is equal to zero, either $f(u)$ or $f(v)$ (or both) must be zero. But this can only occur if either u or v (or both) is a root. This situation causes a branch to box 9 where a test determines whether it was u or v that was a root of the equation. Finally, when the product of s and t is negative, $f(u)$ and $f(v)$ must have opposite signs. In this case, a branch is taken to box 12, where the variables x, z, and n are initialized. The variables x and z are used in the computations in place of u and v so that the input values are not destroyed during the process of computing the successive approximations. The reason for not destroying the input values is that they are needed for output purposes in boxes 19 and 22. The third step in box 12 assigns a value of 1 to a loop counter n which is used to count the number of times that a subinterval is bisected. When 100 bisections have been made and a satisfactory approximation has still not been achieved, execution of the algorithm is aborted. This is done by outputting an error message in box 22 and returning control to in-connector 1.

After the midpoint of a subinterval is computed by averaging the two endpoints of our interval, we assign the value of $f(m)$ to t in the second step in box 13. Notice that this assignment destroys the value of $f(v)$, which was stored as the value of t. Since only one endpoint is needed to determine the subinterval in which the root lies, however, nothing is lost by reusing t for the value of $f(m)$. In boxes 14 and 15 we have two comparisons which determine which subinterval contains the root. If the product of s and t is negative, the left subinterval must contain the root. This is because only then will $f(u)$ and $f(m)$ have different signs. In this

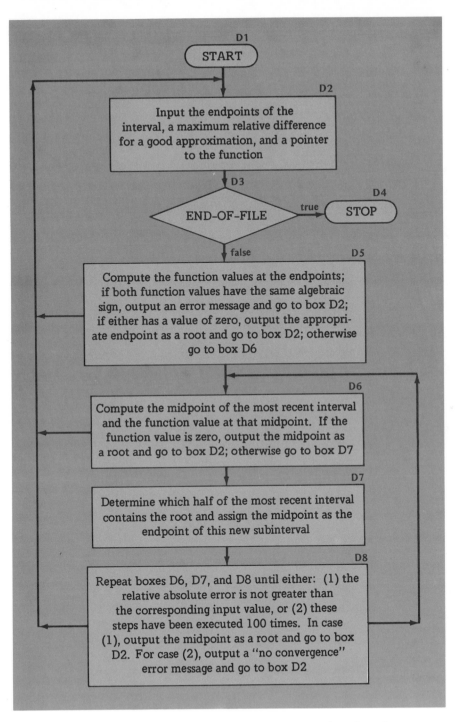

Figure 10.9. Descriptive Flowchart for the Roots-of-an-Equation Problem

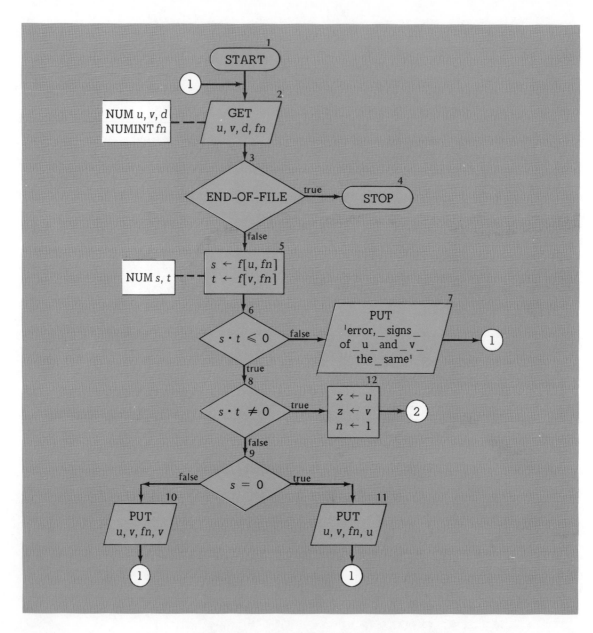

Figure 10.10. Algorithm Flowchart for the Roots-of-an-Equation Problem (continued, opposite page)

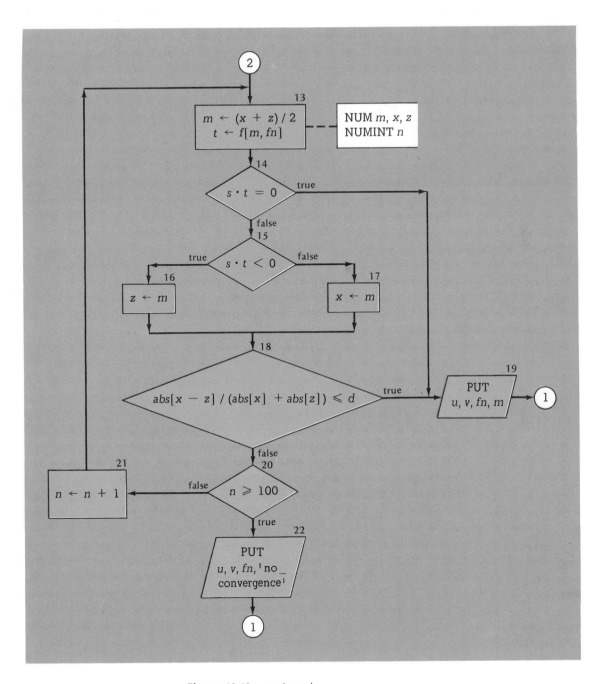

Figure 10.10, *continued*

319

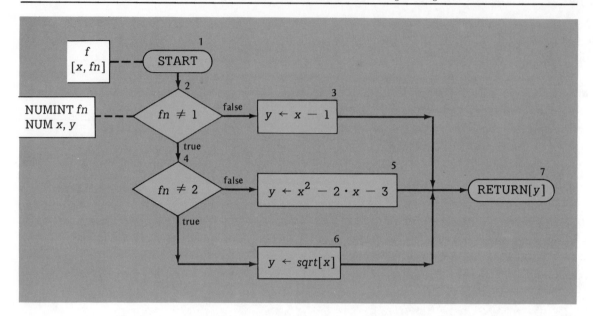

Figure 10.11. Subalgorithm Flowchart to Generate Function Values

case, the midpoint m is assigned to z (which is the stand-in variable for v), thus becoming the new upper bound of our interval. When the product of s and t is a positive value, the right subinterval must be the one that contains the root. This conclusion is reached by a process of elimination, since the left subinterval cannot contain the root when both $f(u)$ and $f(m)$ have the same sign. Thus the right subinterval must contain the root. In this case, the value of the midpoint m is assigned to be the new value of the lower bound x (which is the stand-in variable for u) of our interval. Finally, should the product of s and t be zero, $f(m)$ must be equal to zero and thus m is our root. In this case a branch is taken to box 19, where the value of m is output as the root.

When the value of m is not the root, the next step executed is the comparison operation of box 18. In this box the relative absolute difference is compared with the value of d, which is the maximum difference that will be permitted for a good approximation to a root. If the test indicates that m is a good approximation, the value of m is output by the step in box 19. Otherwise the repetition counter is tested in box 20. If fewer than 100 attempts have been made at approximating the root, n is incremented by 1 in box 21. The next step will be to transfer control to box 13, where another subinterval is generated.

Before the reader accepts the method of bisection as a dandy way of finding the real roots of an equation, some weaknesses of the method must be pointed out. First, although a function may have no real roots, a false root may be found. This can occur when a function comes very close to the x axis but never touches it. Because of rounding error, however, we get a change in signs in an interval and think that we have found a root. A second pitfall may occur when there are two roots that are very close together. In this case we may not be able to find an interval in which the signs change. A third problem is that it is often difficult to define an interval that contains the root of interest. As we noted earlier, the digital graphing algorithm may offer a solution to this problem. Finally, the method of bisection converges rather slowly to an acceptable approximation to the root desired.

more problem analysis

PROBLEMS

8. Develop a trace table for the algorithm of Fig. 10.10; use as input values: $u = 1, v = 4, d = 0.01$, $fn = 2$.

For each of the following problems, develop: (1) a descriptive flowchart, (2) an algorithm flowchart, and (3) a trace table (develop your own input data stream for each of these problems).

9. Modify the algorithm of Fig. 10.10 so that new initial values of u and v are generated should the test in box 6 show that the signs of $f(u)$ and $f(v)$ are the same. Assume at first that there are two roots in the interval. Thus you should move u and v closer together. If after trying four new intervals the signs are still the same, begin widening the interval, beginning from the original values of u and v. This widening process should also be attempted four times.

10. An iterative method for finding approximations to the roots of an equation involves the Newton–Raphson method. Recall that we have already used a special case of this method in the second square-root algorithm developed in Section 5.4.1. This method involves taking an initial approximation x_1 and using the equation

$$x_{i+1} = x_i - \frac{f(x_i)}{f'(x_i)}$$

to generate successive approximations to the root. Develop an algorithm for finding approximations to roots using the Newton–Raphson method. Algorithm input should consist of an initial approxi-

mation, a maximum relative absolute difference, and an integer value that points to a function in a subalgorithm such as the one in Fig. 10.11. Equation (5.8) should be used to compute the relative absolute difference between two successive approximations. Be sure to include a test to be sure that $f'(x_i)$ does not become smaller than 10^{-6} because a small denominator can cause the method to fail.

11. An iterative method sometimes used in finding approximations to the roots of an equation is the *method of successive approximations*. In this method we simply write our function $f(x) = 0$ in the form $x = g(x)$. For example, given $f(x) = x^3 - 2$, we might write $x = x^3 + x - 2$ or $x = (2 + 2x - x^3)/2$ or $x = (x^3 + 3x - 2)/3$ or.... As we can see, there are an infinite number of ways that we can restate a function of the form $f(x) = 0$ to obtain $x = g(x)$. Once restated, however, we can obtain successive approximations to our root x by computing

$$x_{i+1} = g(x_i)$$

Develop an algorithm that begins with an initial approximation and uses the method of successive approximations to compute an approximation to the root of an equation. A function subalgorithm f is needed that contains restated functions of the form $x = g(x)$. Caution should be exercised since this method will converge to the root only when $x = g(x)$ is stated such that $|g'(x)| < 1$ over the interval of the values of x_i.

12. Another method for approximating the roots of an equation is called the *method of false position.* In this method, two initial approximations u and v must be chosen such that $f(u)$ and $f(v)$ are of opposite signs. Then successive approximations may be obtained using the formula

$$x_{i+1} = \frac{x_{i-1} \cdot f(x_i) - x_i \cdot f(x_{i-1})}{f(x_i) - f(x_{i-1})}$$

where $x_0 = u$, $x_1 = v$, and $i = 1, 2, 3, \ldots$. Use the method of false position to develop an algorithm that finds a satisfactory approximation to the root of an equation. Care must be taken at each step to ensure that $f(x_i)$ and $f(x_{i-1})$ have opposite signs.

13. The solution of two simultaneous equations represented by the functions $f(x)$ and $g(x)$ can be obtained by developing a third function

$$h(x) = f(x) - g(x)$$

and solving for $h(x) = 0$. Assume that $f(x)$ is contained in one function subalgorithm f and $g(x)$ in another function subalgorithm g. Modify the algorithm of Fig. 10.10 so that the solution of two simultaneous equations is found given the endpoints u and v of an interval in which they intersect.

14. Modify the algorithm of Problem 10 so that new initial values are generated when a test indicates no convergence. Often in cases such as this a new approximation will permit the algorithm to converge. Your new initial approximations generated should alternate around the most recent approximation before failure by ever-widening amounts.

The algorithm should be considered to have failed after having generated ten new initial approximations.

15. One method of approximating the roots of an equation is the *secant method.* It uses the iterative formula

$$x_{i+1} = x_i - \frac{f(x_i)}{m}$$

where $m = [f(x_i) - f(x_{i-1})]/(x_i - x_{i-1})$. Use the secant method to develop an algorithm that finds a satisfactory approximation to the root of an equation.

16. The extended Newton–Raphson method causes approximations to converge in a cubic fashion on the root of an equation. The extended Newton–Raphson formula is

$$x_{i+1} = x_i - \frac{f(x_i)}{f'(x_i)} - \frac{f(x_i)^2 \cdot f''(x_i)}{2f'(x_i)^3}$$

where $f'(x_i)$ and $f''(x_i)$ are the first and second derivatives of $f(x)$. Use the extended Newton–Raphson method to develop an algorithm that finds satisfactory approximations to the roots of $f(x)$.

17. When the first derivative is difficult to obtain or cumbersome to evaluate, an approximation to the derivative is used in the formula of Problem 10. The approximation is taken as

$$f'(x_i) \approx [f(x_i + \Delta x) - f(x_i)]/\Delta x$$

where Δx is often taken to be $10^{-4} \cdot x$. Modify the algorithm of Problem 10 using our approximation to the value of $f'(x_i)$.

10.4   THE PROBLEM OF FINDING AREA

problem definition and analysis

Another problem that often arises in applied mathematics is that of finding the area under a curve. That is, we need to find the shaded area bounded by the curves $y = f(x)$, $y = 0$, $x = a$, and $x = b$ in Fig. 10.12. The function $f(x)$ is always assumed to be continuous on the interval $a \le x \le b$. That is, it is assumed that $f(x)$ does not have any breaks in that interval. Mathematics provides the methods of integral calculus to solve the problem of finding area. However, in this section we will use an approximating method called the trapezoidal rule, which produces approximations to the area under a curve.

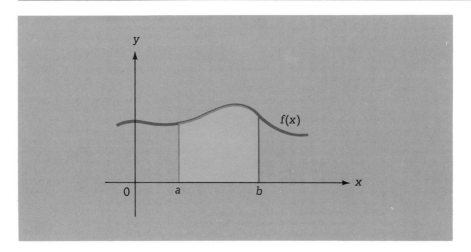

Figure 10.12.   Graph That Shows the Area Under a Curve

The following steps are carried out in approximating area using the trapezoidal rule, where for efficiency subintervals are taken to be of equal length:

1. The interval $a \leq x \leq b$ is divided into n subintervals of equal length h.
2. Then n trapezoids are constructed using the endpoints of the n subintervals.
3. The area of each trapezoid is obtained using the formula

$$area = \frac{f(x_k) + f(x_k + h)}{2} \cdot h \qquad (10.6)$$

where $h = (b - a)/n$, $k = 0, 1, 2, \ldots, n - 1$, and x_k is the value of x at the left endpoint of the kth subinterval.
4. The sum of the areas of the n trapezoids is formed and taken to be an approximation to the area under the curve.

Step 4 can be summarized by the mathematical formula

$$area \approx \sum_{k=0}^{n-1} \left[\frac{f(x_k) + f(x_{k+1})}{2} \cdot h \right] \qquad (10.7)$$

where Σ is simply the summation sign used in Chapter 7. This summation

323

sign simply means to add up a series of items—in this case values of the areas for all n trapezoids. Now, in using the trapezoidal rule we will begin by computing an approximation using $n = 1$, or one subinterval. Then we will divide the interval $a \le x \le b$ into $n = 2$ subintervals and compute a second approximation. Next a third approximation is developed using $n = 3$ subintervals, and so forth until the difference between two successive approximations satisfies some maximum relative absolute difference. Notice that as n increases the length h of each subinterval decreases.

Let us use the function $f(x) = x^3 - x + 1$ as an example, assuming $a = 0$ and $b = 1$. Starting with $n = 1$, we have $h = (b - a)/1 = 1$. Therefore, using Eq. (10.7) we would obtain

$$area \approx \frac{f(x_0) + f(x_1)}{2} \cdot h$$

$$= \frac{f(0) + f(1)}{2} \cdot 1$$

$$= \frac{1 + 1}{2} \cdot 1$$

$$= 1$$

Since the true area can be computed to be 0.75, our true relative error is $(1.00 - 0.75)/0.75 \approx 33$ percent. A graph of the trapezoid used for this first approximation appears in Fig. 10.13(a). Notice that in this example the trapezoid is simply one unit square. The shaded area above $f(x)$ in part (a) is the 33 percent error.

Next let us compute a second approximation using $n = 2$ subintervals. We have $h = (b - a)/2 = 1/2$, and using Eq. (10.7) we would have

$$area \approx \left[\frac{f(x_0) + f(x_1)}{2} + \frac{f(x_1) + f(x_2)}{2} \right] \cdot \frac{1}{2}$$

$$= \left[\frac{f(0) + f(1/2)}{2} + \frac{f(1/2) + f(1)}{2} \right] \cdot \frac{1}{2}$$

$$= \left[\frac{1 + 0.625}{2} + \frac{0.625 + 1}{2} \right] \cdot \frac{1}{2}$$

$$= 0.8125$$

In this case our true relative error is $(0.8125 - 0.75)/0.75 \approx 8.3$ percent. A graph of the two trapezoids used in obtaining this second approximation appears in Fig. 10.13(b). Again, the error is represented by the shaded area above the function $f(x)$. Notice the dramatic reduction in the error resulting from the second approximation.

Let us take a third approximation, this time using three subintervals.

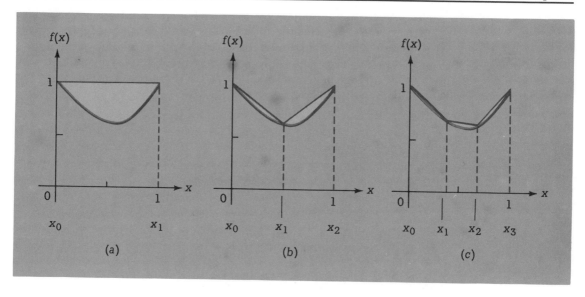

Figure 10.13. Graphs for Three Iterations of the Trapezoidal Rule

The result is $h = (b - a)/3 = 1/3$, and using Eq. (10.7) we would have

$$\text{area} \approx \left[\frac{f(x_0) + f(x_1)}{2} + \frac{f(x_1) + f(x_2)}{2} + \frac{f(x_2) + f(x_3)}{2} \right] \cdot \frac{1}{3}$$

$$= \left[\frac{f(0) + f(1/3)}{2} + \frac{f(1/3) + f(2/3)}{2} + \frac{f(2/3) + f(1)}{2} \right] \cdot \frac{1}{3}$$

$$= \left[\frac{1 + 19/27}{2} + \frac{19/27 + 17/27}{2} + \frac{17/27 + 1}{2} \right] \cdot \frac{1}{3}$$

$$= \frac{21}{27} \approx 0.7778$$

A graph of the three trapezoids used in this case appears in Fig. 10.13(c), with the error again being represented by the shaded area above $f(x)$. Our true relative error has now dropped to $(0.7778 - 0.75)/0.75 \approx 3.7$ percent, a vast improvement indeed. This process could be continued for even larger values of n, with the approximation hopefully improving for each successive approximation. In fact, the only thing that ever causes this method to break down for functions which are continuous and positive on the interval $a \leq x \leq b$ is excessive computational error.

The formula of Eq. (10.7) can be improved by noticing that the value of the function at the right endpoint of the kth subinterval is the same as the value of the function at the left endpoint of the $(k + 1)$th subinterval. That is, the value of the function appears in the sum twice for the endpoint of every interval except for the value of the function at the points a and b. In addition, the value of the function at the right endpoint of the kth subinterval is simply $f(a + k \cdot h)$. Therefore, Eq. (10.7) can be rewritten as

$$area \approx \frac{h}{2}[f(a) + 2 \cdot f(a + h) + 2 \cdot f(a + 2 \cdot h)$$
$$+ \cdots + 2 \cdot f(a + (n - 1) \cdot h) + f(a + n \cdot h)]$$
$$= \frac{h}{2} \cdot \left[f(a) + f(b) + 2 \cdot \sum_{k=1}^{n-1} f(a + k \cdot h) \right] \qquad \textbf{(10.8)}$$

where again $h = (b - a)/n$.

The formula given in Eq. (10.8) can certainly be used for developing our algorithm for approximating the area under a curve using the trapezoidal rule. However, if we double the number of subintervals each time, we have only $n/2$ new subintervals to evaluate on the next iteration of the algorithm. That is, if we denote the approximation to the definite integral for 2^m subintervals as A_m, we have

$$area \approx A_m = \tfrac{1}{2}A_{m-1} + h_m \cdot [f(a + h_m) + f(a + 3 \cdot h_m)$$
$$+ \cdots + f(a + (2^m - 1) \cdot h_m)]$$
$$= \tfrac{1}{2}A_{m-1} + h_m \cdot \sum_{k=1}^{n'} f(a + (2 \cdot k - 1) \cdot h_m) \qquad \textbf{(10.9)}$$

where $h_m = (b - a)/2^m = h_{m-1}/2$; $n' = 2^{m-1}$; and $m = 1, 2, 3, \ldots$. To verify that this holds, let us expand the formula of Eq. (10.8) for $n = 2$ and $n = 4$. For $n = 2$ subintervals we have $h_1 = (b - a)/2$ and, from Eq. (10.8),

$$A_1 = \frac{(b - a)/2}{2}[f(a) + f(b) + 2 \cdot f(a + h)]$$
$$= \frac{b - a}{4}\left[f(a) + f(b) + 2 \cdot f\left(a + \frac{b - a}{2}\right) \right]$$
$$= \frac{b - a}{4}\left[f(a) + f(b) + 2 \cdot f\left(\frac{a + b}{2}\right) \right]$$

Similarly, for $n = 4$ subintervals we have $h_2 = (b - a)/4$, and from Eq. (10.8),

$$A_2 = \frac{(b-a)/4}{2}\{f(a) + f(b)$$

$$+ 2\cdot[f(a + h) + f(a + 2\cdot h) + f(a + 3\cdot h)]\}$$

$$= \frac{b-a}{8}\Big\{f(a) + f(b)$$

$$+ 2\cdot\Big[f\Big(a + \frac{b-a}{4}\Big) + f\Big(a + 2\cdot\frac{b-a}{4}\Big) + f\Big(a + 3\cdot\frac{b-a}{4}\Big)\Big]\Big\}$$

$$= \frac{b-a}{8}\Big\{f(a) + f(b)$$

$$+ 2\cdot\Big[f\Big(a + \frac{b-a}{4}\Big) + f\Big(\frac{a+b}{2}\Big) + f\Big(a + 3\cdot\frac{b-a}{4}\Big)\Big]\Big\}$$

Factoring out and rearranging, we obtain

$$A_2 = \frac{1}{2}\Big(\frac{b-a}{4}\Big)\Big[f(a) + f(b)$$

$$+ 2\cdot f\Big(\frac{a+b}{2}\Big)\Big] + \frac{b-a}{4}\Big[f\Big(a + \frac{b-a}{4}\Big) + f\Big(a + 3\cdot\frac{b-a}{4}\Big)\Big]$$

But, the first set of terms is simply $\frac{1}{2}A_1$, obtained above, while the second set of terms is simply the second term of Eq. (10.9). Therefore, we have

$$A_2 = \frac{1}{2}A_1 + h_2\cdot\sum_{k=1}^{2} f(a + (2\cdot k - 1)\cdot h_2)$$

Although this does not verify Eq. (10.9) in the general case, it can be verified in general by similar algebraic operations. Finally, notice that the variable n' of Eq. (10.9) is not defined to be the number of intervals (2^m) but is rather the number of intervals divided by two (2^{m-1}).

A descriptive flowchart is given in Fig. 10.14 and an algorithm flowchart appears in Fig. 10.15 for approximating the value of an area using the formula of Eq. (10.9). The input values a and b give the left and right endpoints while d gives the maximum relative absolute difference that an acceptable approximation may have. Finally, fn is an integer that indicates which function in a function subalgorithm f is to be used for finding an approximation to the area. The function subalgorithm f would be the same in concept as that of Fig. 10.11. In box 5 of the algorithm the subinterval counter n, the subinterval length h, and the variable al [which corresponds to A_{m-1} in the formula of Eq. (10.9)] are given initial values. Notice that

descriptive and
algorithm
flowcharts

327

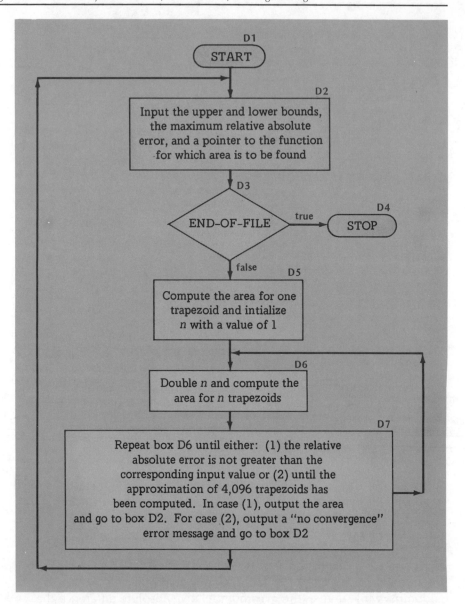

Figure 10.14.   Descriptive Flowchart for the Area Problem

the initial value assigned to al is the area of a trapezoid that consists of one subinterval.

The first step in box 6 doubles the number of subintervals n while the second step halves the length h of the subintervals. Notice that the n of the algorithm is an actual count of the current number of subintervals.

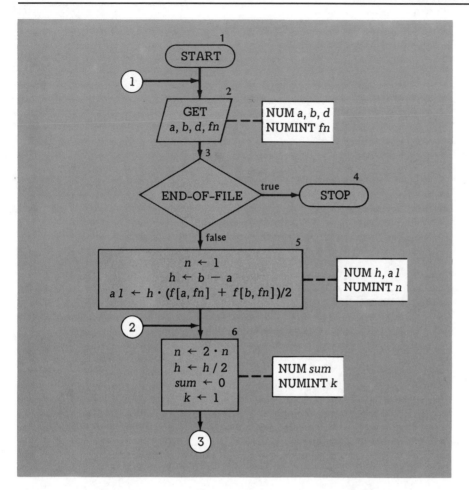

Figure 10.15. Algorithm Flowchart for the Area Problem (continued on page 330)

Therefore, it has a value that is twice that of the *n'* of Eq. (10.9). The
third step in box 6 sets a summing location called *sum* to zero in preparation for forming the sum in the formula of Eq. (10.9). Finally, the last step
in box 6 gives an initial value to the variable *k* that is a loop counter for
the summing loop that consists of boxes 7 and 8. Notice that the variable
h is not subscripted, since only its most recent value is needed both in
computations and in generating its next value. In box 7 the sum of Eq.
(10.9) is formed. Note that *k* is given an initial value of 1 in box 6 and
is incremented by 2 in box 7. Therefore, *k* can only assume the values
of the successive odd integers and is thus equivalent to the multiplier
$(2 \cdot k - 1)$ of h_m in Eq. (10.9). In addition, *k* can never equal *n* since *n* is

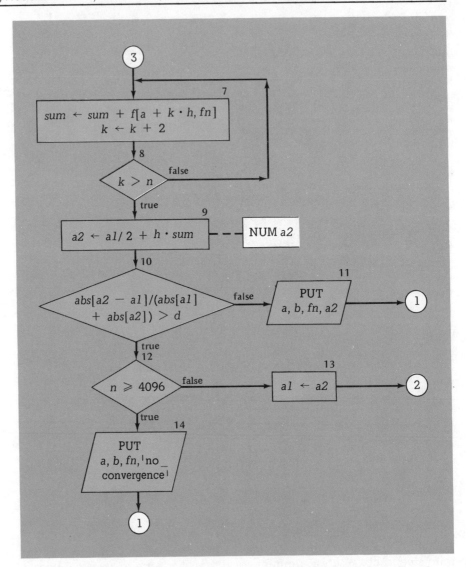

Figure 10.15, *continued*

always an even integer, whereas k is always an odd integer. Thus, the largest value assumed by k will be $n - 1$, or equivalently, $2n' - 1$, as in Eq. (10.9).

The statement in box 9 assigns the next approximation of the area to the variable $a2$ using the formula of Eq. (10.9). Thus, after executing the step in box 9, al contains the previous approximation (for $n/2$ subintervals) while $a2$ contains the most recent approximation (for n subintervals).

Notice that $a2$ is equivalent to A_m of Eq. (10.9). The comparison operation of box 10 compares the relative absolute difference of these two successive approximations to determine whether or not the algorithm has achieved a satisfactory approximation to the value of the area. If it has, the value of the most recent approximation $a2$ is output by the step in box 11. Otherwise, a comparison is made in box 12 to determine whether 4,096 subintervals were used in generating the most recent approximation. If 4,096 subintervals were used, the algorithm aborts by outputting an error message in box 14 and returning control to in-connector 1. This test serves as a safety check so that an unreasonable value of d or rounding error does not cause the algorithm to fail to terminate. If fewer than 4,096 subintervals were used in computing the most recent approximation, then in box 13 the value of the most recent approximation $a2$ is assigned to be the value of the previous approximation $a1$. Then a branch is taken back to in-connector 2, where computation of the next approximation is begun.

Notice in box 10 that Eq. (5.8) of Section 5.4.1 is used in computing the relative absolute difference. In addition, the choice of a maximum of 4,096 subintervals was arbitrary. However, this is usually a sufficient number for evaluating most functions. Finally, on any iteration the amount of error depends on the function $f(x)$. Generally, however, it will not exceed a value on the order of h^2 for the trapezoidal rule algorithm. Thus, for an interval of length 10, the error for $n = 1,024$ subintervals should not exceed approximately $(0.01)^2$.

PROBLEMS

18. Use $f(x) = x^3 - x + 1$ of this section and $d = 0.01$, $a = 0$, and $b = 1$ to develop a trace table for the subalgorithm of Fig. 10.15.

19. Develop three graphs that progressively show the first three approximations generated using the version of the trapezoidal rule given in Eq. (10.9). Use $f(x) = x^3 - x + 1$ in drawing your graphs.

In the following problems, develop: (1) a descriptive flowchart, (2) an algorithm flowchart, and (3) a trace table (develop your own input data stream for each of these algorithms).

20. Use the trapezoidal rule of Eq. (10.8) to develop an algorithm for approximating the area under a curve.

21. Probably the most widely used method for approximating area is *Simpson's rule*. It is popular because it causes faster convergence on a satis-

factory result than does the trapezoidal rule. In its basic form, Simpson's rule uses the formula

$$area \approx \frac{h}{3}[f(a) + 4 \cdot f(a + h) + 2 \cdot f(a + 2 \cdot h)$$
$$+ 4 \cdot f(a + 3 \cdot h) + \cdots + 4 \cdot f(a + (n-1) \cdot h)$$
$$+ f(a + n \cdot h)]$$
$$= \frac{h}{3} \cdot \left[f(a) - f(b) + 2 \sum_{k=1}^{m} f(a + 2 \cdot k \cdot h) \right.$$
$$\left. + 4 \cdot \sum_{k=1}^{m} f(a + (2 \cdot k - 1) \cdot h) \right] \qquad \textbf{(10.10)}$$

where $h = (b - a)/n$ and $m = n/2$ for $n = 4, 6, 8, \ldots$. Develop an algorithm that uses the same input values as does the algorithm of Fig. 10.15 to develop an approximation to an area. Notice that n assumes only even values. The error for Simpson's rule is of the order h^4.

22. If we double the number of subintervals each time a new approximation is generated, we can develop a more efficient version of the Simpson's rule algorithm. Denoting the approximation to the area for 2^m subintervals as A_m, we have

$$area \approx A_m = \frac{1}{2}{\cdot}A_{m-1} + \frac{h_m}{3}{\cdot}\{[f(a + h_m)$$

$$+ f(a + 3{\cdot}h_m) + \cdots + f(a + (2^m - 1){\cdot}h_m)]$$

$$- 2[f(a + 2{\cdot}h_m) + f(a + 6{\cdot}h_m)$$

$$+ \cdots + f(a + (2^m - 2){\cdot}h_m)]\}$$

$$= \frac{1}{2}{\cdot}A_{m-1} + \frac{h_m}{3}\left[4\sum_{k=1}^{n} f(a + (2{\cdot}k - 1){\cdot}h_m)\right.$$

$$\left. -2 \cdot \sum_{k=1}^{n'} f(a + (4{\cdot}k - 2){\cdot}h_m)\right] \qquad \textbf{(10.11)}$$

where

$$h_m = \frac{b - a}{2^m} = \frac{h_{m-1}}{2}, n = 2^{m-1}, n' = 2^{m-2}, \text{ and } m$$

$$= 2, 3, 4, \ldots$$

Notice that this version of Simpson's rule requires that during a particular iteration, twice the terms of the positive sum from the previous iteration be subtracted out. Therefore, all of the terms of

$$f(a + (2{\cdot}k - 1){\cdot}h_m)$$

developed on the *i*th iteration should be stored in a one-dimensional array for use on the $(i + 1)$th iteration. Use the formula of Eq. (10.11) to develop an algorithm for approximating area.

10.5   THE SIMULATION PROBLEM

Monte Carlo method

There is one problem-solving technique we have not touched on that has relevance to almost any field of study. This technique is called the *Monte Carlo method* and involves the use of probability concepts in problem solution. The term "Monte Carlo" is used because the concepts involved were first studied as they relate to games of chance (e.g., poker, black jack, and roulette). Because of the large volume of computations usually involved, Monte Carlo methods are not practical in problem solving unless a computer is available. Thus Monte Carlo methods are rather recent in terms of their use for problem solving and are almost without exception computer-based techniques. In this section we are going to solve one problem using the Monte Carlo method.

probability defined

As we indicated above, the Monte Carlo method involves the use of probability concepts. Therefore, let us begin by examining several basic notions about probability. The classical definition of *probability* is:

> Assume that we have an experiment that has a total of *n* possible outcomes where each outcome can occur in a mutually exclusive and equally likely way. Then the probability that the event *E*, which consists of *m* of these outcomes, occurs is the fraction *m/n*.

The probability of the event *E* occurring is often written as $p(E) = m/n$. As an example, there are fifty-two different outcomes that can occur when drawing one card from an ordinary deck of playing cards. Therefore, the probability of the event that an ace of clubs is drawn when drawing one card is $p(ace\ of\ clubs) = 1/52$, since there is only one ace of clubs per deck. There are four aces in a deck, however, and thus the event of drawing an ace has the probability $p(ace) = 4/52 = 1/13$. As a second example, if we say that the probability of a male child being born is $p(male) = .52$, what we mean is that over a very large series of births, there will be 52 boys per 100 births. Since an event can either occur or not occur, the total probability for all outcomes of an experiment is 1 and the probability of any event occurring always satisfies $0 \leq p(E) \leq 1$.

The set of all possible outcomes of an experiment is called the *sample space* of the experiment. If we assign a number to each outcome that can occur at random (by chance) in an experiment, we have what is called a *random variable*. For example, x may be considered to be a random variable if x is the number of defective television sets produced per hour at a plant over a period of months or years. A *random variate* is a number that is a particular value of a random variable. For example, $x = 5$ defective television sets produced during some hour of production is a random variate. With this brief introduction to probability concepts, let us now take up the concept of a random number.

A *random number* is simply a value of a random variable generated by a random process. Since the physical processes that generate random numbers are difficult to harness to a digital computer, we are going to use pseudo-random numbers in doing our Monte Carlo work. A *pseudo-random number* is a number that behaves as though it is a random number but which is produced by a repeatable process. By *behaves as though it is a random number* we mean that a certain sequence of pseudo-random numbers will satisfy all of the statistical tests that a random number sequence of similar length would satisfy. One advantage of using pseudo-random numbers is that a sequence of them can generally be repeated, thus permitting repetition of an experiment. On the other hand, a sequence of random numbers will not in general repeat itself. Throughout the remainder of this section we will call pseudo-random numbers simply random numbers, even though we know they are only pseudo-random.

The most frequently used type of random number is one that is uniformly distributed over the unit interval. By this we mean that the values assumed by the random variable x can vary over the interval $0 \leq x \leq 1$ and all values in that interval have an equal probability of occurring. A graph of the probability density function for the *uniform distribution* appears in Fig. 10.16. The probability density function is defined to be

$$f(x) = 1 \quad \text{for } 0 \leq x \leq 1$$
$$= 0 \quad \text{for } x < 0, x > 1 \qquad \textbf{(10.12)}$$

We will use random numbers drawn from the uniform distribution in the algorithm that we develop in this section.

random and pseudo-random numbers

uniform random numbers

333

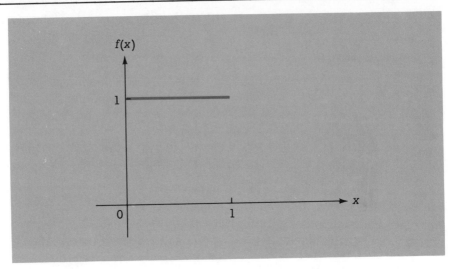

Figure 10.16.   Uniform Probability Density Function

   It is beyond the scope of this text to examine the means by which random numbers from the uniform distribution are generated. Thus we will simply accept the subalgorithm of Fig. 10.17 as one that will produce satisfactory uniform random numbers.

simulation   By far the widest use of the Monte Carlo method is in the area of simulation. In simulation, a model of a system is developed and values are input to this model which cause output to be produced. Since the model is designed to be a representation of the system, by studying model behavior under various conditions we are also hopefully learning how the

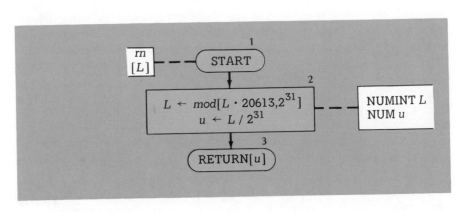

Figure 10.17.   Uniform Random-Number-Generator Subalgorithm

system performs under the same conditions. Thus we are using the model to simulate the performance of the system.

As an example, in planning space flights there are many questions that need to be answered. Moreover, errors in planning can be fatal to the crew. Therefore, a mathematical model of the space flight can be constructed and the actual flight simulated by the use of the model. By changing various things in the model, we can see how these changes will affect various aspects of the flight.

In performing simulation using a digital computer, the models developed will always be mathematical models. That is, the models will always consist of things such as equations and inequalities. In the remainder of this section, let us develop a simple model to simulate the sale of bread at a grocery store.

Let us begin by examining the assumptions included in our bread simulation model. First, we will assume that the grocery store manager has collected data on bread sales over a six-month period. These data indicate that sales for one day have never been less than ten loaves and never greater than seventeen loaves. The frequency with which other quantities of bread have been sold is summarized in Fig. 10.18. This table shows that sales equal: (1) ten loaves five times out of one hundred, (2) eleven loaves ten times out of one hundred, and so forth. In other words, the *Probability of Occurrence* gives the relative proportion of time that the corresponding number of loaves of bread have been sold. The right-hand column simply contains the sum of individual probabilities (given in the middle column) for all quantities of bread sold that are less than or equal to that quantity. For example, for twelve loaves the cumulative probability of 0.30 is derived by summing 0.05, 0.10, and 0.15, which are the probabilities for ten, eleven, and twelve loaves, respectively.

The second assumption is that all bread available for sale on any day is delivered just before the store opens on that day. This bread has

problem definition and analysis

Figure 10.18. Historical Bread Sales Data

Daily Sales (in loaves)	Probability of Occurrence	Cumulative Probability
10	0.05	0.05
11	0.10	0.15
12	0.15	0.30
13	0.20	0.50
14	0.20	0.70
15	0.15	0.85
16	0.10	0.95
17	0.05	1.00

a fixed cost per loaf and is all sold for a fixed retail price. Any bread that is unsold at the end of each day is donated to an orphanage. In addition, the quantity of bread purchased each day is fixed for the period of time simulated.

descriptive flowchart

The descriptive flowchart for this problem appears in Fig. 10.19. The step in box D2 is designed to input the number of sales quantities that have been observed. For the data in Fig. 10.18, this value would be 8, since there are eight rows in the table. In box D5 the daily sales quantities and their corresponding probabilities are input. The daily sales quantities are stored in an array as they are input and the individual probabilities are summed to form cumulative probabilities. These cumulative probabilities are stored in an array as they are computed. Note that a test is included to detect an error in the input probabilities. The step in box D6 is designed to input the values used to perform one simulation experiment. Observe that when the quantity of loaves bought is less than or equal to zero, a branch is made back to box D2. Thus this is taken as a signal that all simulation experiments for this sales table have been completed.

In box D7 a uniform probability is generated, which is then used to look up in the table the sales for that day. The details of how the generated probability is used to look up the sales quantity will be presented in the discussion of the algorithm flowchart. Once sales for the day have been generated, the gross income and net profit for that sales quantity is computed. In addition, accumulated net profit is increased by the amount of the net profit for the day. This is done so that we can compare the profits that result when the simulation experiment is repeated for various purchase quantities. Next the sales quantity, gross income, and net profit for the day are output. The step in box D9 states that the process of generating and outputting sales demand and profit should be repeated for as many days as we wish to simulate. Then in box D10 the input values and accumulated net profit for the simulated time period are output.

algorithm flowchart

The algorithm flowchart for this problem is given in Fig. 10.20. Flowchart box 2 is used to initialize the variable L, which is used by the subalgorithm that generates the random numbers. The step in box 3 is used to input the number of quantities in the sales table. Box 6 is used to initialize the loop variable i and the variable *sum*. In flowchart box 7, the individual sales quantities and their corresponding probabilities are input. Then in box 8 the cumulative probability is computed using the variable *sum* and stored in the array *cpS*. Boxes 9 and 10 are the steps for loop termination and modification, respectively. Thus the loop of flowchart boxes 6 through 10 is used to input the array of sales quantities and compute the array of corresponding cumulative probabilities. The step in box 11 is included to verify that the sum of individual probabilities is equal to 1. The reason the sum of these probabilities must be equal to 1 is that each of the individual probabilities represents the relative fre-

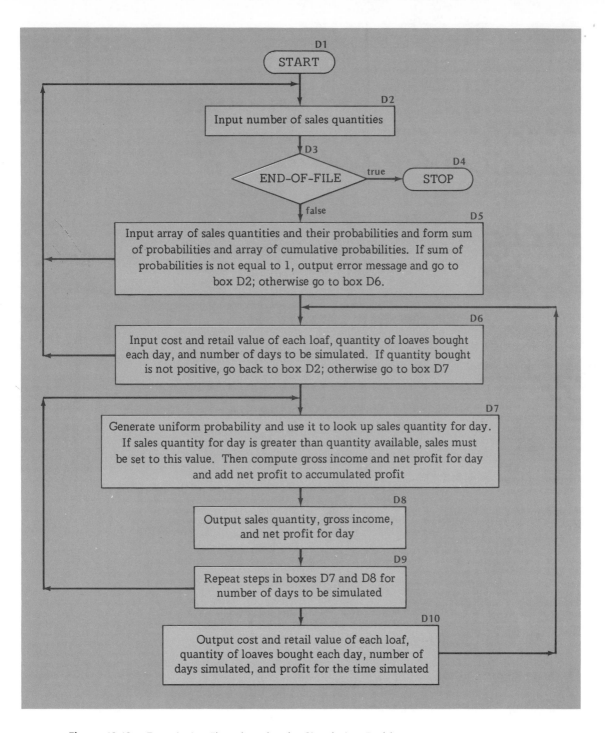

Figure 10.19. Descriptive Flowchart for the Simulation Problem

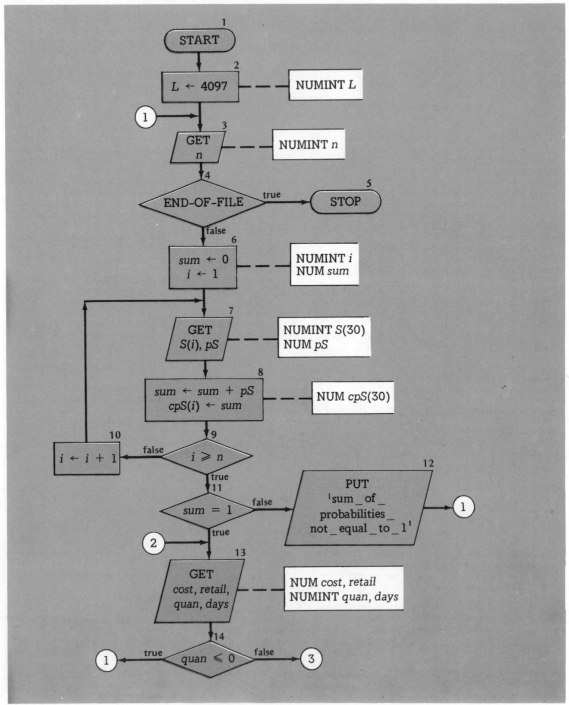

Figure 10.20. Algorithm Flowchart for the Simulation Problem (continued, opposite page)

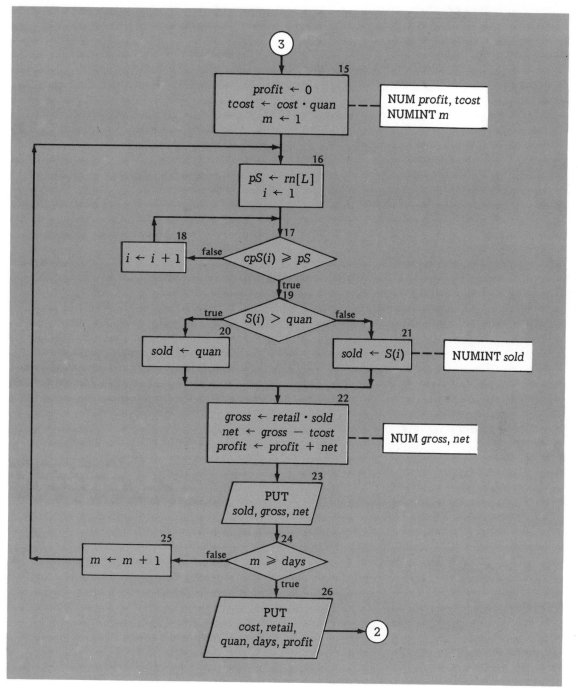

Figure 10.20, *continued*

quency of the respective sales quantities. Therefore, the sum must be equal to 1 because one of the sales quantities must occur.

Input of the values used for each simulation experiment is performed by the step in box 13. The values input are:

1. The cost to the store of each loaf of bread purchased *(cost)*.
2. The price at which the store sells each loaf of bread *(retail)*.
3. The number of loaves of bread the store will purchase each day *(quan)*.
4. The number of days for which the sale of bread is to be simulated *(days)*.

In box 14, a test is made to determine if the quantity of bread purchased is less than or equal to zero. If it is, this signals that no more simulation experiments are to be run using the sales table values currently in the array S. In this case a branch is taken to in-connector 1 where the input of another set of table values and probabilities occurs. Otherwise, a branch is taken to box 15. In this box, the variables used in the simulation experiment are initialized. The variable *profit* is set to zero because it is used to accumulate net profit for all of the days of the experiment. The total cost of the number of loaves of bread purchased each day is computed and assigned to the variable *tcost*. This is done outside of the loop because this total cost does not change through the time of each experiment. Finally, the variable *m* is the loop variable used to control the number of times the loop of boxes 15 through 25 is to be executed.

In box 16, the variable *pS* is assigned the probability returned by invoking the random number subalgorithm *rn*. Recall that the flowchart for this subalgorithm was given earlier in Fig. 10.17. Notice that the variable *L* we initialized in flowchart box 2 is used as the actual parameter when invoking the subalgorithm. This value of *L* is changed by the subalgorithm each time it is invoked, since *L* is used to generate the uniform random numbers. The second step in box 16 initializes the loop variable *i*, which is used in the loop of boxes 16 through 18. This loop is used to look up the sales quantity associated with the random probability generated by the subalgorithm invoked in box 16. The way this is done is to test (in box 17) the random probability generated to determine which is the first of the cumulative probabilities it is less than or equal to in value. Recall that a uniform random number produced by the subalgorithm is a value between 0 and 1. Therefore, we can use it as a cumulative probability that can be compared with those in the array *cpS*. Thus, over a large number of trials each individual sales quantity will be selected with the same frequency as actual bread sales that were observed for the data collected in building the sales probabilities. Note that the loop of boxes 16 through 18 begins this comparison with the smallest cumulative probability. Thus the first value of the array *cpS* that is greater than or equal to the value of *pS* will give the entry in the table that is the sales quantity for the day. That is, the inner loop of boxes 16 through 18 will be exited with *i* pointing to the entry in *S* that contains the number of loaves sold. In box 19 a test is made to be sure that we are not trying to sell more loaves of bread than were purchased. If we are, the step in box 20 is used to assign the quantity purchased by the store as the number of loaves sold. When the number of loaves that could be sold is on hand, however, the value of *S(i)* is assigned to the variable *sold*.

The steps in flowchart box 22 are included to compute the gross income and net profit on the number of loaves sold for the day. Also included in that box is a step that adds the net profit for the day into the accumulated profit for the simulation experiment. In flowchart box 23 is a step that is included to output the number of loaves sold, the gross income, and net profit for the day. Boxes 24 and 25 are the test-for-loop-termination and modification steps, respectively. Finally, box 26 is used to output the input values and accumulated profit for this experiment. The last value output will allow us to compare the results from a number of simulation experiments given various input values. This will be valuable for making management decisions about purchases and pricing.

PROBLEMS

23. Develop an algorithm for dealing at random four bridge hands of thirteen cards each. Assume that the cards of a deck are numbered from 1 to 52 and draw uniformly distributed random integers *x* from the interval $1 \leq x \leq 52$ in generating the bridge hands. Output, however, should include the suit and face value of the cards.

24. The probability of various five-card stud-poker hands can be approximated using the Monte Carlo method. Develop an algorithm that randomly generates hands of five cards each and counts the number of full houses, straights, flushes, and so on. Then the algorithm should use these counts to develop the respective probabilities of obtaining a particular hand.

25. Develop an algorithm that simulates the rolling of a pair of dice and counts the number of times each different point count (2 points, 3 points, . . ., 12 points) comes face up. Then use these fre-

quencies to compute the probability of the various outcomes.

26. Expand the algorithm of Problem 25 to simulate the play of the game of craps. In the game of craps, a player who throws a 7 or an 11 on the first throw wins, whereas a player loses if a 2, 3, or 12 is thrown. Otherwise the number of points face up is called the *point*. The player then continues to roll the dice until either the point turns up again, in which case the player wins, or until a 7 turns up, which is a loss.

27. A roulette wheel contains thirty-eight slots into which a ball may fall, with the slots being numbered from 0 to 36 and 00. The 0 and 00 slots are colored green and the numbers 1, 3, 5, 7, 9, 19, 21, 23, 25, 27, 12, 14, 16, 18, 30, 32, 34, and 36 are colored red, with the remaining numbers being colored black. Develop an algorithm that simulates the spinning of a roulette wheel outputting the frequency with which a ball falls into a slot of each number and color.

SUMMARY

1. Many of the algorithms used to solve mathematical problems are designed to provide approximate rather than exact solutions.

2. Four useful integer functions are the (a) ceiling function, (b) floor function, (c) truncation function, and (d) rounding function.

3. Rounding errors are a result of the fact that computers can represent only finite approximations to real numbers using a binary floating-point system for number representation.

4. The three basic types of rounding error are: (a) input errors, (b) output errors, and (c) computational errors.

5. Input errors are caused by the finite length permitted for computer floating-point numbers and by conversion of numbers from decimal to binary representation.

6. Output errors are caused by the conversion of binary numbers to their decimal equivalents.

7. Computational errors are caused by the finite length of computer floating-point numbers.

8. Because of computational error, the associative and commutative laws of addition and multiplication generally do not hold when performing computer arithmetic.

9. In general, the sum of a series of floating-point numbers with differing magnitudes should be formed in order of increasing magnitude.

10. Caution must be exercised to avoid the practice of taking the difference of two nearly equal quantities because of the resulting loss of significance.

11. A data set is said to be ill-conditioned when small changes in one or more of its values causes a large change in the results.

12. Caution must be exercised in trying to compare for the equality of two floating-point numbers in a computer. Interval comparison, rather than seeking absolute equality, is to be preferred.

13. Developing a digital plot is a useful means of obtaining crude solutions to both single and simultaneous equations.

14. The method of bisection provides a means of finding an approximation to the root of an equation when a root is known to lie in an interval.

15. An approximation to the area under a curve can be found using the trapezoidal rule. The trapezoidal rule proceeds by dividing the interval $a \leq x \leq b$ into n subintervals, constructing trapezoids in each of these subintervals, and then summing the areas of these trapezoids.

16. The error involved in using the trapezoidal rule to approximate a definite integral is on the order of h^2.

17. The most popular method for finding the area under a curve is one that uses Simpson's rule, which uses a quadratic interpolating polynomial.

18. The error involved in using Simpson's rule to approximate a definite integral is on the order of h^4.

19. The Monte Carlo method involves the use of probability concepts in problem solution.

20. A random number is a value of a random variable generated by a random or chance process.

21. In developing Monte Carlo solutions to problems using a computer, we will generally use pseudo-random numbers that are generated by a deterministic process but which behave as though they were random.

22. The most frequently used type of random number is one drawn from a uniform probability distribution that is defined as $f(x) = 1$ for $0 \leq x \leq 1$.

23. A model is a representation of a system that may be used in simulation experiments.

24. Simulation is the process of studying the behavior of a system by experimenting with a model of the system.

The Computer and Society

In the first ten chapters of this book we have explored many aspects associated with the use of a computer in problem solving. We briefly examined notions about what a computer system is and how it solves problems. In addition, we examined a number of ways in which computers are being used and can be used in helping people to solve their problems. Our task in this chapter will be to examine some of the ways in which the computer has affected and may affect our society, its institutions, and the individuals who collectively make up the society.

11.1 ECONOMIC AND INSTITUTIONAL IMPACT

Since the inception of electronic computers in the 1940s, a technological revolution has been occurring in our society. This technological revolution has permitted people to release themselves from the machines and factories that have bound them since the beginning of the industrial revolution, just as the industrial revolution freed them from the labor of the land.

computer revolution

There is, however, one significant difference between the industrial and computer revolution—the telescoping of the time frame for the computer revolution. That is, during the first twenty years of the computer revolution, a level of technological development and implementation has been attained that easily surpasses comparable achievements which required more than one hundred years of the industrial revolution.

Currently we are experiencing an ever-increasing use of computers in all aspects of everyday life, from maintaining airline reservations and tax information to the control of complex industrial processes. In fact, boundless opportunities seem to exist for the application of computer technology to the many activities which transpire within our society or which have not formerly been performed at all. The question we must come to grips with is how the computer revolution is affecting society, both economically and institutionally.

computer impact on productivity

An important aspect of the economic impact of computers involves productivity and employment. *Productivity* may be defined as the annual output per worker. Clearly, as more and more tasks are automated, productivity will increase. This is because fewer people are required to produce the same volume of goods and services. If the cost of the automated

'IT'S TIME WE GOT WITH IT, RIGHT!'

machines is less than the wages of the workers that are replaced, then automation should produce benefits to society through lower prices. Lower prices will mean that a person's income can buy more goods and services than it could before the automation took place. This will, in turn, create a greater demand for other products and services. It is this sequence of developments that is largely responsible for the great jump in the standard of living in the United States during the past thirty years. The computer has been very instrumental in the increases in productivity that have occurred during the past fifteen years to permit these increases in the standard of living.

Although benefits from increased productivity cannot be denied, the picture darkens somewhat when employment is considered. Recall that the factor which permitted prices to drop is that the machines replaced people and performed the same tasks at a lower cost. But what becomes of the people that are now unemployed? In theory, they will take the new jobs created in the industries which now have a greater demand because incomes stretch further. However, there are some problems attached to this argument. First, these other industries have also been automating and therefore can satisfy this increase in demand for their products with the same number of workers (if not fewer). Second, the unemployed worker may not have the skills necessary to acquire an available job. That is, the worker lacks occupational mobility. This means that once a worker is

computer impact on employment

345

displaced from a former job because it has been abolished, another position cannot be easily acquired.

We might say that the solution to the problem is retraining the worker who is displaced. Unfortunately, only recently has this need for retraining become recognized, and to date much of it has been misdirected. That is, much of the retraining has been to prepare people for jobs that are currently obsolete or are soon to become obsolete. In the meantime, the incomes of the unemployed are no longer available to create demand for goods and services. As demand lessens, the work force is further reduced, thus causing a vicious downward spiral. At this point we might say that this discussion is somewhat out of step with the facts. After all, the economy of the United States has gone along pretty well up to this point. But has it really? In the past three decades, reasonably full employment and prosperity have been attainable only during periods of war, either cold or hot. This same period of time has seen the number of persons employed by the various levels of government as a proportion of total employment jump at a significant rate. In addition, there has been a great increase in the demand for services, which has temporarily taken up the slack. This is because automation has been slow in coming to the service industries. But this also is changing, for minimum wage laws have now made service labor costly enough to justify, on a cost basis, the automation of numerous service-type tasks currently or formerly held by human beings. Witness also the reduction taking place in hours worked per year in most industries. All of these factors have thus far tended to shield the impact of the computer revolution on employment.

And this is only the beginning, for the technological changes waiting in the wings pale what we have seen to date in the way of economic impact. For example, the necessary technology exists today to almost completely automate every production plant. Computers can serve as control systems to guide all of the airplanes and trains and process almost all financial transactions. The day is approaching when most teachers could be replaced by computers. This list could be extended on and on.

institutional factors   That many of these things have not yet come about is because the implementation of computer technology has been held back by institutional factors. For example, labor unions have made it very costly and difficult to automate production. One method is by the use of work rules. A second way is by imposing severe economic penalties for terminating employees, such as SUB (supplementary unemployment benefits) and severance pay requirements, together with the seniority system, which requires that the younger workers be dismissed first. A third method is by refusing to permit certain technologies to be introduced. For example, computerized typesetting is now perfected; however, printer's union contracts in many cases will not permit it to be used or so severely restrict its use that it becomes economically infeasible.

'Now Just How Do I Swear In This Witness?'

Another major factor that is retarding implementation of current computer technology is tradition. People are generally adverse to changing the ways in which they do things. Witness, for example, the resistance to discontinuing telephone exchange names in favor of all-numeric telephone numbers. Currently, many people resist the notion of changing to a checkless society where all financial transactions take place electronically between computers. Tradition is not always as tangible as it may seem, for often it is founded in fear. There have been numerous cases where a manager has been reluctant to bring computers into an organization because of the economic fear of losing control to someone who knew more about computer operations. And even when introduction of the computer has been permitted, many managers severely limit its application.

The point we are building up to is that, because there is a lag between the time a technology is developed and the time it sees significant implementation, the full impact of the computer revolution is yet to hit. In the area of unemployment, for example, its impact has thus far been minimized for various reasons mentioned earlier. But the day of reckoning is approaching unless government is to eventually employ almost all of us. And if government does assume this role, what jobs will we be performing that a computer could not do better and at a lower cost? The question of employment problems is one that is going to have to be answered. Furthermore, the answer is going to have to be political rather than technically based as well as one that is adopted as national policy. All that has been attempted here has been to expose the problem, not to solve it. The reason is that too many current values will require reformulation before solutions can be developed.

changes in institutions
Another aspect of how the computer revolution has affected our society relates to our institutions. One example would be a tendency of bigness. Because of the high cost of automation, it appears that the larger an organization becomes, the more able it is to implement this technology. Moreover, the more automated a business, the more competitive it becomes with respect to its less-automated rivals. At one time, economists thought that there were limits to the returns of scale (returns of scale are the profits realized because of the bigness of a business). Today this notion seems outmoded. Witness the fact that IBM and General Motors continue to hold or expand their dominant roles in their industries. Moreover, both firms continue to yield far greater returns on their investments than do their smaller competitors. Furthermore, computers have clearly reversed the trend toward decentralization of companies that was taking place during the precomputer era. The reason for this is that current computer networks make it possible for the executive in the home office to know almost exactly the current status of the various branches and divisions. Thus he regains the ability to remotely control a far-flung empire.

changes in banking
Old institutions are being outmoded by the computer revolution. In fact, it is amazing how myopic most people are to the trend of developments. For example, recently the Federal Reserve Board issued a policy statement declaring that it plans to promote a national computer system for handling financial transactions. The justification is that the banking system is being buried under the paperwork generated by the twenty-eight billion checks currently being written each year. The Board has determined that a check is now processed ten times before it is finally cleared through the writer's bank. Under the computerized system, checks would be all but eliminated. Instead, periodically the amount of your net salary would be credited to your checking account (checkless checking account) in your bank's computer by your employer's computer. When you make a purchase, whether for cash or to be charged, you would have a plate that would cause the amount to be instantly credited to the store's account in its bank's computer and debited to your account, either checking or charge. Periodic payments on such things as cars, homes, and charge accounts would automatically be deducted from your account. Thus the need for checks virtually disappears. All you would get is a periodic state-

ment from your bank's computer telling the sources of funds placed in your account and the destination of funds dispersed from your account.

This all seems innocent enough, but let us consider its institutional impact. First, the postal system would not be burdened by all the checks currently mailed to pay bills and all of the statements on account and reminders that are also mailed. This would leave primarily advertising, parcel post, and personal mail for the Postal Service to handle, thus permitting it to vastly contract its service (and its cost?). Second, printers would no longer be needed to print the checks and messenger services would no longer be needed to transport canceled checks. Third, since everything is computerized relating to your financial transactions, the Internal Revenue Service could simply have its computer audit your account and compute and then deduct the tax owed. Thus bookkeepers and accountants would no longer be needed. Fourth, since we no longer need to make deposits or cash checks, banks can be reduced to computer centers, thus doing away with tellers and plush lobbies and offices.

You might say, what about loans? But since the computer at the bank already has all of your financial records on file, it has probably already evaluated your financial standing and issued you a line of credit. Therefore, a loan officer is not needed to approve loans except in very special cases. But, wait a minute! If all that a bank becomes is simply a computer center, why even have the small banks with their computer centers? Why not just consolidate all financial records at several large central bank computers, such as at the twelve Federal Reserve Banks? After all, most inter-bank transactions would probably clear through Federal Reserve Bank computers anyway. So why not do away with all of the middlemen? Does all of this seem far-fetched? If it does, just consider that it is all possible within the current state of the computer art.

eliminate postal service

Let us change our subject a little and return to the Postal Service (which now handles only advertising, parcel post, and personal mail). Taking personal mail first, why transmit a letter that requires several days to arrive and much physical handling? It would be much more efficient to send correspondence from a computer terminal in your home or office to the terminal of the person who is destined to receive it. In addition, the letter will arrive with very little delay since computers can transmit information at electronic speeds and switch messages quickly, efficiently, and at low cost. You might say, well, maybe I do not want to write a letter all at once. No problem here; just tell the computer to keep the portion of your letter already completed in its memory until you finish it. Then you can give the computer an order to transmit the letter to the addressee. Parcel post is another thing that can be eliminated. After all, it is much more efficient to move items in bulk from one destination to another. Therefore, if I want to send a birthday gift to my mother who lives 1,000 miles away, why not request a store in her home town to deliver it to her? Of course, direct-mail advertising is a nuisance anyway, so very few will miss it. Besides, most advertising can be sent electronically for a lower cost. In conclusion, we can see that in a computerized society there is no need for postal service.

changes in education

What about education? As any student can tell you, much that is taught in schools and colleges is quite factual and repetitive in nature. Moreover, some teachers do not themselves completely understand the concepts they attempt to teach. But computers are very good at handling facts and performing repetitive tasks. Therefore, a majority of teachers can be released and instruction can be taken over by computers. Moreover, since computers can operate twenty-four hours a day, seven days a week, one can spend as much time studying a particular subject as one may desire, and at any time. Thus people can study and learn because they are motivated and it is convenient, not because a class is scheduled to meet at some particular time. In addition, this studying can be done at home, since there will be a computer terminal there from which the student can

'LET'S FACE IT, BASHER, WE'RE OLD HAT!'

communicate with the school's computer. This will vastly reduce the cost of physical plant and transportation of students.

    Finally, let us examine how the political system might change in a computerized society. Under the current system, we have legislators who are supposed to be responsive to the needs of the people and executives who are supposed to propose legislation and administer the system established by currently valid legislation. But this system evolved out of an age when communications were slow, and it would have been too unwieldy to submit all issues to the people as referendums. However, with computer terminals widely available, national as well as state and local issues could be settled completely by polling the people. Thus even the legislative branch of government could be done away with. Of course, this may force a change in the requirements for eligibility to vote on various matters since a better-informed electorate is needed.

changes in the political system

351

We could continue almost interminably discussing how a fully computerized society would cause change in almost every facet of our lives and in virtually all of our institutions. How pervasive the impact of the computer on our institutions is and may become is probably quite clear by now. Therefore, let us turn to the question of collective and individual rights in a computerized society.

11.2   INDIVIDUAL AND SOCIAL IMPACT

As discomforting as the previous discussion on the current and potential economic and institutional impact of the computer on society may be, the personal and societal implications provide even more cause for concern. This concern should go far beyond the loss of identity that people may feel because they are referred to by numbers (such as a student or social security number) in some instances. The concern should be rather with the fact that information about each individual is being gathered at an alarming rate and the point is being reached where it seems likely that the lives of people are potentially subject to the control of other people. Let us explore in more depth this topic of the individual's loss of privacy.

personal records   Today there are many agencies, both public and private, that maintain records on individuals. For example, any person who has ever been a student at any level in the educational system has one or more records in existence. These records contain not just grade reports but a great deal of other personal information, such as health reports, teachers' comments, disciplinary information, and so on. If you have ever been a doctor's patient or been in a hospital, you have a medical record. Every person who has ever used credit has information on file in one or more credit bureaus. The Internal Revenue Service maintains records on anyone who has ever had income tax withheld, and the Social Security Administration keeps similar records. The Census Bureau also maintains information on individuals, as do many other government agencies, such as motor vehicle departments. Insurance companies maintain files on past and present policyholders, and airlines keep records on passengers. The utility companies keep records, particularly the telephone company on long-distance numbers called. Any person who has ever been subjected to security clearance procedures or has been in the military service probably has a detailed record full of personal information.

Almost all of these files, and many more that have not been mentioned, have in common that they contain highly personal information. In many cases, the information is erroneous or simply consists of opinions that are either biased or incorrect. Another property of most such files is that under current laws and regulations a person cannot inspect these

'NO KIDDING — SOME NUT CALLED YESTERDAY TO LOOK AT HIS *OWN* FILE.'

personal records to determine whether or not they contain errors or mis-
leading information. Even worse, a person currently has no control over
who has access to records that contain highly personal information. Thus
at any time a person's privacy may be violated, often without that person's
knowledge. A result of this invasion of privacy would be that an individual's professional or personal reputation (or both) might be destroyed.
These possibilities are alarming enough with non-computer-based information systems, but with computer-based systems the dangers are even
greater in number.

One of the dangers is that all or a substantial part of the information
scattered in various files can now be brought together and stored rather
economically in a central computer. In fact, just such a proposal was made
to Congress by the Bureau of the Budget in the mid-1960s when it recom-
mended the creation of the National Data Center. Under the proposal,
many of the files of various federal agencies were to be centralized in one

**government data
base**

353

computer system to promote efficiency. The advocates of the Center initially proposed to maintain anonymity of the records it kept as much as possible and promised safeguards to prevent unauthorized persons from accessing the files. When the track record of federal agencies is considered, however, there is little reason to feel that the system would maintain its integrity for long. For example, the Social Security Administration currently maintains a computer link with the National Blue Cross Headquarters in Baltimore. The Federal Aviation Administration sells lists of the names and addresses of pilots and other air-related persons registered with it. The Internal Revenue Service sells aggregate income statistics organized by zip code. And the FBI and local law enforcement agencies exchange information freely on the activities of both criminals and suspects. And on and on the list could go.

The original proposal for the National Data Center has long since been defeated in Congress. But those who think that this threat to individual privacy has been laid to rest are badly misled, for a new strategy seems to have appeared. Now computers are proliferating through the various government agencies at the federal, state, and local level. Furthermore, many of these systems are being linked together into networks, and plans are being prepared to link networks of various agencies together. Why isn't Congress stopping this, one might ask? The answer is that the funds are not being provided for anything as clearly defined as a National Data Center. Rather the funds are being appropriated through normal departmental operating budgets and special programs. For example, over $30 million in federal funds have been spent since 1966 on state and local law enforcement computer systems, all of which were to be tied into a national network by the middle 1970s. The Family Assistance Act and Manpower Training Act offered to Congress in 1971 both propose the establishment of computerized data bases. Another proposal has been that all state employment agencies become job clearing houses matching employer needs with the best qualified from among unemployed workers. This would also be undertaken with the primary source of funding being the federal government.

dangers from data bases But why is all of this so alarming? After all, only authorized persons will have access to such information, won't they? Again, based on past history, the answer is no. Even before computers were widely used, files were exchanged between government agencies and often other interests. Credit bureaus, banks, educational institutions, and law enforcement agencies have traditionally exchanged information freely with each other and frequently with the public, even though often only at a price. If matters are not bad enough, there is sufficient reason to question the security of the files maintained on these computerized data bases. Most of the systems used or proposed are online and can be readily accessed from remote terminals. Of course, precautions are built into such systems to

'SORRY, PAL — IT'S INDELIBLE.'

try and prevent unauthorized people from gaining access to files. This is usually achieved through a *password system* which requires that an identifying code be supplied before a file can be accessed. However, as experience has shown at universities such as MIT and Michigan, which have considerable experience with online systems, even a relatively unsophisticated student can crack the code and gain unauthorized access to files. In fact, this can often be accomplished in a matter of only several hours, since the student can use the computer's computational power to help break its own security code. Another possibility is that data can be pilfered by tapping the transmission lines over which computers communicate with each other or with terminal devices (we might end up with a colossal Watergate affair). Yet another possibility is that a dishonest systems programmer can create a secret *door* in the control program of an online system which permits unauthorized persons to get past the computer security system undetected.

test mania   Another aspect of computerized data bases is an ever-growing mania for relying upon tests to evaluate a person academically, psychologically, and socially.   The results of these tests are used with almost blind faith to select students for college admission, scholarships, employment, and promotion, to mention but a few areas.   Yet the validity of almost every test used today is suspect in terms of its ability to predict either behavior or performance.   Many times the student with a high GRE (Graduate Record Examination) score will flunk out of graduate school while students with marginal scores excel in both their studies and their careers. Moreover, most tests are structured in such a way that they are biased toward a particular ethnic group or a particular educational philosophy. Yet these test scores are recorded for all time for open inspection and followed with an almost religious fervor by many administrators.   Whether tests of such questionable validity should be administered or the results be disseminated without an individual's consent raises serious questions about individual privacy.

Another mania that seems to be catching hold is to use the computer to evaluate a person's performance.   For example, in 1969 a plan was announced to rate public school teachers in one southern state by allowing a computer to evaluate the statistics on the academic achievements of their students.   A teacher whose students did poorly based upon computerized statistical analysis would have been dismissed or downgraded under the plan.   Many other such examples can be cited.

11.3   CONCLUSIONS

Much of what has been said thus far in this chapter has been negative. But, the computer offers humanity an opportunity for an improved standard of living never before available.   However, to enjoy these benefits some serious study is required, and many values may need to be revised. In economics, for example, our society has generally adopted a model which states that income will be distributed according to a person's contribution to the output of that society.   In a computerized society, other measures may be needed for deciding how the income will be distributed. Another widely held belief is that work is good and nonwork is bad.   This value will certainly be challenged in a computerized society, for much of the output will be produced by machines under computer control.   Thus, instead of opposing this new technology, we should be carefully and wisely implementing it with a great deal of thought being given at each step of the way.

What about individual privacy? Again, instead of opposing the implementation of the new technology, we need to adopt safeguards. Laws are needed which state that: **protection of privacy**

1. Whenever any public or private agency maintains information on a person, that person must be notified that the record exists.
2. The information being retained cannot be provided to any individual or organization, other than the agency holding the information, without permission of the person to whom the information relates.
3. The name and position of every person who inspects the information must be maintained by the system for audit purposes.
4. Individuals are permitted to inspect their own records and to make copies.
5. Individuals may supply information in writing to supplement information already in their records with such supplementary information becoming a part of the records.

Violation of such a law would carry with it criminal penalties. Extension of this law to all government and private organizations or individuals who might organize files is necessary in a computerized society. In addition, laws should be enacted forcing all such information systems to have elaborate security measures built in, even if the cost becomes rather high. Furthermore, a provision is needed, similar to a statute of limitations, which requires that dated information be destroyed.

An appropriate point upon which to close both this chapter and the book is that the computer, being just a machine, should serve mankind —mankind should not end up serving the machine. Thus, while the implementation of computer technology should be encouraged, the rights of individuals and their society should never be compromised, even in the slightest, for the sake of the machine. The small amount of freedom that has been attained by the individuals in our society should not now be lost because of the invention of a machine with an almost boundless ability to remember, process, and regurgitate information upon command.

PROBLEMS

1. Name two human activities that you think have not been affected by the computer revolution.

2. With the high cost of computers, do you really believe that there are cost savings realized by using them to perform tasks formerly done by humans? Justify your answer.

3. What solutions can you see to the lack of occupational mobility? Are these solutions short-run or long-run solutions?

4. Cite several ways in which you think tradition has prevented computers from being used.

5. Do you really think that it is reasonable to do

away with local banks as we know them in favor of computer centers and a moneyless, checkless society? Justify your answer.

6. What industries do you feel are least affected by the computer? Why?

7. Identify some advantages that you would realize from transmitting all business and personal correspondence using a computer rather than the Postal Service. Be specific.

8. Do you think that teachers can really be eliminated from the educational process in most disciplines? If yes, which disciplines and why?

9. What do you think should be done with regard to the amount of privacy a person should have with respect to personal information collected, retained, and disseminated?

10. Identify several of the favorable things that the computer has performed for various aspects of our society.

SUMMARY

1. Since the inception of electronic computers in the 1940s, a technological revolution has been occurring in our society.

2. Computers have caused a significant jump in worker productivity, although the future impact on productivity will be much greater than that already realized.

3. Institutional factors, such as labor unions, have slowed the use of computers in many areas.

4. Computers have again made corporate centralization a sensible economic strategy. They have also aided in refuting the economic concept of declining returns to scale.

5. Many institutions, such as banks and the Postal System, can easily be eliminated or vastly reduced in size with currently available computer technology.

6. Other institutions that can easily be modified by current computer technology are those involving education and politics.

7. Many confidential records currently exist on computers for each individual in our society. Thus the personal privacy of the individual is in danger unless these records are secure.

8. Proposals, such as the one for a National Data Center, have suggested that all governmental records on each individual should be pooled together in one place. This course of action should be considered dangerous because of the opportunity that it would provide for misuse of the information in the files.

9. Laws are needed to protect the individual from misuse of personal records and to be certain that accurate information is contained therein.

10. Even though the computer can produce many benefits for mankind, individual privacy should never be compromised in the name of implementing computer technology or efficiency.

Appendixes

Pure Number-System Concepts

A number of systems for representing numeric information have existed since the beginning of recorded history. Two such systems familiar to most of us are the system that is based upon Roman numerals and the decimal number system. Because of the problems of representing large numbers and doing arithmetic operations in the Roman numeral system, it is now of little practical value. The decimal system, in fact, is the most widely used system for the representation of numeric information for human use. We will see later in this chapter, however, that modern computers use another number system called the binary system. Let us now study some pure number-system concepts. We use the word *pure* in describing a number system to separate pure numbers from the number systems that use numeric codes to represent numbers.

A.1 REPRESENTATION OF PURE NUMBERS

The decimal number system is based upon a concept called *positional notation*. Essentially this concept states that the *magnitude* of any digit of a number is determined by the *position* of that digit *relative* to an *origin*. In the decimal number system the origin is the decimal point.

positional notation

The magnitude of each digit in a decimal number is determined by multiplying the digit by ten raised to a power. The power of ten used for the multiplier is zero for the digit to the left of the decimal point. This power of ten increases by one for each digit position we move to the left. Similarly, the power decreases by one for each digit position we move to the right. For example, when we write the number 465.32, we really mean

$$465.32 = 4 \times 10^2 + 6 \times 10^1 + 5 \times 10^0 + 3 \times 10^{-1} + 2 \times 10^{-2}$$
$$= 4 \times 100 + 6 \times 10 + 5 \times 1 + 3 \times 0.1 + 2 \times 0.01$$
$$= 400 + 60 + 5 + 0.3 + 0.02$$
$$= 465.32$$

literal expansion

This expanded version of a decimal number in terms of its implicit multipliers (the powers of ten) is called the *literal expansion* of a number. Thus, when we write a decimal number in the conventional manner (for example, 465.32), we are really conveying the meaning of the literal expansion of the number.

radix

In the decimal number system our implicit multipliers involve powers of ten. In general, the number that is raised to a power to be used as an implicit multiplier is known as the base or *radix* of the number system. Thus the radix of the decimal number system is ten. The radix of a number system defines the *number* of different digit values permitted in that system. Since the radix of the decimal number system is ten, ten digit values are permitted in the decimal system. The symbols used for these digit values are the familiar 0, 1, 2, 3, 4, 5, 6, 7, 8, and 9. The origin point of a number is called the *radix point* of the number. For the decimal system we call the radix point the decimal point.

radix point

While decimal numbers are the ones most used by people, computers generally do not use decimal numbers. Instead, computers use a binary number system for representing numeric information. The *binary number system* is similar to the decimal number system with one exception: the radix used in the binary system is the decimal value *two*.* Two other pure number systems widely used for representing numbers in computer science are the *octal* and *hexadecimal number systems*. These number systems are also similar to the decimal number system except that they use *eight* (for octal) and *sixteen* (for hexadecimal) as their radices. The radix points of the binary, octal, and hexadecimal number systems are called *binary, octal,* and *hexadecimal points,* respectively. The octal and hexadecimal number systems are of interest primarily because of the close relationship which they have with the binary number system. This relationship will be explored in Section A.3.

In fact, any integer greater than 1 can be used as the radix of a number system. In general, for r any integer greater than 1, a real number A with n integer and m fractional coefficients a_i, where $0 \le a_i < r$ for $i = n - 1, n - 2, ..., 1, 0, -1 ..., -(m - 1), -m$, can be uniquely represented implicitly as[†]

---

* By convention, the radix of a number system is always given as a decimal number.

† By convention, the radix of a number is denoted by a decimal subscript when any confusion might result with respect to the number system being utilized.

$$A = \pm (a_{n-1}a_{n-2} \cdots a_1 a_0 . a_{-1} \cdots a_{-(m-1)}a_{-m})_r \qquad \textbf{(A.1)}$$

which has as its literal expansion*

$$A = \pm (a_{n-1}r_r^{n-1} + a_{n-2}r_r^{n-2} + \cdots + a_1 r_r^1 + a_0 r_r^0$$

$$+ a_{-1}r_r^{-1} + \cdots + a_{-(m-1)}r_r^{-(m-1)} + a_{-m}r_r^{-m}) \qquad \textbf{(A.2)}$$

Notice in Eq. (A.2) that the radix in the literal expansion is always the base-r rather than the base-10 representation of the radix. This will prove to be important in the conversion of numbers from representation in one number system to representation in another number system.

Figure A.1 lists the binary, octal, and hexadecimal equivalents to the decimal numbers 0 through 15. The commonly accepted symbols for the

Figure A.1   Table of the Binary, Octal, and Hexadecimal Equivalents of the Decimal Numbers 0 Through 15

Number System Radix			
2	8	10	16
0	0	0	0
1	1	1	1
10	2	2	2
11	3	3	3
100	4	4	4
101	5	5	5
110	6	6	6
111	7	7	7
1000	10	8	8
1001	11	9	9
1010	12	10	A
1011	13	11	B
1100	14	12	C
1101	15	13	D
1110	16	14	E
1111	17	15	F

digits associated with each of these number systems have been utilized. Notice that the *binary* system has only two distinct digit symbols† (0 and 1), and the *octal* number system has only eight distinct digit symbols (0,   digit symbols

---

*Observe that for notational convenience the subscripts for the coefficients a_i have been selected so that they will be the same as the exponent of the radix with which each coefficient is associated in the literal expansion.

† The binary digits, 0 and 1, are called *bits,* which is a contraction for *binary digit.*

363

1, 2, 3, 4, 5, 6, and 7). Similarly, the *hexadecimal* number system uses sixteen unique digit symbols (0, 1, 2, 3, 4, 5, 6, 7, 8, 9, A, B, C, D, E, and F). Be careful to note that in the hexadecimal number system the symbols A, B, C, D, E, and F are *numerals* and *not letters* of the English alphabet.

To conclude our examination of the representation of pure numbers, let us look at the literal expansion of numbers in the binary, octal, and hexadecimal systems.

EXAMPLE

$$
\begin{aligned}
1011.11_2 &= 1 \times 10_2^3 + 0 \times 10_2^2 + 1 \times 10_2^1 + 1 \times 10_2^0 + 1 \times 10_2^{-1} \\
&\quad + 1 \times 10_2^{-2} \\
&= 1 \times 1000_2 + 0 \times 100_2 + 1 \times 10_2 + 1 \times 1_2 + 1 \times 0.1_2 \\
&\quad + 1 \times 0.01_2 \\
&= 1000_2 + 10_2 + 1_2 + 0.1_2 + 0.01_2 \\
&= 1011.11_2
\end{aligned}
$$

EXAMPLE

$$
\begin{aligned}
4507.62_8 &= 4 \times 10_8^3 + 5 \times 10_8^2 + 0 \times 10_8^1 + 7 \times 10_8^0 + 6 \times 10_8^{-1} \\
&\quad + 2 \times 10_8^{-2} \\
&= 4 \times 1000_8 + 5 \times 100_8 + 0 \times 10_8 + 7 \times 1_8 + 6 \times 0.1_8 \\
&\quad + 2 \times 0.01_8 \\
&= 4000_8 + 500_8 + 7_8 + 0.6_8 + 0.02_8 \\
&= 4507.62_8
\end{aligned}
$$

EXAMPLE

$$
\begin{aligned}
F23.C7_{16} &= F \times 10_{16}^2 + 2 \times 10_{16}^1 + 3 \times 10_{16}^0 + C \times 10_{16}^{-1} + 7 \times 10_{16}^{-2} \\
&= F \times 100_{16} + 2 \times 10_{16} + 3 \times 1_{16} + C \times 0.1_{16} + 7 \times 0.01_{16} \\
&= F00_{16} + 20_{16} + 3_{16} + 0.C_{16} + 0.07_{16} \\
&= F23.C7_{16}
\end{aligned}
$$

A.2 CONVERSION OF PURE NUMBERS

Several number systems exist, each using a different radix. Therefore, we must have a method for translating numbers from a number system with a given radix to a number system with a different radix. In this section we will examine three algorithms for the conversion of pure numbers between number systems with different radices.

The *method of literal expansion** is the best method for manual conversion of numbers represented by a nondecimal system to numbers in the decimal system. A descriptive flowchart for the algorithm for converting nondecimal numbers to decimal numbers using the method of literal expansion is given in Fig. A.2. Three examples follow in which the number in parentheses at the right of a line indicates the flowchart box number of the step performed in that line.

method of literal expansion

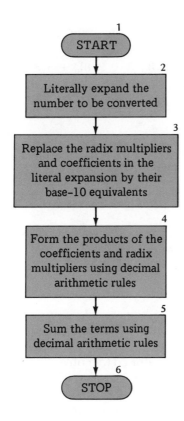

Figure A.2. Descriptive Flowchart for the Algorithm for Converting a Nondecimal Number to Its Decimal Equivalent

Example Convert 10111.101_2 to its decimal equivalent by use of the steps of Fig. A.2.

---

* Sometimes called the *method of transliteration.*

$$10111.101_2 = 1 \times 10_2^4 + 0 \times 10_2^3 + 1 \times 10_2^2 + 1 \times 10_2^1$$
$$+ 1 \times 10_2^0 + 1 \times 10_2^{-1} + 0 \times 10_2^{-2}$$
$$+ 1 \times 10_2^{-3} \qquad \text{(step 2)}$$
$$= 1 \times 2_{10}^4 + 0 \times 2_{10}^3 + 1 \times 2_{10}^2 + 1 \times 2_{10}^1$$
$$+ 1 \times 2_{10}^0 + 1 \times 2_{10}^{-1} + 0 \times 2_{10}^{-2} + 1 \times 2_{10}^{-3} \qquad \text{(step 3)}$$
$$= 16_{10} + 4_{10} + 2_{10} + 1_{10} + 0.5_{10} + 0.125_{10} \qquad \text{(step 4)}$$
$$= 23.625_{10} \qquad \text{(step 5)}$$

Example   Convert 3105.64_8 to its decimal equivalent by use of the steps of Fig. A.2.

$$3105.64_8 = 3 \times 10_8^3 + 1 \times 10_8^2 + 0 \times 10_8^1 + 5 \times 10_8^0 + 6$$
$$\times 10_8^{-1} + 4 \times 10_8^{-2} \qquad \text{(step 2)}$$
$$= 3 \times 8_{10}^3 + 1 \times 8_{10}^2 + 0 \times 8_{10}^1 + 5 \times 8_{10}^0 + 6$$
$$\times 8_{10}^{-1} + 4 \times 8_{10}^{-2} \qquad \text{(step 3)}$$
$$= 1536_{10} + 64_{10} + 5_{10} + 0.75_{10} + 0.0625_{10} \qquad \text{(step 4)}$$
$$= 1605.8125_{10} \qquad \text{(step 5)}$$

Example   Convert $3F9.AC_{16}$ to its decimal equivalent by use of the steps of Fig. A.2.

$$3F9.AC_{16} = 3 \times 10_{16}^2 + F \times 10_{16}^1 + 9 \times 10_{16}^0 + A \times 10_{16}^{-1}$$
$$+ C \times 10_{16}^{-2} \qquad \text{(step 2)}$$
$$= 3 \times 16_{10}^2 + 15 \times 16_{10}^1 + 9 \times 16_{10}^0 + 10 \times 16_{10}^{-1}$$
$$+ 12 \times 16_{10}^{-2} \qquad \text{(step 3)}$$
$$= 768_{10} + 240_{10} + 9_{10} + 0.625_{10} + 0.046875_{10} \qquad \text{(step 4)}$$
$$= 1017.671875_{10} \qquad \text{(step 5)}$$

An exact equivalent decimal number can be obtained when converting from a nondecimal number to the decimal system.

Two algorithms are required for converting decimal numbers to their nondecimal equivalents. The two algorithms taken together constitute what is known as the *multiplication/division method*. This method requires that a decimal number to be converted be *separated* into its integer and fractional parts. The descriptive flowchart given in Fig. A.3 is for an algorithm used to convert the integer portion of a decimal number to its nondecimal equivalent. Three examples follow in which the steps of Fig. A.3 are used to convert decimal integer values to some nondecimal equivalents. Notice that when converting integers from the decimal system to a nondecimal system exact equivalents are obtained. In addition, observe that in our structuring of the examples, the remainders must be read from bottom to top in forming the converted numbers.

multiplication/division method

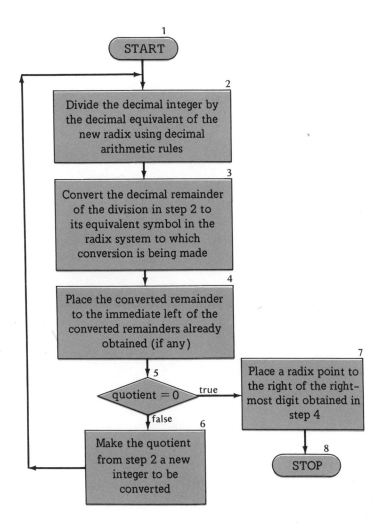

Figure A.3. Descriptive Flowchart for the Algorithm for Converting a Decimal Integer to Its Nondecimal Equivalent

Example Convert 237_{10} to its binary equivalent by use of the steps of Fig. A.3.

Algorithm Iteration	Division	Quotients	Remainders
	2)237		
1	2)118	118	1
2	2)59	59	0
3	2)29	29	1
4	2)14	14	1
5	2)7	7	0
6	2)3	3	1
7	2)1	1	1
8	0	0	1

Therefore, $237_{10} = 11101101_2$.

Example Convert 1237_{10} to its octal equivalent by use of the steps of Fig. A.3.

Algorithm Iteration	Division	Quotients	Remainders
	8)1237		
1	8)154	154	5
2	8)19	19	2
3	8)2	2	3
4	0	0	2

Therefore, $1237_{10} = 2325_8$.

Example Convert 1246_{10} to its hexadecimal equivalent by use of the steps of Fig. A.3.

Algorithm Iteration	Division	Quotients	Remainders
	16)1246		
1	16)77	77	14
2	16)4	4	13
3	0	0	4

Therefore, $1246_{10} = 4DE_{16}$.   (Note that the remainders 14 and 13 had to be converted to their hexadecimal equivalents, E and D, respectively, according to the step in box 3.)

A descriptive flowchart for the algorithm for converting a decimal fraction to its nondecimal equivalent is given in Fig. A.4. Three examples follow in which the steps of Fig. A.4 are used to convert decimal fractions to some nondecimal equivalents. In general, exact nondecimal equivalents

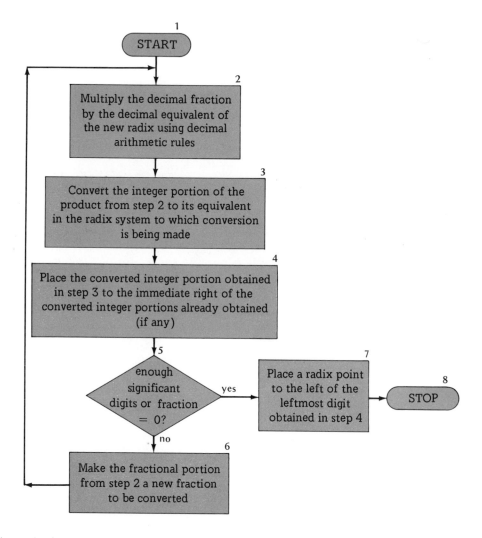

Figure A.4.   Descriptive Flowchart for the Algorithm for Converting a Decimal Fraction to Its Nondecimal Equivalent

of decimal fractions cannot be obtained when converting a fraction from the decimal to a nondecimal system. However, the numbers in our examples were chosen so that they would convert to an exact equivalent. Observe in our structuring of the examples that the integers are read from top to bottom in forming the converted fractions.

Example   Convert 0.8125_{10} to its binary equivalent by use of the steps of Fig. A.4.

Algorithm Iteration	Multiplication	Integer	Fraction
1	$2 \times 0.8125 = 1.6250$	1	0.6250
2	$2 \times 0.6250 = 1.2500$	1	0.2500
3	$2 \times 0.2500 = 0.5000$	0	0.5000
4	$2 \times 0.5000 = 1.0000$	1	0.0000

Therefore, $0.8125_{10} = 0.1101_2$.

Example   Convert 0.8125_{10} to its octal equivalent by use of the steps of Fig. A.4.

Algorithm Iteration	Multiplication	Integer	Fraction
1	$8 \times 0.8125 = 6.5000$	6	0.5000
2	$8 \times 0.5000 = 4.0000$	4	0.0000

Therefore, $0.8125_{10} = 0.64_8$.

Example   Convert 0.65625_{10} to its hexadecimal equivalent by use of the steps of Fig. A.4.

Algorithm Iteration	Multiplication	Integer	Fraction
1	$16 \times 0.65625 = 10.50000$	10	0.50000
2	$16 \times 0.50000 = 8.00000$	8	0.00000

Therefore, $0.65625_{10} = 0.A8_{16}$.   (Note that the integer value 10 had to be converted to its hexadecimal equivalent, A.)

A.3   SPECIAL CASES

A special case exists that sometimes makes number conversion between two radix systems a relatively simple operation. This special case holds when either of the radices of the systems involved in conversion is an integer power of the other radix. Two good examples would be that 8 and 16 are both integer powers of 2. Therefore, conversion in either direction between binary and octal or binary and hexadecimal can take advantage of the relationship that exists between these systems. A descriptive flowchart for an algorithm for conversion of a binary number to its octal or hexadecimal equivalent appears in Fig. A.5; conversion in the opposite direction can be performed using the descriptive flowchart of Fig. A.6.

Example   Convert 11101010011.10111_2 to its octal equivalent by use of the steps of Fig. A.5.

$$011 \quad 101 \quad 010 \quad 011 \quad . \quad 101 \quad 110_2$$
$$3 \quad\quad 5 \quad\quad 2 \quad\quad 3 \quad . \quad\quad 5 \quad\quad 6_8$$

Therefore, $11101010011.10111_2 = 3523.56_8$.

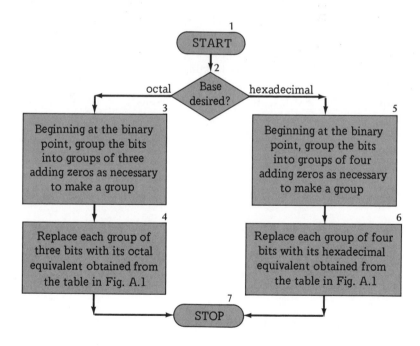

Figure A.5. Descriptive Flowchart for an Algorithm for Converting a Binary Number to Its Octal or Hexadecimal Equivalent

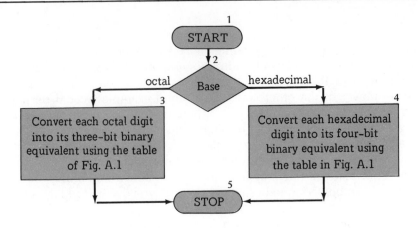

Figure A.6. Descriptive Flowchart for an Algorithm for Converting an Octal or Hexadecimal Number to Its Binary Equivalent

Example   Convert 111101010011.10111_2 to its hexadecimal equivalent by use of the steps of Fig. A.5.

$$\begin{array}{ccccccc} 1111 & 0101 & 0011 & . & 1011 & 1000_2 \\ F & 5 & 3 & . & B & 8_{16} \end{array}$$

Therefore, $111101010011.10111_2 = F53.B8_{16}$.

Example   Convert $2AF.C5_{16}$ to its binary equivalent by use of the steps of Fig. A.6.

$$\begin{array}{ccccccc} 2 & A & F & . & C & 5_{16} \\ 0010 & 1010 & 1111 & . & 1100 & 0101_2 \end{array}$$

Therefore, $2AF.C5_{16} = 001010101111.11000101_2$.

Example   Convert 3740.562_8 to its binary equivalent by use of the steps of Fig. A.6.

$$\begin{array}{ccccccccc} 3 & 7 & 4 & 0 & . & 5 & 6 & 2_8 \\ 011 & 111 & 100 & 000 & . & 101 & 110 & 010_2 \end{array}$$

Therefore, $3740.562_8 = 011111100000.101110010_2$.

Since we have a simple means for converting numbers to and from binary, we can easily convert between the octal and hexadecimal number systems.   The method would be to first use the algorithm of Fig. A.6 followed by the algorithm of Fig. A.5.

Example   Convert 7302.152_8 to its hexadecimal equivalent by use of the steps of Figs. A.6 and A.5.

$$
\begin{array}{ccccccc}
7 & 3 & 0 & 2 & . & 1 & 5 & 2_8 \\
111 & 011 & 000 & 010 & . & 001 & 101 & 010_2
\end{array}
$$

Therefore, $7302.152_8 = 111011000010.001101010_2$.

Converting the latter to hexadecimal by use of the steps of Fig. A.5:

$$
\begin{array}{cccccc}
1110 & 1100 & 0010 & . & 0011 & 0101_2 \\
E & C & 2 & . & 3 & 5_{16}
\end{array}
$$

Therefore, $7302.152_8 = EC2.35_{16}$.

Similarly, by applying the descriptive flowchart of Fig. A.6 and then the steps of Fig. A.5, we can easily convert hexadecimal numbers to their octal equivalents.

A.4   COMPLEMENTS

An often-used concept in computer arithmetic is that of the complement of a number.   The two types of complements most often found are: (1) the radix complement and (2) the radix-minus-1 complement.   The *radix complement* (denoted C_r) of a real number u_r which consists of n integer digits and m fractional digits in the base-r system may be defined as

radix complement

$$
C_r = 10_r^n - u_r \tag{A.3}
$$

Alternatively, observe that the radix complement C_r is the number such that

$$
C_r + u_r = 10_r^n \tag{A.4}
$$

That is, the radix complement of an $(n + m)$-digit number is that number which, when added to the number of which it is the complement, results in the radix raised to the nth power.   This sum will thus be a number consisting of a 1 followed by n zeros to the left of the radix point and m zeros following the radix point.   The radix-minus-1 complement of a number is simply the radix complement of that number less 1 in the low-order position.

Example   Form the radix complement of 567.83_{10}.

$$\begin{array}{r} 1000.00_{10} \\ -567.83_{10} \\ \hline 432.17_{10} \end{array}$$ 10s complement of 567.83_{10}

Example   Form the radix complement of 561.03_{8}.

$$\begin{array}{r} 1000.00_{8} \\ -561.03_{8} \\ \hline 216.75_{8} \end{array}$$ 8s complement of 561.03_{8}

Example   Form the radix complement of 1011011.011_{2}.

$$\begin{array}{r} 10000000.000_{2} \\ -1011011.011_{2} \\ \hline 0100100.101_{2} \end{array}$$ 2s complement of 1011011.011_{2}

In the last example, note that the 2s complement of a binary number may be obtained simply by changing all 1 bits to 0 and all 0 bits to 1, and then adding 1 to the result. Computers represent numbers internally using the binary system in which flipping bits is a very simple procedure. Thus complements are easily obtained on a computer system.

A.5   PURE NUMBER ARITHMETIC

addition Regardless of the base system used, the rules for performing arithmetic operations are the same for combining pure numbers of the same radix system. For example, the only change required in doing addition in a nondecimal number system is to keep track of when a carry into the next digit position occurs. In the decimal number system we have a carry of 1 when the sum of the two respective digits and any previous carry is larger than nine. In general, if the sum of the two digits and any previous carry is less than the radix, the carry digit is a zero. Otherwise, there is a carry of 1 into the next digit position to the left and the sum is reduced by the value of the radix.

Example   Form the sum of 1011101.1101_2 and 111110.0010_2.

$$1011101.1101_2$$
$$+\,111110.0010_2$$
$$\overline{10011011.1111_2}$$

Example   Form the sum of 556.77_8 and 4634.072_8.

$$556.770_8$$
$$+\,4634.072_8$$
$$\overline{5413.062_8}$$

Subtraction can be performed on pure numbers by use of the borrowing method learned in elementary schools. However, most modern computers perform subtraction by adding the radix complement of the subtrahend to the minuend. If a carry occurs out of the leftmost digit position, the carry is dropped and the sum will then be the difference of the two original numbers. However, if no carry occurs out of the leftmost digit position, the sum is the radix complement of the difference. In the latter case, the sum can simply be complemented and a minus sign affixed to the recomplemented number.   **subtraction**

    Care must be taken in complementing the subtrahend. This is because the subtrahend must be extended to the length of the minuend using leading and trailing zeros before forming the complement. The method of complements is used in computers for subtraction because complementation of binary numbers is very easy to accomplish. In addition, the complexity and related expense of developing separate subtraction circuitry is not needed when using the method of complements. Following are examples of subtraction using the method of complements for both the binary and decimal number systems.

Example   Subtract 1011101.11_2 from 11011111.101_2 by use of the method of complements.

$$11011111.101_2$$
$$\underline{10100010.010_2} \quad \text{2s complement of } 01011101.110_2$$
$$110000001.111_2$$

Dropping the 1 that carried out of the leftmost digit position, the difference becomes 10000001.111_2.

Example   Subtract 93.75_{10} from 223.625_{10} by use of the method of complements.

$$223.625_{10}$$
$$906.250_{10} \qquad \text{10s complement of } 093.750_{10}$$
$$\overline{1129.875_{10}}$$

Dropping the 1 that carried out of the leftmost digit position, the difference is 129.875_{10}.

Example Subtract 11011111.101_2 from 1011101.11_2 by use of the method of complements.

$$01011101.110_2$$
$$00100000.011_2 \qquad \text{2s complement of } 11011111.101_2$$
$$\overline{01111110.001_2}$$

Since there was no carry out of the leftmost digit position, this is the 2s complement of the result. Complementing the sum and affixing a minus sign, we obtain the difference as -10000001.111_2.

Example Subtract 223.625_{10} from 93.75_{10} by use of the method of complements.

$$093.750_{10}$$
$$776.375_{10} \qquad \text{10s complement of } 223.625_{10}$$
$$\overline{870.125_{10}}$$

Since there was no carry out of the leftmost digit position, this is the 10s complement of the result. Complementing the sum and affixing a minus sign, we obtain the difference as -129.875_{10}.

multiplication and division   Multiplication and division of pure numbers in a nondecimal system is performed by use of the same notions we are familiar with in the decimal number system. Examples of binary multiplication and binary division are given here to illustrate this point.

Example Multiply 10110.101_2 by 101.01_2.

$$10110.101_2$$
$$\times 101.01_2$$
$$\overline{101\ 10101}$$
$$10110\ 101$$
$$\underline{1011010\ 1}$$
$$1110110.11001_2$$

Example Divide 1110110.11001_2 by 101.01_2.

$$101\ 10.\ 101$$
$$101.01_\wedge \overline{)\ 1110110.11_\wedge 001}$$
$$\underline{10101}$$
$$100010$$
$$\underline{10101}$$
$$1101\ 1$$
$$\underline{1010\ 1}$$
$$11\ 01\ \ 0$$
$$\underline{10\ 10\ \ 1}$$
$$10\ 101$$
$$\underline{10\ 101}$$
$$0$$

Observe that the rules for placing the binary point in the above product and quotient are similar to those for placing the decimal point in the multiplication and division of decimal numbers. Thus, the number of binary places in a product is the sum of the number of binary places in the multiplicand and the multiplier.

PROBLEMS

1. Give the literal expansions of the following numbers:

a. 312.075_{10}

b. -469.588_{10}

c. 5603.1217_8

d. $9AE.C5F_{16}$

e. $-3B1.8FC_{16}$

f. -402.607_8

g. 101101.1011_2

h. 111000.11101_2

i. 529.673_{10}

j. $4FF.C03_{16}$

2. Convert the following numbers to their decimal equivalents by use of the steps of Fig. A.2:

a. 1011.011101_2

b. -11110.11101_2

c. 10001.10001_2

d. 576.3204_8

e. 107.5177_8

f. -1706.1125_8

g. $A8C.12F_{16}$

h. $-8E0.4B_{16}$

i. $A9D.3CF_{16}$

j. 562.413_{16}

3. Convert the following decimal numbers to their equivalents in the base given by use of the steps of Figs. A.3 and A.4:

a. 781.32_{10} to binary

b. -519.06_{10} to binary

c. 3276.549_{10} to binary

d. 812.475_{10} to octal

e. -9678.520_{10} to octal

f. 476.5204_{10} to octal

g. 4983.627_{10} to hexadecimal

h. -56772.37_{10} to hexadecimal

i. 607.91_{10} to hexadecimal

j. 1412.257_{10} to hexadecimal

4. Convert the following numbers to their equivalents in the base given by use of the steps of Figs. A.5 and A.6:

a. 10110110110.1011101_2 to hexadecimal

b. 1001101110.0010111_2 to octal

c. $DA5.6C_{16}$ to binary

d. 703.6251_8 to binary

e. $6A5.78C_{16}$ to octal

f. $-AF.CA_{16}$ to octal

g. 2074.362_8 to hexadecimal

h. -4621.703_8 to hexadecimal

5. Use the most convenient method from among those discussed in this chapter to convert the following numbers to their equivalents in the base given. State the figure number(s) of the algorithm(s) used in each case.

a. 527.003_8 to decimal

b. $A25.C7_{16}$ to octal

c. 542.983_{10} to binary
d. 1011101.101_2 to decimal
e. -4763.25_{10} to hexadecimal
f. 77325.63_8 to hexadecimal
g. $7A3.2F_{16}$ to binary
h. -11011.1011011_2 to octal
i. 374.256_8 to binary
j. $-88AA.F3_{16}$ to decimal
k. -110110.10111_2 to hexadecimal
l. -4987.63_{10} to octal
m. 45.6832_{16} to octal
n. 17.9638_{10} to hexadecimal
o. -49.8763_{10} to binary
p. 1488.734_{10} to hexadecimal
q. $AC12_{16}$ to octal
r. 1110111011.10111_2 to octal
s. $F43.A0C_{16}$ to decimal
t. 703.24_8 to decimal

6. Form the radix complement of each of the following numbers:
a. 540.67_{10}
b. 347.15_8
c. $5C8.9E_{16}$
d. 439.82_{10}
e. 101101.110_2
f. 10100.000_2
g. 205.634_8
h. $4FA.27_{16}$
i. 1111.00111_2
j. 3199.689_{10}

7. Perform the following addition operations:
a. $11101.11011_2 + 1011101.1_2$
b. $1.1011101_2 + 1011.110001_2$
c. $110.11001_2 + 1100.001_2$

d. $10001.11001_2 + 100011.101_2$
e. $101011.1011_2 + 11101.1101_2$
f. $205.634_8 + 1726.357_8$
g. $1607.5432_8 + 42.67375_8$
h. $4FD.37_{16} + AFC.2DF_{16}$
i. $56.E3C_{16} + 4FC.235_{16}$
j. $D476.92F_{16} + D27.B22_{16}$

8. Perform the following subtraction operations by use of the method of complements:
a. $456.78_{10} - 213.82_{10}$
b. $5475.25_{10} - 42.64_{10}$
c. $312.98_{10} - 782.6_{10}$
d. $47.9_{10} - 583.625_{10}$
e. $1011101.110_2 - 101.101_2$
f. $10101.101_2 - 111011.1011_2$
g. $110000.011_2 - 111.1101_2$
h. $1.11011_2 - 111100.1_2$
i. $732.5_8 - 216.12_8$
j. $42.4_8 - 175.63_8$

9. Perform the following multiplication operations:
a. $101101.101_2 \times 10.111_2$
b. $-1101.10111_2 \times 1.101_2$
c. $47.52_8 \times 47.63_8$
d. $-7043.2_8 \times 413_8$
e. $4F2C_{16} \times 32E_{16}$
f. $4C.56_{16} \times 421_{16}$

10. Perform the following division operations:
a. $101101.101_2 / 101.11_2$
b. $4763.2_8 / 2.53_8$
c. $-743.25_8 / 5.67_8$
d. $-1101.11011_2 / 1.101_2$
e. $4F2C.3_{16} / 4.2_{16}$
f. $CE03_{16} / 2F_{16}$

Flowchart Numeric Functional Operators

Mnemonic Functional Operator*	Operation Description
abs[x]	Return the magnitude of x.
ceil[x]	Return the least integer which is greater than or equal to x.
cos[x]	Return the trigonometric cosine of x.
exp[x]	Return the exponential of x, i.e., e^x.
floor[x]	Return the greatest integer which is less than or equal to x.
log[x]	Return the natural logarithm of x.
log10[x]	Return the base-ten logarithm of x.
max[x,y]	Return the greater of the two values if x is not equal to y; if x equals y, return the value of x.
min[x,y]	Return the lesser of the two values if x is not equal to y; if x equals y, return the value of x.
mod[n,m]	Return the value (for $n \geq 0, m > 1$) of $n - m \cdot trun[n/m]$.
round[x]	Return floor[x + 0.5].
sin[x]	Return the trigonometric sine of x.
sqrt[x]	Return the square root of x.
trun[x]	Return the integer that is formed by dropping the fractional portion of x (if any).

*Where: n is the integer result of evaluating and truncating any arithmetic expression.
      m is the integer result of evaluating and truncating any arithmetic expression.
      x is the result of evaluating any arithmetic expression.
      y is the result of evaluating any arithmetic expression.

APPENDIX
C

Selected References
with Annotations

The following list of references is not intended to be exhaustive but rather is designed to give the interested student a start toward locating additional literature in the area of computer science. For the same reason all references listed are textbooks; journal articles have intentionally been omitted. The classification system: (1) introductory, (2) intermediate, and (3) advanced is designed for a beginning undergraduate student, not for a graduate major in computer science. This text, for example, would be classified as introductory.

INTRODUCTORY

Gear, C. W. *Introduction to Computer Science* (Palo Alto, Calif.: Science Research Associates, Inc., 1973). A reasonably formal treatment of algorithm design concepts designed primarily for computer science majors with a good preparation in mathematics.

Hull, T. E., and D. D. F. Day. *Computers and Problem Solving* (Reading, Mass.: Addison-Wesley Publishing Company, Inc., 1970). The first part of this text contains a FORTRAN-based introduction to algorithm design; part two presents a number of interesting problems culled from various disciplines.

Ralston, Anthony. *Introduction to Programming and Computer Science* (New York: McGraw-Hill Book Company, Inc., 1971). Introduces concepts of algorithm design primarily through the use of ALGOL and several other higher-level programming languages.

Rice, John K., and John R. Rice. *Introduction to Computer Science* (New York: Holt, Rinehart and Winston, Inc., 1969). An introduction to computers and algorithm design that requires a good preparation in mathematics. Algorithms are presented primarily in English, FORTRAN, and ALGOL.

Rothman, Stanley, and Charles Mosmann. *Computers and Society* (Palo Alto, Calif.: Science Research Associates, Inc., 1972). A survey of how computers are used in contemporary society.

Sanders, Donald H. *Computers in Society* (New York: McGraw-Hill Book Co., 1973). An easy-to-read survey on how computers are used in our society.

Sherman, Phillip M. *Techniques in Computer Programming* (Englewood Cliffs, N.J.: Prentice-Hall, Inc., 1970). A well-written text on various aspects of designing and implementing algorithms for computer execution.

Sterling, T. D., and **S. V. Pollack.** *Computing and Computer Science: A First Course with PL/I* (New York: Macmillan Publishing Co., Inc., 1970). An introduction to computer science which contains a number of interesting and varied topics, such as Turing machines and metalanguages.

Walker, Terry M. *Introduction to Computer Science: An Interdisciplinary Approach* (Boston: Allyn and Bacon, Inc., 1972). Introduces students of all disciplines to computer science and computer problem-solving techniques. The book utilizes only a flowchart language to present algorithm-design concepts. However, programming language companion texts are available that present the most popular programming languages

Walker, Terry M., and **W. W. Cotterman.** *An Introduction to Computer Science and Algorithmic Processes* (Boston: Allyn and Bacon, Inc., 1970). Introduces students to topics in computer science through the use of a flowchart language, FORTRAN, and PL/I as the languages for algorithm design. It contains algorithms for many varied problems as well as material on number systems, computer systems, systems analysis and design, and data structures.

INTERMEDIATE

Daniels, Alan, and **Donald Yeates** (eds.). *Systems Analysis* (Palo Alto, Calif.: Science Research Associates, Inc., 1971). A very readable introduction to concepts associated with the design and implementation of business information systems.

Elson, Mark. *Concepts of Programming Languages* (Palo Alto, Calif.: Science Research Associates, Inc., 1973). A good survey of programming languages and their concepts.

Gear, C. William. *Computer Organization and Programming,* 2nd ed. (New York: McGraw-Hill Book Company, Inc., 1974). An excellent exposition on computer design and programming systems.

Gordon, Geoffrey. *System Simulation* (Englewood Cliffs, N.J.: Prentice-Hall, Inc., 1969). An excellent, well-written introduction to computer simulation modeling concepts and techniques.

Hellerman, Herbert. *Digital Computer System Principles,* 2nd ed. (New York: McGraw-Hill Book Company, Inc., 1973). Provides an excellent introduction to computer system design concepts as well as programming and operating systems using the APL language.

Lohnes, Paul R., and **William W. Cooley.** *Introduction to Statistical Procedures: With Computer Exercises* (New York: John Wiley & Sons, Inc., 1968). An introductory statistics text with a computer orientation and nominal mathematics background required. Topics covered are the more common ones used for research in the social sciences.

Lott, Richard W. *Basic Systems Analysis* (San Francisco: Canfield Press, 1971). A thorough discussion of the concepts associated with the analysis, design, and implementation of a computer-based business information system.

Miller, Arthur R. *The Assault on Privacy* (Ann Arbor: The University of Michigan Press, 1971). Probably the most authoritative book currently available on the subject of the computer and individual privacy. It is well researched and makes for delightful reading.

Struble, George. *Assembler Language Programming: The IBM System/360* (Reading, Mass.: Addison-Wesley Publishing Company, Inc., 1969). A thorough, well-written text on assembly language programming for the IBM System/360. This text should provide a good understanding of the architecture of the most widely used contemporary computer system.

ADVANCED

Acton, Forman S. *Numerical Methods That Work* (New York: Harper & Row, Publishers, 1970). A very pleasant, well-written introduction to topics in numerical analysis.

Arden, Bruce W., and **Kenneth N. Astill.** *Numerical Algorithms: Origins and Applications* (Reading, Mass.: Addison-Wesley Publishing Company, Inc., 1970). An excellent introduction to numerical analysis which uses flowcharts and FORTRAN programs to present algorithms.

Berztiss, A. T. *Data Structures: Theory and Practice* (New York: Academic Press, Inc., 1971). A sound exposition on discrete mathematical structures, their applications, and their computer representation.

Galler, B. A., and **A. J. Perlis.** *A View of Programming Languages* (Reading, Mass.: Addison-Wesley Publishing Company, Inc., 1970). A well-written advanced treatment of algorithms, programming languages, and data structures. This book should be read by anyone who desires a sound theoretical background in these subjects.

Gries, David. *Compiler Construction for Digital Computers* (New York: John Wiley & Sons, Inc., 1971). An excellent text on the design of compilers.

Grove, Wendell E. *Brief Numerical Methods* (Englewood Cliffs, N.J.: Prentice-Hall, Inc., 1966). A very readable and concise introduction to numerical analysis.

Harrison, Malcolm C. *Data Structures and Programming* (Glenview, Ill.: Scott, Foresman and Company, 1973). A good discussion of data structures as it relates to programming languages. Includes coverage of the list and string processing languages (LISP and SNOBOL), as well as APL and ALGOL 68.

Knuth, Donald E. *The Art of Computer Programming,* Vol. 1, *Fundamental Algorithms,* 2nd ed. (Reading, Mass.: Addison-Wesley Publishing Company, Inc., 1973). Chapter 2 provides an indepth study of the topic of information structures. In fact, this chapter probably represents the current standard on the subject in computer science.

Rosen, Saul (ed.). *Programming Systems and Languages* (New York: McGraw-Hill Book Company, Inc., 1967). A collection of seminal articles on various aspects of computer programming systems and languages covering the period up through 1965.

Sammet, Jean E. *Programming Languages: History and Fundamentals* (Englewood Cliffs, N.J.: Prentice-Hall, Inc., 1969). A thorough survey of programming languages, past and present.

Sobel, Herbert S. *Introduction to Digital Computer Design* (Reading, Mass.: Addison-Wesley Publishing Company, Inc., 1970). A well-written text on the logical design of digital computer hardware systems.

Wegner, Peter. *Programming Languages, Information Structures, and Machine Organization* (New York: McGraw-Hill Book Company, Inc., 1968). A well-written text covering many of the fundamental concepts relating to computers and computer programming systems.

Brief Glossary of Computer Terms

absolute address: The address permanently assigned to a location in computer main memory.

access: The act of fetching an item from or storing an item in any computer memory device.

access time: The time needed to access data in a computer memory device.

accumulator: A register in which the result of an arithmetic or logic operation is formed.

acoustic coupler: A device that allows a telephone to be used as a communications link between a remote terminal device and a computer.

acronym: A word that is formed using the initial letter or letters in a name or phrase. An example is PL/I, which is derived from *Programming Language/I*.

address: An identification, represented by a group of symbols, that specifies a register, main memory location, auxiliary memory location, or computer-related device (e.g., a remote terminal).

ADP: An acronym for *Automatic Data Processing*, which is the processing of data by automatic means.

ALGOL: An acronym for *ALGOrithmic Language*, a procedure-oriented programming language that is widely used in Europe and in academic circles.

algorithm: A procedure that consists of a set of unambiguous rules which specifies a sequence of operations that provides the solution to a specific class of problems in a finite number of steps.

algorithmic language: A computer programming language designed for representing algorithms.

alphabetic data: Data items that consist solely of blanks and the letters of the English alphabet.

alphanumeric data: Data items that consist of letters of the English alphabet, blanks, decimal digits, and special characters.

analog: The representation of data by means of continuously variable physical quantities.

analog computer: A computer that represents data in analog form and which operates on data using physical processes (usually electricity).

analysis: The methodical investigation of a problem, including the reduction of the problem to subproblems that are easier to identify and understand.

analyst: A person who defines problems and develops algorithms for their solution.

annotation: A descriptive comment or explanatory note.

ANSI: An acronym for the American National

Standards *I*nstitute, which is a group that establishes standards for devices, languages, coding systems, and many other things.

application program: An algorithm represented as a computer program which is designed to solve a user's problem (as contrasted with a computer system problem).

arithmetic and logical unit (ALU): The portion of a digital computer's central processing unit in which arithmetic and logical operations are performed.

array: A group of data items (or sets of data items) arranged in a specific order in one or more dimensions.

artificial intelligence: That branch of computer science concerned with the development of computer algorithms that perform functions normally associated with human intelligence (e.g., reasoning, learning).

ASCII: Acronym for *A*merican *S*tandard *C*ode for *I*nformation *I*nterchange, which is the standard code used to represent characters for storage in a computer memory and for interchange between computer systems and their associated devices.

assembler: A computer program that translates assembly language program statements into machine language instructions.

assembly language: A computer-dependent, machine-oriented computer programming language.

associative memory: A memory in which data are accessed by the contents of locations, not by the position in memory or by the use of an address. Also called *content-addressable memory.*

asynchronous: Operating independently, usually using start and stop signals.

automation: The performance of various operations or processes by automatic means.

auxiliary memory: Any computer memory or memories used to supplement main memory.

background processing: The execution of lower-priority computer programs during time periods when higher-priority programs are not requiring execution.

band width: The capacity of a transmission line, which is generally given in bits per second.

batch processing: A technique in which a number of similar data items or transactions are grouped or batched for sequential processing by a computer.

baud: A unit of signaling speed equal to one bit per second.

BCD: An acronym for *Binary Coded Decimal,* which is the representation of decimal digits using a binary code. BCD is also sometimes defined more broadly to include binary coding systems such as EBCDIC.

binary digit: By convention, the digits 0 or 1.

binary numbering system: The number system that uses a base or radix of 2.

bit: Acronym for *BI*nary digi*T*.

bit string: A string of binary digits in which each binary digit is taken to be an independent unit.

block: A set of data items, symbols, records, program statements, or other objects that are taken to be a unit.

block diagram: A diagram of a system or computer in which the principal parts are represented by boxes of various shapes which show the basic functions and functional relationships among the constituent parts.

blocking: The practice of grouping several logical records together as one physical record (or block) in memory media (e.g., magnetic tape, magnetic disc).

bootstrap: A technique by which a process contains the components required to load or initialize itself.

branch: A transfer of control operation in a procedure.

breakpoint: A point in an algorithm where execution of the algorithm may be interrupted without the loss of results obtained up to that point.

buffer: A memory area or device that is used to compensate for any differences in rate of data flow or to allow for the asynchronous operation of computer system components.

bug: An error in an algorithm or program or an equipment malfunction.

byte: A group of adjacent bits that are operated upon as a unit. Often a byte is the number of bits required to represent one alphabetic or special character using a given coding scheme (ASCII or EBCDIC).

card punch: A device used to punch data represented as holes into paper cards for the purpose of computer output.

card reader: A device used to input data represented as holes in paper cards into a computer's main memory.

cathode ray tube (CRT): An electronic tube with a screen that is used in computer terminals to display input and output data.

central processing unit (CPU): The portion of a computer used to control the components of a computer hardware system and in which information processing is performed. The CPU consists of a control unit and an arithmetic and logical unit.

character: A letter, digit, punctuation mark, or other special symbol used for the representation of information. In a computer, characters are usually represented using binary codes.

character string: A string of characters.

COBOL: An acronym for *CO*mmon *B*usiness *O*riented *L*anguage, a procedure-oriented programming language that is widely used in commercial data processing applications.

CODASYL: The Conference Of *DA*ta *SY*stem Languages, a committee made up of representatives of industry and government for the purpose of establishing standards for commercial data languages.

code: A set of unambiguous rules that are used to describe the representation of data. Also, a system of rules and conventions that are used in forming, receiving, transmitting, and processing signals that represent data. Also, the process of writing a procedure by use of a computer programming language.

collate: The operation of combining the records of two or more ordered files to form one ordered file.

compiler: A computer program that translates a source program written in a procedure-oriented programming language into an object (or target) program that is usually represented in a machine-oriented language.

concurrent: The occurrence of more than one event or activity in some given time interval.

console: The hardware device in a computer system that is used for communication between human operators and the system.

constant: A literal value that remains unchanged during the execution of a procedure.

control unit: The part of the CPU that controls the operation of the computer system.

core storage: A type of memory device that has commonly been used for main memory; often used incorrectly as synonomous for main memory.

counter: A device that is used to record the number of occurrences of an event.

CRT: An acronym for *Cathode-Ray Tube*, a device used to display computer input and output data.

cybernetics: The discipline that utilizes theories and studies on communication and control in living organisms and machines.

data: Any representation of facts, concepts, or instructions in a well-defined manner for the purpose of human or machine communication, processing, or interpretation. Alternatively, data are any information represented in a systematic way.

data base: A set of data files integrated together for use in processing for a number of different applications. Also called a *data bank*.

data cell: A random-access auxiliary storage device in which data are recorded on magnetic strips arranged in cells.

data processing: Any sequence of one or more operations performed upon data to achieve a desired result.

data reduction: The process of transforming raw data into a more useful form, usually reducing its volume.

deadlock: A condition in which competing demands for computing resources prevent the execution of two or more processes from proceeding.

debug: To locate and correct errors in an algorithm or malfunctions in computer hardware.

decision table: A table that contains all contingencies and the decision rules that cause various actions to be taken for each of these contingencies. Decision tables can be used instead of algorithm flowcharts for problem description and documentation.

decode: The process of applying a set of unambiguous rules to transform data to some previous representation.

diagnostic: A message produced by a compiler or other computer program which identifies some error or malfunction that has been detected.

digit: A symbol used to represent the value of any of the unsigned integers less than the radix of that number system.

digital computer: A device in which arithmetic and logic operations are performed only on data represented in a discrete form, with the results always being discrete data.

digitize: The process of transforming continuous data values into a discrete (or digital) form.

direct access: Pertaining to computer memory devices in which access time is not related to the location of the data in that memory. Also called *random access.*

documentation: A description of a program or system made up of any or all of: algorithm flowcharts, decision tables, source program listings, system flowcharts, card layouts, and text.

downtime: The length of time a computer system or one or more of its components is not available for processing because of a software or hardware malfunction.

EBCDIC: An acronym for *Extended Binary Coded Decimal Interchange Code,* an eight-bit binary code used for data representation in computer memory.

echo check: A method used to check the accuracy of data transmission by returning the received data to the sender for comparison.

edit: To alter the form or format of data for output or other purposes.

effective address: The address formed by address modification (such as indexing or indirect addressing) which is used to specify the current operand.

emulate: To cause one computer to perform in a manner identical to that of a second computer such that the first computer can execute programs and perform operations that were written for the second computer even though the design and/or data representation systems of the two computers are not identical.

encode: The process of applying a set of unambiguous rules to transform data from its original form to some coded representation.

ENIAC: An acronym for *Electronic Numerical Integrator And Calculator,* the first operational (in 1946) electronic computer.

error: Any discrepancy between a computed, measured, or observed value and the true, specified, or theoretically correct value.

execution time: (1) The time required by a CPU to execute an instruction once the instruction has been moved to the CPU, or (2) the total time a CPU spends in executing a program from the time execution begins to the point where it terminates.

facilities management: The use of an independent organization to operate a computer facility on a contract basis.

fail soft: A system in which the failure of one or several hardware components does not cause all processing to cease but rather in which processing continues, usually at a degraded level of performance.

fetch: The process of locating a data item or instruction in memory and transferring it to some other memory device.

field: A group of characters that is treated as a unit of data; a field is a part of a record.

file: A collection of logically related records that are treated as a unit.

fixed-length record: Relates to a file in which the various records must contain the same number of characters.

fixed-point: Numbers represented as signed integers, with no digits to the right of the decimal point.

floating-point: Numbers represented as a value times a fixed base raised to some power. In computer memory, only the value and the power portion of floating-point numbers are stored.

flowchart: A graphical representation for the definition, analysis, or solution of a problem, in which symbols of various shapes are used to represent operations, data flow, equipment, and so on.

foreground processing: The execution of higher priority computer programs while not processing lower priority programs that are awaiting execution.

FORTRAN: An acronym for *FOR*mula *TRAN*slator, a procedure-oriented computer programming language that is used primarily for solving scientific problems.

generator: A computer program that produces values (e.g., random numbers) or other programs (e.g., report-writing programs) as output.

graphic: A symbol generated by a process such as printing, handwriting, or drawing.

graphics: The use of a computer to draw symbols and/or figures on a cathode-ray-tube device or a plotter.

hardware: The electronic, magnetic, and mechanical devices of a computer system (i.e., the physical components of the computer); contrast with *software*.

heuristic: The directed trial-and-error method of problem solving in which problem solutions are discovered by evaluating the progress made toward the end result; contrast with *algorithm*.

hexadecimal numbering system: The number system that uses a base or radix of 16.

Hollerith code: A coding system used to represent alphanumeric information on punched cards that consist of eighty columns and twelve rows.

hybrid computer: A computer that has both digital and analog capabilities (i.e., data are represented and processed in both analog and discrete form).

immediate address: The case in which the address portion of a machine-language instruction contains the value of an operand rather than its address.

index: (1) Any symbol (usually an integer) that is used to uniquely identify an element in an array; or (2) an ordered list that contains references to the contents of a file or document, together with pointers to the location of those contents in the file or document.

indexed sequential file: A file in which records are ordered sequentially based on a logical key; records in such files can be accessed either directly or by sequential processing.

indirect address: A machine-level address that points to a main memory location which contains either the address of the operand or another indirect address.

information: The meaning assigned to data by human beings using some system of representation.

information retrieval: The methods and procedures used for storing and retrieving specific data and/or references based on the information content of documents.

input/output: Relating to the input of data to computer main memory, or the output of data from computer main memory, or both.

instruction: A set of symbols that defines an operation to be performed and the data or unit of equipment that is to be used.

instruction counter: A counter in the control unit that points to the location in main memory in which the next instruction to be executed resides.

integrated management information system: A computer-based management information system that is designed by considering the whole of information sources and needs within an organization. This can be contrasted with a system in which these sources and needs are broken up into mutually exclusive processing tasks performed on multiple unrelated data files.

interface: A common or shared boundary between two computer devices or systems.

interleave: An arrangement whereby the parts of one sequence of objects or events are alternated with the parts of one or more other sequences of objects or events in such a way that each sequence retains its identity (usually for the purpose of overlapped execution of the sequences).

interpreter: (1) A translator program in which each source language statement is translated into target code and the target code for that statement is immediately executed, or (2) a device that prints at the top of a punched card the symbols represented by the holes that have previously been punched in the card.

interrupt: A signal that causes the CPU to terminate execution of the currently executing program so that execution of another program can begin or resume; termination of the interrupted program generally occurs in an orderly manner so that its execution can be resumed from the point of interruption at a later time.

inverted file: A file in which the natural order is reversed.

item: A group of characters that is treated as a unit of data; an item is a part of a record (item is a synonym for *field*).

iteration: A single cycle of a repetitively executed series of algorithm steps.

job: A set of logically related tasks that constitutes a unit of work for a computer.

job stream: The input to an operating system that consists of one or more jobs.

K: An abbreviation for a unit of measure in computers, which generally means 2^{10} (1,024) but also may mean 1,000.

key: A sequence of one or more characters within a record that is used to identify the record.

keypunch: A device actuated by a keyboard that is used to punch holes in a card to represent data.

label: One or more characters used to identify an item.

latency: The elapsed time between the request for data from a memory device and the beginning of data transfer.

line printer: A device that prints all of the characters of a line in one operation on continuous paper forms.

list: An ordered set of records.

location: A place in computer memory having a unique address that is used to store data and instructions.

logical record: The set of fields that are logically related to each other, considered independent of their physical location.

loop: A sequence of one or more algorithm steps that is executed zero or more times until some termination condition is satisfied.

machine language: The language the instructions of which the computer CPU can execute directly.

macro instruction: A pseudo-instruction in a source language that causes the substitution of a number of predefined source language instructions.

magnetic card: A card with a magnetic surface on which data can be recorded magnetically using binary codes.

magnetic core: One type of memory medium capable of storing one binary digit.

magnetic disc: A memory medium on which data are stored in concentric circles on circular platters that are coated with a magnetic substance.

magnetic drum: A cylinder on which data are stored magnetically in bands that wrap around the cylinder.

Magnetic Ink Character Recognition (MICR): The machine recognition of characters printed with a magnetic ink (used primarily on bank checks).

magnetic tape drive: A device used to read and write data that are recorded on magnetic tape using binary codes.

main frame: Synonomous with CPU.

main memory: The part of computer memory from which data can be stored or fetched directly by the CPU.

management information system (MIS): A computer-based information system designed to provide managers with the information needed to plan, organize, direct, and control the operations and activities of an organization.

master file: A file that contains relatively permanent data.

memory: The set of computer components used for the storage of data and instructions.

memory protection: The control of access to any portion of memory (either real or virtual, main or auxiliary) to prevent unauthorized or accidental access to or alteration of the contents.

merge: The operation of combining the records of two or more ordered files to form one ordered file, where the order of the records in the combined file is the same as the order of the records in the original files.

microprogram: A series of pseudo-instructions that are translated by micrologic (a semipermanently stored set of primitive instructions) in the computer during execution.

microsecond: One millionth of a second (10^{-6} second).

millisecond: One thousandth of a second (10^{-3} second).

minicomputer: A small, relatively inexpensive (unit cost of less than $100,000) computer.

modem: Acronym for *MOdulator-DEModulator*, a device that converts digital data into analog form and modulates it for transmission over com-

munication lines and then converts it back to digital form at the receiving station.

multiplexor: A device that combines signals received from a series of low-speed lines and interleaves them for transmission over a high-speed line.

multiprocessing: The simultaneous execution of more than one instruction sequence (program) by a computer (requires more than one CPU) or a computer network.

multiprogramming: The simultaneous processing of more than one independent program by interleaving the execution of their instruction sequences in one CPU.

nanosecond: One billionth of a second (10^{-9} second).

natural language: A language in which the rules are determined by current usage rather than predefined on some logical basis.

object code: The output of a language translator (a compiler or interpreter) that is the result of translating a program written in a source code.

octal numbering system: The number system that uses a base or radix of 8.

offline: Any device that is not under the control of the CPU.

online: Any device that is under the control of the CPU.

operand: An object that is operated upon during the execution of a computer instruction.

operand address: The part of a machine-language instruction that points to the main memory location where the operand is located.

operating system: A collection of computer programs that: (1) facilitate the processing of the algorithms that people write to tell a computer how to solve a type of problem, and (2) schedule the resources of the computer among these user algorithms.

operation code: The portion of a computer in-

389

struction that directs the computer CPU to perform an operation (also called an op code).

Optical Character Recognition (OCR): The process by which printed characters are read by light-sensitive devices for computer input.

overflow: A condition where the result of some operation is too large to be stored in the amount of memory space allocated to that value.

overlay: The technique by which the same area of main memory is sequentially loaded with different sections of code from the same program.

pack: The technique of storing several data items in one data field or main memory location.

page: A group of contiguous memory locations (usually of fixed length), data, or code that is moved in and out of main memory as a unit.

parallel: Any operation performed simultaneously using separate facilities or devices.

parameter: A variable that is assigned a value that remains constant for a specific purpose or process.

parse: The operation of separating an input symbol string into its basic components and categorizing these components.

pattern recognition: The identification of forms, shapes, or configurations using automatic techniques.

physical record: A group consisting of one or more logical records that is input or output in a single operation as one unit.

picosecond: One trillionth of a second (10^{-12} second).

PL/I: An acronym for *Programming Language/I*, a procedure-oriented programming language designed for solving problems of almost any type.

pointer: A data item that indicates the memory location of an item or record of interest.

polling: The process of interrogating a number of devices or processes in a sequential manner to determine whether or not they require service.

positional notation: A numeration system in which a number is represented by an ordered set of digits such that the value represented by each digit is determined by its position relative to the radix point as well as by the value of the digit itself.

postmortem: The analysis of any operation or process subsequent to its completion.

problem-oriented language: A computer programming language that allows the method for the solution to a problem to be described using terminology related to the particular problem area.

procedure-oriented language: A computer programming language that is used to implement for computer execution procedures for a wide variety of problem types.

process control: The monitoring and control of a production process by a computer.

program: The implementation of a procedure by use of a computer programming language. A program consists of an ordered set of instructions that tells a computer CPU how to accomplish a specific task.

protection: Any device, program segment, or data segment that has access to it (or any of its parts) is controlled to prevent unauthorized or accidental access to or alteration of the contents.

punched card: A card in which data are represented by a certain pattern of holes, which are punched in the card.

punched paper tape: A roll of paper tape in which data are represented by the pattern of holes that are punched in the tape.

pure code: Any procedure that does not modify itself in any way during execution.

radix: The base of a number system; an integer that tells the number of symbols used in a number system.

random access: Synonym for direct access.

real time: An information system in which outputs are available in time to affect the process that generates future inputs.

record: A collection of related data items that are treated as a unit.

recursive: Anything that might call upon itself. A recursive procedure is one that invokes itself.

relative address: A number that represents the displacement of an absolute address from a base address.

reliability: The probability that a device will perform without failure during some time period.

remote access: The input to and/or output from a computer of information from devices that are not in close proximity with the computer.

remote batch processing: The input of information to a computer or output of information from a computer in batches from a small computer not in close proximity with the larger computer.

response time: The interval between an event and the response of the compuer to the event. In time-sharing, this would be the elapsed time between the transmission of a request for processing and the beginning of the computer's response, which is output at the terminal.

RPG: An acronym for *Report Program Generator,* a problem-oriented language used to assist in the solution of problems that involve a large amount of formatted printed output.

scan: To examine a file or record item by item in a sequential manner.

semantics: The meaning assigned to statements, words, or phrases in a language.

serial access: A method of sequentially processing records organized in a linear order in a file in their natural order (i.e., access time to a record is dependent upon the location of the desired record in the file).

simulation: The process of representing and analyzing the properties and behavior of a physical or proposed system by constructing and experimenting with a computer model of the system.

simultaneous: The occurrence of two or more events at the same instant of time.

software: The set of programs used to instruct the computer in problem solving; consists of the operating system programs and applications programs.

source program: A computer program written in a programming language that must be translated to machine language before it can be executed by a computer.

special character: A graphic character that is not a letter of the English alphabet, a numeric digit, or a space character.

subalgorithm: Any algorithm that is subordinate to another algorithm. That is, a subalgorithm must be invoked by an algorithm that is already being executed.

synchronous: Any device or process that is controlled by a clock which emits signals at regular intervals, in which the device or process may only begin at the beginning of the interval.

syntax: The rules that determine what the legal constructions are in a language.

systems analyst: A person who studies the activities, methods, techniques, and procedures of systems for the purpose of computerizing those systems. The systems analyst usually provides the programmer with detailed program specifications, including a systems flowchart and file and record descriptions.

systems flowchart: A diagram that utilizes specially shaped symbols to illustrate the flow of source documents, data, and output documents. All activities and procedures that involve the collection of data, the processing of the data, and the output and dissemination of data are precisely documented.

tag: A field which consists of one or more characters that is attached to a record for the purpose of identification.

target program: Synonomous with *object program.*

telecommunications: The transfer of data between two or more points using either public or private communications media.

teleprocessing: The processing of data from remote sites by use of telecommunications facilities.

terminal: A device used to input data to or output data from a computer, often from remote points.

throughput: The total amount of useful work performed by a computer in a given unit of time.

time-sharing: The concurrent use of one computer system by more than one user or program by allocating short time intervals of processing to each active user. The objective is to provide each user or program with short response times to requests for processing such that the user will have the impression that the computer's resources are dedicated to that user.

total system: An integrated management information system that operates in real-time.

trace: A diagnostic technique to provide a listing of the results of the execution of each source language statement (or certain type of source language statement).

transactions file: A file that contains data generated during some time period, which is processed in conjunction with a master file for purposes of producing reports, statements, and the like, and for the updating of the master file.

translator: A computer program that accepts as input a source program and produces as output an object (or target) program. Translators are either compilers or interpreters.

trap: A branch taken to a fixed location upon the occurrence of an abnormal event (e.g., overflow, attempt to execute an instruction with an illegal operation code) so that an error-handling procedure can be executed.

Turing machine: A mathematical model of a computing device that alters its internal state and reads from, writes on, and moves in one of two directions a tape of conceptually infinite length, with such operations always based on its current state.

turnaround time: The elapsed time between the submission of input for processing and the receipt of the output of that processing.

unbundling: The separation of pricing for computer hardware, certain computer software, and other computer-related services.

underflow: The condition that occurs when a floating-point result is smaller in magnitude than the smallest value that a particular computer can represent.

unpack: The process of separating two or more data items that have been previously stored in one memory location or field.

utility routine: A computer program contained in the operating system that performs some often-needed function (e.g., sorting, input/output, diagnostics).

variable: A label used to identify one or more main memory locations in which one or more constant values are stored, where these constant values may be changed during program execution.

variable-length record: Relates to a file in which the various records may contain a different number of characters.

verify: The process of checking the accuracy of data transcription by comparing it with a second transcription performed on the same record.

virtual machine: The computer system as it appears to the user. For example, by use of emulation, one computer can be made to execute programs written for another computer. In this case, the computer being emulated is the virtual machine and the computer executing the program is the real machine.

virtual memory: The main memory as it appears to the user, which may be vastly larger in capacity than the real (or actual) main memory on a particular computer. Virtual memory is accomplished by having the operating system subdivide a program and keep in real memory only those parts of the program currently being referenced, with the remaining parts being stored in auxiliary memory.

word: A group of adjacent bits that are operated upon as a unit. The number of bits that a word consists of is defined for each computer system.

word length: The storage capacity of a word, as expressed by the number of bits, bytes, or characters that a word may contain.

zero suppression: The operation of replacing with spaces all leading (left-hand) zeros in a number.

392

INDEX

[*Words defined in Appendix D* (Brief Glossary of Computer Terms) *are not listed in this index.*]